Blackstone's Guide to the

CRIME AND DISORDER ACT 1998

Roger Leng, LLB
Reader in Law, University of Warwick

Richard D. Taylor, MA, LLM, Barrister
Forbes Professor of English Law and Head of Department of Legal Studies,
University of Central Lancashire

Martin Wasik, LLB, MA, Barrister
Professor of Law, Manchester University

BLACKSTONE PRESS LIMITED

First published in Great Britain 1998 by Blackstone Press Limited,
Aldine Place, London W12 8AA. Telephone 0181-740 2277

© R. Leng, R. D. Taylor, M. Wasik, 1998
The contributors hold the copyright for their respective contributions.

ISBN: 1 85431 848 9

British Library Cataloguing in Publication Data
A CIP catalogue record for this book is available from the British Library.

Typeset by Montage Studios Limited, Horsmonden, Kent
Printed by Ashford Colour Press, Gosport, Hampshire

Blackstone's Guide to the

CRIME AND DISORDER ACT 1998

Contents

Preface

The authors would like to express their customary appreciation to the publishers for their patience and understanding in the face in particular of the complications caused by two of us moving house during the period immediately following the Act receiving the Royal Assent on 31 July. This event, as tends also to be the case with removal dates, was in considerable doubt right up to the last moment (due to a clash between the Lords and the Commons which is discussed in the Introduction).

Our special thanks also go to Laurence Eastham for his skilful editing at a time when he himself was also in the process of moving house, an event which is supposed to be high up on the stress factor scale but which, at times, seemed to pale into insignificance compared with the task of making sense of this multi-faceted Act.

Roger Leng
Richard Taylor
Martin Wasik
22 October 1998

Introduction

The Crime and Disorder Act 1998 is the first major criminal justice legislation of the Labour Government, elected on 1 May 1997 with a manifesto commitment to be 'Tough on crime, tough on the causes of crime'. In practice, the Act shows us that being 'tough on crime' means dealing with those who make their neighbours' lives hell through their persistent petty offending and anti-social behaviour; measures to control dangerous sex offenders; and restrictions on cautioning, to ensure that repeat young offenders must face their responsibilities in court. 'Tough on the causes on crime' may perhaps mean a preparedness to invest in long-term solutions rather than quick fixes, and a willingness to engage with, and to respond to, criminological research with measures designed to prevent and change offending behaviour, rather than simply to condemn it.

It would be wrong, however, to read the Act simply as one party's vision of the future. The politicisation of law and order issues in recent years has meant that both the Conservative and Labour parties have competed with each another to present themselves as sound on these matters and to support policies likely to go down well with the majority of the electorate. This has been exemplified by the way in which Labour, when in opposition, trod cautiously in its opposition to the Conservative Government's Crime (Sentences) Act 1997, then surprised its traditional supporters by implementing much of that Act as soon as it came into power. Many of the provisions of the present Act promote policies which were developed under the former administration, or reflect concerns that would have been addressed whichever Government was in power. Anti-social behaviour orders and sex offender orders, carry forward the policies foreshadowed in the Protection from Harassment Act 1997, and the Sex Offenders Act 1997. Provisions allowing magistrates to sit alone, introducing early administrative hearing in magistrates' courts, and removing committal proceedings for indictable only offences, are all responses to long-standing concerns about delay in the criminal justice process, a subject crystallised by the influential 'Narey Report', *A Review of Delay in the Criminal Justice System*, published in February 1997.

As a result of the apparent political consensus on criminal justice matters, and feeding on public concerns (fanned by the press) about predatory sex offenders, out-of-control juvenile offenders whom the courts were powerless to deal with, and 'neighbours from hell', the Act had a relatively easy and largely uncontroversial ride through Parliament, although there were unexpected problems in its latter stages. Almost at the last minute, an amendment to bring the age of consent for homosexual sexual activity into line with heterosexual sexual activity, at 16 (House of Commons

Report Stage 22nd June) nearly resulted in the Bill being delayed over the summer recess. There was even talk of the Bill being lost altogether. The amendment was passed on a free vote, by a majority of 240, but when the issue went back to the House of Lords together with other Commons amendments, it was rejected. Their Lordships felt that the proposed change would 'fail adequately to protect vulnerable young people'. Many supporters of the amendment pressed the Government to reverse this defeat in the Lords, but Home Secretary Jack Straw argued successfully against this course of action when the matter returned to the Commons on 28 July. There were only a few days left before the summer recess, and further delay would wreck the timetable for implementing many of the Bill's provisions in September 1998. The Government, Mr Straw pointed out, had given an undertaking on 21 October 1997 and lodged with the European Court of Human Rights, with respect to the stay of proceedings brought by two individuals with the backing of Stonewall, the Gay Rights organisation, in which they had challenged the differential age of consent. The undertaking was to hold a free vote in the Commons on the issue and, if the House voted in favour of equalisation, to bring forward amending legislation, consideration of which would be completed by the end of the 1998/99 session. This undertaking could still be met by introducing legislation in the next session, by which time a review group could have examined further the complex proposals, favoured by many in the House of Lords, to introduce safeguards against the abuse of trust of vulnerable young people. If accepted, such safeguards might be enacted at the same time as the change to the age of consent. This approach was accepted by the Commons, reluctantly by some, with the result that the Bill did become law, and received the Royal Assent at the latest stage possible before the summer recess on 31 July.

Although many of the Act's provisions were not opposed in principle (the age of consent issue apart) the Parliamentary debates did air a number of real concerns about how the Act's provisions would operate in practice. Two of the queries which recurred throughout the debates were, first, whether any significant new money would be forthcoming to translate the various elaborate schemes for crime prevention measures into workable reality and, second, whether the Anti-social Behaviour Orders and Sex Offenders Orders contained in the Act so compromised basic principles of justice as to fall foul of the European Convention on Human Rights. The Government sought to meet the doubters on the first point by announcing on 21 July, a £250 million package of investment in what Mr Straw claimed to be the 'biggest crime cutting initiative in the world'. Although close inspection of the figures indicates that much of the planned expenditure is to fall under heads other than law and order, some new money is being made available, both to the local authorities and to the probation service, to reflect their new responsibilities. The second query is as yet unanswered: with the imminent incorporation of the European Convention into English law by the Human Rights Act 1998, it would be ironic, but not surprising, if the heightened awareness of human rights issues in legal circles required the Government to reconsider some of the provisions in the Crime and Disorder Act in the face of challenge in the courts.

The provisions of the Act

Part I of the Crime and Disorder Act tackles the prevention of crime and disorder on a number of different fronts. By section 17, local authorities are placed under a specific duty to consider the crime prevention implications of all their decisions, and are given more specific duties to co-operate with the police and other agencies in conducting local crime audits, and the formulation of periodic crime prevention strategies under section 6. Particular problems associated with persistent anti-social behaviour, and the threat posed by sex offenders in the community are addressed by new civil orders under ss. 1 and 2 of the Act. These orders will permit the courts to prohibit a wide range of specified conduct, with breach of an order made a serious criminal offence, punishable by up to five years' imprisonment. A number of further measures are designed to address the causes of juvenile crime. The parent of a child who offends may, under s. 8, be placed by the court under a parenting order which includes a requirement that the parent attend counselling or guidance sessions. Children below the age of criminal responsibility who offend, or who are at risk of doing so, may be made the subject of a child safety order under s. 11. That order will place the child under the supervision of a social worker, for up to three months. Where it is feared that crime is linked to the problem of unsupervised children on the loose late at night, or with high levels of truancy, local authorities are given new powers to establish local curfew schemes under s. 14, for the removal of young children from the streets at night, or truancy schemes under s. 16, by virtue of which constables may remove suspected truants to schools or other designated places. Chapter III of Part I extends the special powers of stop and search which were made available to the police under s. 60 of the Criminal Justice and Public Order Act 1994. The new Act empowers them, for a limited period in a certain locality, to require the removal of masks or other items which are being worn to conceal a person's identity.

Part II of the Act addresses the substantive criminal law, and makes two important changes. The first is the introduction of a range of racially aggravated offences, and the second is the abolition of the presumption of *doli incapax* for children aged between 10 and 14. Although it remains an open question whether the creation of distinct new offences is the best way of combating racist violence, and although persuasive argument can be mounted for preserving a 'twilight' zone of responsibility for young juveniles, both these provisions made it to the statute book with little or no amendment. Indeed, during the Bill's passage through Parliament, criminal damage was added to the range of racially aggravated offences, and to the abolition of *doli incapax* was added the extension to children under 14 of the provisions permitting adverse inferences to be drawn from their failure to testify in court. The provisions on racially aggravated offences should be read alongside the new statutory requirement in s. 82 of the Act that racial aggravation must be taken into account as an aggravating factor in sentencing in relation to *any* offence in which it is proved. The relationship between this sentencing provision and the substantive racially aggravated offences is far from straightforward, as will be seen in the course of discussion in Chapter 3 of this Guide. The abolition of the death penalty for treason and piracy, the only offences for which it still remained at least in theory available, was also added to this Part of the Act, although it might more logically have come within Part IV, which contains most of the provisions relating to sentencing

Part III of the 1998 Act contains a number of substantial reforms to the criminal justice system. A new national and local structure for youth justice is established. At the national level, the Youth Justice Board is created under s. 41, the Board being given powers to monitor the performance of the youth justice system as a whole, and to advise the Home Secretary. Locally, councils are given responsibility under s. 38, in co-operation with the police, probation service and health authorities, to provide a range of youth justice services and also to draw up annual youth justice plans. Liaison amongst the various partners in providing youth justice services is to be placed in the hands of Youth Offender Teams, by virtue of s. 37. In a further important change, the former system under which children and young persons might receive a formal caution from a police officer, rather than be prosecuted for their offences, is abolished and replaced by a more rigid system of 'reprimands' and 'warnings' under ss. 65 and 66. A reprimand may be administered for a first offence, to be followed by a warning for a subsequent offence. Where a warning has been given, the youngster must be referred for assessment to the youth offending team, who will arrange a rehabilitation programme if appropriate. Part III of the Act also contains the provisions designed to implement the government's pledges to remove unnecessary delays from the criminal justice process. It provides, *inter alia*, for lay staff in the CPS to undertake much of the work of the Service in relation to summary proceedings, and for single justices and justices' clerks to perform many functions which previously had to be performed by the full court. Committal proceedings are to be abolished for indictable-only and 'related' offences, and overall time limits (as opposed to custody lime limits) are to be introduced for the first time. Many of these significant changes are to be tested through pilot schemes before being brought into force across the whole of the country. Some may represent only an interim stage on the road to more radical criminal justice reforms — such as the proposals to give qualified CPS staff rights of audience in the Crown Court; the recommendations of the Glidewell Report on the CPS, and in particular its future relationship with the police; and further consideration being given to the highly controversial Narey proposal to abolish the accused's right of election for Crown Court trial.

Sentencing of offenders is the main topic addressed in Part IV of the Act. The courts are given new powers to pass 'extended sentences' on offenders convicted of violent or sexual crimes. A new custodial sentence for young offenders, the detention and training order, is established, although it will not be implemented until next year. The detention and training order will replace the secure training order (on the statute book since 1994 but brought into force only in 1998 to reflect the fact that one such centre is now operational) and, for those aged 15, 16, and 17, the sentence of detention in a young offender institution. New community sentences, the drug treatment and testing order, and the action plan order, are to be piloted for 18 months, as is a new non-custodial sentence for young offenders, the reparation order. Reparation by the offender to the victim is an important theme in Part IV, and this approach to criminal justice is being given a significant role in legislation for the first time. As can be expected from any modern legislation on criminal justice, there is much further adjustment to sentencing law and procedure, often tucked away in the Schedules to the Act. Section 80 of the Act places the Court of Appeal under a duty to issue sentencing guidelines, a practice which the Court itself devised in the 1970s and has been building upon ever since. Section 81 establishes a Sentencing Advisory Panel. The role of the Panel will be to advise the Court of Appeal on the content of sentencing guidelines, and to prompt the Court when the Panel thinks that old guidelines require updating, or new ones should be issued.

Part V of the Act deals with a number of miscellaneous and supplemental matters including new powers for courts to remand children and young persons to secure accommodation under ss. 97 and 98, and a group of seven sections on early release and recall of prisoners.

Implementation and Extent

The bulk of the provisions in the Act extend to England and Wales only, but s. 36, which abolishes the death penalty for treason and piracy, applies variously to England and Wales, Scotland, Northern Ireland, the Isle of Man and the Channel Islands.

The Act includes a number of provisions applicable to Scotland which are not considered separately in this Guide, but reference is made to some of the Scottish provisions where that has proved useful for purposes of comparison. The most significant changes affecting Scotland are:

(a)   Chapter II of Part I, which is concerned with the prevention of crime and disorder, and to which is linked s. 115;

(b)   s. 33, which creates racially aggravated offences in Scotland;

(c)   Chapter II of Part IV, which deals with extended sentences for violent and sexual offenders, and drug treatment and testing orders; and

(d)   ss. 108–112 and 117(2), which concern early release arrangements in Scotland.

Section 118 indicates that legislation will be passed for Northern Ireland by Order in Council concerning:

(a)   sex offender orders (as ss. 2–4);

(b)   abolition of *doli incapax* (as s. 34);

(c)   avoiding adjournments in youth courts (as s. 47(5));

(d)   the accused's presence at trial via television link (as s. 57); and

(e)   drug treatment orders (as ss. 61–64).

Such Orders may be passed subject to annulment by either House of Parliament, rather than subject to the affirmative resolution procedure.

The Act will be brought into force in stages on days to be appointed by the Home Secretary (s. 121(2)). Exceptionally, some measures relating to sentencing in Scotland have retrospective effect. Different days may be appointed for different purposes, or in different parts of the country, in order to allow for some provisions to be piloted in particular areas in advance of general implementation. Some provisions, such as those relating to parenting orders, will not operate in a particular locality until the courts have received notification from the Home Secretary that suitable arrangements are available in that area. Transitional provisions are provided in sch 9. In the event that anything has been forgotten, the Home Secretary retains a power to make further transitional provision and savings, as appear necessary, in the orders by which particular provisions are brought into force (s. 121(3)).

A handful of provisions relating to the Youth Justice Board, the power of justices to sit alone, football spectators and some amendments to the Criminal Justice Act 1991 were implemented immediately on 1 August 1998 (Crime and Disorder Act 1998 (Commencement No. 1) Order 1998 (SI 1998/1883). A large number of provisions were brought into force on 30 September 1998 (Crime and Disorder Act 1998 (Commencement No. 2 and Transitional Provisions) Order 1998 (SI 1998/2327). Implementation of a further group of provisions is planned for December or

'Winter' 1998. These relate to truancy, sex offender orders, masks and face coverings, and the new procedure for indictable-only offences. Longer term projects are: home detention curfews (early 1999), the Sentencing Advisory Panel (April 1999), anti-social behaviour orders (April 1999), detention and training orders (Summer 1999), time limits (Autumn 1999) and the recall to prison of short term prisoners (early 2000). Another source of information on implementation of the Act is Home Office Circular 38 / 1998, which is available on the Home Office Web site (along with much other useful material relating to the Act) on http://www.homeoffice.gov.uk.

The Act commenced its Parliamentary journey on 2 December 1997, as a House of Lords Bill of 96 sections. As is now customary with these Bills, by the time it received the Royal Assent on 31 July 1998 it had grown considerably, on this occasion to 121 sections. Its Second reading in the Lords was on 16 December 1997, with its Committee Stage being on the 3, 10, 12, and 24 of February, and 3 of March 1998, and the Report and Third Reading being on the 17, 19 and 31 of March. The Bill was introduced into the Commons on April 1, Second reading was on the 8 and it was considered in Standing Committee B from the 28 of April until the 11 of June. Report and Third reading were on 22 and 23 June respectively, the Commons amendments were considered by the Lords on the 22 of July and the only one not agreed to (on the homosexual age of consent) was considered by the Commons on July 28.

Chapter 1
Community Safety

This chapter is concerned with a group of provisions in Part I of the Act which have a common aim of making communities safer. These provisions create new controls over persons who have engaged in anti-social behaviour and dangerous sex offenders and require local authorities to formulate plans for the reduction of crime and disorder. Community safety also underlies a further group of provisions, dealt with in Chapter 2, which address offending by the young and seek by various forms of active intervention to prevent children adopting criminal lifestyles.

ANTI-SOCIAL BEHAVIOUR ORDERS

Background

The anti-social behaviour order, which is introduced by s. 1, is inspired by a number of factors. Modern criminological research indicates the damaging effect on the lives of people who are the victims of persistent petty offences or anti-social behaviour, such as littering, excessive noise, obstruction and abuse, not amounting to any discrete offence. Such behaviour is particularly problematic where committed by a group of antagonists and where the parties are neighbours. Contrary to earlier assumptions that the better-off in society are the most likely targets of crime, it is now recognised that it is in the poorer communities that the worst effects of victimisation are felt. Although attempts have been made to provide or utilise remedies for these problems under housing legislation and civil law, these remedies have proved inadequate. Even if an appropriate remedy is available, it may be frustrated through lack of legal assistance for the victim, or actual or feared intimidation and reprisals.

A political consensus that these problems should be addressed resulted in two pieces of legislation to deal with harassment passed by the former Conservative Government, and Labour proposals which are now enacted as the anti-social behaiour order (ASBO). The first Conservative legislation on this issue was found in s. 154 of the Criminal Justice and Public Order Act 1994 which inserted a new s. 4A into the Public Order Act 1986. This created a new offence of causing intentional harassment, alarm or distress by using threatening, abusive or insulting words or behaviour or disorderly behaviour, or displaying any writing, sign or other representation which is abusive or insulting; the offence is punishable by up to six months' imprisonment. It supplemented the existing offence of using threatening, abusive or insulting words or behaviour likely to cause harassment, alarm or distress under s. 5 of the 1986 Act, which does not require proof of either intent or that harm is actually caused, and is punishable only by a fine (see Wasik, M. and Taylor, R., *Blackstone's Guide to the Criminal Justice & Public Order Act 1994*, pp. 98–100).

The Conservative Government's second attempt to deal with the identified problems was the Protection from Harassment Act 1997 (see generally Lawson-Cruttenden, T. and Addison, N., *Blackstone's Guide to the Protection from Harassment Act 1997*). Although prompted by problems relating to stalkers, the Act was also aimed at nuisance neighbours and racial abuse. The Act created a novel mix of civil and criminal remedies. Harassment, which is defined as a course of conduct which a reasonable person would consider amounted to harassment of another (s. 1), is made an offence under s. 2 and may be subject to a civil action for damages and/or an injunction under s. 3. Notably, an injunction may be granted on the basis of actual or apprehended harassment. This is significant because it allows an injunction to be granted where past harassment cannot be proved. Breach of such an injunction is made an offence under s. 3(6), punishable by imprisonment for up to a maximum of five years (s. 3(9)). In the course of sentencing an offender for an offence of harassment or for breach of an injunction, the court has a power to make an order restraining further harassment of the victim or any other person. Breach of such a restraining order would itself amount to an offence punishable by up to five years' imprisonment (s. 5(5) and (6)). The offence-creating sections came into force only on 1 September 1998: before that date breach of an order could be treated as contempt of court only. As a result, there is as yet no experience of the operation of the new provisions.

The Labour Party's proposals for a 'community safety order' to deal with anti-social behaviour were first floated in a consultation paper published in 1995, and developed in a further paper, *Protecting our communities*, in 1996. Once in Government, similar proposals were published in the Home Office consultation paper, *Community Safety Order*, published in September 1997.

The ASBO

The ASBO is a radical new mechanism, designed to overcome some of the deficiencies of existing law. It has a new label, but this is essentially the same beast as the community safety order which was proposed in earlier consultation papers. Although its purpose has generally been welcomed, its unusual form has provoked criticisms and objections both inside and outside Parliament. The ASBO provisions are expected to be implemented in April 1999.

An order may be sought by a 'relevant authority' meaning either a local authority or a chief constable, and only after consultation between these parties (s. 1(1) and (2)). For this purpose the relevant local authorities are councils for districts and London boroughs, the City of London, the Isle of Wight and the Isles of Scilly and, in relation to Wales, county or county borough councils (s. 1(12)). The dual power of application and the requirement of consultation reflects the new duties on councils and the police to co-operate in strategies to reduce crime and disorder (ss. 5 and 6). It also reflects the fact that allegations of anti-social behaviour may come first to either the police or to councils as housing providers. Placing responsibility for making an application on the relevant authorities overcomes the problem that an aggrieved person who seeks a remedy may be deterred by intimidation. In this respect, the new procedure should prove more effective than the power to seek an injunction under the Protection from Harassment Act 1997 for which personal application is required.

The ASBO is conceived as a local remedy to deal with a local problem. Thus, the application must be made to the magistrates' court whose commission area includes the place where it is alleged that the relevant anti-social behaviour took place (s. 1(3)). This, coupled with the requirement that generally any prohibition contained in the order must be designed to protect persons within a particular local government area (s. 1(6)), fits the principle of local responsibility for crime and disorder, but may arbitrarily limit the effectiveness of the provision in practice. Thus, it would be difficult to use an ASBO where the alleged anti-social behaviour was committed through a variety of media such as post, telephone and electronic mail and was aimed at a group of people, perhaps members of a family, living in different parts of the country.

An application may be made in relation to any person aged 10 or over. This is in marked contrast to the corresponding provision in s. 19, applicable to Scotland, which applies only to persons over the age of 16. It is remarkable that an amendment which would have extended the scope of that provision to 12-year-olds was resisted by the Scottish Office minister (*Hansard*, Commons, Standing Committee B, 4 June 1998, cols 724–726), whereas an amendment which would have raised the threshold age for the English provision to 13 was similarly resisted by a Home Office minister (*Hansard*, Commons, Standing Committee B, 30 April 1998, cols 74–78). The explanation given for including young children within the potential scope of ASBOs is that frequently anti-social behaviour involves a number of members of a single family and the actions of the children may be as harassing as those of older family members. Placing responsibility on children as young as 10 is consistent with the Government's 'no more excuses' policy and the abolition of the presumption of *doli incapax* for children of this age. However, in practice, experienced magistrates may doubt whether the ASBO regime is appropriate for a child who *ex hypothesi* is acting under the influence of older members of his family, when such older family members are before the court.

The anti-social behaviour

The primary condition which must be fulfilled before an order is made is that a person has acted in an anti-social manner, meaning a manner which caused or was likely to cause harassment, alarm or distress to one or more persons not of the same household as himself (s. 1(1)). The requirement that the offender and victim should not be of the same household is designed to exclude domestic disputes, but may cause problems in relation to various forms of multi-occupancy. The court must disregard any act of the defendant which he shows was reasonable in the circumstances (s. 1(5)), although it is up to the defendant to raise and prove this. The actions which justify the making of the order must have been committed after the commencement date for s. 1.

A recurrent theme in debate in Parliament was questioning the need for the new provision in the light of the existing remedy under the Protection from Harassment Act 1997. The answer is provided by the Government's consultation paper *Community Safety Order*, which suggested that the new order would cover behaviour which was anti-social but not necessarily harassing and that whereas the 1997 Act would serve for harassment of a particular individual or family, the ASBO could be used for harassment directed at a community (para. 3).

Concern was also expressed about the breadth of the formula. Various peers and MPs queried whether the ASBO might be used against merely eccentric behaviour or where a householder was distressed by her neighbour's conduct in keeping geese or planting a high hedge, whether the conduct covered by the formula might vary according to region, or whether the order might be used in a discriminatory way and whether the provision would be used against the mentally ill cared for in the community. These queries were answered by Lord Williams of Moston, who denied that the formula was vague and expressed confidence in the ability of magistrates to understand and apply the relevant concepts. He also pointed out that the result of a finding that anti-social behaviour had occurred would be a prohibitory order which would merely require the subject to behave in a decent way towards fellow citizens (*Hansard*, Lords, 3 February 1998, cols 512–514).

Dealing with similar points in the Commons, Alun Michael for the Home Office argued that a threshold level for ASBOs would be established by three mechanisms: first, the application must be made by the police or local authority who might be expected to filter out trivial cases; secondly, the two-year minimum duration for the order would deter applications relating to less serious forms of anti-social behaviour; thirdly, guidance to be issued by the Home Office would set out firm advice on the threshold to be applied (*Hansard*, Commons, Standing Committee B, 30 April 1998, col. 43). The consultation paper *Community Safety Order* had promised a provision in the statute which would have required local authorities and the police not to exercise their powers in a manner which discriminated on grounds of race, religion, disability, sex or sexual orientation (para. 10). Since no such provision has found its way into the statute, it will presumably appear in the forthcoming guidance.

Mr. Michael also argued that the ASBO would be up-tariff in the sense that: 'A number of attempts will have been made to use different prohibitions, the threat of eviction or prosecution, or efforts will have been made to get the different parties together to resolve issues ...' (ibid, col. 96). Whether this is the case remains to be seen. As will be discussed below, the procedural advantages attached to an ASBO may make it a first rather than a last resort for the police and local authorities.

It should be noted that it is sufficient to show that harassment, alarm or distress were likely, but not that anybody actually experienced such emotions. It was suggested in the consultation paper that this drafting would effectively excuse those affected by the behaviour from the need to act as witnesses and would allow evidence to be given by professional witnesses, such as local authority staff (para. 13). This suggestion is problematic. In the normal cases where a council officer or police officer does not observe the allegedly harassing behaviour, such officer's evidence would be based upon the complaints he or she had received and would be hearsay. Although this may be admissible under s. 1 of the Civil Evidence Act 1995 if the proceedings are treated as civil, the maker of the original statement may be called to be cross examined by leave of the court under s. 3. In any event, courts might be unwilling to infer the effects of the defendant's behaviour on particular individuals without hearing evidence from those persons directly.

The procedure

New Magistrates' Court Rules, The Magistrates' Courts (Sex Offender and Anti-Social Behaviour Orders) Rules 1998, will be issued in Autumn 1998. The draft rules are sketchy as to procedure but clues can be gleaned from guidance published by the Home Office and Government statements in Parliament.

As already mentioned, it is intended that the application for an ASBO should be treated as a civil procedure by way of complaint under s. 53 of the Magistrates' Courts Act 1980 and subject to the civil burden of proof on a balance of probabilities. This has been criticised on the ground that the ASBO is the first stage of a process that can lead to a conviction for a serious offence and as such should be subject to the criminal burden of proof beyond reasonable doubt. The Government has justified adopting the civil standard on two grounds. The first justification is that an application for an ASBO does not lead directly to a conviction and is akin to an application for an injunction. The second justification is that the similar procedure for obtaining an injunction under the Protection from Harassment Act 1997 is subject to the civil standard. This argument is not entirely convincing. Applications for bind overs, which operate in a similar manner to ASBOs, are also by complaint in the magistrates' court but it has been held by the Divisional Court that where a person has been acquitted it would be improper to bind him over unless the judge is satisfied beyond reasonable doubt that the defendant posed a potential threat (*Middlesex Crown Court, ex parte Khan* (1997) 161 JP 240).

The basis for arguing that a criminal standard of proof should apply to ASBOs is that the procedure is, properly considered, criminal rather than civil. The attributes which suggest that this should be considered a criminal proceeding are that:

(a)   the imposition of an ASBO will attract publicity and stigma in the same way as a criminal conviction;

(b)   prohibitions attached to an ASBO may significantly restrain the defendant's freedom and should be seen as penalties; and

(c)   where a defendant is convicted for contravening an ASBO the sentencing court is barred from imposing a conditional discharge (s. 1(11)), suggesting that the imposition of the ASBO is itself seen as a form of conditional discharge on first conviction (see generally Gardner *et al* 'Clause 1 — the hybrid law from hell' (1998) *Criminal Justice Matters*, no. 31, pp. 25–27).

The proposed procedure in the magistrates' court was described in para. 16 of the Home Office consultation paper. Once an application had been made by either the police or local authority, the person in question would be informed of this, the grounds for it and the date of the hearing. It is not made clear whether this would require disclosure of the evidence or a summary of it as required for either-way offences tried summarily. In principle this level of disclosure should be the minimum required by natural justice and anything less could lead to a challenge as to the fairness of the trial under Art. 6 of the European Convention on Human Rights. The consultation paper suggested that it would be for the defendant to decide whether to attend court to challenge the application, however this was contradicted by Mr. Michael in Committee when he suggested that the court would have power to issue an arrest warrant to secure the defendant's attendance (*Hansard*, Commons, Standing

Committee B, 30 April 1998, col. 74). This view appears to be correct since where a hearing is by complaint, the defendant may be summoned and in the event of non-attendance, powers to adjourn or issue a warrant for arrest are found in ss. 54–57 of the Magistrates' Court Act 1980. If the defendant did not appear, the court would have the power to grant an order *ex parte*, but the order would not take effect until it had been served on the defendant.

At para. 6, the consultation paper suggests that normally the court would expect to have the views of both the police and the local authority and that these 'views' would form part of the evidence. This passage is misleading. It appears to confuse a submission made by the applicant as to the scope of the order sought with evidence on which the court could base the necessary findings of fact. Under the s. 1 procedure there are clearly two parties, the 'relevant authority' which makes the application (i.e., police or council) and the defendant. Whereas the relevant authority which did not make the application could give evidence, it would be very odd if that authority could express a 'view' to the court. If this were to occur it would confuse and lengthen the proceedings. It would also be improper for a court to 'expect' evidence from any particular quarter. The question of what evidence is called should be for the parties to the application.

At the Committee stage in the Commons, it was suggested that there would be a presumption that an application would go ahead on the first hearing in court and that adjournments would be allowed only exceptionally. The justification offered by Mr Michael was that speed was needed to stop the nuisance, that time would already have passed because attempts would have been made to deal with the problems without recourse to s. 1 and that if the defendant could frustrate the procedure by not turning up this might lead to intolerable delay (*Hansard*, Commons, Standing Committee B, 30 April 1998, col. 96). The flaw in this argument is that intolerable delay is not a corollary of allowing the defendant adequate time to prepare his case. It is to be hoped that in practice magistrates will not allow fairness to an accused to be sacrificed in the interests of avoiding delay.

The terms of the order

A court may make an ASBO only if satisfied that it is necessary to protect persons from further anti-social acts by the defendant (s. 1(1)). Correspondingly, the prohibitions which may be imposed by an ASBO are those necessary for the purpose of protecting persons in the local government area (or specified adjoining areas) from further anti-social acts by the defendant (s. 1(6)). The court has wide discretion as to what prohibitions to impose although these might include curfew orders, orders excluding the defendant from a particular place, or orders not to make contact with named individuals.

It appears that the 'relevant authority' should specify what prohibitions are requested at the time the application is made. This is implicit in s. 1(6) which states that a relevant authority should not specify prohibitions which are designed to take effect in an adjoining local government area without first consulting the relevant council and chief constable.

The duration of the order is at the discretion of the court subject to a minimum of two years (s. 1(7)). In its consultation paper the Government suggested that, because the order was protective, the duration of the order should not reflect the nature of the proved conduct, but rather the period of time necessary to protect the community (para. 15). Both the applicant and the defendant may apply to have the order varied or discharged (s. 1(8)) except that an ASBO cannot be discharged within the first two years, except with the consent of both parties (s. (9)). The effect of the two-year bar might be neutralised by a court leaving an order in operation whilst discharging all of the substantial prohibitions within it.

These provisions could cause problems for courts since there is no bar on an aggrieved defendant making repeat applications to vary an order. However, a court might be able use its inherent jurisdiction to restrict applications to vary to cases where there were fresh circumstances or considerations. In doing this a court might rely upon *Nottingham Justices ex parte Davies* [1981] QB 38, in which the Divisional Court upheld a rule of this sort in relation to repeat bail applications.

Breach of an order

Doing anything which is prohibited by an ASBO, without reasonable excuse, is an offence, punishable on summary conviction by a fine not exceeding the statutory maximum or up to six months' imprisonment, or both or on conviction on indictment to a fine or imprisonment for up to five years, or both. As a consequence of a sentence of five years' imprisonment being possible, the offence will be arrestable. In sentencing for breach of an ASBO the court may not impose a conditional discharge (s. 1(11)) but there is no bar on an absolute discharge. This position was explained on the basis that it was necessary to retain the option of an absolute discharge as a safety valve for negligible breaches. The reason for barring a conditional discharge is that its purpose and that of the ASBO are essentially the same: 'to enjoin the individual not to offend further — not to continue the behaviour that led to the appearance in court' (per Alun Michael, *Hansard*, Standing Committee B, 5 May 1998, col. 137).

Dealing with breaches may not be entirely straightforward. The theory which prompted the creation of the ASBO is that harm to victims stems from an aggregate of different types of anti-social conduct. Accordingly, it is envisaged that an ASBO might include prohibitions on criminal activities such as property damage and assault, on 'sub-criminal' activities such as trespass, noise, or abuse, but also perhaps on activities such as speaking to or writing to the victim, which in other circumstances might be considered neutral. Difficult prosecution decisions will have to be made where a breach is clear but it involves an act such as simply approaching and speaking to the victim.

It also remains to be seen to what extent a defendant charged with breach will be able to challenge the terms of the original order. A simple analogy with contempt of court by breach of an injunction would suggest that the order should not be questioned. However, the special features of the ASBO suggest that a challenge should be possible. The effect of the ASBO is to place an individual under prohibitions particular to himself — a form of personalised criminal law. These prohibitions may be imposed in his absence. Although the order must be served on the defendant before it may take effect and he has a right of appeal, he may have chosen not to exercise this right. If and when a breach occurs, the act may be criminal only because of the order and for no other reason. Criminal responsibility for breach of an ASBO is the result of a two-stage process. The first stage is the imposition of the order by the magistrates' court. The second stage is the finding of guilt at a trial for breach. Particularly where the alleged breach does not involve criminal acts, the most important stage in the ascription of criminal responsibility will be the first. It would be unfair, and probably also a breach of Art. 6 of the European Convention on Human Rights, if a person could be convicted of a serious offence without the opportunity to challenge the key earlier determination on which his conviction is based.

SEX OFFENDER ORDERS

Background

The creation of the sex offender order (SOO) in s. 2 is one of a number of recent initiatives designed to deal with the risks presented by certain types of sex offender following release from custody. Concern about this issue has arisen as a result of cases in which released sex offenders have committed further attacks or killed following release.

The problem was partially addressed in the Sex Offenders Act 1997 which created a registration system for sex offenders which requires that the offender lodge his name and address with the police and notify them if he stays at any one address for a period of more than 14 days in the course of a year. The period of required registration is a minimum of five years but may be indefinite, according to the seriousness of the offence(s) as indicated by the type and duration of the sentence imposed. Failure to register as required is an offence punishable by fine or up to six months' imprisonment. The 1997 Act has the modest aim of allowing the police to monitor the whereabouts of sex offenders. The weakness of the 1997 Act is that it applies only to persons who were serving some form of sentence, whether a community sentence or in custody, or were under supervision, or detained following an insanity verdict at the time when the Act came into force on 1 September 1997 or to persons who are convicted or cautioned for a sexual offence after that date. Whereas this restriction avoids criticisms of retrospectivity, it excludes from the register a number of persons who have been convicted of sex offences in the recent past and who may present a danger.

An attempt to address the dangers posed by sex offenders in the context of children's homes was made in the Children (Protection from Offenders) (Miscellaneous Amendments) Regulations 1997 (SI 1997 No. 2308), which require that persons responsible for running children's homes must obtain information about possible criminal convictions before employing any person in a position involving contact with children. A more general attempt to address the problem is found in the provision for extended supervision on release for sexual and violent offenders under ss. 58 and 59 of the present Act, which are discussed in Chapter 7.

The proposal on which the SOO is based was first discussed in the Home Office consultation paper *Community Protection Order*, published in November 1997. The current provision closely follows that proposal, albeit with a more informative name. Although novel in form, the SOO is rooted in modern criminal policy, since it exploits the existing registration procedure introduced by the Sex Offenders Act 1997 and adopts a two-stage procedure in which a criminal sanction is founded upon an earlier civil order, which was pioneered in the Protection from Harassment Act 1997 and which is now also the basis for the ASBO under s. 1. The success of the SOO will depend upon the effectiveness of procedures under the 1997 Act to monitor and keep track of sex offenders. This may also be an area of fruitful collaboration with other agencies such as the local authority who may be able to provide housing in places which reduce the opportunities for further offending.

Sex offenders

Section 2 relates to sex offenders. That term is defined by s. 3(1) by reference to offences listed in sch. 1 to the Sex Offenders Act 1997. Those offences are:

(a)   rape (under Sexual Offences Act 1956, s. 1);
(b)   intercourse with a girl under 13 (s. 5 SOA);
(c)   intercourse with a girl between 13 and 16 (s. 6 SOA);
(d)   incest by a man (s. 10 SOA);
(e)   buggery (s. 12 SOA);
(f)   indecency between men (s. 13 SOA);
(g)   indecent assault on a woman (s. 14 SOA);
(h)   indecent assault on a man (s. 15 SOA);
(i)   assault with intent to commit buggery (s. 16 SOA);
(j)   causing or encouraging prostitution of, intercourse with, or indecent assault on a girl under 16 (s. 28 SOA);
(k)   an offence under s. 1 of the Indecency with Children Act 1960;
(l)   inciting a girl under 16 to have intercourse (Criminal Law Act 1977, s. 54);
(m)   offences relating to indecent photographs of children under s. 1 of the Protection of Children Act 1978;
(n)   smuggling pornography involving children (Customs and Excise Management Act 1979, s. 17);
(o)   possession of indecent photographs of children (Criminal Justice Act 1988, s. 160)

Consensual offences of unlawful sex with a girl between 13 and 16, buggery and indecency between men are not treated as sexual offences for the purposes of the 1998 Act where the offender was aged under 20 when the offence was committed. The offences listed at (d) to (i) above are also excluded when the other party to the relevant act was aged over 18, except where the offender was sentenced to prison for 30 months or more or to a restriction order. This rule is designed to exclude consensual sexual offences which would not attract a heavy penalty and other less serious offences. Presumably, this age limit will be reduced to 16 for offences involving sexual acts between men when this becomes the relevant age of consent in legislation promised for the Parliamentary session 1998–9.

Also included in the list of relevant sexual offences are corresponding Scottish offences and offences under service law.

A person is a 'sex offender' for the purpose of the 1998 Act if he has been convicted of or cautioned, reprimanded or warned for an offence listed above, or found to be not guilty by reason of insanity or found to be under a disability and to have done the act charged in relation to a listed offence.

A person will also be a sex offender if he has been punished under the law of a foreign jurisdiction for an act which both constituted an offence under the law of that jurisdiction and would have constituted a relevant sexual offence if it had been committed in the United Kingdom (s. 3(1)(d)). It may be difficult to establish that the facts on which a foreign conviction was based conform precisely to the elements of an offence in the UK. For this reason, where it is shown that the defendant has been convicted abroad, the offence may be presumed to be a relevant sexual offence unless and until the defendant serves a notice. This notice must state that the offence for which the defendant was convicted would not amount to an offence in the UK, indicating why he was of that opinion and requiring the applicant (ie the chief constable seeking the SOO) to prove that the offence did correspond to a relevant sexual offence (s. 3(6)). The court also has a power under s. 3(7) not to presume that an offence punished abroad corresponds to a relevant sexual offence but to put the applicant to proof of this issue, even where the defendant has not issued a notice under s. 3(6). These provisions are designed to avoid a detailed analysis of foreign law where it is fairly obvious that the conviction abroad relates to a qualifying sexual offence. This advantage may be lost if defendants with foreign convictions choose to contest the question of whether such convictions qualify as sexual offences.

The application for an order

Applications must be made by the police, in the name of the chief constable, to the magistrates' court whose commission area includes any place where the actions of the defendant which prompted the application took place (s. 2(1) and (2)). Applications will be by complaint, subject to new rules of court (The Magistrates' Court (Sex Offenders and Anti-social Behaviour Orders) Rules 1998. The applicant must prove:

(a)   that the defendant is a sex offender as defined above; and
(b)   that the defendant has acted in a way which gives reasonable cause to believe that a SOO is necessary to protect the public from serious harm from him (s. 2(1)).

The acts of the defendant on which the order is based must have occurred since the commencement date for s. 2 (1 December 1998) and also since the conviction or punishment which cause him to be categorised as a sex offender (s. 3(2)).

Concern was expressed in Parliament about the breadth of the formula used to define the conduct which may trigger the imposition of a SOO (see generally *Hansard*, Standing Committee B, 5 May 1998, cols 147–194). It was made clear that the acts causing concern need not be criminal but might involve hanging around outside schools or in public parks or other places where children gather. Unlike the ASBO where the issue of an order is triggered by behaviour which is itself harmful, a SOO may be triggered by behaviour which merely indicates a risk of future harm.

An order cannot be made unless it is proved that the necessary conditions are fulfilled. It has been asserted that because this is a civil rather than a criminal procedure, the standard of proof must be on a balance of probabilities rather than to the criminal standard beyond reasonable doubt. The Act makes no mention of burden of proof on this issue, neither do draft versions of rules of court available at the time of writing. As with the ASBO, criticisms have been made that the SOO is really a criminal procedure and should be treated as such. In relation to the SOO, the issue is made less significant by the fact that what has to be proved is not a certain fact but merely that there is a 'reasonable cause to believe' in the need for an order. Even if the criminal burden of proof were applied, it would still be possible for magistrates to issue an order without being certain that the defendant had acted as alleged or that he posed a risk.

The order

The making of a SOO will have two main consequences for the defendant. First, the defendant will be made subject to the existing registration scheme under the Sex Offenders Act 1997 for the duration of the order (s. 2(5)) if not already subject to registration. Secondly, the order may prohibit the defendant from doing anything prescribed by the order (s. 2(3)). The scope of the prohibitions to be applied is restricted under s. 2(4) to 'those necessary for the purpose of protecting the public from serious harm from the defendant'. This seems to allow a wide discretion to magistrates (see Gillespie 'Paedophiles and the Crime and Disorder Bill' [1998] 1 *Web Journal of Current Legal Issues*). In appropriate cases, prohibitions might relate to staying away from particular places, not seeking particular sorts of work, not speaking to children or giving presents to children. More restrictive orders, for instance involving curfews or requiring the defendant to move from his own home, would appear to be possible in extreme cases but would run the risk of being struck down as being contrary to the European Convention on Human Rights.

An order will run for the period specified by the magistrates, which will be not less than five years (s. 2(5)). The order may be varied or discharged on application to the court which made the order by either party, except that an order cannot be discharged within five years except with the consent of both parties (s. 2(7)). The power to vary might be used to add extra prohibitions or to extend the period of the order where the defendant's behaviour had shown further cause for concern. New rules of court will be published relating to such applications to vary or discharge. As well as the power to apply for variation or discharge, the defendant has a right of appeal under s. 4 which is considered below.

Breach of the order

Breach of the prohibitions contained in a SOO, without reasonable excuse, is made an offence, punishable summarily by a fine not exceeding the statutory maximum or imprisonment up to six months, or both, or on conviction on indictment by a fine or imprisonment not exceeding five years, or both (s. 2(8)). In the event of conviction, the court is barred from imposing a conditional discharge (s. 2(9)). The theory underlying this is apparently that on the occasion of the making of the order the defendant did something wrong and benefited by receiving a warning as to his future conduct rather than punishment. It would thus be futile to issue a second such warning in the form of a conditional discharge. The problem with applying this theory to particular cases is that the original order may have been issued on the basis of conduct, such as going swimming, which is normally innocuous. In this situation the defendant cannot be considered to have benefited by being warned on the first occasion and it might be quite appropriate to impose a conditional discharge rather than sentence on the first occasion on which the order is breached.

As with ASBOs, the police, CPS and the courts are likely to have great difficulties where the conduct in breach of a SOO is trivial, such as going to a park, and which does not exhibit any patent threat to children or others. The problems will arise in determining whether a prosecution should be brought in such a case and, if a conviction is obtained, what would be an appropriate sentence.

APPEALS AGAINST ORDERS

Appeals against the making of both anti-social behaviour orders and sex offender orders lie to the Crown Court under s. 4. In determining an appeal, the Crown Court has wide powers under s. 4(2):

(a)   to make such orders as may be necessary to give effect to its determination of the appeal; and
(b)   to make such incidental or consequential orders as appear to it to be just. Any order made by the Crown Court on appeal (apart from an order that the magistrates should re-hear the application) is to be treated as if it were an order of the magistrates' court from which the appeal was brought for the purposes of the powers of that court to vary or discharge the order (s. 4(3)).

It should be noted that there is no right of appeal by a local authority or chief constable against a refusal by the court to make either sort of order. Of course any of the parties would have the normal right to appeal by way of case stated to the Divisional Court of the Queen's Bench Division on the ground that the magistrates' decision was either wrong in law or in excess of jurisdiction. Since courts are given wide discretion in the granting of either type of order, there may be little scope for challenge on the basis of errors of substantive law. However, the procedures to apply are to be determined and set out in new court rules and the operation of these procedures may provide more possibilities for challenge.

CRIME AND DISORDER STRATEGIES

Sections 5 and 6 place local authorities and police forces under a duty to co-operate in the formulation and implementation of crime reduction in the local authority area. These provisions were foreshadowed in the Home Office consultation document *Getting to Grips with Crime: A New Framework for Local Intervention*, published in 1997, which in turn adopted proposals first made in *Safer Communities: The Local Delivery of Crime Prevention through the Partnership Approach*, a report by an independent working group, convened by the Home Office Standing Conference on Crime Prevention and chaired by James Morgan (Home Office, 1991).

Although the current legislation is the first attempt at formal implementation, the Morgan Report has already had a considerable impact on the development of multi-agency crime prevention initiatives. Thus, a *Survey of Community Safety Activities in Local Government in England and Wales*, published by the Local Authorities Association in 1996, found that 62 per cent of authorities were involved in multi-agency partnerships and over 50 per cent had a budget for community safety projects. The current legislation should therefore be seen not as a new initiative, but rather an attempt to build upon and encourage existing initiatives, to formalise procedures and to create a degree of consistency across different areas.

Responsibility for strategies

The Act reflects the view that crime prevention strategies should target manageable geographical areas and should address the needs of recognisable communities. For this reason strategies are to be developed at district/borough level. Thus, under s. 5(4) the local government areas for which strategies must be formulated are districts, London boroughs, the City of London, the Isle of Wight and the Isles of Scilly, and in Wales counties and county boroughs. Primary responsibility for formulating a strategy for the reduction of crime and disorder in each such area is placed jointly on relevant local councils (s. 5(1)(a)) and the chief officers of every police force whose area lies within the relevant local authority area. The relevant councils will be:

(a)   the council for the area where this is a unitary authority (e.g., a London or metropolitan borough); or
(b)   in relation to districts where the council is not a unitary authority, the district council plus the council for the County which includes that district.

Because county councils will be involved in the preparation and implementation of strategies relating to a number of districts, the county councils will need to take responsibility for co-ordinating the various plans.

The arrangement under which responsibility rests jointly on the local authorities and chief officers of police is seen as the best way to encourage true partnership and collective action and expresses the concept that the police and the councils have equal stakes in the process. The possibility that one or other of the agencies should take the lead in crime prevention was considered but rejected by the Government not only for reasons of principle but also because of the practical difficulties which might arise if one body was seen to be attempting to exercise control over the personnel or resources of another (*Getting to Grips with Crime* 1997, p. 3). One difficulty with the new scheme is that police force areas are not coterminous with local authority boundaries. A consequence of this is that in formulating strategies councils may have to work with more than one police force, who in turn may have to be involved in the formulation and implementation of strategy in more than one area.

Detailed *Guidance on Statutory Crime and Disorder Partnerships*, has now been published and is available from the Home Office. In order to fulfil their joint responsibilities, chief constables and local authorities will need to appoint particular personnel to act on their behalf. The recent guidance has emphasised that it will be for each agency to decide on the appropriate level at which it should be represented (para. 1.19).

In formulating a strategy the relevant council and chief constable(s) (designated the 'responsible authorities' (s. 5(1))) are under a mutual duty to co-operate with every police authority, probation committee and health authority whose area of responsibility coincides with any part of the relevant local government area. The Home Secretary may also prescribe by order other bodies or persons who benefit from and are subject to the same mutual duty to co-operate in the formulation and implementation of the strategy (s. 5(2)). Examples of such bodies given in the

Government consultation paper were local schools and education and training institutions, youth services and the CPS.

It will be particularly important that local crime strategies are developed in a way which is consistent with the annual policing plans which police authorities are required to produce. This should not cause too many problems, particularly since the review of crime levels and patterns which the new legislation requires can be used by police authorities to gain a clear view of policing needs and priorities across their areas.

The Home Secretary may also prescribe by order other descriptions of person or body to be invited to participate in the formulation or implementation of the strategy. Where such an order has been made, the responsible authorities will be under a duty to invite participation by one such person or body fitting the relevant description (s. 5(3)). The consultation paper gave a number of examples of the sorts of bodies which might be invited to participate in a less formal way, these included: local residents and voluntary groups; faith communities; Drug Action Teams; Area Criminal Justice Liaison committees, the fire service (in relation to arson protection) and the British Transport Police in areas where the rail infrastructure is an integral part of the community.

Review of local crime and disorder

Before embarking upon the formulation of a crime prevention strategy, the responsible authorities must undertake a lengthy process of auditing the levels of crime and disorder in their area (s. 6(2)). The process will have four stages. First, a review of levels and patterns of crime and disorder must be carried out. It is a requirement that account is taken of the knowledge and experience of persons in the area. This suggests that it would not be sufficient to rely upon police records of reported crime or court records of prosecution, but rather research similar to that conducted for the *British Crime Survey* should be carried out. This would involve surveys of residents to discover what forms of crime they had experienced and what impact it had had on their lives. Detailed advice on the organisation and commissioning of the relevant research is found in Chapter 3 of the guidance published by the Home Office. The second and third stages would be to analyse the results of that review and to publish the results in a report. The fourth stage would be to obtain the views on that report of the local residents and bodies in the area, to include any bodies which the responsible authorities are required to invite to participate in formulating the strategy, as prescribed by the Home Secretary under s. 5(3). Views of residents might be obtained by holding public meetings or otherwise.

The requirement to publish the review of local crime and solicit local opinion is a clear expression of the Government's aim to democratise criminal justice and to involve citizens in crime prevention. It is clear that, if these aims are to be achieved, efforts must be made to ensure that the report is published widely and in terms which make sense to ordinary citizens rather than to professional criminologists and experienced politicians.

Each crime prevention strategy must be designed to operate for a three-year period, after which time it must be renewed (s. 6(1) and (7)(a)). The first such strategy must operate from a date to be set by the Home Secretary. Presumably, a sufficient lead-in period will be allowed to enable the completion of the crime audit procedures discussed above.

The effect of these provisions is to commit local authorities and police forces to what will be virtually a rolling programme of surveying, analysing, reporting and consultation, followed by strategy formulation. Although the *Survey of Community Safety Activities in England and Wales*, published in 1996, indicated that 62 per cent of authorities had undertaken crime pattern analysis, it seems probable that guidance will be required from the Home Office to assist local authorities and police forces in what for some will be a new function.

The strategy

The strategy must include both objectives and long-term and short-term performance targets against which the extent to which the objectives have been achieved can be measured (s. 6(4)). Examples of performance targets given in the Government consultation document included the number of homes fitted with alarms, the number of young people attending clubs and reductions in the number of burglaries or incidents of town centre disorder per month. It must be specified what persons or bodies are pursuing what objectives. Responsibility for pursuing particular objectives can be placed upon the responsible authorities, co-operating probation authorities and health authorities, other co-operating bodies as prescribed by the Home Secretary under s. 5(2)(c) and any body invited to co-operate as prescribed under s. 5(3), or by agreement with any other person or body (s. 6(4)).

Once formulated the strategy, including objectives and performance targets, must be published in the relevant area (s. 6(5)(d)). The published document must also include details of the co-operating persons and bodies, details of the review of crime patterns and levels and details of the locally published report (s. 6(5)(a) to (c)).

In the course of implementing the strategy, the responsible authorities are under a continuing duty to keep it under review and to make any changes to it that appear necessary or expedient (s. 6(6)).

Scrutiny by the Home Secretary

The process for reviewing crime and devising a strategy to tackle it is primarily designed as one for which the local council and chief constable will be accountable to the people rather than to some higher authority. In its consultation paper, the Government described the role of the Home Office as helping to identify and spread good practice and the hope was expressed that local partnerships would provide copies of strategy and progress documents to the Home Office to aid this function (*Getting to Grips with Crime*, p. 5). This is not mandatory, although s. 7 provides a long-stop power for the Home Secretary to require the responsible authorities for a particular local government area to report on the exercise of their functions. The Home Secretary must specify on which matters a report is required (s. 7(1), may specify the form which the report is to take (s. 7(2)), and may require that the report should be published in a manner which appears to him to be appropriate (s. 7(3)).

Local authorities' duty to consider crime and disorder implications

A further initiative arising out of the consultation paper *Getting to Grips with Crime* is the new duty imposed by s. 17 on each local authority 'to exercise its various functions with due regard to the likely effect of the exercise of those functions on, and the need to do all that it reasonably can to prevent, crime and disorder in its area'. This duty applies to all local authorities, joint authorities, police authorities, National Park authorities and the Broads Authority (s. (2)).

The effect of this new duty for local government was described in the consultation paper in the following terms: 'The proposals are not about requiring local government to deliver a major new service, or to take on substantial new burdens. Their aim is to give the vital work of preventing crime a major new focus across a very wide range of local services.... It is a matter of putting crime and disorder considerations at the heart of decision making ...' (p. 6). For the Government, this new focus is seen as a potential money-saver — for instance if a strategy were succesful in combating vandalism it might thereby reduce repair bills — and for this reason no additional money from central government is to be provided to accompany this new duty.

Chapter 2
Youth Crime and Disorder

Part I of the Act contains a group of provisions which are designed to address the causes of youth crime. These relate to parenting orders, child safety orders, local child curfew schemes and powers to remove suspected truants from the streets to return them to school or some other designated place. The provision relating to truants will come into force on 1 December 1998. The remaining provisions will be piloted, alongside the youth justice measures considered in Chapter 4, from 30 September 1998 for a period of 18 months in four areas. One purpose of the pilot study will be to enable the drafting of suitable rules of court relating to parenting orders and child safety orders.

PARENTING ORDERS

Sections 8 and 9 provide new powers for courts to make parenting orders where a child has been dealt with for an offence, anti-social behaviour or truancy and where such an order is desirable for the purpose of preventing a recurrence of the problem which led to the original court proceedings. Pre-existing measures for parental responsibility for juvenile offending impose sanctions and burdens on the hapless parents. The new order is innovative in addressing the problems of parenting in a constructive way by requiring parents to participate in weekly counselling or guidance sessions for a period of up to three months.

Background

The central theme of the Government's White Paper *No More Excuses* (Cm 3809, 1997) and the earlier consultation paper *Tackling Youth Crime* was 'taking responsibility', applicable to both young offenders and their parents. Although this principle has considerable political and practical appeal, by treating children and parents together it may obscure the essential difference between the nature of the responsibility which attaches to the two groups. The child is responsible because she or he committed a wrongful act and may therefore be punished for it. It is true that in some cases a parent may have contributed to the commission of the crime by some dereliction of duty but this will generally not be known or proven. Thus, if as a general principle or rule parents of young offenders are to be responsible, this must be in the sense of having a duty to attempt to prevent further offending behaviour. If such a responsibility is to exist it will be one which is imposed by law as flowing from the status of parent, rather than flowing directly from the earlier criminal act.

The distinction between the responsibility of the young offender and that of the parent can thus be expressed as follows: the young offender is responsible for the earlier crime; the parent has responsibilities in relation to guiding the future conduct of the young offender.

A criticism of the pre-existing law on parental responsibility for youth crime is that by appearing to sanction or punish the parent it blurs the distinction between responsibility for the crime and the parent's responsibilities in relation to the child. Thus, parents are made liable for financial penalties imposed on their children under s. 57 of the Criminal Justice Act 1991, and may be bound over to exercise proper parental control of a child offender, subject to forfeiture of a recognisance of up to £1,000 for failure to do so, under s. 58 of the Criminal Justice Act 1991. In the latter case, unreasonable refusal to be bound over can itself be treated as the equivalent of a summary offence, punishable by a fine not exceeding level 3 on the standard scale (currently £1,000).

A second criticism of the existing regime of parental responsibility is that it adds to the burdens of families who are already experiencing difficulties and may ultimately lead to children being taken into care and the break-up of a family. The burdens imposed on parents may be quite unrealistic, for instance where a single working mother of three children is bound over to control a wayward delinquent 16-year-old. Although requiring parents to take responsibility for their children's offending was the central plank of the former Government's juvenile justice policy (*Crime, Justice and Protecting the Public*, HMSO, 1990), it is now recognised that the relevant provisions of the 1991 Act are not popular with magistrates, and accordingly are little used. Recognising this, the present Government's policy places a new emphasis on offering training and support to help parents to change and control their children's offending behaviour, whilst retaining the possibility that parents who neglect their responsibilities may be answerable to the courts. Similar proposals had been made in a consultation paper, *Preventing Children Offending*, published by the former Conservative Government (Home Office, 1997). Notwithstanding the change of emphasis, a detailed study of the new provisions discloses many of the faults of the scheme which they supplement.

The parenting order

A court may make a parenting order in a number of circumstances specified in s. 8(1), these are:

(a) where the court makes a child safety order in respect of a child under the age of 10, under s. 11;

(b) where the court makes an anti-social behaviour order or a sex offender order in respect of a child or young person;

(c) where a child or young person is convicted of an offence; or

(d) where a parent or other person in a parental role is convicted of an offence relating to the truancy of a child or young person under ss. 443 or 444 of the Education Act 1996.

The condition which must be fulfilled for a parenting order to be made is that such an order would be desirable in the interests of preventing the conduct which gave rise to the order (s. 8(6)). Thus, in relation to an anti-social behaviour order, a child safety order or sex offender order, the issue for the court is whether a parenting order would be desirable in preventing a repetition of the conduct which led to the original order against the child or young person (s. 8(6)(a)). Where a youngster has been convicted of an offence or a parent has been convicted of an offence relating to his child's truancy, the issue for the court is whether a parenting order would be desirable in preventing further offences by the child or further truancy offences by the adult (s. 8(6)(b) and (c)).

The test of whether an order would be desirable to prevent future misconduct is borrowed from s. 58 of the Criminal Justice Act 1991, which deals with binding over the parents of young offenders. Notwithstanding that pedigree, it remains unclear how the courts should interpret desirability. As stated the test seems to be entirely subjective. However, it would hardly be satisfactory if a bench of magistrates justified the imposition of an order on the basis that they found it desirable even though there was no indication that it would serve any useful purpose, and even though it would cause demonstrable problems for the family in question. It is submitted that a better approach would be to apply a three-stage test. The first stage would involve determining whether there were reasonable grounds to believe that a parenting order might have some effect in preventing the misconduct in question. The second stage would be to consider what adverse consequences for the parent or child, or indeed any other affected party, might flow from the imposition of an order. At the third stage the court would determine the ultimate question of whether in the circumstances it was desirable to impose an order, by weighing the likely advantages and disadvantages of doing so.

Even where a court is satisfied that a parenting order would be desirable in the interests of preventing a repetition of the objectionable conduct, the court generally retains a discretion not to impose an order. This follows from s. 8(2) which states that the court 'may' make an order where it is satisfied that the relevant conditions are fulfilled. An exception to this general rule is made where a person under the age of sixteen is convicted of an offence. In this case the court must make a parenting order if it is satisfied that the relevant conditions are fulfilled (s. 9(1)(a)), and if it is not so satisfied, must state in open court that it is not and why it is not (s. 9(1)(b)). It is not clear why the commission of an offence as the basis for an order should be treated differently from the other grounds. The relevance of the age of sixteen would appear to be that a young person of this age may have removed himself from parental control in which case a parenting order would be futile.

Circumstances in which an order should not be made would include: where it is clear that the parents are already making sensible efforts to control the child and will continue to do so, or where the parents need help but are willing to seek and receive this on a voluntary basis. This point was made by Lord Williams of Moston, speaking for the Government at the Committee Stage in the Lords:

What we are trying to provide is a regime which will assist parents, not dragoon them unmercifully … We would prefer voluntary counselling and parenting guidance, but for those who do not wish it … a sanction may be of assistance. (*Hansard*, Lords, 10 Feb 1998, cols 1076-1077).

It is important that the stigma of a parenting order should not be applied needlessly. If this is to be avoided, it would appear that the Government must make provision for those who need parenting advice and are willing to receive it voluntarily, as well as for those who are required to receive it by court order. At the other end of the scale, an order should not be imposed where it would be futile, for instance in circumstances in which it is clear that a parent has lost control of the child and has no realistic prospect of regaining it.

The terms of the order

The core of the parenting order is a requirement to attend counselling or guidance sessions, no more than once a week for a period of up to three months (s. 8(4)(b)). The sessions to be attended will be specified by the 'responsible officer', who will be a probation officer, social worker or member of a youth offending team (s. 8(8)). The delegation of this responsibility to an official should provide a degree of flexibility and permit variations in the programme without the need for further court hearings. The court has a discretion to waive the requirement to attend counselling or guidance sessions where a parent has attended such sessions under an earlier parenting order (s. 8(5)).

As well as attending parenting sessions, the parent may be required to comply with further requirements specified in the order, for a period not exceeding 12 months (s. 8(4)(a)). Such requirements may be imposed which the court considers desirable in the interests of preventing repetition of the misconduct which led to the making of the order or further offences (s. 8(7)). The White Paper *No More Excuses* (p. 14) gave the following as examples of additional requirements which might be imposed in appropriate cases: a parent might be required to escort his child to school or to ensure that a responsible adult would be at home to supervise the child during the evenings.

Both the court, in imposing requirements, and the responsible officer, in issuing directions relating to the attendance at counselling or guidance sessions, must try to avoid conflicts with the parent's religious beliefs and clashes with periods during which the parent is normally at work or attending an educational establishment (s. 9(4))

Because the core of the parenting order involves attendance at counselling or guidance sessions, it will not be practical to make such orders until local arrangements have been made to provide such sessions. Accordingly, a court must not make a parenting order unless it has been notified by the Home Office that suitable arrangements are in place in the area in which it appears to the court that the relevant parent resides or will reside (s. 8(3)). The term 'area' is not defined, nor is there any requirement that the training sessions must be reasonably accessible to the parent, except to the extent that attendance must not conflict with times of work or attendance at an educational establishment under s. 94(b). It therefore appears that a person might be ordered to attend sessions at a considerable distance from his home, but within the same 'area' according to the definition applied by the Home Office. In such circumstances, a person charged with the offence of failing to comply with the order might raise the defence of reasonable excuse under s. 9(7).

Before making an order, the court must explain to the parent(s) in ordinary language the effect of the order and of the requirements to be imposed and that failure to comply with the order without reasonable excuse is punishable as a summary offence (s. 9(3)).

The affected parent

The parenting order may be made in respect of a person who is a parent or guardian, or somebody who fulfils the definition of parent for the purpose of the Education Act offences. Since a number of persons may fulfil the definition of parent or guardian, this may give the court a discretion concerning who is to be subject to the order. In practice, this is most likely to be the person who attends court as parent under s. 34A of the Children and Young Persons Act 1933 (as inserted by s. 56 of the Criminal Justice Act 1991). This conclusion is reinforced by two factors: first, that before making an order the court is required to explain it to the affected parent under s. 9(3) and this would not be possible for a parent who was not before the court; secondly, under s. 8(6) the court should not make an order which would be futile, and it would be very difficult to be satisfied on this issue without having the parent who is to be subject to the order before the court.

In the not unusual situation where of two parents only one takes a constructive interest in the welfare of the child, the effect of limiting parenting orders to those parents who attend court will be to further burden the interested parent whilst leaving the uninterested parent untouched. This raises doubts about the ability of the new provision to force the laxest parents to take a positive role in preventing youth crime.

Unlike s. 57 of the Criminal Justice Act 1991, which controversially extends responsibility for financial penalties incurred by a child to the local authority where the child is either in care or provided with accommodation, only natural persons may be subject to parenting orders.

Appeals against parenting orders

A person against whom a parenting order has been made who wishes to challenge it has a choice of courses. As well as the right of appeal provided by s. 10, an aggrieved parent may also seek a discharge or variation of the order from the court which made it under s. 9(5) (discussed below). Notably, the application for discharge or variation is not contingent upon proof of a change of circumstances and could be made immediately after the imposition of the order. In theory this leaves the parent with a straight choice of means to challenge an order. In practice it seems very unlikely that a court would countenance discharge or variation soon after an order is made and in the absence of a change of circumstances. This suggests that the first resort of an aggrieved parent will be an appeal under s. 10, with an application under s. 9(5) as a fallback option if that fails. Interestingly, there seems to be nothing to prevent an applicant under s. 9(5) relying upon grounds precisely similar to those which had been unsuccessful in a dismissed appeal.

The formal right of appeal under s. 10 may be to the Crown Court, Court of Appeal (Criminal Division) or the High Court, depending upon the original ground for making the order.

Appeal is to the Crown Court where a parenting order follows: the making of either an anti-social behaviour order or a sex offender order against a child or young person (s. 10(1)(b)); the conviction of a child or young person in a youth court (s. 10(4)(a)), or the conviction of the parent for an offence relating to the child's truancy (s. 10(5)). In all of these cases an aggrieved parent may also appeal by way of case stated to the High Court on the ground that the court's determination was wrong in law or is in excess of jurisdiction, under s. 111(1) of the Magistrates' Courts Act 1980.

Appeal will be to the Court of Appeal where the parenting order is made following a conviction of a child for an offence where the child or young person has been tried in the Crown Court (s. 10(4)).

Appeal is to the High Court (ie the Divisional Court of the Queens Bench Division) where a parenting order follows the making of a child safety order under s. 11 by a magistrates' court sitting as a family proceedings court (s. 10(1)(a)).

The powers of the court hearing the appeal also vary according to the ground for making the order. Where the parenting order follows the making of either an anti-social behaviour order or sex offender order against the child or young person, the Crown Court or High Court has broad powers to make such order as may be necessary to give effect to its determination of the appeal; and may also make such incidental or consequential orders as appear to it to be just (s. 10(2)(a) and (b)). Where the Crown Court or High Court makes an order under these powers, generally the order of the court determining the appeal is to be treated as the order of the original court for the purposes of s. 9(5) and (6), which give the original court powers to vary and discharge parenting orders, and also for the purposes of s. 9(7), which makes breach of a parenting order a summary offence (s. 10(3)). This does not apply where the appeal court directs a magistrates' court (including a youth court) to re-hear an application for a parenting order. In practical terms this means two things:

(a) that the jurisdiction of the Youth Court to vary or discharge a parenting order remains even though the terms of the original order have been varied on appeal;

(b) that failure to comply with a parenting order will be an offence whether or not it has been varied on appeal.

Where the parenting order follows the conviction of the child for an offence or the conviction of the parent for an offence relating to truancy, the appeal is treated as if it were an appeal against sentence (s. 10(4) and (5)). Thus, the case will either be heard in the Crown Court (where the original trial took place in a youth court or magistrates' court) or in the Court of Appeal (in the exceptional case where a child has been tried on indictment in the Crown Court). This is a convenient rule because it ensures that an appeal against the imposition of the parenting order may be dealt with by the same court which would deal with any appeal against sentence by the child (where the parenting order follows the child's conviction) or any appeal by the parent against sentence (where the parenting order follows conviction of the parent for an offence relating to truancy).

Variation and discharge

The court which made a parenting order has wide powers of variation and discharge, on application by either the responsible officer or the parent (s. 9(5)). The court's powers are:

(a) to discharge the order as a whole;

(b) to cancel any provision of the order; or

(c) to insert in the order (either in addition or in substitution for any of its other provisions) any new provision which the court could have included in the order in the first place.

The test for exercising these powers of discharge or variation is what the court considers appropriate. The only limitations are that there appears to be no power to extend the period of the order, which in any event is subject to a maximum of twelve months, and, where an application to discharge an order has been dismissed, no further such application may be made by any person except with the consent of the court which made the order (s. 9(6)).

The procedure is most likely to be used to accommodate changes in circumstances, for instance to vary the obligation to attend guidance sessions where a parent moves home or becomes ill. The procedure is sufficiently flexible to respond to problems relating to the child or young person which have arisen since the first hearing. Thus, for instance, if following the imposition of a parenting order a child begins to truant from school, the order could be varied to require the parent to accompany the child to school each day.

No procedure is specified under s. 9(5) except that an application must be made by either the parent or the responsible officer. Rules of court are to be made relating to this procedure and they are expected to require notification to the other party and to grant a right to be heard on the issue.

CHILD SAFETY ORDERS

The child safety order relating to children under ten, introduced by s. 11, reflects three of the core policies underlying the Act. These are: first, that preventing crime is better than responding once it has occurred; secondly, that young offenders and their parents must take responsibility for their offences; and thirdly, that measures should target not just crime, but also undisciplined or anti-social behaviour which tends to accompany crime. The new order responds to research which suggests that offending may be greatly influenced by a child's early influences and that patterns of offending behaviour may be established at a young age (Graham, J. and Bowling, B., *Young people and crime*, Home Office, 1995). In practice child safety orders are likely to be used in conjunction with parenting orders under s. 8.

The label 'child safety' is somewhat misleading since the order is not directly concerned with the child's welfare but rather addresses the child's potential offending behaviour. The order may be made by a magistrates' court and is triggered by the child's misconduct. The effect of the order is to place the child under supervision for a period of (normally) three months and to subject the child to certain restrictions or requirements.

Although the order was generally supported in its passage through Parliament, it has been criticised elsewhere. For instance the National Association of Probation Officers have argued that the effect of the order is to 'reduce the age of criminal responsibility to zero' and criticised its negativity, feeling that a provision which positively encouraged care and support would achieve more (NAPO, *Briefing on the Crime and Disorder Bill*, February 1998). The Family Policy Studies Centre have expressed concern that the provision blurs the age of criminal responsibility and, in particular, may lead young children to believe that they are offenders. It pointed out that the provision does not make clear who has responsibility for seeing that a child complies with requirements under an order and the fear is expressed that the use of orders may increase the numbers of children entering the court and care systems (FSPC, *The Crime and Disorder Bill and the Family*, 1998).

Making of the order

Jurisdiction to make child safety orders is vested in the magistrates' family proceedings court, which may make an order only if it has been notified by the Home Secretary that arrangements for implementing such orders are available in the area (s. 11(2)). The choice of the family proceedings court as the venue, rather than the youth court as originally proposed, is a concession to those critics who view the order as a means of criminalising children.

Application for an order must be made by a local authority with social services responsibilities, presumably represented by a social worker (s. 11(1)). This underlines the extent to which the new crime prevention measures require co-operation between police and local authorities, since most commonly it will be the police who become aware of the misconduct which triggers the application to make an order. Placing this responsibility on the local authority should ensure that the application is made in full knowledge of other social work interventions in relation to the child or the family.

When applying for an order, the local authority should report to the court on the child's family circumstances and the likely effect of the order on those circumstances, since such information must be considered by the court before an order may be made (s. 12(1)).

Before making an order the court must be satisfied that one or more of four conditions, set out in s. 11(3), are fulfilled. These are:

(a) that the child has committed an act which, if he had been aged 10 or over, would have constituted an offence;

(b) that a child safety order is necessary for the purpose of preventing the commission by the child of an act which would have constituted an offence if committed by a child aged 10 or over;

(c) that the child has contravened a ban imposed by a curfew notice under s. 14 (see below);

(d) that the child has acted in a manner that caused or was likely to cause harassment, alarm or distress to one or more persons not of the same household as himself.

The standard of proof to be applied in determining whether a condition is fulfilled is the civil standard on a balance of probabilities (s. 11(6)).

The grounds for making the order are so wide that it would be hard to imagine a child who did not qualify. Thus, taking sweets from a friend or even a risk that a child might do so would qualify under (a) and (b), a curfew contravention might involve 10 minutes innocent play after 9 p.m. by a child who did not understand the curfew and who was not wearing a watch, and condition (d) might be satisfied by raucous play to the annoyance of an elderly neighbour. Because of the breadth of these conditions it seems that youth offending teams and courts must devise further criteria to distinguish the trivial from cases where intervention would be helpful. The huge discretion granted to enforcers and courts may also be fertile ground for discrimination, perhaps unconscious, between groups of children on class, race or other grounds. This should be addressed and guarded against.

The procedure to be adopted by the court in making an order is unclear until new rules of court are promulgated. The Act contains no particular provision for summoning either the child or the child's parents or guardians to attend. Reliance cannot be placed on s. 34A of the Children and Young Persons Act 1933, which requires a court to order the attendance of a parent or guardian where a 'child or young person is charged with an offence or is for any other reason brought before a court'. This provision is inapplicable because, even where the basis for application is conduct corresponding to an offence, the child is not 'charged with an offence', and neither could the child be said to be 'brought before the court' since there is no power to do so. Section 12(2) which requires that an explanation is given to a parent or guardian before an order is made, assumes the presence of the parent or guardian, but provides no power to bring such person before the court. Presumably these problems will be addressed in the expected rules of court.

If the court is to be satisfied that one or more condition is fulfilled, there must first be at least the opportunity for an adversarial contest, or alternatively some method for taking the equivalent of a plea. For instance, where the ground for applying for the order is that the child had committed a quasi-crime under (a) and this is denied by the child, there must be some means of determining the facts. It appears that the court will have to devise some procedure for doing this with little assistance from the Act, which does not specify whether the child or the parent or both should be considered parties to the action. In draft guidance on child safety orders published in July 1998, the Home Office has expressed the view that the parties to the proceedings will be the local authority as applicant and the parents or guardians of the child (para. 3.5). This view is supported by s. 12(4), which gives a parent or guardian a right to apply to court to vary or cancel an order. This strongly implies that a parent has powers to appear and make representations at the original hearing, and probably also to call evidence relating to the issue of whether or not one of the conditions is fulfilled. In principle, the parent should be able to make representations concerning any requirement which it is proposed to impose on the child.

Before making an order, the court must consider information about the child's family circumstances and the likely effect of the order on those circumstances (s. 12(1)). This information may be supplied orally, since there is no requirement that the information must be supplied in writing. The duty on the court to consider the likely effect of the order implies that the court should exercise its discretion against making an order where to do so would cause greater problems for the family. It seems sensible that such reports will be supplied either by social services or by the youth offender team, although the duties of the local authority and the youth offender team relate only to 'the provision of reports or other information required by the courts in criminal proceedings against children ...' (s. 38(4)(e)), whereas an application for a child safety order is a civil proceeding. It would seem right in principle to request information about the family circumstances from the parents and not simply to rely upon a social worker's report.

The court must also, before making an order, explain to the child's parent or guardian in ordinary language the effect of the order and any requirements included in it, the consequences which may follow if the child fails to comply with any of those requirements, and that the court has power to review the order on the application either of the parent or guardian or of the officer responsible for supervising the child under the order (s. 12(2)). The explanation required will be complex and difficult to formulate in a way which would be readily understandable to a lay person. It is to be hoped that some body, perhaps the Home Office or Magistrates' Association, will draft a model explanation for the guidance of courts performing this difficult task.

The terms of the order

A child safety order made under s. 11 places a named child under the age of 10 under the supervision of a responsible officer, who may be either a social worker or member of a youth offending team (s. 11(8)) The draft Home Office guidance suggests that, where a child safety order is combined with a parenting order, it would be convenient for the same responsible officer to be appointed in respect of both. Even where a formal parenting order is not made, the imposition of requirements under a child safety order will inevitably mean that the responsible officer must work with the parents. An order will operate for a period of up to three months, or in exceptional circumstances, 12 months (s. 11(4)). An order will also require the child to comply with requirements specified by the court.

The normal maximum duration of three months does not appear to be consistent with the purposes of the order which are to address the child's offending behaviour and influence the child away from a lifestyle conducive to offending. It seems unlikely that work having lasting benefits for the child could be done in such a short period. It is also inconsistent that a parenting order may run for up to 12 months without the need to demonstrate exceptional circumstances. What the courts will consider to be exceptional circumstances remains to be seen. In theory, the courts should not treat the mere fact that a longer period of supervision is needed to be effective as an exceptional circumstance, since this would probably apply to the majority of cases.

The requirements which may be imposed upon the child are those which the court considers desirable in the interests of:

(a)   securing that the child receives appropriate care, protection and support and is subject to proper control; or

(b)   preventing a repetition of the kind of behaviour which led to the child safety order being made (s. 11(5)).

As far as practicable, such requirements should avoid any conflict with the parent's religious beliefs, and any interference with the times at which the child normally attends school (s. 12(3)).

The draft Home Office guidance indicates that requirements imposed under an order will need to be tailored to the problems or behaviour and underlying causes which prompted the making of the order. The requirements would also necessarily take account of locally available schemes and facilities. The following were suggested as requirements which might be imposed:

(a)   attendance at a school or extra-curricular activities such as sporting activities or homework clubs;

(b)   avoiding contact with disruptive and possibly older children;

(c)   not visiting areas, such as shopping centres, unsupervised;

(d)   being home during certain hours, probably the evenings; or

(e)   attending particular courses or sessions to address specific problems (e.g., educational support or behavioural management).

Discharge, variation and appeals

Procedures are provided for both the discharge and variation of child safety orders on application of either the responsible officer or the parent or guardian, under s. 12(4), and for appeals against the making of an order, under s. 13. Since either procedure can lead to the complete discharge of an order, an aggrieved parent has two possible rights of appeal, although in normal circumstances the fact that the order runs for a maximum of three months should deter appeals.

Under s. 12(4), the court has a wide discretion to discharge the order, cancel any provision in it, or insert (either by addition or substitution) any provision which could have been included in the order from the outset. An application may be made only while the order is in force, and thus cannot be made for the sole purpose of vindicating a grievance after an order has run its course. The test to be applied is what appears appropriate to the court. There is no requirement of a change of circumstances. However, since the power to discharge or vary is vested only in the court which made the original order, it seems unlikely that any application will be entertained without some change of circumstances. Presumably such applications will normally be heard *inter partes*, although it appears that once the order is in force the responsible officer is treated as a party rather than the local authority which applied for the original order. Once an application for discharge has been dismissed, no further application for discharge may be made by any person except with the consent of the court which made the order (s. 12(5)). This is designed to avoid the court's time being wasted by repeat applications.

Under s. 13, an appeal against the making of a child safety order lies to the Divisional Court. Unlike the provision for variation or discharge, which nominates the parent as party to the proceeding, it is not stated who may appeal. In the absence of such a statement, the child is presumably the appellant, and may be represented by a parent or other person as next friend. There is no right of appeal for the local authority against a refusal to grant an order. On hearing the appeal the court may make whatever orders are necessary to give effect to its determination of the appeal and may make such incidental or consequential orders as appear to it to be just. For the purposes of any later proceedings to vary or discharge an order or for breach of the order, any order made by the Divisional Court on appeal is to be treated as if it were an order of the magistrates' court from which the appeal was brought (s. 13(2)). Necessarily, this rule does not apply to an order of the Divisional Court directing that an application should be re-heard by the magistrates' court.

Breach of a child safety order

The magistrates' court is given powers under s. 12(6) where it is satisfied that a child has failed to comply with any requirement of a child safety order, following an application by the responsible officer. The court's powers are:

(a) to discharge the order and substitute a care order under s. 31(1)(a) of the Children Act 1989; or

(b) to vary the original order, either by cancelling any provision in it or by inserting or substituting for an existing provision any provision which could have been included in the child safety order when first made.

Where a court decides that in consequence of the breach a care order should be made, s. 12(7) provides that it will not be necessary to establish the normal conditions for a care order under s. 31(2) of the Children Act 1989 (i.e., that the child is suffering, or is likely to suffer significant harm due to unreasonably poor parental care or that the child is beyond parental control). It appears that breach of a child safety order provides a new route into care which is not subject to the traditional safeguards. It is important that courts do not treat a care order as a natural response to breach. Whether or not s. 31(2) formally applies in the case of breach, it would seem sensible for the courts to adopt some form of threshold test akin to that provision to avoid the needless imposition of care orders.

CHILD CURFEW SCHEMES

Section 14 provides power to impose local short-term curfews for children under the age of 10. The policy to introduce such powers had been announced by Jack Straw as Shadow Home Secretary in 1996. Notwithstanding considerable opposition to the proposals, they were carried forward through the consultation paper *Tackling Youth Crime* (1997) and the White Paper *No More Excuses* (Cm 3809, 1997).

The problem which the scheme addresses, as described in the consultation paper, is that 'unsupervised children gathered in public places can cause real alarm and misery to local communities and can encourage one another into anti-social and criminal habits' (para. 114). The White Paper which followed placed a rather different emphasis: 'for their own good, and to prevent neighbourhood crime or disorder, young children should not be out unsupervised late at night' (para. 5.6).

Critics in both the press and Parliament expressed scepticism about the scale of the problem, pointing out that the Government did not rely upon any hard evidence and that, in any event, the police have existing powers under s. 46 of the Children Act 1989 to take children into temporary custody. Although this power is expressly for the purpose of preventing significant harm to the child, rather than to the community, it could reasonably be argued that to prevent a child being drawn into criminal or disorderly acts is to protect the child from harm. The National Association of Probation Officers suggested that, if the purpose of the measure was to encourage communities to take control of their youngsters, this might be better achieved by real efforts to support and revitalise communities.

Other criticisms which were summarised in a briefing paper issued by the Family Policy Studies Centre focused on the possibility of considerable regional variations; the need for additional resources for enforcement; and that children on the streets may be genuinely escaping from abuse, violence or alcohol or drug abuse in the home (FPSC, *Briefing on the Crime and Disorder Bill*, 1998). A further criticism that exercise of the power would breach Art. 5 of the European Convention on Human Rights would probably not stand up to scrutiny in view of the margin of appreciation permitted to domestic law in relation to matters of public order and child welfare.

The power to declare a local child curfew

The power to make a local child curfew scheme under s. 14(1) is vested in a local authority, including for this purpose: district councils, London borough councils, the Common Council of the City of London, the councils for the Isle of Wight and the

Isles of Scilly and, in Wales, county and county borough councils (s. 14(8)). A scheme will come into operation only if confirmed by the Home Secretary, who may also fix the date on which it is to come into operation (s. 14(5)).

A precondition for making a curfew scheme is that the authority consults with every chief constable whose force area covers any part of the authority's area and also such persons or other bodies as the authority considers appropriate (s. 14(3)). Where a local authority is served by two police forces, it seems that the duty to consult a chief constable applies even where the local area in which the proposed curfew is to operate falls outside that chief constable's police area. Although the duty to consult does not require that consent is obtained, it is unlikely that a local authority would go ahead without the agreement of the police who would have responsibility for enforcing the scheme.

The local authority has total discretion over whether or not to consult other persons or bodies. Consultation with community groups may have benefits in gaining local support for any scheme, or perhaps for achieving voluntary understandings about how local children should be dealt with which might render a scheme unnecessary. In view of the Government policy to encourage partnerships in dealing with crime, it may be that the Home Secretary would be unwilling to confirm a scheme which was proposed without appropriate local consultation.

A local scheme will involve a ban on children of specified ages (under 10) being in a public place within the specified area covered by the scheme. The curfew will operate during specified hours between 9 p.m. and 6 a.m., unless the child is under the effective control of a parent or responsible person aged 18 or over (s. 14(2)). Different age groups may be banned during different hours (s. 14(6)). By restricting the exception to cases in which the child is under the effective control of an adult, the provision makes clear that it is not sufficient if an adult is merely at hand, unless that adult is exercising control, which presumably means actively preventing the sorts of conduct which the curfew is designed to prevent. Thus, a child could not avoid a curfew simply by running with a gang of youngsters some of whom were aged over 18.

A child will only be in breach of a curfew if found in a public place (s. 14(2)). For this purpose 'public place' bears the same meaning as in Part II of the Public Order Act 1986 (s. 14(8)). Under the 1986 Act, this includes all highways, pavements and verges, footpaths and bridleways and 'any other place to which at the material time the public or any section of the public has access, on payment or otherwise, as of right or by virtue of express or implied permission' (Public Order Act 1986, s. 16). The issue is whether the public are allowed access at the relevant time and so, for instance, a snooker club would be a public place notwithstanding that the manager could refuse entry to any person and that it closed at midnight.

A scheme will normally come into force one month after confirmation or on a different date fixed by the Home Secretary (s. 14(5)). The ban can last for a maximum of 90 days, suggesting that the provision is designed for short-term street-clearing exercises rather than long-term regimes. There is however nothing to stop a local authority seeking a succession of consecutive bans in relation to the same area.

The notice which must be given of the scheme must specify the area and the relevant age groups and times during which the ban will operate (s. 14(1) and (6)). The curfew notice must be posted in some conspicuous place or places within the specified area, and in a manner which the local authority considers desirable for giving publicity to the notice (s. 14(7)). This requirement is not wholly unambiguous. At first glance it might appear that, however extensive the area in which the curfew is to operate, a single prominently placed notice will suffice. An alternative interpretation would be that whether or not the notice is conspicuous should be judged relative to the area in which the ban is to operate. Thus, if a curfew is to operate in a large area, say a whole housing estate, a notice should be conspicuous in every part of that estate. Whatever the correct interpretation of the term, wide publicity will be necessary if curfews are to have any effect in practice, and no doubt local authorities will recognise this.

Contravention of curfew notices

Contravention of curfew notices is dealt with by s. 15. A constable who finds a child whom the constable has reasonable cause to believe is acting in contravention of a ban imposed by a curfew notice may take the child to the child's home, unless the constable has reasonable cause to believe that if taken home the child would be likely to suffer significant harm (s. 15(3)).

The requirement of a reasonable cause to believe requires that the constable acts upon some objective evidence as to all the relevant factors, i.e. the child's age and the absence of effective control by an adult. Once a constable has such reasonable cause for belief that amounts to a defence to any civil action where in fact a mistake has been made. This would apply, at least in theory, to a mistake about the scope of an order in terms of area, age group, hours or operative dates, if there was reasonable cause for the mistake. In practice it would rarely be reasonable for a constable to make a mistake about such matters.

The provision does not give the constable a power to use force in removing a child and taking the child home. The issue might arise if either the child resists or other youngsters or adults with the child resist the removal. Under common-law principles a constable may use reasonable force in exercising a lawful power, although judging what is reasonable in the circumstances might be problematic.

It is implicit that a constable removing a child should check the child's explanation to discover whether the child is absent from home through fear. Although s. 15(3) does not indicate what action should be taken if the constable has cause to believe that the child may suffer harm if taken home, s. 46 of the Children Act 1989 provides a power in such circumstances to remove a child to suitable accommodation, i.e., the police station or the care of social services, for his own safety. This power may also be employed where a constable takes a child home but finds nobody, or no responsible adult, in.

Where a constable has reasonable cause to believe that a child is in contravention of a curfew, the constable must also inform the local authority of this as soon as is reasonably practicable (s. 15(2)). When this is done, the local authority are placed under a duty to enquire into the circumstances of the child and to initiate the investigation within 48 hours of receiving the report of the contravention (s. 15(4)).

Conclusion

The need for curfew schemes has been doubted in many quarters and the scheme has been opposed by groups concerned with civil liberties and child welfare. The scheme will be put into effect only if local authorities take the initiative and if police forces are prepared to make taking children off the streets a high priority. Whether this will happen to any great extent must be questioned. Local authorities may be deterred by the relatively elaborate procedure (involving local consultation, confirmation by the Home Office, and publicity); and the fact that once in place a scheme will operate only for a maximum of three months before needing renewal. Police forces and police officers may not be convinced that the scale of the problem justifies resort to such a power, where to do so is inherently likely to generate confrontation with individuals and groups in the local community.

ROUNDING UP TRUANTS

Section 16 creates a new police power to detain children found playing truant in a public place and to remove them, either back to their own school or to a place designated for this purpose. The provision was added during the Bill's Commons Committee stage following a recommendation of the Schools Exclusion Unit which reported on 11 May 1998. Although the initiative did not emanate from the Home Office it sits well with the core policies underlying the Act. The measure is multi-agency since implementation will involve co-operation between the police, the local authority education department and particular schools. Although the measure has educational and social purposes, its primary rationale is the prevention of youth crime. The hypothesis is that truanting children, away from their homes and in the absence of adult control, are particularly likely to commit crime or indulge in the forms of anti-social behaviour which are dealt with elsewhere in the Act. The Government supports this hypothesis by quoting a Metropolitan Police study which showed that 5 per cent of offences committed by children occurred during school hours (*Hansard*, Standing Committee B, 9 June 1998, col. 778). The measure is therefore consistent with the Government's policy to target resources on early intervention to prevent crime rather than to respond to crime once it has occurred.

The new power will not be generally available to the police, but may be brought into operation in a particular area where two conditions are fulfilled, which effectively require agreement between the police and the education authority. The first condition is that the local authority has designated premises for the purpose of receiving truants and have so notified the chief constable (s. 16(1)). The premises may be a school or some other place such as a local authority office. In debate, Home Office Minister Mr. Mike O'Brien indicated that local authorities would be given a free hand in designating premises but that it was expected that in many cases children would ultimately be removed to their own schools. The second condition is that a superintendent or higher ranking police officer has directed that the relevant powers should be exercisable in a particular area and for a particular period (s. 16(2)).

The effect of these twin conditions is that the powers may be put into operation in areas where there is a particular truancy problem and where both the police and the education department have the resources to deal with it in this way. The fact that the scheme will be put into operation for a definite period reflects the belief that operating the power for a limited period would have both immediate and long-term effects, and therefore may not need to be repeated. This was the experience of an experimental scheme in Kent which was influential on the Government's thinking (*Hansard*, Standing Committee B, 9 June 1998, col. 785).

Where the scheme has been put into operation, if a constable finds a child or young person in a public place and has reasonable cause to believe that the child is of compulsory school age, and is absent from school without lawful authority, the constable may remove the child to the designated premises or to his or her school (s. 16(3)). 'Public place' has the same meaning as in Part II of the Public Order Act 1986 and will include places such as shopping centres and bowling alleys, where the public, or a section of the public, are either granted access or may be if payment is made. By the exclusion of private premises, it is made clear that the measure is not aimed at truancy *per se*, but rather truancy in situations where it is most likely to lead to offending or anti-social behaviour.

A child's absence from school will be taken to be without lawful authority unless it falls within the lawful grounds set out in s. 444 of the Education Act 1996, which covers leave, sickness, unavoidable delay or days set aside for religious observance. It should be noted that a child who is being lawfully educated other than at school under s. 7 of the Education Act 1996, or a child who is excluded from school, will not be covered by the provision because neither could be described as absent from school.

The power under s. 16(3) operates only where the constable has reasonable cause to believe the relevant conditions apply. Since the scheme will operate only in areas where truancy is a problem and by agreement with the education department, the officer's belief may be supported by information supplied by local schools. Nevertheless, officers may have difficulties in applying the test in relation to youngsters who are unco-operative, particularly in areas which are served by more than one school or where local schools have different term dates or hours of work. Although officers would have a defence to a civil or criminal action if they acted on the basis of a reasonable belief, they might be unwilling to act in relation to children of 14 or 15 who claimed to be above the school-leaving age. This might leave the most problematic group of truants untouched by the provision.

The constable's power is to remove the child to school or designated premises. This is not an arrest in the traditional sense of detention for the purpose of instituting proceedings and thus statutory provisions relating to arrests will not apply. It seems probable however that common-law principles relating to arrests would apply, particularly the requirement to explain reasons and the power to use reasonable force to effect the arrest. The duty to explain reasons for an arrest was established by the House of Lords in *Christie* v *Leachinsky* [1947] AC 573. In that case, Viscount's Simon's rationale for requiring reasons to be given was simply that the arrested person as a citizen was entitled to know why he was being seized. The power under s. 16 may not be described as an arrest but it nevertheless involves the deprivation of liberty of a person who is, however young, a citizen. It seems axiomatic that the rule in *Christie* v *Leachinsky* must apply.

It is also probable that the common-law rule entitling a constable to use reasonable force to effect a lawful arrest should apply. If it did not, the constable would be left in the strange position of having a legal power over a young person which could be resisted by simple refusal to co-operate. On the other hand it should not be assumed that degrees of force which might be justified in relation to arrest would be lawful in this context. In relation to arrest, the use of quite a high degree of force may be justified by the social interest in bringing suspected offenders to justice. It is less clear how great the social interest is in rounding up truants, and therefore less clear what degree of force could be used. It may be that officers will be advised not to use force in exercising powers under s. 16, even if this undermines the purpose of the provision and leads to a loss of authority for the individual officer. Two good reasons can be suggested for such a policy: first, that this is the only sure way for the officer to avoid possible civil or criminal action; secondly, that use of force in these circumstances might have a damaging effect on relations between the police and young people.

Chapter 3
Criminal Law

This chapter deals with the two major changes to the substantive criminal law introduced by Chapter III of the Act, i.e., the creation of a number of racially aggravated offences and the abolition of the presumption of *doli incapax* in relation to children. It will also deal with the related matter of the effect of a child's silence at trial and the quite separate matter of new police powers to require removal of masks etc. which are to be found in an adjacent part of the Act.

RACIALLY AGGRAVATED OFFENCES

Background

Concern about racially motivated criminal conduct has grown in recent decades and has been manifested in a variety of ways. The offence of inciting racial hatred (the latest manifestations of which are now to be found in ss. 18 to 23 of the Public Order Act 1986) was created by the Race Relations Act 1965, but the offence was always controversial because of its potential conflict with freedom of expression and has proved both difficult to enforce and largely ineffective in dealing with racism. Since 1988 the police have recorded separately any incident within the 1985 Association of Chief Police Officers' (ACPO) definition 'in which it appears to the reporting or investigating officer that the complaint involves an element of racial motivation; or any incident which includes an allegation of racial motivation made by any person'. The number of incidents reported under this test rose from 4,383 in 1988 to 7,734 in 1992, an apparent increase of 77 per cent, although some of this increase may have been due to changes in recording practice. Figures from the British Crime Survey relating to the same period suggest that the true figure was between 13,000 and 14,000 incidents reported annually and that there was a considerable gap between the number of racial incidents reported to the police and the number actually recorded (Home Office research and statistics directorate: research findings No 39, August 1996). A survey by the Police Research Group for the year 1996/7 (Home Office press release, 24 November 1997) found wide variations between forces in the information on racial incidents that is recorded and counted and a wide range of interpretations of the ACPO definition of a racial incident. Irrespective of the differences in recording procedures, the numbers of racial incidents actually recorded by the police continued to rise from 7,734 in 1992 to 12,222 in the period April 1995 to March 1996.

Whatever might be the true figure of actual racial incidents under whichever definition, the clear perception of racially motivated crime as a significant problem (and notorious cases such as the stabbing to death in 1993 of a black youth, Stephen Lawrence, as a result of what a coroner's jury has now found to be a racist attack by five white youths) led to calls during the passage of the Criminal Justice and Public Order Act 1994, supported by the Home Affairs Committee (3rd report Racial Attacks and Harassment, Session 1993–4, HC 71) to create a new offence of racially motivated violence (see Wasik, M. and Taylor, R., *Blackstone's Guide to the Criminal Justice & Public Order Act 1994*, pp. 98–99) but this was resisted by the then Home Secretary, Michael Howard. Instead, the offence of intentionally causing a person harassment, alarm or distress was created and inserted as s. 4A of the Public Order Act 1986, an offence which could include incidents of racial harassment, but which, on the other hand, could have little application to incidents of racial violence. The same comment could also be made about the summary offence under s. 2 of the Protection from Harassment Act 1997 and even the more serious indictable offence under s. 4 of that Act covers only causing fear that violence will be used rather than being apt to deal with the actual use of violence.

The lack of specific reference to racial motivation in the harassment offences mentioned above and the lack of any specific aggravating elements relating to racial motivation in the major offences of violence led to the Labour Party including a commitment to create new offences of racially motivated violence and racial harassment in its manifesto for the 1997 election. Following its election, the government issued a Home Office consultation paper in September 1997, entitled *Racial Violence and Harassment*, seeking views on how it should implement its manifesto commitment. The consultation paper's proposals for a series of offences of racial violence and racial harassment, based on existing general offences of violence and harassment, form the basis of what has now been enacted in ss. 28 to 33 of the Act. The consultation paper also proposed to put on a statutory footing the decision in *Ribbans* (1995) 12 Cr App Rep (S) 698 to the effect that a proven racial element should be taken into account as an aggravating factor when sentencing, a proposal now enshrined in s. 82 of the Act.

The new offences

To describe the offences as new is to some extent misleading as they are all essentially parasitic on existing offences under the Offences Against the Person Act 1861 (plus common assault), the Criminal Damage Act 1971, the Public Order Act 1986 and the Protection from Harassment Act 1997. The new offences are committed where a person commits one of the relevant existing offences 'which is racially aggravated' as defined in s. 28. They have effect from 30 September 1998.

The relevant existing offences are set out in subsection (1) of each of ss. 29 to 32 as follows:

s. 29(1)   (a) an offence under s. 20 of the 1861 Act (malicious wounding or grievous bodily harm);

(b) an offence under s. 47 of the 1861 Act (actual bodily harm);

(c) common assault.

s. 30(1)   an offence under s. 1(1) of the Criminal Damage Act 1971 (simple
               criminal damage).

s. 31(1)   (a) an offence under s. 4 of the Public Order Act 1986 (fear or provocation
               of violence).

            (b) an offence under s. 4A of the Public Order Act 1986 (intentional
               harassment, alarm or distress);

            (c) an offence under s. 5 of the Public Order Act 1976 (harassment, alarm
               or distress).

s. 32(1)   (a) an offence under s. 2 of the Protection from Harassment Act 1997
               (harassment).

            (b) an offence under s. 4 of the Protection from Harassment Act 1997
               (putting in fear of violence).

The test of racial aggravation

Each of the above existing offences becomes the corresponding new offence under
ss. 29 to 32 if the test of racial aggravation in s. 28 is satisfied. The test is satisfied if
(s. 28(1)):

(a)   either at the time of committing the offence, or immediately before or after
doing so, the offender demonstrates towards the victim of the offence hostility based
on the victim's membership (or presumed membership) of a racial group; or

(b)   the offence is motivated (wholly or partly) by hostility towards members of
a racial group based on their membership of that group.

The individual relevant offences will be commented on later but first it is necessary
to analyse the test of racial aggravation common to them all.

As has been stated above, there are two alternative grounds of racial aggravation,
common to each of which is the notion of hostility towards a person or persons based
upon their membership of a racial group, i.e., racial hostility.

In alternative (a) racial hostility is required to be *demonstrated* at or immediately
before or after the time of the offence whereas in alternative (b) racial hostility is
required to be the *motivation* (in whole or in part) for the offence. The two types of
aggravation could therefore be described as *demonstrated racial hostility* and *racially
hostile motivation*. The second type of aggravation represents the central target at
which the legislation is aimed, where the motive for the offence is a racial one.
However, the difficulties inherent in proving motive led the Government to include
the first type of aggravation (demonstrated racial hostility) as an alternative less
subjective, and therefore more easily provable, type of aggravation which it is
envisaged will be the more frequent type of aggravation on which actual prosecutions
will be based.

The Government's recognition of the difficulties involved in proving racially
hostile motivation is summed up in para 8.2 of its consultation paper:

Ministers recognise that the creation of offences which required the prosecution to
prove that the offence was motivated on racial grounds would create a difficult
hurdle to be overcome by the prosecutors. The prosecution would need to
distinguish a racial motive from other possible motives and would have to

demonstrate the degree to which a person had been influenced by various motives: There may be a whole range of different circumstances and motives at work in such cases, and this may put a conviction in doubt for all but the most overtly racist incidents.

The consultation paper continued:

8.3   The government intends that the new offences should cover cases where the prosecution is able to show racial motivation but it believes that for most racial incidents of violence and harassment a much more realistic test will be necessary.

8.4   It proposes therefore that the new offences should be committed where it is shown to the usual standard of proof in criminal cases that the offender demonstrated racial hostility at or around the time of the basic offence, or that the motivation for committing that offence was racial hostility.

8.5   This sets the threshold for the new offences at a level which is likely to catch all the cases where there is any evidence of racism.

It is significant to note that the demonstration of racial hostility is not strictly a means of proving or inferring hostile motivation (which might have been a more justifiable or acceptable basis on which to proceed) but is a separate and independent (and likely to be the most frequent) ground of racial aggravation. The ensuing discussion will air some of the difficulties in this somewhat broad and essentially ersatz form of racial motivation and will suggest some interpretations which will keep the concept of demonstrated racial hostility within reasonable bounds. One important limitation which should however be noticed at the outset in s. 28(1)(a) is that the demonstration of hostility must be at the time of the offence or *immediately* before or after it. This at least answers some of the worries that have been discussed in the United States (see Hare 1997 OJLS 415 at 426–431) about the potential 'chilling effect' on freedom of speech if a person's previous utterances could be used against him as evidence of his hostility towards a particular racial group. There is however nothing in s. 28(1)(b) (racially hostile motivation) to exclude non-contemporaneous statements of the accused as evidence of the *motivation* for the offence, but of course such statements would still have to be shown to be more relevant than prejudicial before they could be admitted.

Returning to the broader and more worrying ground of demonstrated racial hostility under s. 28(1)(a), some reservations about the width of this independent ground were expressed during the passage of the Bill by a number of peers. As Lord Monson put it (*Hansard*, Lords 12 February 1998, col. 1266) this ground:

is positively Orwellian in that it seeks to police people's emotions. It increases maximum sentences by up to 300% for offences which have nothing to do initially with race or nationality and where there is no racial motivation, but where, in the course of the attack, some hostility or resentment may emerge accidentally.

How legitimate this type of concern may be, and the true ambit of the section, can be better judged by considering some examples given in the course of the debates. Some of these examples may seem a little trivial or unreal compared with the reality confronted by the often vulnerable victims of racial violence but they are useful non-emotive illustrations by means of which some of the characteristics of the new concepts can be outlined and highlighted. Lord Monson gave the example of an enraged car driver whose car has been run into by the car behind him and who takes a swing at the driver who, by his accent is clearly from the North East, saying:

> 'That is for smashing my car, you Geordie so and so.' He would probably be found guilty of common assault and sentenced to a maximum of six months' imprisonment. However if the careless driver lived 30 or 40 miles further north and the aggrieved driver heard him speaking with a Scottish accent, he could well take a swing at him saying, 'that is for damaging my car you Scottish so and so'. Under the terms of the Bill he would be liable for two years' imprisonment — four times as much.

The most obvious point to emerge from this type of example is the perceived arbitrariness of the contrast or dividing line between groups of people who are not protected by special provisions and those who are. It is a point that one is always going to be able to make in respect of rules protecting particular groups of people and it is a point neither particularly compelling nor particularly germane to the issue currently being discussed. The more legitimate or relevant point of the example is the fact that the offence appears to be aggravated purely because some racial or national adjective happens to be applied to the victim even though the motivation for the offence is nothing to do with the victim's race or nationality. However, closer consideration of the wording of s. 28(1)(a) may lead to the conclusion that in these circumstances even this ground of aggravation is not made out. Section 28(1)(a) requires the offender to demonstrate 'hostility based on the victim's membership (or presumed membership) of a racial group'. In Lord Monson's example, the hostility is primarily based on the fact that the driver is responsible for damaging the assailant's car. The mere fact that he recognises that his victim is Scottish and uses that adjective in describing him does not necessarily mean that he is demonstrating hostility based on the fact that he is Scottish, although a court might in some circumstances be willing to infer that the hostility is, partially at least, based on this ground. Since the word 'hostile' is quite a strong one, it is suggested that the courts should not be too ready to draw such an inference where the reference to race or nationality etc. is essentially incidental and there is clearly some other ground for the hostility (but cf. the discussion of s. 28(3)(b) below) based on the individual victim and/or what the victim has done rather than his membership of a racial group which is mentioned in passing. (See also the discussion by Hare at p. 430, illustrated by the case of *Cole* [1993] Crim LR 300 where the racial adjective was arguably used as much to identify the victim as to indicate racial hostility.) This would keep the ambit of s. 28(1)(a) within sensible limitations whilst leaving it open to deal with other cases where the racial hostility is clearly demonstrated (e.g., where the aggrieved motorist, on recognising that his victim is Scottish, takes the opportunity to say 'that's what all you drunken/idle/useless Scots deserve in any case). In such a case, the assailant is demonstrating racial hostility towards Scots independently of any hostility towards the individual based on the fact that he has damaged his car. The case is clearly within s. 28(1)(a) even though there was no racial motivation for the attack which was originally motivated by the damage to the assailant's car.

Lord Monson's example may be contrasted with another given later in the same debate by Lord Carlisle of Bucklow at col. 1269 which concerned a Scotsman and a

Welshman falling out in a public house after attending a Scotland v Wales rugby match. If the Scotsman punches the Welshman and calls him a bloody so and so that may be an offence of assault occasioning actual bodily harm. If the punch is accompanied by the words 'you bloody Welsh so and so' it probably becomes a racially aggravated assault since the hostility is based arguably as much on the victim's membership of the racial group (Welsh people) as on any disagreement about the match. In this example, to the extent that the defence could argue that the hostility was based on differing views about the match (differences which any interested spectators might share) as opposed to hostility to Welsh, there might still be a possibility of arguing that the hostility is not racial. Conversely of course, racial hostility can be demonstrated without any words being used. If a gang of soccer hooligans singles out Scottish (or Dutch or any other nationality of) football supporters for violent attention, then the selective violence against those individuals as opposed to anyone else attending the same event may amount to a demonstration of hostility based on the victim's membership of a racial group. Even in this situation, the defendant may argue that the hostility is not based on the membership of the racial group but on the fact the victim (whatever the nationality) is attending the match in support of the Scottish football team and wearing their colours. In other words the hostility is not towards Scotsmen but towards people who support their football team. This latter argument would be tenable not only under s. 28(1)(a) but also under s28(1)(b) (racially hostile motivation) since the same phrase 'hostility ... based on membership of a racial group' is at the heart of that subsection also. What is perhaps clear from the foregoing discussion is that this concept of 'hostility based on membership of a racial group' is not as clear as it might be given its crucial role in the definition of these new racially aggravated offences, and the concept provides plenty of ambiguities which defence lawyers will seek to exploit.

An attempt to pre-empt some of these arguments is to be found in s. 28(3) which states:

> it is immaterial for the purposes of paragraph (a) or (b) of subsection (1) above whether or not the offender's hostility is also based, to any extent, on
> ...
> (b) any other factor not mentioned in that paragraph.

The prosecution would seek to rely on this subsection, for example, to rebut the argument previously put in relation to the car accident illustration, that the hostility was based on the fact that the victim had crashed into the defendant's car rather than on the victim's race. However, s. 28(3)(b) does not completely meet the point since it merely states that the fact that there is another reason for the hostility *besides* racial hostility is immaterial. It does not remove the need for the prosecution to prove positively that there was a demonstration of racial hostility or invalidate a defence argument that the *only* cause of the defendant' hostility was the fact the victim had crashed into his car. It does however cover the sort of case referred to earlier where there is clear evidence of racial hostility in addition to hostility because of the victim's individual conduct, i.e., where the defendant does not merely mention the victim's nationality in passing but emphasises the appropriateness of causing harm to people of the victim's nationality by saying something like 'that is what all [Scotsmen]/ [members of your racial group] deserve/should receive'.

The definition of 'membership' in s. 28(2) might also be thought to militate against some of the arguments which, it is suggested above, some defendants may seek to rely on. Take for example the argument about hostility towards supporters of a national football team rather than hostility towards people of that nationality:

'membership', in relation to a racial group, includes association with members of that group.

It might be argued that, insofar as there are non-Scottish followers of the Scottish football team, this does not matter as they are associated with members of the group, Scottish nationals. This argument is flawed because it rests on the definition of membership rather than of a racial group and does not alter the fact that the defendant's hostility is towards supporters of a particular football team rather than towards a racial group. By way of contrast, the extended definition of membership is applicable where, for example, a white youth attacks a white girl and says 'that is what you get for going out with black boys'. There is clearly hostility towards a racial group (black people) of which the actual victim would not be a member except for the extended definition in s. 28(2) which gives her membership by association.

The football supporters example might however be different if the assailant(s) believed that Scottish football supporters were invariably or ordinarily Scottish; in that case the hostility could be said to be based on the victim's presumed membership of a racial group and, by s. 28(2), presumed means 'presumed by the offender' and, by s. 28(3)(a), it would be immaterial that the hostility is also based on the fact that these Scots (or presumed Scots) are also football supporters.

The definition of membership to include association with members of a racial group is only stated to be applicable to s. 28(1)(a) (demonstrated racial hostility) and is not in terms applicable to s. 28(1)(b) (racially hostile motivation). This is due to, and points up the fact that s. 29(1)(b) does not require hostility 'towards the victim of the offence' as such but merely hostility 'towards members of a racial group'. The victim will normally be a member of that racial group and hence will be included within the ambit of the racial hostility but the offence is equally made out under s. 28(1)(b) even if the victim is not a member of the racial group towards whom the hostility is established as the motivation for the offence. Thus, to take the example of the white girlfriend again, if the attack on the white girl is shown to be motivated by her friendship with the black youth or youths, the hostility towards members of a racial group (black people) is made out without any need to prove that she, the actual victim of the offence, is technically a member of the racial group by association.

The definition of racial group in s. 28(4) uses almost the same wording as is to be found in the definition of racial hatred in s. 17 of the Public Order Act 1986 which refers to 'a group of persons defined by reference to colour, race, nationality (including citizenship) or ethnic or national origins' (the 1998 Act has 'race, colour' and the 1986 Act 'colour, race', but there is no apparent significance in that). These definitions are also almost identical to the definition of racial group in the Race Relations Act 1976 (save that the 1976 Act has no reference to citizenship). Thus, in accordance with the House of Lords decision in *Mandla* v *Dowell Lee* [1983] 2 AC 548 on the meaning of the definition in the 1976 Act, Sikhs would constitute a racial group qualifying as being defined by ethnic origins, as would Jews and also it would seem, Gypsies but not Rastafarians (see *Blackstone's Criminal Practice*, **B11.153**).

The fact that Rastafarians may not come within the definition of a racial group does not necessarily mean that an attack on a group of Rastafarians is not a racially aggravated offence. If D attacks a group of black people with dreadlocks such an attack may be based on hostility both towards Rastafarians and also towards Afro-Caribbean or black people in general. Section 28(3)(a) makes it clear that it is no defence for D to say that his hostility was partly based on 'the fact or presumption' that the victims belonged 'to a religious group' (Rastafarians) if there was also a more general hostility towards black people or Afro-Caribbean people or any other racial group of which the victims were members.

Having considered the two ways in which an offence may be racially aggravated, we can now turn to the relevant individual offences to which the concept of racial aggravation may be applied so as to turn them into the more serious offences created by ss. 29 to 32.

Section 29: Racially aggravated assaults

Section 29 selects three offences against the person as suitable to form the basis of three new corresponding racially aggravated offences:

(a)   s. 20 of the Offences Against the Person Act 1861 (malicious wounding or grievous bodily harm);
(b)   s. 47 of the Offences Against the Person Act 1861 (assault occasioning actual bodily harm), and
(c)   common assault.

The most obvious result of creating the aggravated form of these three offences is that the maximum penalty on indictment is increased. In the case of the first two offences, the increase is from five years to seven years (s. 29(2), and in the case of common assault it is from six months to two years (s. 29(3)). Indeed the effect on common assault is more significant even than that because common assault is normally only a summary offence which can be tried only on indictment where s. 40 of the Criminal Justice Act 1988 applies (founded on same facts as a count charging an indictable offence or part of a series of offences etc.). The effect of s. 29 is that there is a new offence of racially aggravated common assault which is triable on indictment quite independently of the conditions in s. 40 of the Criminal Justice Act 1988.

The rationale for selecting these offences and not other offences against the person such as wounding with intent contrary to s. 18 of the Offences Against the Person Act 1861 was that:

where the basic offence already carries a maximum sentence of life imprisonment, as under section 18 of the Offences Against the Person Act 1861, the racially aggravated offence is not in practical terms required as the sentence cannot be increased. In other words, there is nothing to be gained, if there is no increased sentence, in placing the additional burden on the Crown Prosecution Service to meet the racially aggravated test. For that reason, we have not included murder and manslaughter in the list of offences (Alun Michael, Home Office Minister of State, *Hansard*, Commons, Standing Committee B, 12 May 1998, col. 325).

Section 82 of the Act, which requires the court to treat racial aggravation as a factor increasing the seriousness of the offence for sentencing purposes is intended to deal with such offences which already carry the penalty of life imprisonment (or a high maximum penalty). The racially aggravated offence with an increased maximum is only required where the existing offence does not carry a sufficiently high maximum penalty. This explanation then begs the question: why not just increase the maximum penalty for the specified offences and allow the racial aggravation to be taken into account in sentencing? The Government's response to this was as follows:

> if we simply increase the sentence across the board and say for example that the sentence for a s. 47 offence for all purposes is [seven years rather than five years] that has an effect across the board on sentencing. That becomes the maximum. The courts then determine where they put all the offences, whether or not racially motivated, on that scale. That would be moving all the goalposts for every single offence to the top when the purpose of these clauses is to increase them because of racial motivation (Lord Falconer, *Hansard*, Lords, 12 February 1998, col. 1292)

Whatever the Government's reasoning, the statute does seem to have produced a somewhat inelegant combination of some offences against the person being given corresponding new racially aggravated offences with higher maxima and yet other closely related offences being left untouched, with racial aggravation to be a factor taken into account at the sentencing stage. Nor is it merely a matter of inelegance, there are some real practical difficulties lying in wait for both the prosecution and the courts and also some odd clashes of principle.

Where there is evidence of causing grievous bodily harm with intention to do so and also evidence of racial aggravation, there may be some delicate decisions to be made. Ordinarily, the prosecution can be safe in the knowledge, following *Mandair* [1995] 1 AC 208, that if the intent to cause grievous bodily harm under s. 18 of the 1861 Act is not made out, there can still be an alternative verdict of maliciously inflicting grievous bodily harm contrary to s. 20 of the 1861 Act. However, the racial aggravation which would have been taken into account at the sentencing stage if s. 18 had been made out surely cannot be taken into account in sentencing under s. 20 since the proper course would have been to charge and prove the aggravated offence now available under s. 29(1)(a) of the 1998 Act (racially aggravated malicious infliction of grievous bodily harm). Having said that, s. 82 appears to require the court to take into account the aggravation on all offences other than those under ss. 29 to 32, which logically means it should be taken into account on a conviction under s. 20 of the 1861 Act or indeed any of the other offences on which the offences under ss. 29 to 32 are based. This would lead to the odd situation that there is no advantage in charging the aggravated offence unless the appropriate sentence taking account of the aggravation will be higher than the maximum for the normal offence (e.g., higher than five years in the case of s. 20).

The more principled course would be for the prosecution to include the racially aggravated offence under s. 20 in the indictment, but they may be reluctant to do this since this may give the wrong signals to the defence (that the prosecution are willing to consider a guilty plea to that lesser charge rather than the s. 18 offence). However, if the charge is not included at the outset, the defence may resist the inclusion in the course of the trial of the racially aggravated s. 20 offence (as opposed to the normal s. 20 offence, which is available as an alternative verdict).

To try to avoid some of these difficulties, amendments were moved in the Lords, for example by Viscount Colville of Culross (*Hansard*, 17 March, col. 699) to provide for a racially aggravated form of the s. 18 offence with which the accused could be charged. This would have allowed the racially aggravated s. 20 offence as an alternative verdict without the latter having to be specifically charged in the indictment. The Government rejected these amendments which in their view 'would require the prosecution to meet the additional hurdle of proving racial aggravation without providing any additional sentence. Where there is evidence of racial aggravation, [s. 82] already enables the court to impose a higher sentence' (Lord Falconer, col. 701). This response rather glosses over the point that the racial aggravation has to be proved at some point if it is to be taken into account, even under s. 82 by the judge in sentencing, (following a *Newton* hearing if necessary) even if it is not proved before the jury. The creation of the racially aggravated s. 18 offence would not cause a problem if the racial aggravation was not proved because the ordinary s. 18 offence would clearly be an alternative verdict under s. 6(3) of the Criminal Law Act 1967 and this would have the merit that issues of racial aggravation would be out in the open and proved to the satisfaction of the jury whether the basic offence turned out to be under s. 18 or s. 20. The Government however was adamant in its view that in practice any difficulties could be overcome by the good sense of prosecutors and at 11.45 p.m. Viscount Colville noted the lateness of the hour and conceded defeat but commented:

Unless we get over the problem, I am afraid that the use that will be made of the Bill's provisions will not be as extensive or appropriate as would otherwise be the case ... I do not expect any further amendments to be brought forward, but I do expect the goverement to consult with the CPS on the matter. I believe that the CPS will express very strong views as regards the correct way to handle such matters. If there are strong views then, for goodness sake, let us ensure that they are used consistently across the whole length and breadth of the country because that is the other thing that is likely to go wrong.

The most sensible and likely way out of the difficulties referred to above is that the prosecution will always include a count of the racially aggravated s. 20 offence when they charge under s. 18 and there is any evidence of racial aggravation (to be taken into account at the sentencing stage on a conviction under s. 18). Indeed, even in cases where there is no racial aggravation, the current CPS Charging Standards say (para. 11.5) that despite s. 20 being an alternative verdict to s. 18, a separate count to cover the s. 20 offence should be included in the indictment where there is a realistic likelihood of the jury convicting of the lesser offence. Including the racially aggravated s. 20 offence need not send any signals about any perceived weakness in the s. 18 charge since the evidence of racial aggravation should signal to the defence why this course has been taken. The task of the judge summing up to the jury will not however be made easier by this practice. The judge will have to explain that on the more serious charge (i.e. the s. 18 offence) the jury need not concern themselves with the evidence of racial aggravation (which we have already seen under s. 28 is not necessarily a straightforward concept) but that they can rest assured that the evidence they have heard on that will be taken into account in sentencing if the accused is convicted; what should concern them is whether they find the intention to cause grievous bodily harm is proved. On the less serious but racially aggravated s. 20 charge, they must be told that the intention to cause grievous bodily harm is not required but that they must find the test of racial aggravation to be satisfied. There may well be a danger that, where the racial aggravation is extreme, a jury may feel that a verdict of guilty of the aggravated s. 20 offence better reflects the criminality involved; they may even acquit of the s. 18 offence, which may seem less appropriate to them since it does not specifically refer to the racial aggravation which they find to be the central feature of the case. The accused will then end up with a less severe sentence than if convicted of the s. 18 offence, even where the jury would almost certainly have convicted had there been a racially aggravated form of s. 18.

All these complexities and nuances are the result of having a flawed and unprincipled compromise between making racial aggravation a factor in the sentencing stage and creating specific racially aggravated offences with enhanced penalties where the racial aggravation has to be proved as an ingredient of the offence before conviction. The compromise and the difficulties could have been avoided by providing that the maximum penalty for the selected offences should be increased where racial aggravation is established at the sentencing stage (but the maximum penalty would remain the same in other cases to avoid ratcheting up the sentencing tariff for all instances of the offence concerned). This admittedly would have lost the denunciatory impact of creating new offences which was the other justification relied on by the Government for the approach which it has adopted, but a provision increasing maximum penalties in circumstances of racial aggravation would itself have had an almost equal denunciatory or condemnatory effect and one wonders how much more impact the formal creation of new criminal offences will really have on the man or woman in the street.

Despite the above difficulties illustrated by the relationship between the s. 18 offence and the racially aggravated s. 20 offence, there is no doubt about the relationship between offences under ss. 20 and 47 of the 1861 Act on the one hand and the new racially aggravated forms of those offences on the other. The basic offence under the 1861 Act is clearly an alternative verdict to each of the aggravated offences under s. 29(1)(a) and (b) by virtue of s. 6(3) of the Criminal Justice Act 1967 if the element of racial aggravation is not made out since the basic offence is expressly included in the allegations in the indictment.

The position is somewhat different in relation to racially aggravated common assault under s. 29(1)(c). If the element of racial aggravation is not made out on a trial on indictment, common assault is not an alternative verdict since, following ss. 39 and 40 of the Criminal Justice Act 1988, common assault is a summary offence and is therefore not 'within the jurisdiction of the court of trial' within the meaning of the Criminal Law Act 1967 and can only be included in an indictment if done so expressly under the terms of s. 40 of the Criminal Justice Act 1988. Therefore, where racially aggravated common assault is charged on indictment (unlike common assault simpliciter, it is an indictable offence triable either way), it will always be wise to include a separate count of common assault; this will always be justified under the terms of s. 40 of the Criminal Justice Act 1988 since the common assault charge will always be founded on the same facts as the racially aggravated common assault.

Although common assault is not an alternative verdict to racially aggravated common assault (unless expressly included as a separate charge in the indictment), racially aggravated common assault clearly is an alternative verdict to racially aggravated assault occasioning actual bodily harm. However, if the racially aggravated actual bodily harm charge fails because neither the racial aggravation element nor the bodily harm element is proved, again common assault simpliciter is not available unless a separate count has been included. Thus on a charge of racially aggravated actual bodily harm, it would normally be prudent to include a common assault count even though there is no need to specify a racially aggravated common assault.

Whatever the current complexities of the interrelationship between the various racially aggravated assaults and existing offences against the person, and however satisfactorily or unsatisfactorily these are worked out in practice, the issues will be required to be revisited quite soon. The Government intends to introduce long-awaited legislation modernising non-fatal offences against the person following its consultation paper *Violence: Reforming the Offences Against the Person Act 1961*, published by the Home Office in February of this year. The consultation paper essentially proposed, *inter alia*, the replacement of the offences under ss. 18, 20, 47 of the 1861 Act and common assault by four more modern and intelligibly worded offences with graduated maximum penalties from life, through seven years, then five years down to six months for the least serious. Given the proposal of seven years for the second most serious offence (equivalent to the s. 20 offence) which is the same as is now available for the racially aggravated s. 20 offence, it will be interesting to see what increased penalty the Government will propose for the racially aggravated form of this new offence assuming that a racially aggravated form of this offence will still be considered necessary.

Section 30: Racially aggravated criminal damage

Whilst the Government, as has been seen, persistently resisted attempts to introduce an offence of racially aggravated wounding with intent, pressure to include an offence of racially aggravated criminal damage eventually succeeded and what became s. 30 was introduced into the Bill at Third Reading in the House of Lords on 31 March 1998. Criminal damage had originally not been included because the Government had intended to include only those offences which were in the broad sense directed against the person. However, it was pointed out that racially motivated offences of criminal damage are in reality very often directed towards the owner or occupier of property or indeed designed to terrorise or harass or dismay members of racial groups irrespective of the ownership of the property. The example was given of racist graffiti on bus shelters and there was also reference to the racist killing of Stephen Lawrence and the fact that more recently a plaque erected in his memory had been vandalised. A further consideration in support of including criminal damage as one of the racially aggravated offences is that the value of the property damaged may not be a good measure of the seriousness of the offence where there is racial aggravation and yet ordinary criminal damage must be tried summarily where the value of the property damaged is £5,000 or less (Magistrates' Courts Act 1980, s. 22 and sch. 2).

The new racially aggravated offence under s. 30 is not subject to the above restriction and indeed on indictment carries a maximum penalty of 14 years' imprisonment as opposed to the normal ten-year maximum (one reason explicitly given for the choice of 14 years was that if the offender was aged under 18 and the case a serious one, the offender could then, if appropriate, be dealt with under s. 53 of the Children and Young Persons Act 1933).

Section 30(3) deals with the question of who should be regarded as the victim of the offence and was explained by Lord Falconer as follows (*Hansard*, Lords, 31 March 1998, col. 202):

The other potential problem with this offence was reconciling the victim of the offence with the victim of the racial hostility. To take the example cited in earlier debates, in cases where racial hostility was demonstrated to tenants of a house which was damaged, there had been doubts about whether the tenants could always be said to be the victims of the damage itself.

The definition of those to whom damaged property belongs for the purposes of the 1971 Act is however wide enough to cover all those who have custody, control or a proprietary interest in or a charge over property that is destroyed or damaged. This is the definition that is adopted in subsection (3) of the new clause.

Section 30(3) does not necessarily yield a simple answer to all questions relating to the victim of the offence. First of all it is only of relevance (and the question of who is the victim is only of relevance) where demonstrated racial hostility is being relied on within s. 28(1)(a). In relation to s. 28(1)(b) (racially hostile motivation), there is no specific mention of the victim and 'hostility towards members of a racial group based on their membership of that group' is sufficient irrespective of whether there is an identifiable victim and whether or not that victim is a member of the racial group (see above). This makes racially hostile motivation the only possible ground of aggravation if the owner of the property damaged cannot, even in the extended sense provided for in s. 30(3), be regarded as the victim of the offence (e.g., racist graffiti or slogans daubed on a bus shelter). The difficulty then would be the normal one of proving motivation — the very reason the alternative concept of demonstrated racial hostility was introduced. Proving motivation might sound straightforward where the criminal damage constitutes racist graffiti etc., but the defence may be able to claim that the graffiti was done purely as a means of self-expression (or for some other reason) and not *because of* hostility towards members of a racial group even though the graffiti happened to carry a racist message.

Even under s. 28(1)(a) (demonstrated racial hostility), where the notion of the victim of the offence is an essential ingredient, there may be some difficulty surrounding the phrase 'demonstrates towards the victim of the offence hostility', which suggests hostility towards the individual (albeit on the grounds of his or her membership of a racial group) whereas the criminal damage may be thought to demonstrate hostility towards all members of the racial group as opposed to who happens to be the individual owner of the property. This may be arguable in particular if the owner of the property is unknown to an accused who has selected a property at random in an area which he knows to be populated exclusively or predominantly by members of a racial group.

One problem that would at first glance not appear to complicate s. 30 is that of alternative verdicts since it is reasonably clear that if the element of racial aggravation is not made out the basic offence of criminal damage is still available as an alternative verdict. This would appear to remain true even if the value of the property damaged is less than £5,000 so that the offence would normally have been tried summarily. Unlike common assault, criminal damage remains an indictable offence triable either way (see sch. 1 to the Interpretation Act 1978 and *Blackstone's Criminal Practice*,

D3.1) and hence still falls 'within the jurisdiction of the court of trial' within the meaning of s. 6(3) of the Criminal Law Act 1967. However, because of dicta in *Mearns* [1991] 1 QB 82 (see *Blackstone's Criminal Practice*, **D16.29**) it might be safest to include a separate count of simple criminal damage as is permitted by s. 40(3)(d) of the Criminal Justice Act 1988, although it is submitted that the better view is that this is not strictly necessary.

The offence of racially aggravated arson does not appear to exist since s. 1(3) of the Criminal Damage Act 1971 only requires 'an offence committed under this section' to be charged as arson and this does not cover the offence of racially aggravated criminal damage under s. 30 of the CDA 1998 even if it is committed by fire. As the maximum penalty for arson on indictment is life imprisonment, the Government's view no doubt is that racially aggravated arson is not needed.

Section 31: Racially aggravated public order offences

Section 31 selects three offences of descending severity, under ss. 4, 4A and 5 of the Public Order Act 1986, as the ones for which it is necessary to have specific corresponding racially aggravated offences. The basic offences are summary only and thus the maximum penalties are limited to six months (in the case of s. 5, the maximum penalty is a fine); it is for this reason that they are selected and riot, violent disorder and affray are not, since their maximum penalties are already considered to be adequate. In the case of the two offences already punishable with imprisonment (ss. 4 and 4A), the racially aggravated forms of the offences become indictable and triable either way with a maximum penalty of two years' imprisonment on indictment. In the case of s. 5 of the Public Order Act 1986, the racially aggravated form of the offence remains summary but the maximum penalty is increased from a fine at level three to a fine at level four. Section 31(2) and (3) provide for powers of arrest roughly corresponding to those already provided for in relation to the basic offences in the Public Order Act 1986, although the rider to s. 31(3) gives slightly more information than is contained in s. 5(4) of the Public Order Act 1986, which provides the corresponding power of arrest for the basic offence.

Section 31(6) expressly provides, in relation to the two (relatively) more serious offences under ss. 4 and 4A, that the basic offence is an alternative verdict to the racially aggravated form of offence. This is necessary since the basic offences are not themselves indictable nor is there provision for them to be expressly included in an indictment under s. 40 of the CJA 1988. In relation to the least serious of the three offences (based on s. 5 of the Public Order Act 1986) there can be no question of alternative verdicts as even the racially aggravated offence remains summary and the alternative verdict procedure does not apply in magistrates' courts.

Despite the relative clarity of s. 31(6), there is still a potential problem concerning alternative verdicts where more serious charges of violent disorder or affray are also being considered. By s. 7 of the Public Order Act 1986, an offence under s. 4 of that Act is an alternative verdict to violent disorder or affray. However, the racially aggravated form of s. 4 is not made an alternative verdict to those offences and there is no racially aggravated form of violent disorder or affray (although racial aggravation is to be taken into account in sentencing under s. 82 of the 1998 Act). The issue is the mirror image of the problem discussed earlier in relation to s. 18 and 20 of the Offences Against the Person Act 1861 with the same dilemmas as to which and how many counts to include in the indictment and how to direct juries when the most serious count in the indictment does not specifically allege racial aggravation but one of the less serious counts does. The Government thought once more that the difficulties could be ironed out with common sense in practice. The only difference perhaps is that with the s. 18/s. 20 issue the Government will perforce have an opportunity to revisit the issues when the offences against the person are themselves recast whereas this is less likely to happen with the public order offences.

Section 31(7) is of similar effect to s. 30(3) in relation to criminal damage in that it provides that the victim for the purposes of the racially aggravated form of the offence under s. 5 of the Public Order Act 1986 is the person likely to be caused harassment, alarm or distress.

Section 32: Racially aggravated harassment

Section 32 provides for racially aggravated versions of the two offences under the Protection from Harassment Act 1997, an Act that was passed primarily to deal with so-called stalkers although its ambit is not limited to that type of conduct. There are two offences under the 1997 Act, simple harassment under s. 2 and putting another in fear of violence (on at least two occasions) under s. 4. The s. 2 offence is triable only summarily with a maximum six months' penalty whereas the offence under s. 4 is much more serious and carries a maximum penalty of five years on indictment. The racially aggravated forms of these two offences are both made indictable and triable either way and the maximum penalties are increased to two years and seven years respectively (consistently with the identical increase in penalties for racially aggravated common assault and offences under ss. 20 and 47 of the Offences Against the Person Act 1861). Racially aggravated harassment is expressly made an arrestable offence (as is the basic offence of harassment) and racially aggravated putting in fear of violence is, like its corresponding basic offence under s. 4 of the 1997 Act, automatically an arrestable offence by virtue of its maximum penalty of seven years.

Alternative verdicts are expressly provided for as follows:

(a)   By virtue of s. 32(6), racially aggravated harassment under s. 32(1)(a) is an alternative verdict to a count of racially aggravated putting in fear of violence under s. 32(1)(b).

(b)   By virtue of s. 32(5), a conviction for the summary offence of harassment under s. 2 of the Protection fron Harassment Act 1997 is an alternative verdict to racially aggravated harassment under s. 32(1)(a). However there is no express provision for an alternative verdict of the summary offence of harassment where the original charge is *racially aggravated* putting another in fear of violence even though the summary offence is, by virtue of s. 4(5) of the 1997 Act, expressly made an alternative verdict to the basic offence of putting in fear of violence. There may therefore be situations where it is prudent to include a count of racially aggravated harassment alongside a count of racially aggravated putting in fear even though the former is expressly made an alternative verdict in s. 32(6) since the express count of racially aggravated harassment brings with it the possibility of an alternative verdict of basic harassment (the summary offence). Apart from these express provisions dealing with alternative verdicts, as a result of the operation of s. 6(3) of the Criminal Law Act 1967, putting another in fear of violence is an alternative verdict to racially aggravated putting another in fear of violence.

Unlike some of the earlier racially aggravated offences, the above provisions on alternative verdicts do seem reasonably certain in their effect but they can hardly be regarded as simple or clear either to describe or to apply, and the good sense envisaged by the Government on the part of prosecutors and courts is going to be required in bucketfuls if the provisions are to be applied smoothly and without difficulty.

Whilst it is not within the aims of this book to deal with provisions relating solely to Scotland, one cannot help noticing that there is only one new racially aggravated offence (harassment) created (by s. 33) in respect of Scotland. There racial aggravation is otherwise left to be dealt with as a factor in sentencing, given the wide latitude provided by the fact that the relevant substantive offences are non-statutory and that the racial aggravation can be specifically libelled in the indictment or specified in the complaint as envisaged in s. 96 which, unlike its near equivalent for England (s. 82), expressly requires it to be 'proved that an offence has been racially aggravated' (s. 96(1)).

ABOLITION OF THE PRESUMPTION OF *DOLI INCAPAX*

At 22 words long, s. 34 ties equally, but deceptively, with s. 108 as the shortest in the Act; it succinctly provides: 'The rebuttable presumption of criminal law that a child aged 10 or over is incapable of committing an offence is hereby abolished'.

Prior to the Act children and young persons were divided into three categories for the purposes of criminal responsibility:

(a)   those aged under 10, who could not be criminally responsible;

(b)   those aged between 10 and 14, who were presumed to be incapable of criminal intent (*doli incapax*) unless the presumption could rebutted by the prosecution);

(c)   those who had reached the age of 14, who were treated as equally responsible as adults (but for whom there were special procedural and sentencing rules).

The effect of s. 34 is that the three categories are now only two and children under 10 are not criminally responsible whilst those over 10 are, thus giving us one of the lowest ages of criminal responsibility anywhere in Europe or indeed the world. To appreciate the effects of s. 34, and the arguments which have been brought to bear both in favour and against it, a certain amount of background must be set out.

At common law, the minimum age of responsibility was even lower, being set at seven years (although this was of course mitigated by the *doli incapax* rule). The minimum age was raised in 1933 to eight and in 1963 to the present age of 10, although the Ingleby Committee in 1960 had recommended that it be raised to 12.

For children above the age of criminal responsibility, the presumption of *doli incapax* represented an attempt to recognise the variable development of individual children and their capacity to appreciate the wrongfulness of different types of actions. The presumption of *doli incapax* could be rebutted only by the prosecution proving that the child knew that what had been done was seriously wrong (not just naughty or mischievous).

The *doli incapax* rule has long been criticised on the grounds that the greater the need for intervention in the child's life, the less likely is it that the child can be held criminally responsible. As Glanville Williams notoriously put it ([1954] Crim LR 493), 'the worse the child's upbringing and the more warped his standards, the safer he is from the correctional treatment of the criminal law'. In practice, for many years the rule was not often successfully invoked since comparatively little evidence was required to show that the child did indeed know that what was done was seriously wrong. However, practice was not consistent and from time to time cases would come before the appeal courts (see e.g., *JM* v *Runeckles* [1984] 79 Cr App Rep 255) to determine whether or not sufficient evidence had been adduced to show that the particular child had 'mischievous discretion' as it was called (i.e., was *doli capax* as opposed to *incapax*).

For these sorts of reasons, the Ingleby Committee had in 1960, as mentioned above, recommended the abolition of the rebuttable presumption of *doli incapax*, although this has to be seen in the context of their view that the age for automatic exemption from criminal responsibility should be raised to twelve, thus rendering the protection of the rebuttable presumption less important and taking out of the criminal process those most likely to be properly found *doli incapax*. The Children and Young Persons Act 1969 also provided a framework for complete exemption for children under the age of 14 (except for homicide) by means of s. 4, but this section was never brought into force and indeed was repealed in the Criminal Justice Act 1991, reflecting a general shift from a predominantly rehabilitative ideal towards one where notions of desert and just punishment were given more credence as effective principles to achieve reductions in crime and criminal behaviour.

In practice, in the period between the 1969 Act and Criminal Justice Act 1991, the *doli incapax* rule continued to be applied or ignored without too much apparent difficulty save for the odd case that went to the appeal courts, but it was thrust back into the limelight by a number of developments in the 1990s.

First, on 24 November 1993, amidst not just national but worldwide publicity, two 10-year-olds were convicted of the murder of the two-year-old James Bulger whom they had abducted from a shopping precinct in Liverpool. The vivid and public demonstration of the type of offences which very young children were capable of committing has had an enormous and continuing impact on the public's attitude to children, particularly as the legal arguments and public controversy about the appropriate trial procedure and sentencing regime for these children have continued ever since (see *Secretary of State for the Home Department, ex parte Venables* [1997]AC 407, HL and also *Venables and Thompson* v *UK*, C-24724/94 and C-24888/94, declared admissible by the European Commission on Human Rights.)

Second, Parliament recognised the assumed increasing sexual precocity of children by passing the Sexual Offences Act 1993, which abolished the previous irrebuttable presumption (distinct from the *doli incapax* presumption) that a boy under the age of 14 was incapable of sexual intercourse or of any offence such as rape of which sexual intercourse was a necessary component. The result of that has been an increasing number of trials younger and younger children for the offence of rape, allegedly committed in most cases against equally young complainants.

Such prosecutions have also been facilitated by changes to rules of evidence and procedure in the Criminal Justice Acts 1988 and 1991 whereby child witnesses and victims (essentially those aged under 14 or, in the case of sexual offences, under 17) can give evidence by means of pre-recorded video evidence and can be cross-examined (or can give the whole of their evidence if no pre-recorded video is made) by means of a live video link to a place outside the courtroom and away from its full pressure, trauma and stress. Children's evidence is also now given unsworn and there is no longer any duty to enquire into the child's ability to understand the duty to speak the truth before a child can be allowed to give evidence, although a child witness will not be allowed to give evidence if it appears to the court 'that the child is incapable of giving intelligible testimony'. Even children under 10 therefore, provided that they are able to give intelligible testimony, can give evidence even though they cannot be liable for any criminal offence including perjury. These changes are of course primarily designed to enable child witnesses to give evidence against adult offenders who have assaulted or abused them but they also come into play in relation to juvenile offenders whose offences are often committed against other juveniles.

The Bulger case and the impact of the Sexual Offences Act 1993 provided the background for the leading case of *C (A Minor) v DPP* [1996] AC 1, which was the third factor to put the *doli incapax* presumption firmly back into the melting pot. In *C (A Minor) v DPP* a 12-year-old was seen tampering with a motorcycle with a crowbar and when challenged ran away. He was convicted in the juvenile court of the offence under the Criminal Attempts Act 1981 of interfering with a motor vehicle with intent to commit theft but appealed on the grounds that no evidence had been given to show that he knew that his actions were seriously wrong.

The Divisional Court ([1994] 3 WLR 888) accepted that insufficient evidence had been given of the child's knowledge of wrongfulness, the fact that he had run away being consistent as much with mere naughtiness as with anything more serious, but held that the presumption of *doli incapax* was now outdated and should no longer be regarded as part of the law:

whatever may have been the position in an earlier age, when there was no system of universal compulsory education and when perhaps children did not grow up as quickly as they do nowadays, this presumption at the present time is a serious disservice to our law ... it is unreal and contrary to common sense (Mann LJ)

Although some might have agreed with the sentiments expressed in this judgment, there was considerable surprise at the boldness of the court in abrogating a centuries-old rule of the common law. Questions were asked about the legitimacy of a retrospective broadening of the basis of responsibility, although one could argue that no-one could have been adversely misled by the change since a child sufficiently sophisticated to consider whether his actions were criminal under the law as previously understood would by definition have had to be capable of appreciating their wrongfulness and therefore would have been liable to be convicted under either test.

On appeal to the House of Lords ([1996] AC 1), the House agreed that the law was in need of reform but held that this was a matter for Parliament and therefore reversed the Divisional Court decision, emphasising the need for evidence of the child's capacity independently of the acts alleged to constitute the crime itself.

The net result of the attempt by Mann LJ to reform the law and remove the presumption seems to have been that a rule which was only infrequently invoked and which generally was given little attention except in the most serious cases acquired a much higher profile. There was a positive rash of cases trying to work out what exactly is required to rebut the presumption, which consequently seemed to become more difficult to do. As Sir John Smith notes in his commentary on one of these cases (*A v DPP* [1997] Crim LR 125), 'sometimes the authoritative enunciation of established principles results in their more strict application than hitherto'.

Thus in *CC (A Minor) v DPP* [1996] 1 Cr App Rep 375, D, aged 11, together with J, attacked a 12-year-old on a bicycle and placed a lock knife against the boy's throat to demand money. The prosecution gave no specific evidence to rebut the presumption of *doli incapax* but the magistrates convicted of Public Order Act offences since it was almost inconceivable that a boy of the appellant's age would not know that it was seriously wrong to place a knife against someone's throat to demand money. The convictions were quashed since the prosecution had not proved that the boy was normal for his age and that could not be assumed. Even though very little evidence would be needed, none had been provided in this case other than the evidence of the acts constituting the crime.

In *A v DPP* [1997] 1 Cr App Rep by contrast, although the accused again refused to answer any questions about his conduct, his conviction for indecent assault was upheld. The appellant had seen the threats made to a girl who was then taken to the twentieth floor of a block of flats where she was raped and assaulted by three boys including the appellant. Here the court managed to rebut the presumption by means of evidence of conduct of the accused immediately before and after the offence, but distinct from the acts constituting the offence itself, as required by the House of Lords in *C (A Minor) v DPP*. However it was a fine distinction and there were many other cases on either side of the line which led to a situation of confusion and inconsistency.

Although, as noted above, as long ago as 1960 the Ingleby Committee recommended abolition of the presumption, this was in the context of a recommended increase in the age of responsibility from 10 to 12. The Draft Criminal Code (Law Com No. 143) prepared for the Law Commission by a team of academics did not contain the presumption but the Law Commission's own report (Law Commission No. 177, 1989) recommended retaining the presumption unless the age of responsibility could be raised, thereby echoing the Ingleby Committee position changes. The Conservative Government's position in 1990, as outlined in the White Paper, *Crime, Justice & Protecting the Public* (Cm 965), was also in favour of retaining the presumption.

However, the increased profile of the rule in the intervening years and the shifts and difficulties in the courts described above provided the context in which the Labour Party in its May 1996 consultation paper, *Tackling Youth Crime; Reforming Youth Justice*, found the rule to be 'most unsatisfactory'. Following the election, the Government duly issued a Home Office consultation paper, *Tackling Youth Crime*, in September 1997 which commenced by stating that:

A central aim of the government's youth justice reforms is to encourage young offenders and their parents to take responsibility for their actions. For a young offender to accept responsibility for his or her offence and to face up to the harm which they have caused to the victim is both a valuable moral lesson and a first step to rehabilitation.

The Government argued that the *doli incapax* presumption was archaic, illogical and unfair in practice in the following respects (but see Charlotte Walsh, [1998] 3 *Web Journal of Current Legal Issues* for a cogent criticism of these arguments):

Archaic in that it does not recognise the way in which children mature so quickly today and also in that it harks back to a time when punishments for a wide variety of crimes could be very serious whereas today the emphasis particularly with children is on rehabilitation rather than punishment.

Illogical since the presumption is that children 10–14 do not know right from wrong but if evidence is given that the child is of normal development for that age, the presumption is rebutted!

Unfair because of difficulties of gaining independent evidence if the child refuses to say anything under police questioning or in court.

The result, said the Government, was that some children are not prosecuted or convicted and the opportunity is missed to take appropriate action to prevent re-offending. The consultation paper concluded that the presumption should be abolished and the child's age and maturity continue to be taken into account at sentence. (Consistently it was claimed with the UN Convention on the Rights of the Child — but see especially Art. 40).

The initial consultation paper was followed by a White Paper entitled significantly 'No More Excuses — a new approach to tackling youth crime in England and Wales' where the intention to abolish the presumption was confirmed and the need to do so summed up by an example given at para. 4.7

The presumption of *doli incapax* gives rise to genuine difficulties in practice. In a recent case a boy who had been cautioned at the age of twelve embarked upon a spree of offending over the next twelve months, resulting in his eventual conviction for offences including criminal damage, arson, robbery, witness intimidation, common assault, assault occasioning actual bodily harm, theft from a vehicle, theft of a vehicle and driving while disqualified.

The prosecution of these offences was hampered by the need in each case to rebut the presumption of *doli incapax*. The boy attended a special school and the prosecution relied on the headmaster who had known the boy for five years to give evidence rebutting the presumption. Rather than allow the prosecution in subsequent cases to present this evidence in writing the defence insisted on the headmaster being called in person in every contested case. He thus had to attend court on a number of occasions and gave evidence in at least two trials. The defence appealed against conviction arguing among other things that the headmaster should not have been called to give evidence to rebut the presumption because he was himself a victim of the offender. The appeal was rejected and the sentence finally passed one year after the cases had first come to court.

The alternative of reversing the presumption rather than abolishing it (so that the defence would have to provide evidence of the accused's lack of knowledge of right and wrong) was discussed briefly but not favoured by the Government as it might lead, in the Government's view, to similar complexities as under the current law. This is perhaps unfortunate. The current law is predicated on the assumption that some children aged between 10 and 14 lack the capacity to appreciate the wrongfulness of their actions (without which it is not right to hold them criminally responsible). Reversing rather than abolishing the presumption would at least have given such children the opportunity of proving this, albeit with the burden now on the defence.

Amendments were tabled at several stages in the passage of the Bill to reverse rather than abolish the presumption but the Government consistently resisted this compromise. For the sake of making the criminal process swifter and more efficient, the opportunity to prove that an individual child lacked criminal capacity will be denied and children will be held criminally responsible where arguably it is inappropriate and pointless.

In a letter to *The Times* on 16 December, Frances Crook, Director of the Howard League for Penal Reform said that the Bill 'could turn out to be one of the most sweeping attacks on civil rights this century, resulting in dramatic use of prison custody for children and anyone identified as different and difficult'. Earlier the letter commented that:

> the Bill's abolition of *doli incapax* means that primary school age children will be treated the same as adults by the courts, expected to comprehend fully the implications of their actions and the court procedure. The detention and training order means that a child as young as 12 could be held in a youth prison and the Home Secretary will have the power to reduce that to 10-year-olds. Girls of this age could go to adult women's prisons. The government is ignoring the fact that in recent years some 35 teenagers have taken their own lives in prisons.

Similar sentiments were expressed by the National Association for the Care and Resettlement of Offenders, and a number of other bodies such as JUSTICE, Liberty and Barnardos expressed concern to the Home Office that abolition of the presumption was taking place without any increase in the minimum age of responsibility. During the passage of the Bill, Government ministers made frequent reference to the fact that 111 out of the 180 respondents to the consultation process favoured abolition of *doli incapax* (the corollary being that that over a third were not in favour although a substantial minority favoured reversal rather than abolition).

Whilst some of the fears expressed about the abolition of the presumption are undoubtedly well founded, it may not be entirely true that 'children will be treated the same as adults by the courts, expected to comprehend fully the implications of their actions'. Independently of the presumption of *doli incapax*, responsibility for most serious offences in English law depends on proof of a subjective awareness or foresight of at least the risk of the harmful consequences of one's actions and the age of the accused will no doubt continue to be a factor in deciding whether the particular accused had the necessary foresight. As against that, there are still a number of serious offences where an individual's lack of capacity to foresee or appreciate the consequences of his or her actions is not relevant because the courts have adopted an objective standard of liability. These include most obviously the offence of manslaughter and, perhaps more significantly, criminal damage, where the decision in *Elliot* v *C* [1983] 1 WLR 939 still stands as confirmation of the objective interpretation of recklessness which means that a child who is incapable of appreciating the risk of damage which he or she is creating is still acting recklessly and is guilty of the offence if the risk would have been obvious to a reasonable person. This is of course a problem not just for child defendants but also for adults who lack the normal capacity to foresee the results of their actions. It is therefore entirely accurate in this context to say that children will be treated the same as adults by the courts and the presumption of *doli incapax* will not be available to mitigate the harshness of objective tests of responsibility such as that applicable to criminal damage.

Mitigation of the effects of the abolition of the rule may have to be effected by the CPS who, as Lord Williams of Mostyn for the government acknowledged, (*Hansard*, Lords, 19 March 1998, col. 839) 'will also continue to bear in mind whether or not it is in the public interest for a prosecution to be brought'. Lord Williams continued, less sympathetically perhaps, to point out that the public interest does not limit itself only to the public interest in the welfare of a prospective defendant child'. Earlier, Lord Williams had pointed to the other aspects of the public interest which the Government had in mind:

> We have to bear in mind the legitimate and reasonable concerns of victims ... They are also entitled to a reasonable regard for their rights and freedoms just as one has to have a proper and tender regard for young children. We believe we have the balance right here ... what one wants is early intervention; not early savage punishment but early assistance. It does a child no favours to let it drift on without knowing, particularly in a modern sophisticated society, that if it commits criminal acts there will be sanction.

There are those who feel that our modern society has not reached a particularly high degree of sophistication if it regards a criminal conviction as an appropriate way of illustrating the consequences of doing wrong to a child as young as ten who is not allowed to show that it did not appreciate that it had been doing anything seriously wrong in the first place. Even if one accepts that in very many cases the child does understand the seriousness of what it has done, not all of the 7,125 children proceeded against in magistrates' courts in 1996 will have done so. Given the abolition of the presumption, the number who are convicted despite not having this understanding seems set to rise unless the abolition of *doli incapax* can be publicised in primary schools up and down the land so as to put children on notice that the criminal courts will accept no more excuses for any criminal acts which they perpetrate (after 30 September 1998, the date of implementation) and that they should somehow develop their understanding of right and wrong a little more quickly than hitherto.

EFFECT OF A CHILD'S SILENCE AT TRIAL

Unlike the voluminous literature and extensive consideration devoted to the *doli incapax* rule before its abolition by the Act, the change to the law on the effect of a child's failure to give evidence at his trial was introduced at Third Reading in the Lords (31 March 1998) with no prior warning, save for a brief mention in passing at the Report Stage 12 days earlier (*Hansard*, Lords, 19 March 1998, col. 839). The change made by s. 35 takes effect by means of an amendment to s. 35 of the Criminal Justice and Public Order Act 1994, which permits a court or jury to draw inferences from an accused person's failure to testify or to answer any question but which hitherto applied only to any person '*who has attained the age of fourteen years*' (1994 Act , s. 35(1). The italicised words are now repealed and inferences are permitted to be drawn from the accused's failure to testify or answer any question, whatever the age of the accused.

The Government sought to justify this change by reference to two arguments from consistency:

(a)   consistency with the abolition of *doli incapax* — if children are equally responsible as adults they should equally be expected to be able to provide an innocent explanation if they have one;

(b)   consistency with ss. 34, 36 and 37 of the 1994 Act which have never been limited to persons aged over 14 but which allow adverse inferences to be drawn from failure to mention facts when questioned or charged, or when asked by a constable, to account for objects etc. or to account for presence at a particular place.

Neither of these arguments seems particularly convincing. As to the first, even if a child understands the seriously wrong nature of his act, there will be few such children who have any real understanding of the nature of inferences which a court can draw or of their true significance in the trial process. The Government argument looks for consistency between two concepts which are in reality quite different. As to the second argument, the same comment can be made. Failure to answer questions when sat in a police station with a friend and/or adviser to consult is quite a different matter than failure to go into the witness box or to answer a question when alone in the witness box.

Baroness Mallalieu put the arguments against the change quite well (*Hansard*, Lords, 31 March, col. 205):

> When a defendant is aged between 10 and 14, in reality the decision whether to give evidence is not taken by the child. It is the decision of the advocate. The child does what he is advised to do. Indeed he is usually quite incapable, no matter how carefully it is explained, of understanding the meaning of 'adverse inferences' or what the consequences of the choices open to him are. There may be very good reasons ... for not advising the child not to give evidence. He may be inarticulate and not able to give a proper account of himself. He may be frankly terrified and likely to be an appalling witness.... In practice I suspect that there will be few cases where a magistrate or judge would think it right to direct a jury or indeed to direct themselves that adverse inferences should be drawn form a child's failure to give evidence where counsel has so advised. However, I wonder whether the noble Lord can tell me where the pressure for this change comes from. I am not aware of any difficulties.

In response, Lord Williams indicated that there had been no consultation with the Bar Council, the Law Society or the Criminal Bar Association or indeed with anyone else, the arguments from consistency being thought to be enough. He did however concede that he 'would tend to agree ... that in practice adverse inferences would be perhaps relatively rarely drawn' (col. 207).

This reassuring sentiment should however be contrasted with the outcome of the case of *Friend* [1997] 1 WLR 1433, decided under the unamended s. 35, where the accused was 15 but had a mental age of nine but the Court of Appeal upheld the trial judge's ruling that the accused's mental condition did not make it undesirable under s. 35(1)(b) for him to give evidence and thus his failure to give evidence permitted adverse inferences to be drawn. The measures now available to make it easier for young witnesses to give evidence seem to have been factors influencing the court to find that the accused on the facts could be expected to give evidence and these factors may also prove to be an influence in relation to children who are actually, rather than just mentally, aged below 14.

One possible oversight in the amendments made by s. 35 of the 1998 to s. 35 of the 1994 Act relates to the phrase 'having been sworn' in s. 35(2) and (5) of the 1994 Act. The presence of this phrase implies that a failure to answer a question, as opposed to the more common failure to go into the witness box in the first place, can only give rise to an adverse inference if the accused is giving sworn evidence. Since children under 14 now never give sworn evidence (following s. 51 of the Criminal Justice Act 1991 inserting s. 33A into the Criminal Justice Act 1988) it would seem to follow that an adverse inference cannot be drawn from their failure to answer questions. The only weakness in this argument is that the phrase 'having been sworn' does not appear in section 35(3) of the 1994 Act which is the subsection which actually authorises the drawing of adverse inferences. However, it would be very odd (not to say misleading for the accused) for s. 35(2) to require a court to satisfy itself that a warning had been given about the consequences of failure to answer a question *having been sworn* if an adverse inference could be drawn whether or not the witness had been sworn. For this and other reasons it would seem that a new or supplementary practice direction is going to be required beyond the current one governing s. 35 (*Practice Direction (Crown Court: Defendant's Evidence)* [1995] 1 WLR 657).

The point just discussed is a somewhat technical one and in one sense arises by accident, since the phrase 'having been sworn' was probably adopted as meaning 'after having started to give evidence' at a time when the section could not apply to unsworn evidence of children under 14 anyway. It also, of course, has no application to the much more common case where the accused fails to testify at all. It does nevertheless point up the fact that whilst the law considers children under 14 to be too young to give sworn evidence or to understand the significance of the oath, it does not consider them too young to be irrebuttably presumed to understand whether their conduct is seriously wrong or to understand the significance of the adverse inferences which may be drawn from their failure to testify.

The change to the effect of a child's silence at trial has come into force, as with the change to *doli incapax*, from 30 September 1998. Although it is a matter of evidence, it does not affect trials for offences *committed* before commencement (sch. 9, para. 2).

POWERS TO REQUIRE REMOVAL OF MASKS ETC.

These new powers (ss. 25 to 27) were introduced into the Act at a relatively late stage with the stated aim of:

> making the police more effective in dealing with people who wear masks to avoid being identified when they carry out violent offences.... The police can already take firm action when they have reasonable suspicion that people are committing or about to commit offences. They currently lack a power to demand the removal of face coverings before trouble starts and before they have reasonable suspicion against any individual (Mr Mike O'Brien, Under Secretary of State for the Home Office, *Hansard*, Commons, Standing Committee B, 9 June 1998, col. 788).

The new powers, which could have significant potential impact on civil liberties unless carefully circumscribed, are given substance through s. 60 of the Criminal Justice and Public Order Act 1994, a section which itself was regarded as introducing a remarkably broad new power (see Wasik, M. and Taylor, R., *Blackstone's Guide to the Criminal Justice & Public Order Act 1994*, p. 98). The original s. 60 conferred a power on a police officer of the rank of superintendent or above to give authorisation for 24 hours, in respect of a locality within his area, for special stop and search powers to be exercised by any constable in uniform. The authorising officer had reasonably to believe that incidents involving serious violence may take place in the locality (the authorisation could be by an inspector if he believed that incidents involving serious violence were imminent) and the actual power was to stop and search for offensive weapons and dangerous instruments. The novel and striking thing about this power given to the constable was that, within the area of the authorisation, it applied irrespective of 'whether he has any grounds for suspecting that the person or vehicle is carrying weapons or articles of that kind'.

Section 60 had already been extended in various respects by amendments effected by s. 8 of the Knives Act 1997, which reduced to inspector the rank of officer required to make the authorisation (although in such a case the inspector has to cause an officer of the rank of superintendent or above to be informed as soon as is practicable). More significantly perhaps, the amendment broadened the grounds for making an authorisation to include a reasonable belief that persons are carrying dangerous instruments or offensive weapons as an alternative to the reasonable belief that incidents involving serious violence may take place. The amendment also increased the length of time for which the original period of 24 hours could be extended under s. 60(3) from a further six hours to a further 24 hours.

Section 25 now further amends s. 60 of the Act not in terms of the criteria for giving an authorisation but in terms of the powers of constables once an authorisation is given. By a new s. 60(4A) the constable is to have power:

(a)   to require any person to remove any item which the constable reasonably believes that person is wearing wholly or mainly for the purpose of concealing his identity;
(b)   to seize any item which the constable reasonably believes any person intends to wear wholly or mainly for that purpose.

It should be noted that there are two separate powers in the new s. 60(4A): a power to require removal of an item and a power to seize an item but there is no power to search for face coverings etc. because it was acknowledged that it would be going 'too far to have a power to stop and search for face coverings [as] they are not in the same category of knives and offensive weapons. However it is reasonable for police officers to be able to seize face coverings that they come across whilst searching for other things, or because such coverings are being carried openly.' (Mr O'Brien, *Hansard*, Commons, Standing Committee B, 9 June 1998, col. 789).

Although much of the discussion in Committee was concerned with opposition amendments concerned to ensure that the powers could adequately deal with masked hunt saboteurs or animal rights activists etc. (and more whimsically and topically, Scottish football fans travelling to the World Cup, because of the difficulties the French authorities were having in identifying such fans in full Scottish dress and woad from their passport photographs), none of these are the main groups at which the powers are aimed. As Mr O'Brien explained:

The new clause does not relate only to hunt saboteurs.... The provisions are designed to deal with the serious disturbances that occur in many of our housing estates in urban and rural areas.... For example, the provisions will deal with youths, with balaclavas covering their faces, who hijack cars and drive them at high speeds around housing estates. (*Hansard*, Commons Standing Committee B, 9 June 1998, col. 804.)

It was recognised by the Under Secretary that the power needed sensitive handling and that legitimate and peaceful protesters might want to conceal their identity for good reasons (e.g., farm workers protesting about hunting but worried about repercussions on their employment if their identity was revealed) and there was no intention to undermine such a peaceful and legitimate protest. He continued by pointing out that 'if there is an anticipation of violence at such a protest, it is in the overall public interest that such farm workers should remove their facial coverings, or leave the scene. They could have that choice'.

These sentiments seem admirable but there appears to be nothing in the new powers *requiring* the constable to give the protester the choice, although it is to be hoped that constables would use the power sensitively and allow a protester who clearly was prepared to leave the locality peacefully the opportunity to do so without having to reveal his or her identity. It should be noted that s. 60(8) of the 1994 Act, which makes it a summary offence to fail to stop as required under s. 60, is amended to make it also such an offence, under s. 60(8)(b), to fail to remove a face covering etc. when required to do so. Furthermore, an offence under s. 60(8)(b) is made an arrestable offence as a result of s. 27(1) amending s. 24(2) of the Police and Criminal Evidence Act 1984. Section 27(2) inserts a new s. 60B into the 1994 Act to confer a power of arrest without warrant in Scotland in relation to offences under s. 60(8).

Another issue of great potential sensitivity is of course the issue of face coverings etc. worn for religious purposes, Muslim women being the most obvious example. The Under Secretary made it plain there was no intention to interfere with the wearing of face coverings for this and other legitimate purposes and pointed to the requirement that the constable exercising the power must reasonably believe that the person concerned is wearing a face covering wholly or mainly for the *purpose* of concealing his identity. It was, however, acknowledged that this could be a difficult judgment and, it might be added, could be a highly charged one were the police to be dealing with a large protest involving large numbers of people of a particular religious persuasion wearing face coverings consistently with that religion but which the police might feel were being used to conceal identity or even with a dual purpose. In this latter connection it should be noted that the constable's belief has to be that the wearing is 'wholly or mainly' for the purpose of concealing identity. The Government anticipated that 'officers will see that it is for them to exercise the best possible judgement'.

The original s. 60 of the Criminal Justice and Public Order Act 1994 authorised the seizure of offensive weapons and dangerous instruments (such as knives) but made no provision as to what should happen to such items after they had been seized. Section 26 inserts a new s. 60A which empowers the Secretary of State to make regulations 'regulating the retention and safe keeping, and the disposal and destruction in prescribed circumstances, of such things' (s. 60A(2)). These regulations, it would appear, will provide for seized face coverings etc. as well as offensive weapons etc. although the regulations 'may make different provisions for different classes of things or for different circumstances' (s. 60A(3)).

The new powers in relation to face coverings conferred by the amendments effected by ss. 25 to 27 will come into force on 1 December 1998 and, by s. 121(6)(a), they will also extend to Scotland.

Chapter 4
Youth Justice

This chapter deals principally with the new system for youth justice established by ss. 37 to 42. It also deals with reprimands and warnings to young offenders under ss. 65 and 66 and the new powers for courts to remand children and young persons to secure accommodation under ss. 97 and 98.

THE YOUTH JUSTICE SYSTEM

Sections 37 to 42 create a new structure for the youth justice system at both local and national levels. These provisions reflect the principle, established by s. 5, that responsibility for tackling crime should be shared between the police and local authorities. The new structures also provide a framework for the development of programmes to steer youngsters away from crime in conjunction with parenting orders, child safety orders, rehabilitation for warned offenders, reparation orders, action plan orders and supervision orders.

The purpose of the new structures is found in s. 37, which makes the prevention of offending the principal aim of the youth justice system. This aim will inform the work of local authorities who are placed under new duties: to provide various youth justice services (s. 38), to co-operate with the police and other agencies in establishing youth offending teams (s. 39) and to formulate annual youth justice plans (s. 40). Locally the new youth offending teams will play a vital role in co-ordinating the efforts of the various agencies engaged in youth justice work.

Nationally, such local efforts to tackle youth crime will be overseen by a new Youth Justice Board whose duties are to monitor the youth justice system and to advise the Home Secretary (s. 41). Government rhetoric in the consultation papers and the White Paper on which this Part of the Act is based, and in Parliament during the passage of the Act, has emphasised flexibility, local decision-making and local 'ownership' of youth justice services. However, a degree of control is reserved to the Home Secretary through guidance issued under s. 42(3) local authorities and their partners in delivering youth justice services must act in accordance with such guidance.

These provisions will come into force on 30 September 1998 in relation to four areas in which pilot schemes will be operated. These schemes will start in October and will run for a period of 18 months until general implementation. The provision concerning appointments to the Youth Justice Board was brought into force in advance of the other provisions in order to enable the Board to commence its work as soon as possible. Areas other than those affected by the pilot schemes will be expected to have appointed youth offending teams and to have formulated a youth justice plan in readiness for general implementation in 2000–2001.

Aim of the youth justice system

Section 37 provides that it shall be the principal aim of the youth justice system to prevent offending by children and young persons and that it shall be the duty of all persons and bodies carrying out functions in relation to the youth justice system to have regard to that aim in addition to any other duty to which they are subject. In this context the youth justice system means the criminal justice system insofar as it relates to children and young persons (s. 42(1)). This superficially unexceptionable proposition was controversial during its passage through Parliament and may cause difficulties in practice for a number of the professional groups involved in the youth justice system.

In their White Paper *No More Excuses*, the Government referred to:

confusion about the purpose of the youth justice system and principles that should govern the way in which young people are dealt with by youth justice agencies. Concerns about the welfare of young people have too often been seen as in conflict with the aims of protecting the public, punishing offences and preventing offending.

If there was such confusion, in relation to both social workers and probation officers, this is explicable. For social workers, responsibilities in relation to youngsters passing through the youth justice system were developed piecemeal as an adjunct to the social worker's prime responsibility for the welfare of the child or young person. For probation officers, although they have always acknowledged a duty to try and turn offenders away from crime, they have argued that this long-term aim is not best pursued by the sorts of quasi-policing measures which might be needed to prevent offending in the short term. Criticism in Parliament of s. 37 focused on the extent to which it might deflect various professional groups from their proper roles.

Notwithstanding these concerns, a close reading of s. 37 indicates that it may have little impact on the duties of criminal justice actors. First, although crime prevention is to be the principal aim of the youth justice system, this is not stated to be the principal aim of any particular agency within that system. Thus, for instance, the principal aim of a social worker receiving a child into care during police detention will rightly remain the welfare of the child. The duty imposed by s. 37(2) is simply to have regard to the aim of the system, and it is expressly conceded that the actor will have other duties to which he must have regard.

Concerns that s. 37 may alter a lawyer's duties in respect of his client are also misplaced. Whereas it has always been the case that a defence lawyer cannot either legally or ethically positively facilitate a crime by the client, the duty to advise in the client's best interests and to maintain the client's confidences are respected by the common law (see, e.g., *Derby Magistrates' Court, ex parte B* [1996] AC 487) and could not be displaced by a mere duty to have regard to the aim of preventing crime.

Duty to provide youth justice services

The Act introduces a new label, 'youth justice services', for the collection of services provided by local authorities and the probation service in relation to the detention of young suspects and their supervision before trial, the sentencing process and the execution of sentences upon young offenders. In recent years the nature and extent of such services, and hence the options available to the police and the courts, have varied according to area. Section 38 now places responsibility for the provision of such services on local authorities, acting in co-operation with relevant chief officers of police, police authorities, probation committees and health authorities.

The Act does not specify the manner of the required co-operation between the various services. However, the Government's consultation document, *New National and Local Focus on Youth Crime*, suggested that this might be effected through a chief officers' group, chaired by the local authority chief executive and comprising the chief officers of the social services and education departments, the probation service, the police and the health authority. This group would have a management and planning role and would also have to liaise with other bodies such as local Drug Action Teams and the Criminal Justice Liaison Area Committees. The group's most important role would be to supervise and monitor the work of the youth offender teams, to be set up under s. 39, which will have responsibility for co-ordinating the work of the various services at operational level.

The key question of who pays for these services is answered only vaguely, and this may be expected to be a source of friction between the co-operating bodies. Under s. 38(3), the local authority and each of the co-operating bodies is given power to contribute towards the funding of youth justice services, either by making payments directly or by contributing to a fund to be established by the local authority for this purpose. The financial contribution of each participating body would not necessarily match the secondment of its staff to youth justice work. The Government had made clear both in its consultation document and in Parliament that it expected that youth justice services would be funded from existing resources and that no new provision would be made. At the same time, chief officers were instructed that they should be personally involved in managing youth justice services and agencies are being placed under new duties relating to crime prevention. It is clear that youth justice is to be given a high priority and the Home Secretary's change of heart in announcing on 21 July 1998 that new funds would be made available is welcome. However, the Home Secretary has made clear that all agencies are to be expected to achieve efficiency improvements recommended by the Audit Commission in its report *Misspent Youth*, and should also seek value for money in purchasing youth justice services from outside providers.

The youth justice services to be provided are listed in s. 38(4), although the Home Secretary may vary or add to the list by order (s. 38(5)). The present list comprises:

(a) the provision of persons to act as appropriate adults to safeguard the interests of children and young persons in police detention;

(b) the assessment of children and young persons who are given a final warning under s. 66, for the purpose of determining their suitability for a rehabilitation programme (as provided for by s. 66(2)), and the provision of such programmes;

(c) the provision of support for children and young persons remanded or committed on bail while awaiting trial or sentence;

(d)   the placement of children and young persons under the age of 17 remanded to local authority accommodation while awaiting trial or sentence under s. 23 of the Children and Young Persons Act 1969;

(e)   the provision of reports relating to bail decisions and social enquiry reports or other information required by courts in criminal proceedings against children and young persons;

(f)   the provision of 'responsible officers' to supervise parenting orders under s. 8, child safety orders under s. 11, reparation orders under s. 67, and action plan orders under s. 69;

(g)   the supervision of children and young persons sentenced to a probation order, a community service order or a combination order;

(h)   the supervision of children and young persons sentenced to a detention and training order under s. 73 or a supervision order under s. 71;

(i)   the post-release supervision of children and young persons under s. 37(4A) or 65 of the Criminal Justice Act 1991 or s. 37 of the Crime (Sentences) Act 1997.

(j)   the provision of secure accommodation for the purpose of detention and training orders under s. 75.

Youth offending teams

Plans for the establishment of local youth offender teams (YOT) were set out in the consultation document *New National and Local Focus on Youth Crime*. The Government acknowledged, and wished to build upon, the considerable developments in co-operation and inter-agency projects in delivering youth justice services at a local level. For instance Home Office Circular 30/1992, issued jointly with the Welsh Office, had encouraged co-operation between social services and the probation service in relation to 16 and 17-year-old offenders. Arrangements also existed in most areas for the division of responsibility for younger offenders between social services and the probation service. Although formerly social services had responsibility for offenders under 16 and the probation service for offenders above that age, it was recognised that a more effective service could be provided by joint youth justice teams which could offer a wider range of services and continuity as young offenders grew older. Other areas had more broadly based inter-agency teams which might include representatives from the police, the education services and voluntary organisations. Such partnerships were recognised as being particularly effective in providing 'caution plus' programmes, bail support schemes and activities for young people subject to supervision orders. The need to place inter-agency YOTs on a statutory footing arises as a result of the Government's policy to draw upon the best practice developed at local level and to create programmes to tackle youth offending throughout the country.

Under s. 39, the duty to establish YOTs falls on local authorities, acting in conjunction with relevant chief officers of police, health authorities and probation committees (s. 39(1) and (3)). The local authorities in question are county councils, district councils which do not fall under a county council, London borough councils, the Common Council of the City of London and, in Wales, county councils and county borough councils (s. 42(1)(a) and (b)). This level of local government was chosen because it provides social and education services, which are important components of the YOT scheme. A local authority may establish more than one YOT if appropriate and is also free to co-operate with neighbouring authorities to set up one or more YOT (s. 39(2)). This might be appropriate where a unitary authority is surrounded by an adjacent county council.

Section 39(7) gives YOTs two functions:

(a)   to co-ordinate the provision of youth justice services for all those in the local authority's area who need them; and

(b)   to carry out such functions as are assigned to the team in the youth justice plan formulated by the authority under s. 40.

This prescription leaves considerable leeway as to the precise role of the YOT. The Government have issued an *Interdepartmental Circular on Establishing Youth Offender Teams* (Home Office, June 1998), although this emphasises that the precise roles of YOTs must be determined locally. At one extreme a YOT might be little more than a liaison body between the various parties carrying out the functions under the local youth justice plan. At the other extreme, a YOT might become a form of executive agency providing or purchasing youth justice services and active in the development of new forms of intervention and local policy. The functions which may be assigned to a YOT under a youth justice plan may include functions in fulfilment of the local authority's duty to take reasonable steps designed to encourage children and young persons not to commit offences, under para. 7(b) of sch. 2 to the Children Act 1989 (s. 40(3)).

The *Interdepartmental Circular on Establishing Youth Offender Teams* suggests that if such a team is not already in operation in a particular area it would be necessary to form a steering group to oversee its establishment. The steering group should contain representatives of all the contributing agencies, who should either be the chief officers or at sufficient level of seniority to negotiate on behalf of the services they represent. A youth offender team manager would be appointed by the steering group and be accountable to it, but perhaps with day-to-day accountability to the chief officer of one of the participating agencies. Team managers might be drawn from any of the participating agencies since the skills and experience of the individual would be more important than a particular background.

The precise method of funding YOTs and their work remains unclear. Local authorities, chief officers of police and probation committees are empowered to make payments towards such expenditure or to contribute to a fund for this purpose (s. 39(4)) but it appears that levels of contribution may have to be negotiated on a local basis.

Under s. 39(5) a YOT must include: a probation officer, a local authority social worker, a police officer, a representative of a local health authority, and a person nominated by the chief education officer. This is not an exclusive list and the local authority, after consulting the prescribed membership of the YOT may invite any other person considered appropriate to join the team. The Government consultation document suggested as examples of bodies which might be represented the local authority youth service and voluntary organisations already engaged in work with young offenders. The Government also expressed the view that YOTs should remain manageable in size but emphasised that there should be sufficient flexibility for membership to be determined locally.

The Government's rationale for requiring that particular agencies would be represented on a YOT is to supply particular skills and to ensure integration with the work of the relevant agencies (*New National and Local Focus on Youth Crime*, paras 35–42). Thus, social workers would be able to supply information about young offenders who had already received help from social services for some other reason. It was considered particularly important that the YOT should make necessary connections with other work being done with a young offender or the offender's family by the local authority.

Probation officers would supply their particular skills in assessing young offenders and working with them in the community to change their behaviour. Although the Government stopped short of legislating to shift responsibility for the supervision of particular groups of offenders, it made clear that it considered that much of the supervision work with offenders aged 13 or 14 should be carried out by probation officers rather than social workers. The Government has also indicated that it may be appropriate for probation officers to undertake the supervision of even younger children. This is implicit in s. 71(5) which removes the bar on probation officers supervising 10–12 year olds except in certain circumstances, formerly found in s. 13(2) of the Children and Young Persons Act 1969.

The consultation paper set out a number of potential roles for police officers on YOTs. First, such officers could ensure good liaison with colleagues administering final warnings to young offenders (under s. 65). Apart from the formal requirement to inform the YOT when a young offender is warned, liaison will be important in view of the duty to explain to the young offender at the time of the warning about the available rehabilitation programmes which accompany warnings. It will also be important for the police to pass on any information which they have about the young offender which may be relevant to the YOT's duty to assess the young offender with a view to rehabilitation under s. 66(2)(a). Officers in the YOT team would also have a role in ensuring that the team's policies were translated into police work, by ensuring that in dealing with young offenders the police in general would highlight the effects of crime on victims and the community, and warn young offenders of the problems associated with having a criminal record. Police officers might also be involved in reparation work with young offenders and victims and help with offenders by providing supervised leisure activities, as well as playing more traditional policing roles in checking the observance of curfews and attendance at projects and investigating alleged breaches of orders.

Representation of the local authority education department on the YOT would reflect the links between offending and truancy and exclusion from school. It is envisaged that the person appointed as the education representative might have experience working with truants or excluded children. The representative's particular contribution to the team might involve ensuring that the education department fulfilled its statutory duties to enforce school attendance and provide education for excluded children and also ensuring that young offenders' education needs are addressed.

Of the bodies which must be represented on YOTs, health authorities have the least experience of direct involvement in youth justice work. It is envisaged that the health authority representative will have a particular input in relation to offenders with drug, alcohol or mental health problems. It will be important to ensure that adequate provision is made for relevant treatment or counselling and that this may be drawn upon for the purposes of the rehabilitation programmes which will accompany formal warnings under s. 66, action plan orders under s. 69, and post-release supervision.

Youth justice plans

Section 40(1) places local authorities under a duty to formulate and implement annual youth justice plans. In formulating such a plan a local authority must consult chief officers of police, probation committees and health authorities whose areas cover any part of the local authority area. In fact more than simple consultation will be required. Since the plan must set out how youth justice services in the area are to be supplied and funded, and how the YOTs are to be composed and funded, it seems clear that the plan must represent an agreement between the parties.

In the course of debate in Parliament, the question arose whether there should be specific duties to consult with representatives of significant ethnic minorities within an area (*Hansard*, Commons, Standing Committee B, 14 May 1998, cols 390–391). The guidance now published on the establishment of YOTs requires ethnic monitoring to determine whether particular groups are being treated equitably and in order to retain the confidence of all ethnic groups in society. It also advises that consideration be given to consulting relevant representative groups (para. 92).

The local authority must submit each annual plan to the Youth Justice Board for England and Wales and must also publish it in a manner, and by such date, prescribed in directions given by the Home Secretary (s. 40(4)). Further to the duty to submit the annual plan, all of the partner bodies in youth justice — local authorities, chief constables, police authorities, probation committees and health authorities — may be required to submit specified information or make supplementary reports on particular matters to the Youth Justice Board in pursuance of the Board's duties to monitor and advise the Home Secretary on the operation of the youth justice system and to monitor the extent to which the aim of taking steps to prevent offending by children and young persons is being achieved (s. 41(8)). Where such reports are submitted, the Board may also order the authority which provided the report to publish it in a manner which the Board considers appropriate (s. 41(9)).

As well as monitoring by the Youth Justice Board, it was suggested in the consultation paper (para. 45) that further inspections of YOTs would take place which might take one of two alternative forms. The first alternative was that HM Inspectorates of Constabulary and Probation, the Social Services Inspectorates and Ofsted might be asked to carry out joint inspections of YOTs. The second alternative was that the Youth Justice Board would undertake inspections and for this purpose would have inspectors seconded to it from the relevant inspectorates. In either case, inspections would be informed by the national standards to be drawn up by the Home Secretary after advice from the Youth Justice Board.

The Youth Justice Board

Section 41 establishes the Youth Justice Board for England and Wales as a non-departmental public body sponsored by the Home Office. The precise implications of this status are hazy although it is clearly not designed to be independent of Government since by s. 41(7) the Board must comply with any directions given by the Home Secretary and act in accordance with any guidance given by him.

The Board's membership will consist of between 10 and 12 persons appointed by the Home Secretary; they must include persons who appear to him to have extensive recent experience of the youth justice system (s. 41(3) and (4)). During the passage of the Act, the Government resisted suggestions that particular constituencies, such as youth panel magistrates or representatives of victims' organisations, should be represented on the Board, although it was pointed out that such persons would qualify.

Board members may be full-time or part-time; appointments will be for five years with the possibility of renewal up to a maximum continuous period of 10 years. A chairman will be appointed and there is also a power to appoint a chief executive. The Home Secretary retains the power to sack any member or the chairman without cause by declaring the office vacant, subject to the payment of compensation. There is also a power to remove a member or the chairman for dereliction of duty, bankruptcy, criminal conviction or unfitness (s. 41(11) and sch. 2).

The Board's functions are primarily concerned with monitoring and advice to the Home Secretary, with some limited executive functions which may be added to by the Home Secretary.

The duty to monitor the youth justice system and the provision of youth justice services under s. 41(5)(a) is supported by the duty on YOTs to submit their annual plans to the Board, and by the Board's power to require information or a report on a particular matter from the various bodies involved in the provision of youth justice services locally (s. 41(8)). The Board also has a specific duty to monitor the extent to which the aim of preventing offending by children and young persons is being achieved, and any relevant standard met (s. 41(5)(c)).

Under s. 41(5)(b), the Board is required to advise the Home Secretary on:

(a)   the operation of the system and the provision of youth justice services;

(b)   how the principal aim of the system, to prevent offending by children and young persons, might most effectively be pursued;

(c)   the content of national standards relating to the provision of youth justice services, or such standards relating to accommodation for detained children and young persons; and

(d)   the steps that might be taken to prevent offending by children and young persons.

The Board's executive functions are:

(a)   to publish information obtained from local providers of youth justice services (s. 41(5)(e));

(b)   to identify, make known and promote good practice in:

(i)   the operation of the youth justice system and provision of youth justice services;

(ii)   the prevention of offending; and

(iii) working with children and young persons who are at risk of becoming offenders (s. 41(5)(f));

(c)   to make grants, with the Home Secretary's approval, to local authorities or other bodies for the development of good practice or the commissioning of research in relation to good practice (s. 51(5)(g)); and

(d)   to commission such research themselves (s. 41(5)(h)).

The possibility that the Board's role may expand in future is provided for by s. 41(6), which permits the Home Secretary, by order, to amend, subtract, add to or alter any of the Board's functions or to provide that any of his own functions in relation to youth justice may be exercised concurrently by the Board.

Disclosure of information between youth justice agencies

Fears expressed by some youth justice agencies that they would be hampered in co-operating with other agencies by restrictions on the disclosure of information under the data protection legislation are dispelled by s. 115. The section empowers any person to disclose information to any of the public agencies involved in the delivery of youth justice services where this is necessary or expedient for the purpose of any provision of the Act.

REPRIMANDS AND WARNINGS

It has long been accepted that prosecution is not necessarily the most appropriate response to detected offending and, accordingly, there is no rule requiring prosecution. This is particularly the case in relation to young offenders whose offending may be trivial in nature, who are likely to grow out of crime and for whom the experience of being dealt with in the formal criminal justice system may be counterproductive in terms of creating a negative self-image or being influenced by other offenders. Although no doubt it has always been the case that some trivial offending has been ignored or subject to a decision to take no action, the caution was developed as a more formal alternative to prosecution. Since 1985 the practice of cautioning has been subject to guidelines issued by the Home Office. Notwithstanding the guidelines being tightened in 1994 to discourage repeat cautioning, police forces were nevertheless allowed considerable discretion in terms of decision-making processes and the criteria employed. For this reason, the extent and manner of cautioning has varied considerably between different areas with some areas developing imaginative programmes for offenders, known collectively as 'caution plus'.

The development of 'caution plus' addressed the perceived shortcoming of cautioning, which was that it amounts to no more than a warning and does little to address offending behaviour. The essence of 'caution plus' is that, in parallel with the caution, the young offender should engage in some further activity which assists the offender in confronting his own offending behaviour. Typically the plus element has involved some form of reparation to the offender or to the community, or some form of educational activity, counselling or therapy. Although the term 'caution plus' will no longer be used once this Act is brought into force, the concept will survive in the guise of the 'rehabilitation' order which may accompany a formal warning under s. 66.

Sections 65 and 66 replace cautions for children and young persons with a new system of reprimands and warnings. Cautions for these age groups will be abolished from the commencement of the provisions (s. 66(8)). The purpose of the reform is to create a predictable staged process under which a child or young person may expect to be reprimanded for a first offence, warned for a second and prosecuted for a third.

As with the former system of cautioning, responsibility for decision-making and administering reprimands and warnings rests with the police. The new system however will differ from the old in the extent to which other agencies — social services, the probation service and the education authority — play a role. The former cautioning scheme encouraged consultation and liaison between agencies in exercising the discretion whether to caution rather than prosecute. The new scheme, which is considerably more rigid and makes explicit reference to various judgments made by a constable, would seem to preclude inter-agency decision-making, although, as will be discussed below, the other agencies will have important roles in devising and operating the rehabilitation programmes which may accompany formal warnings.

The administration of a caution involved three stages: a determination that there was sufficient evidence to prove guilt; taking the suspect's admission of guilt; and the imposition of a sanction. (The caution, and now the reprimand and warning, are properly considered as sanctions because, although not immediately onerous, they are recorded in police, educational and social services files and may have a considerable impact on later decisions about the young person and upon her or his life opportunities.) A criticism of the former scheme was that it was inappropriate for these functions to be the responsibility of police officers without legal or other external scrutiny and safeguards. Although for juveniles the consent of both the suspect and parents was required, such consent was easily obtained since the alternative was prosecution.

The new scheme of reprimands and warnings, however, follows the old in leaving the issue of guilt and the imposition of the sanction to the police. This indicates trust in the police and a preference for efficiency and speed in decision-making over checks and safeguards. Paradoxically, by attempting to confirm the autonomy of the police in these matters, the Act has probably exposed police decision-making to a greater possibility of scrutiny by way of judicial review.

The new scheme in outline

An offender who has not previously been reprimanded or warned may be reprimanded, provided that various pre-conditions (discussed below) are satisfied (s. 65(2)). A second reprimand is therefore ruled out. In the transitional period a first caution administered before s. 65 is brought into force will be treated as a reprimand, and a second or subsequent caution will be treated as a warning (sch. 9, para. 5). A warning may be administered even though the offender has not previously been reprimanded if a constable considers the offence is sufficiently serious to require a warning rather than a reprimand. The Home Secretary may issue guidance as to when a first offence is so serious as to require a warning (s. 65(6)(a)(ii)). Where a person who has been warned commits a further offence, the police have no option to either reprimand or warn (s. 65(2) and (3)), except where two years have elapsed since the earlier warning and the offence is not considered serious (s. 65(3)(b)). The implication is that once a person who has been warned commits a further offence within two years a prosecution must follow, and no doubt that will normally be the case. However, as discussed below (see The public interest), it is arguable that, even where a further reprimand or warning is ruled out, the police retain a discretion to take no action on an otherwise prosecutable case where it would not be in the public interest to prosecute.

The preconditions for reprimand and warning

The preconditions for both reprimand and warning are set out in s. 65(1) as follows:

(a) a constable has evidence that a child or young person ... has committed an offence;

(b) the constable considers that the evidence is such that, if the offender were prosecuted for the offence, there would be a realistic prospect of his being convicted;

(c) the offender admits to the constable that he committed the offence;

(d) the offender has not previously been convicted of an offence; and

(e) the constable is satisfied that it would not be in the public interest for the offender to be prosecuted.

Evidence

The requirement that a constable should instigate the reprimand procedure only on the basis of evidence which he considers sufficient for a realistic prospect of conviction appears to be designed to ensure that the procedure is not applied on the basis of mere suspicion. The meaning of 'evidence' in this context is problematic. The term cannot be limited to evidence which might be admissible in court since in many situations admissibility will depend upon specific determination which may be made only by a court. Equally, it seems that the notion of evidence for the purposes of s. 65 must bear some relationship to the rules of evidence. Thus, a court called upon to determine the legality of a reprimand might well hold it unlawful if based purely upon an anonymous telephone call (which would be inadmissible in court as hearsay), an allegation made by a mentally incompetent person (inadmissible due to incompetence), or purely on the basis of the suspect's criminal record.

It is also not made clear whether the requirement of an admission by the offender comes into play only once a constable considers that there is sufficient evidence to convict, or whether such admission may itself supply or contribute to the constable's assessment of sufficiency. The fact that in law uncorroborated guilty pleas and confessions are sufficient for conviction may suggest that a suspect's admission should be sufficient for reprimand or warning. There are however differences between mere admissions in police stations and guilty pleas and confessions respectively. Whereas the police station admission may be made without legal advice and may be witnessed only by the police, the guilty plea is taken in open court in response to a case which has been vetted by the CPS, and normally follows legal advice. A conviction may be founded solely upon a confession only if a magistrates' court or jury are satisfied of its admissibility, authenticity and credibility.

These distinctions indicate that consistency does not require that a reprimand or warning could be based upon an admission alone. Perhaps the strongest argument for interpreting s. 65 as requiring both an admission and an independent assessment of evidential sufficiency is that if the admission itself could do double duty and supply evidential sufficiency the requirement of an evidential basis and an assessment of sufficiency set out in s. 65(1)(a) and (b) would be of no effect. The better view therefore seems to be that in order to justify a reprimand or warning there must be an admission plus an evidential basis for guilt which the constable assesses to be sufficient quite apart from the admission.

The test of 'realistic prospect of ... conviction' is the same as that applied by the CPS in deciding whether a prosecution should proceed and has been interpreted as requiring at least a 51 per cent chance of conviction. In the CPS context, applying the test involves not only an assessment of the prosecution case, but also a consideration of any defences that might be raised and matters which might affect success at trial, such as the possible unavailability of a witness. Presumably, in relation to decisions whether to reprimand or warn, the first two factors would be relevant but not the third, since it would be incongruous to consider practical issues concerning the trial where the objective is to avoid such a trial.

The test involved is objective in the sense that the constable must have evidence (under 65(1)(a)) but subjective in terms of whether the constable considers that there is a realistic prospect of conviction. The choice of a subjective test will not totally preclude judicial review since a decision that there was a realistic prospect of conviction founded on patently insufficient evidence might be quashed as unreasonable (*Associated Picture Houses* v *Wednesbury Corporation* [1948] 1 KB 223).

The admission

It is not made clear what will suffice for an admission. In principle, as a conviction cannot be founded upon an ambiguous plea, so a reprimand or warning should not be founded upon an ambiguous admission. Ambiguity might arise, for instance, where an admission is tempered with an excuse or where the young person makes plain that admitting the offence is done only to avoid prosecution rather than as an acknowledgment of guilt. Such ambiguities may be exposed where the putative admission is taped rather than recorded on paper.

In order to avoid the risk of ambiguity, it would be good practice for an officer taking an admission for the purpose of a reprimand or warning to ask the suspect to admit to each of the elements of the offence. For instance, in relation to an offence of theft, the offender might be asked if he stole the bag, if he knew that it belonged to Mr. Smith, if he intended to keep it and if he knew that ordinary people would consider what he did dishonest.

No previous convictions

A prior conviction for an offence, however trivial, is an absolute bar to the administration of a warning or reprimand. Although this will limit police discretion, it does not mean that the police must necessarily prosecute if they have sufficient evidence to do so against a child or young person with a prior conviction. As will be argued below, in such cases the public interest may dictate that no further action is taken.

The rigidity of this bar may cause problems in circumstances where because of faulty record keeping or misunderstanding, the police administer a reprimand or warning to an offender who has been convicted previously. Theoretically, a reprimand or warning administered in such circumstances would be a nullity and the young person could be prosecuted for the later offence. Whether this would be a sensible course of action, perhaps some time after the offence, is another matter.

The public interest

The final precondition to the administration of reprimand or warning is that the constable is satisfied that it would not be in the public interest for the offender to be prosecuted. The role of public interest in prosecution decision-making is well established and has been elucidated in successive Home Office Guidelines on Cautioning and Codes for Crown Prosecutors. The Act makes no specific provision for the issuing of general guidance on the meaning of public interest, suggesting that the police are to be expected to refer to existing sources of guidance in applying the test.

As will be discussed below, under s. 65(6)(a) the Secretary of State is required to publish guidance relating to one aspect of public interest — the issue of the seriousness of the offence, as it relates to two particular decisions. The two decisions in question are:

(a)   whether an offence is not so serious as to require a charge to be brought, and can therefore be dealt with by warning even though the offender had been warned previously within the last two years (under s. 65(3)(b));

(b)   whether an offence is so serious as to require a warning in circumstances in which a reprimand would otherwise be appropriate (under s. 65(4)).

It is notable that in these two contexts the degree of seriousness operates to vary the appropriate response to an offence as between charge and warning, or reprimand and warning, respectively. It does not appear to be contemplated that triviality of an offence might be a factor suggesting that no formal action is taken. Inconsistently, the current Code of Practice for Crown Prosecutors indicates that non-prosecution should be the proper course in any case in which the court would be likely to impose a very small or nominal penalty or where the loss or harm caused is minor (*Blackstone's Criminal Practice*, appendix 5).

The clash between the rigid structure of prosecution decision-making imposed by the Act and the discretion confirmed by the Code for Crown Prosecutors will be apparent in two situations: first, where a suspect who has no previous convictions refuses to admit a trivial offence; secondly, where a person who has previously been warned commits a further trivial offence, or an offence attended by strong mitigating circumstances.

In the first of these situations, under the old regime a caution would have been ruled out because of the absence of an admission but it would not have been in the pubic interest to prosecute, and so the proper course for the police would have been to take no further action. If a charge was brought in such circumstances, the CPS Code prescribed that the case should be dropped. Under the new system, introduced by the current Act, taking no further action is not contemplated as an option. Section 65 seems to imply that prosecution is the normal response where a constable has evidence to prove an offence and that the only alternatives are to reprimand or warn where the offence is admitted. This implies a duty to prosecute in the absence of an admission, however trivial the offence and whatever public interest factors are present. This is inconsistent with the CPS Code, under which the absence of an admission does not bar the dropping of a case where triviality or other public interest factors indicate that this is the appropriate course.

The second problem arises in relation to a person who, having been previously warned, commits a further trivial offence or one subject to mitigating circumstances. Although formerly the case might have been treated as one in which the public interest militated against charge, s. 65(2) bars a reprimand and s. 65(3)(a) bars a further warning (unless two years have passed since the earlier warning: s. 65(3)(b)). The message is clear: that the offender may only go up-tariff. If reprimand and warning are excluded, by implication so is a decision to take no further action.

Should s. 65 be interpreted as excluding the possibility of no further action being taken in the two situations discussed here, the police would be forced to prosecute, against the public interest, in circumstances where if the CPS adhere to the Code, the case will inevitably be dropped. It can hardly be imagined that it was the intention of Parliament that the police should indulge in such pointless and wasteful exercises. This suggests strongly that, although not acknowledged in the Act, a police discretion to take no further action remains, and indeed would be the proper course for trivial offences which are not admitted, or which follow earlier warnings. If this is right, it would be paradoxical for a suspect who denies a provable offence to be treated more leniently than one who admits it. This in turn might suggest that no further action does or should remain an option for offenders whether they admit the offence or not.

Offenders other than children or young persons

An oddity of the new scheme is that it applies only to children and young persons. For offenders aged 18 or over, the non-statutory cautioning scheme will continue to apply. Although the present Home Office guidelines discourage repeat cautions, they are not ruled out. It would seem therefore that an 18-year-old offender might have the benefit of a third caution rather than a prosecution in circumstances in which his 17-year-old accomplice must be prosecuted.

Special cautioning schemes

Prior to the 1998 Act, the general cautioning scheme under Home Office guidelines was supplemented by other special schemes such as the national scheme relating to soliciting for the purpose of prostitution and kerb-crawling and local schemes relating to minor offences like being drunk and disorderly in a public place. These schemes reflect the particular offences in question. Thus, the cautioning scheme for soliciting conceives the prostitute as both offender and victim and operates both as a stage to be passed before a prosecution can be brought and as an opportunity for the offender to be put in touch with caring agencies who may assist with problems underlying her work as a prostitute. On the other hand, cautioning schemes relating to drunkenness offences are primarily designed to conserve police resources in areas beset by a substantial problem of public drunkenness.

Section 65(8) which provides that: 'No caution shall be given to a child or young person after the commencement of this section', would appear to abolish both the general scheme and special cautioning schemes insofar as they apply to persons under 18. It may be however that some special cautioning schemes survive for the following reason. Under the applicable definition of caution, borrowed from Part V of the Police Act 1997, the caution must be 'in respect of an offence which at the time when the caution is given, he has admitted'. The cautioning scheme for soliciting for prostitution which has operated under Home Office guidelines since 1959 does not require that the offence is admitted: indeed an appeal may be taken to the magistrates' court where a woman denies the offence for which she has been cautioned (Street Offences Act 1959, s. 2). Thus, any scheme like that relating to soliciting, where a caution may be administered without a prior admission, would fall outside the prohibition in s. 65(8).

It should also be noted that in the past police forces have employed responses to crime short of prosecution described in other ways, for instance as 'informal warnings'. There seems nothing to stop them doing so again for particular crimes requiring flexibility of response. Should this occur, the effect of abolishing cautioning may be little more than to change the terminology employed.

The administration of reprimands and warnings

A reprimand or warning for an offender aged under 17 must be administered by a police officer at a police station, in the presence of an appropriate adult (s. 65(5)(a)). The Home Secretary is placed under a duty to publish guidance as to the category of constable who may administer a reprimand or warning and as to the form which reprimands and warnings are to take and the manner in which they are to be given and recorded (s. 65(6)(b) and (c)). It seems likely that the guidelines to be issued will require that the relevant officer is of at least the rank of inspector, as currently required by the cautioning guidelines.

An 'appropriate adult' in relation to a child or young person is (s. 65(7)):

(a)   a parent or guardian;

(b)   in relation to a child in the care of a local authority or voluntary organisation, a person representing that authority or organisation;

(c)   a local authority social worker; or

(d)   if no person within those categories is available, any responsible person aged 18 or over other than one employed by the police in any capacity.

This meaning of 'appropriate adult' is the same as in PACE Code C, para 1.7, which relates to attendance at police interviews with juveniles. No priority is indicated as between categories (a), (b) and (c), although it is generally accepted that a social worker should be asked to attend only if a parent or representative of an organisation with parental authority is unable to do so.

In the context of police interviews, the definition of appropriate adult has been significantly modified by the notes of guidance appended to Code C and case law. Thus, a person suspected of involvement in the offence or who is estranged from the juvenile will not be an appropriate adult (Code C, Note 1C), neither will a solicitor attending the interview in that capacity (*Lewis* [1996] Crim LR 260) nor a person attending the police station in the capacity of lay-visitor (Code C, Note 1F), nor a parent who lacks the mental capacity to properly perform the function of appropriate adult (*Morse* [1991] Crim LR 195). These exceptions are eminently sensible, but it is doubtful whether they can apply to the definition of appropriate adult in s. 65, since that section is unambiguous. Thus, if s. 65(7) states that a father may be an appropriate adult, he will be so whatever his state of mental health, sobriety or relationship with his child. It is very doubtful that this result was intended and it perhaps indicates the pitfalls of importing directly into statute provisions of administrative codes which do not bind the courts.

The constable administering a reprimand or warning is required to explain in ordinary language to the offender and appropriate adult (for offenders aged under 17) that the reprimand or warning may be cited in court as part of the offender's record for the purpose of sentencing following any future conviction. In relation to a warning, the constable must also explain that, following the warning, the offender will be referred to a youth offending team for assessment and might be required to take part in a rehabilitation programme. The effects of any guidance to be issued by the Home Secretary about the content of rehabilitation programmes and about how failures to participate in such programmes should be recorded must also be explained. The offender must also be told that in the event that he is convicted of a further offence within two years, the court would be barred from imposing a conditional discharge (s. 65(5)(b).

The effects of reprimands and warnings

Both reprimands and warnings may be cited as part of a person's record in future criminal proceedings in any court for the purpose of sentencing (s. 66(5)). This marks a change from the convention relating to juvenile cautions, which was that they might be cited in the future proceedings in the youth court but not in magistrates' courts or the Crown Court. Apart from this, the reprimand will operate as no more than an admonition and warning as to future conduct, much like the caution which it replaces.

A warning, however, will have three further significant consequences for a young offender. First, once warned, further offending if detected will normally lead to a prosecution. Secondly, once warned, an offender will not normally be eligible for a conditional discharge if convicted of a further offence within two years (s. 66(4)). Thirdly, a warning must always lead to a referral to the local youth offending team who will assess the young offender and, unless it is considered inappropriate, will arrange for him to participate in a rehabilitation programme.

The bar to conditional discharges for offenders who had previously received a warning proved controversial during the passage of the Act through Parliament. The idea was criticised on the ground that it removed sentencing discretion from the courts and, in particular, might force a court to impose a sentence which it considered neither useful nor justified. The Government defended the bar on the ground that the conditional discharge functions as a form of warning coupled with the threat of sanction in relation to future offending. In these respects it functioned in a similar way to the warning, and it was felt that the impact of a warning would be diluted if a young offender believed that further offending would be met with a conditional discharge. Paradoxically, a prior warning does not preclude the even more lenient disposal of absolute discharge.

The sorts of rehabilitation programmes offered by youth offending teams for warned offenders will inevitably depend upon the resources available to such teams. Guidance will be published by the Home Secretary as to what should be included in such programmes (s. 66(3)). In many cases a rehabilitation programme may differ little from reparation orders imposed upon convicted young offenders under s. 67.

No sanction is prescribed for failure to participate in a rehabilitation programme. However, the Home Secretary is to issue guidance as to the manner in which failure to participate in a rehabilitation programme should be recorded and to whom such failures should be notified (s. 66(3)(b) and (c)). Any report on the failure of a person to participate in a rehabilitation programme may then be cited at the sentencing stage of later criminal proceedings as part of the offender's record (s. 66(4)(c)). The significance which such a report might have is not clear since the warning, which accompanied the rehabilitation order, will also be cited. Being reported for failure to co-operate in a rehabilitation scheme will not appear to amount to a very severe sanction for a young offender who does not contemplate re-offending or does not contemplate being caught.

REMAND OF CHILDREN AND YOUNG PERSONS TO SECURE ACCOMMODATION

Sections 97 and 98 give courts the power to order that children and young persons remanded without bail should be housed in secure accommodation. However, at the time of writing no date has been set for implementation.

Background

The treatment of children or young persons who are remanded without bail pending trial has presented a problem for some years. Traditionally, remand has been to the care of the local authority under s. 23 of the Children and Young Persons Act 1969. However, local authority care is not suitable for juveniles who are dangerous or likely to re-offend or abscond, unless secure accommodation can be provided. Prior to 1991, many local authorities provided some secure accommodation for remanded juveniles but this proved to be inadequate for the numbers requiring such accommodation. Accordingly, s. 23 provided that male juveniles who were charged with offences punishable with imprisonment for fourteen years or more, for violent offences, or who had a history of absconding, might be remanded to a remand centre or prison.

Remanding juveniles to adult penal institutions was not considered satisfactory in principle and was abolished for female juveniles in 1979 once sufficient secure places were available. Measures to abolish the remand of juvenile males to adult institutions were found in s. 60 of the Criminal Justice Act 1991, but these were contingent on the building of a suitable number of secure units. That objective has yet to be accomplished and accordingly s. 60 has not yet been brought into force. Prior to the current Act, the operative law was found in a 'transitional' form in s. 23 of the Children and Young Persons Act 1969 (provided for by s. 62 of the CJA 1991) which was designed to operate until sufficient secure units had been built. Further amendments to s. 23 were contained in s. 20 of the Criminal Justice and Public Order Act 1994. These were never brought into force and will be repealed by s. 97(5) of the 1998 Act.

Prior to the coming into force of this part of the 1998 Act, the relevant law under the transitional version of s. 23 may be summarised as follows. The basic rule is that remanded juveniles must be placed in local authority accommodation. Exceptions are made for males of fifteen or over who are:

(a)   charged with offences which for an adult would be punishable with fourteen years imprisonment;

(b)   charged with violent or sexual offences; or
(c)   who have a history of absconding or a history of offending whilst on bail.

Such juveniles may be remanded to a remand centre or prison on the ground of need to protect the public. In addition, Youth Courts may remand a juvenile of either sex aged fifteen or over to secure local authority accommodation (if available) under s. 60(4) of the CJA 1991.

The new provisions

In its White Paper *No More Excuses*, (p. 20) the Government noted that local authorities were providing more secure places although these were not expected to meet demand. A need was expressed for additional court powers to remand children between twelve and fourteen and girls of fifteen or sixteen to local authority secure accommodation. These powers are now granted by s. 97. Concern was also expressed about vulnerable fifteen and sixteen year old boys remanded to adult institutions and accordingly, it was proposed to change the law to allow such youths to be remanded to secure accommodation if a place could be identified. This is provided for by s. 98.

Section 97(2) amends s. 23 of the C&YPA 1969 and lowers from fifteen to twelve the age at which a security requirement may be attached to remand to local authority care. The implementation of this reform will be subject to the Home Secretary prescribing by age and/or sex, categories of juvenile to be affected. Thus the provision can be implemented in stages, presumably starting with the older age groups, as secure accommodation becomes available. A security requirement may not be imposed in relation to a child or young person who is not legally represented unless the defendant has either been refused legal aid on means grounds or had been informed of his or her right to legal aid but has declined it (subs. (3) inserting a new subs. (5A) in s. 23 of the C&YPA 1969).

The long term aim is to abolish the remand of juveniles to adult penal institutions and s. 98 is designed to ameliorate problems in the interim. In this capacity s. 98 will supersede and repeal s. 62 of the CJA 1991 and the 'transitional' version of s. 23 of the C&YPA which it created.

Section 98 is novel in form and operation. It modifies s. 23 of the C&YPA 1969 only in relation to male juveniles aged fifteen or sixteen who do not qualify for remand to local authority secure accommodation. When s. 98 is brought into operation there will be two versions of s. 23 one applicable to this group of male juveniles, the other applicable to juveniles in general.

Much of the alternative version of s. 23 introduced by s. 98 follows the existing law. Thus, remand to an adult institution is possible only for offences punishable with fourteen years imprisonment in the case of an adult, or violent or sexual offences, or where there is a history of absconding or offending whilst on bail, and where there is a need to protect the public (s. 23(5)). A decision that a juvenile falls within these criteria may be made by a court only after consulting a probation officer, a social worker or a member of a youth offending team (s. 23(4)). A juvenile may not be remanded to an adult institution unless he or she has been refused legal aid on means grounds or has been offered legal aid but refused it (s. 23(4A)). For qualifying juveniles there is a clear order of priority of remand institution. Thus, the remand should be to local authority secure accommodation, or if this is not available, to a remand centre, or if this is not available, to a prison (s. 23(4)). Where a juvenile has been remanded to local authority accommodation without the imposition of a security requirement, the court retains the power to impose such a security requirement or remand the juvenile to a remand centre or prison at a later date if the relevant criteria are satisfied (s. 23(9A)).

The major departure from the pre-existing law relates to juveniles to whom the criteria in s. 23(5) apply but for whom the court makes a finding that by reason of physical or emotional immaturity or a propensity of the juvenile to harm himself or herself, it would be undesirable for him or her to be remanded to a remand centre or prison (s. 23(5A)). Where this finding is made the juvenile may be remanded to local authority secure accommodation where this available (s. 23(4)).

Chapter 5
Criminal Procedure

The majority of the provisions discussed in this chapter could be subtitled, 'reducing delays', a policy which has become a major theme in criminal justice legislation in recent years and which has been given renewed emphasis by the new Labour Government. The policy is implemented through a variety of provisions some of which modify the procedure in magistrates' and youth courts and provide for single justices and clerks to deal with certain matters and increase the powers which can be delegated to lay staff in the CPS. Other provisions provide for committal proceedings to be by-passed for indictable-only and related offences whilst another group of provisions tinker with powers relating to bail in the hope of decreasing the number of wasted adjournments. Television links between courts and prisons are to be introduced to reduce delays caused in pre-trial hearings and to avoid the need for the accused to be produced in court on every occasion. Some of the above measures will be introduced initially on a pilot basis but this chapter also deals with powers to introduce, once the measures to reduce delays have been put into effect, strict time limits for the various stages of criminal proceedings with even stricter limits for cases involving juveniles.

A highly critical Public Accounts Committee Report in 1994/5 (Administration of the Crown Court, HC 173) commented that 'it was a matter of serious concern that so little progress has been made over the years in reducing the time taken to bring cases to trial' but recognised that the Lord Chancellor's Department was only one of several participants in the criminal justice system and that some of the causes of delay lay outside their direct control. In October 1996 the Lord Chancellor's Department, the Home Office and the Law Officers' Department set up a review under Martin Narey reporting to an interdepartmental steering committee, 'To identify ways of expediting the progress of cases through the criminal justice system from initiation to resolution, consistently with the interests of justice and securing value for money'. The report (*Review of Delay in the Criminal Justice System*) was published by the Home Office in February 1997 and has become known as the Narey Report. The new Labour Government accepted many though not all of the Report's recommendations in its response published as an annex to its own consultation paper, *Reducing Remand Delays*, published by the Home Office in October 1997. This consultation paper opened by noting that:

The government made a specific manifesto commitment to bring remand delays down to national targets. This is distinct from, although relevant to, the separate specific pledge to halve the time to get persistent young offenders from arrest to sentencing.... However, tackling the problem of delays in the criminal justice system as a whole is also a high priority for the government ... it is taking longer for cases to be brought to completion in recent years despite significant reductions in the number of cases coming to the criminal courts. In far too many custody cases, custody time limits are not being met. Urgent changes are needed to improve current performance.

The Government declared its intention to deal with these problems in two ways:

(a) by introducing more efficient procedures as recommended by Narey;

(b) by strengthening the system of statutory time limits to ensure that targets are met, (something which could only realistically be done once the means to comply with them had been established via the efficiency improvements).

Sections 43 to 57 contain the measures designed to implement this strategy and will be discussed in the logical order indicated above, i.e., first the measures intended to reduce delays and increase efficiency and then the new system of time limits which it is intended that these efficiency gains will enable to be introduced.

REDUCING DELAYS AND INCREASING EFFICIENCY

49. Powers of magistrates' courts exercisable by a single justice etc.

The powers conferred by this section were presaged by Chapter 5 of the Narey report, headed Managing Cases in Magistrates' Courts, where it was said:

The importance of case management has been recognised in the area of civil justice by Lord Woolf's proposed reforms, and in the Crown Court by the adoption of Plea and Direction hearings. On the evidence of what I have seen, it seems clear that there is a great deal that could be achieved in magistrates' courts through more rigorous management of the case before it goes to trial....

Ideally lay magistrates should do this but for a number of reasons they are not well suited to the role. The need for a bench of three lay magistrates to reach agreement between themselves is not conducive to decisive action: and where a court does act firmly, there is frequently no continuity, so that the next time the case comes to court it will probably be before a differently constituted Bench which may either be less inclined to press matters or not be aware of the opinions and attitude of the earlier Bench. The first of these difficulties could be overcome, and the second possibly reduced, by allowing hearings concerned with case management to be heard by a single justice.

The report then went on to conclude that in fact case management would be best carried out by justices' clerks (and other senior staff to whom they may delegate their powers) rather than single justices with the added side-effect of enabling magistrates 'to concentrate on determining the bail or custody status of defendants and deciding on guilt and sentencing, for which they are best qualified'. The report suggested a long list of powers which could be given to justices' clerks, some of which were clearly administrative, such as marking an information withdrawn, but others of which were clearly judicial in nature, such as ordering the separate or joint trials of several co-accused.

In its response, the Government indicated qualified agreement stating that:

> there is a role both for magistrates and in appropriate circumstances Clerks to the Justices. Further consideration will be given to which of the powers identified in the report ... could properly be delegated to Clerks. As a preliminary step, the Crime and Disorder Bill will include a provision authorising a single justice to exercise these powers; those which are considered appropriate will then be delegated to Clerks by means of secondary legislation.

Accordingly, clause 40(1) of the Bill as originally introduced into the House of Lords empowered a single justice to exercise a long list of powers taken virtually word for word from the Narey report and subclause (2) made provision for rules to be made to enable justices' clerks to exercise some or all of these functions. Section 49(1) and (2) substantially reproduce these provisions but what is now s. 49(3) was added to the Bill at Third Reading in response to concerns expressed by peers at earlier stages, including those of Lord Bingham CJ at Second Reading where (*Hansard*, Lords, 16 December 1997, col. 561) he accepted that whilst there were:

> some powers ... which can quite unobjectionably be exercised by a justices' clerk, for example, (b) to mark an information as withdrawn; (c) to dismiss an information ... where no evidence is offered by the prosecution ..., some powers listed in the clause are quite different, for example in (f) to require 'a medical report and for that purpose to remand the accused in custody or on bail'
>
> To send a defendant to prison is a judicial act; it is not an order which anyone not exercising judicial authority should make, and it is certainly not a matter of administration.
>
> ... I object to the possibility that some of these powers might by rule be exercised by the justices' clerk because such a rule would erode the fundamental distinction between the justices and the justices' legal adviser.... If the justices' clerk were to be entrusted with these important decisions and judgments, judicial in character, the time would inevitably come when people would reasonably ask whether he or she should not be left to get on and try the whole case.

Section 49(3) therefore prohibits any rules being made to delegate some of the more sensitive and judicial functions listed in subsection (1), the prohibited areas of delegation being set out in the five sub-paragraphs of s. 49(3).

It should be noted that s. 49(1) does not contain an exhaustive list of the situations where a single justice can act as there were already a number of situations where a single lay justice was authorised to act alone including, for example, s. 18(5) of the Magistrates' Courts Act 1980, which enables mode of trial proceedings to be presided over by a single lay justice (although in practice this does not normally happen). Furthermore by s. 45 of the Justices of the Peace Act 1997:

> Rules made in accordance with section 144 of the Magistrates' Courts Act 1980 may (except to the extent that any enactment passed after this Act otherwise

directs) make provision enabling things authorised to be done by, to or before a single justice of the peace to be done instead by, to or before a justices' clerk.

The power to delegate functions to a justices' clerk therefore already existed quite apart from s. 49(2) but the limitations in s. 49(3) on what can be delegated serve as an example of an Act 'otherwise directing' within the bracketed words in s. 45 of the 1997 Act. Quite apart from the prohibited areas of delegation, the rules made by virtue of s. 49(2)(a) may make any delegation 'subject to any specified restrictions or conditions' (additional to those in s. 49(3)) and by s. 49(2)(b) 'may make different provision for different areas'. This latter phrase is designed to facilitate the piloting of the new powers for six months from the end of September 1998 in different areas (Tyneside, Croydon, Blackburn/Burnley, Northamptonshire, North Staffordshire and North Wales).

The justices' clerk to whom the powers may be delegated is one within the same meaning as s. 144 of the Magistrates' Courts Act 1980 but this does not mean delegation will be limited to the fully qualified justices' clerk properly so called within the meaning of s. 43 of the Justices of the Peace Act 1997. Section 45(2) of the Justices of the Peace Act 1997 provides for rules to be made enabling delegation to take place from a justices' clerk to 'a person appointed by a magistrates' courts committee to assist him', i.e., to deputy or assistant clerks. At Commons committee stage (*Hansard*, Commons, Standing Committee B, 14 May 1998, col. 414), the Government resisted an amendment to ensure that only clerks with five years' experience would be able to exercise the powers delegated under s. 49:

It is necessary that the clerk to the justices should be satisfied that the person exercising the powers under the 1997 Act is competent, proper, professional and qualified. The Hon Member appears to be worried that someone who is completely inexperienced and unqualified could exercise the powers. That will not happen.

The Opposition spokesman (Mr Clappison) was not completely satisfied with this response, questioning just how much experience would be necessary. He did not press the matter further, but no doubt the level of delegation will be one of the aspects of the operation of the powers which will be monitored during the pilots.

It is envisaged that the powers given to single justices and to be delegated to clerks under s. 49 will be utilised through a more developed system of pre-trial reviews which it was noted in Chapter 5 of the Narey Report have become:

increasingly common in courts throughout the country over the past few years. They have developed locally in a variety of ways and there is no single model but it is clear that, properly conducted, PTR's can make a significant contribution to case progress.... The most effective PTR's seem to be those where through local consent the Clerk is given a great deal of latitude in managing the case ... where this co-operation is not forthcoming PTR's will be ineffective ...

... I would expect PTR's to be useful in the great majority of contested cases, but there would be circumstances (for example, where it was possible to resolve preliminary issues on paper) in which a PTR would contribute nothing. I therefore recommend that it should be for the courts to decide whether a PTR should take place in particular cases.

This recommendation was accepted by the Government with no specific mention of pre-trial reviews as such in the Act, it being left to the courts to develop their own non-statutory framework but using the powers of single justices and clerks as provided for in s. 49.

Section 50: Early administrative hearings

As the name suggests, these hearings would take place at an earlier stage than a pre-trial review and, as with pre-trial reviews, the practice of holding them, conducted by clerks, has already developed on a non-statutory basis in some magistrates' courts:

> so that the defendant can hear what the court expects from him in terms of obtaining legal representation and supplying evidence to enable the court to consider a legal aid application. The clerk also explains to the defendant the nature of the forthcoming proceedings and the implications of the charge against him. In some cases this prompts a guilty plea; where the case is contested, experience has shown that overcoming defendants' inertia in applying for legal aid helps to reduce the number of adjournments (Narey Report, Chapter 5).

The Narey Report goes on to describe how the hearings worked at Bexley, one of the pioneers in the field:

> Defendants are bailed to appear, the first Tuesday or Thursday after [charge] at a hearing conducted by the Clerk to the Justices . . . or a senior clerk. An independent volunteer helps the defendant to complete the legal aid application forms and to select a solicitor from a list of local firms. The clerk explains to the defendant the procedures of the court and the charges he is facing and ascertains whether the defendant appears to be eligible for legal aid. If so the volunteer makes a telephone appointment with the solicitor on the defendant's behalf and the clerk sets as the date of the first hearing a day on which the solicitor is due to be in court (this link with the listing process is important).
>
> Uncertainty over the extent of powers for the police to bail a defendant to appear at an EAH [early administrative hearing] or for the clerk to extend that bail to the first substantive appearance has discouraged many courts from adopting EAH's and there is a strong case for legislating so as to put them on to a proper footing. I recommend that this should be done.

Section 50 is designed to do give effect to this recommendation although with some differences of detail. Section 50(1) provides for the first appearance after charge (except for cases falling under s. 51, indictable-only and related offences: see below) to be before a court consisting of a single justice, or by virtue of s. 50(4), a justices' clerk. At such a hearing, an early administrative hearing, s. 50(2) directs that:

> (a)   the accused shall be asked whether he wishes to receive legal aid; and
> (b)   if he indicates that he does, his eligibility for it shall be determined; and
> (c)   if it is determined that he is eligible for it, the necessary arrangements or grant shall be made for him to obtain it.

By s. 50(3) the single justice (or clerk) may exercise such of his powers as a single justice (or as a clerk, as the case may be) as he thinks fit and on adjourning the hearing may remand the accused in custody or on bail *except* that by s. 50(4) (in the case of a clerk rather than a single justice), there is no power to remand in custody or, without the consent of the prosecutor and the accused, to impose bail conditions other than those (if any) which have already been imposed.

In connection with bail, it should be noted that there is a related change introduced by s. 54(2) which adds a requirement to attend an interview with a legal adviser as a possible condition of bail under s. 3(6) of the Bail Act 1976 and thus this is a condition of bail that a single justice may choose to impose at an early administrative hearing. Paragraph 33 of the Home Office consultation paper, *Reducing Remand Delays* (October 1997), proposed this power, noting that 'failure to obtain legal advice or representation is one of the most common reasons for delay, resulting in ineffective first hearings and routine adjournments'.

Section 50 was brought into force on 30 September 1998 and does not appear to be subject to piloting. The ability of clerks as opposed to single justices to conduct early administrative hearings is not subject to any regulations being made, although a clerk would only be able to carry out the functions referred to in s. 50(2) (which is the main point of an early administrative hearing) and to continue to remand on bail in accordance with s. 50(4), but not to impose any new conditions (including the condition as to interview with a legal adviser) unless both prosecutor and the accused consent. In other words, clerks will have no other powers of a single justice to exercise under s. 50(3)(a) until such time as regulations giving them any such powers are made in accordance with s. 49(2).

Section 51: No committal proceedings for indictable-only offences

The notion that cases should not be sent for trial before a jury unless there has been a thorough examination of whether there is a case to answer by means of a committal hearing has been gradually and persistently eroded for over thirty years, ever since the Criminal Justice Act 1967 introduced 'paper committals' without consideration of the evidence. Since then we have seen the introduction of the notice of transfer procedure for serious or complex fraud introduced by the Criminal Justice Act 1987 and a similar procedure for certain offences involving child victims or witnesses in the Criminal Justice Act 1991. More recently, the attempt in the Criminal Justice and Public Order Act 1994 to abolish committal proceedings altogether and replace them with transfer for trial proved impractical to implement. Instead the Criminal Procedure and Investigations Act 1996 introduced a new modified form of committal in which no oral evidence is given and no witnesses called. At the same time the 1996 Act introduced the plea before venue procedure which also has the effect of removing the need for committal for trial where the accused is prepared to indicate an intention to plead guilty.

Chapter 6 of the Narey Report also noted the trend away from committals and that one of the chief remaining reasons for starting indictable offences off in the magistrates' court was to enable a decision about venue to be made (i.e., summary trial in the magistrates' court or trial on indictment in the Crown Court). However, with offences triable only on indictment rather than triable either-way, there is no decision about venue to be made, 'therefore, the question is not how they could be moved more quickly from magistrates' courts to the Crown Court, but whether they need to spend any of their life in the magistrates' court at all'. This question was made more pertinent by the statistic noted in the Narey Report that indictable-only cases currently spend about half their life in magistrates' courts, on average 87 days in the magistrates' court before committal. The Narey Report therefore concluded that indictable-only cases should begin their life in the Crown Court, which would also be the appropriate court for considering representations in advance of the trial that there was no case to answer, something recommended for indictable-only cases by the Royal Commission on Criminal Justice (Cm 2263, (1993), Chapter 6, para. 28).

The Narey Report went on to point out that:

> The Crown Court, now closely involved in case management through plea and directions hearings, is well placed to manage cases from the outset. The PDH in an indictable-only case would, if this recommendation were accepted, take place much earlier in the life of the case, with the potential to effect very significant reductions in the time taken to complete it. An earlier PDH would also provide a clear point at which a plea of guilty might attract the maximum sentence discount.

The Narey Report also considered there would be advantages in terms of security of prisoners since persons accused of these most serious offences would not have to be produced at the less secure magistrates' courts but instead at Crown Court centres, and perhaps not even there to the extent that video links to such centres could be established (see the discussion of s. 57 below).

Section 51 and sch. 3 give effect to the Narey Report's proposals on indictable-only offences and are planned to be piloted from 4 January 1999. It is not quite true to say that such cases start their life in the Crown Court since the first appearance at least of the accused will be in the magistrates' court but if he:

> appears or is brought before a magistrates' court ('the court') charged with an offence triable only on indictment (the indictable-only offence), the court shall send him forthwith to the Crown Court for trial—
>   (a)   for that offence, and
>   (b)   for any either-way or summary offence with which he is charged which fulfils the requisite conditions (as set out in [s. 50(11)]).

Section 50(11) provides that an offence fulfils the requisite conditions if it appears to the court to be 'related' to the indictable-only offence (and in the case of summary offences is punishable by imprisonment or disqualification from driving).

The notion of 'related' is explained in s. 50(12)(c) and (d).

For either-way offences 'related' has a similar meaning to the same term in s. 38A(6) of the Magistrates' Courts Act 1980 (as inserted by s. 51 of the Crime Sentences Act 1997 in relation to the plea before venue procedure). Thus, under s. 51(12)(c), if the either-way offence 'could be joined in the same indictment' as the indictable-only offence which is itself of course the phrase used in r. 9 of the Indictment Rules 1971 and which is therein satisfied if the charges 'are founded on the same facts, or form or are a part of a series of offences of the same or a similar character (see *Blackstone's Criminal Practice*, **D9.24–D9.27** for discussion of this test).

Summary offences are dealt with under s. 51(12)(d). A summary offence is 'related' to an indictable-only offence if it 'arises out of circumstances which are the same as or connected with those giving rise to the indictable-only offence', a test which echoes that in s. 41 of the Criminal Justice Act 1988 under which magistrates already have a limited power to commit for 'trial' in respect of summary offences. *Blackstone's Criminal Practice*, **D7.23** notes that, in respect of s. 41, 'committal with a view to sentence on a guilty plea' would be more accurate since the summary offence is not included in the indictment and is put to the accused in the Crown Court only if he is convicted of an indictable offence and if the accused pleads not guilty to the summary offence, the Crown Court has no further power in the matter which can only be revived in the magistrates' court. Exactly the same is true of a related summary offence under s. 51 of the 1998 Act by virtue of para. 6 of sch. 3, which is why s. 51(9) provides that the trial of the information of the summary offence is treated as adjourned (so that if necessary the matter can be revived in the magistrates' court). Furthermore, just as under s. 41(4) of the 1988 Act, the Crown Court can still deal with a summary offence to which there is a not guilty plea if it is one that falls within s. 40 of the 1988 Act, and thus can be and is thereby included in the indictment (see 1998 Act, sch 3, para. 6(8)).

The position is different with 'related' triable either-way offences under s. 51(12)(c). These will obviously be included in the indictment and tried in the Crown Court in the normal way provided that on arraignment the indictment still contains an indictable-only offence (i.e., the indictable-only offence or offences have not been removed following an application to dismiss under para. 2 of sch. 3 or for any other reason). However, if before arraignment no indictable-only offence remains in the indictment, the justification (that related offences should be tried together) for having automatically committed the accused for trial on the triable either-way offences is no longer applicable. Consequently, in such a case, paras 7 to 15 effectively require the Crown Court to go through the plea before venue procedure (paras 7 and 8) and, if appropriate (where the accused does not indicate an intention to plead guilty), conduct a mode of trial hearing (paras 9–15). The ironic result of a procedure designed to reduce delay could be that a triable either-way offence which was always suitable for summary trial goes to the Crown Court as an offence related to an indictable-only offence but is not tried there (because the indictable-only offence is dismissed before arraignment) and is then sent back to the magistrates for trial where it could have been tried in the first place!

So far we have considered the simple case under s. 51 where an *adult* appears before a magistrates' court charged with an indictable-only offence and, *on the same occasion*, is charged with 'related' summary and/or triable either-way offences. Section 51(2) makes essentially similar provision for where an adult who has *already* been sent for trial on an indictable-only offence under s. 51(1), *subsequently* appears in the magistrates' court charged with related summary or either-way offences. There is however an important difference in that under s. 51(1), the magistrates' court 'shall' send the related offences to the Crown Court along with the indictable-only offence whereas under s. 51(2) the magistrates 'may' do so. In other words the magistrates must send related offences to the Crown Court under s. 51(1) but merely have a discretion to do so under s. 51(2). Section 51(3), which deals with persons charged with a related either-way offence *jointly* with a person who is being, or who has been, sent for trial for an indictable-only offence (to which the either-way offence is related), makes the same distinction. If the indictable-only offence has been sent for trial on a *previous* occasion, the court has discretion on whether to send the related jointly charged either-way offence to the Crown Court, whereas if both charges are before the magistrates *on the same occasion* there is no discretion and both offences must be sent to the Crown Court. If the jointly charged person is sent to the Crown Court for trial on the either-way offence under s. 51(3), again the court must, as in the case of a person charged with an indictable-only offence under s. 51(1), also send *him* for trial on any related either-way or summary offences with which he is charged. Section 51(5) and (6) makes similar provision for children and young persons charged with an indictable offence jointly with an adult sent for trial for that offence. The court 'shall' send the child or young person to the Crown Court on the jointly charged indictable offence if it considers it necessary in the interests of justice to do so but under s. 51(6) it has a discretion in relation to related either-way or summary offences, irrespective of whether the adult has been previously sent for trial or is being sent for trial on the same occasion.

The intended operation of the above provisions was described in the House of Lords by Lord Falconer, Solicitor-General, in moving a number of technical amendments as follows (*Hansard*, Lords, 24 February 1998, col. 550)

Clause 42 is designed to secure the prompt removal to the Crown Court of indictable-only offences, but it is not sufficient for these offences alone to be sent to the higher court. If a defendant faces other charges triable either-way which are related to the indictable-only offence it may be necessary for those charges to accompany it to the Crown Court That is why where an adult is sent to the Crown Court for trial for an indictable-only offence, Clause 42 requires the court also to send there any related either-way charge which is before the court on that occasion either against him or against another adult jointly charged with him. But because of the reference to 'that occasion' the clause does not take account of the situation where the defendant has already been sent to the Crown Court for trial for an indictable-only offence and there is a subsequent appearance in court on a related either-way charge either by that person or by another adult jointly charged with him. For example, a suspect may be caught and charged with an either-way offence jointly with the main suspect only after the latter has been arrested and appeared in court. The effect of these amendments is to give the magistrates' court a discretion to send the defendant to the Crown Court for trial on that related charge.

In deciding whether to exercise this discretion the court will be able to take into consideration the stage which the indictable-only case has reached. The appearance on the related charge may follow soon after the indictable-only one, in which instance it would be right for that case to be sent forward too so that they can be dealt with together. If, on the other hand, the indictable-only case had already progressed a long way, it is possible that sending the related charge up to the Crown Court to join it would lead to extra delay, in which case the discretion would be exercised against sending it up to the Crown Court.

Although s. 51, by sending cases directly to the Crown Court, by-passes committal proceedings and hence the opportunity to submit that there is no case to answer, the accused still has an opportunity to have the charge dismissed in advance of the trial by making an application to the Crown Court under para. 2 of sch. 3. The procedure is closely modelled on that available where a charge has been transferred to the Crown Court under either of the existing notice of transfer schemes under the Criminal Justice Act 1987 for serious or complex frauds (see *Blackstone's Criminal Practice*, **D8.15–D8.19**) or the Criminal Justice Act 1991 for certain cases involving child witnesses (see *Blackstone's Criminal Practice*, **D8.20**). As under those provisions, in contrast with the position in committal proceedings since the new modified form of committals was brought into force during 1997, oral evidence by witnesses can be given with the leave or by order of the judge (para. 2(4)) if it appears that the interests of justice require him to do so. This would happen only in wholly exceptional circumstances, but it is surprising that the existing provisions are copied now that oral evidence cannot be given in committal proceedings. Given also that the application may relate to sexual offences, it is also noteworthy that there is no absolute bar on requiring the complainant to give oral evidence at an application to dismiss such a charge, thus potentially putting such a complainant at risk of having to go through the distressing business of giving evidence twice over, once at the dismissal application and once at the subsequent trial. This should be contrasted with para. 5(5) of sch. 6 to the Criminal Justice Act 1991 prohibiting any leave or order being given to enable or require certain child witnesses to give oral evidence on the hearing of such an application. When challenged about the possible abuse of the dismissal procedure which some defendants in sexual cases may seek to exploit, the Government minister (Mike O'Brien, *Hansard*, Commons, Standing Committee B, 14 May 1998) referred to the similarity with the 1991 Act as a justification for leaving the discretion with the trial judge without pointing out, or perhaps being aware, that para. 5(5) of sch. 6 to that Act created an absolute bar on child victims or witnesses giving oral evidence at a dismissal hearing. Although Mr O'Brien said 'it may sometimes — extremely rarely I hope — be right that evidence would be given by a victim in such a hearing' he seemed content to leave it to the judge's interpretation of what the interests of justice required him to do and that is how para. 2(4)of sch. 3 leaves it.

Section 52(1) makes it clear that where a person is sent for trial under s. 51 it may be on bail or in custody in accordance with normal principles and s. 52(3) deals with the question of when criminal damage is to be treated as an indictable offence for the purposes of s. 51. Somewhat surprisingly in view of the aim to reduce delays (and in the light of the word 'forthwith' throughout s. 51), but understandably in the light of the complexity of s. 51, s. 52(5) authorises a magistrates' court to adjourn any proceedings under s. 51 and in the meantime to remand the accused.

Section 53: Powers of CPS non-legal staff

Section 53 is a highly controversial section. It arises from Chapter 3 of the Narey Report, Managing the Decision to Prosecute, which made a number of recommendations designed to reduce delays caused by the interface between the police and the CPS. The radical nature of the proposals and the potential impact of the reasoning behind them on the independence of the decision to prosecute can be judged by considering the following extracts from the chapter.

Better use of administrative staff
I have concluded that it would be necessary and sensible for the CPS to use
administrative staff for some of the duties currently carried out by lawyers. There
are two main areas of work. The first involves the initial consideration of the file
when received from the police. The Prosecution of Offences Act allows the
Director of Public Prosecutions to delegate work to Crown Prosecutors but when
in 1988, the then DPP attempted further to delegate the review of files to executive
officers the First Division Association took the DPP to judicial review; the court's
judgment was that:

> *'in the discharge of his functions under the Act the DPP may not lawfully*
> *delegate to any person not being a Crown Prosecutor the decision whether in*
> *any criminal proceedings (1) [there is] the evidence to proceed and/or (2) the*
> *prosecution is in the public interest'*

I recommend that the Prosecution of Offences Act be amended to grant the DPP
the necessary powers to confer on lay staff the powers of a Crown Prosecutor,
subject at all times to direction by legally qualified staff. Administrative staff,
properly trained and supported, would then be able to review files prosecuting
uncontested cases.

For uncontested cases I recommend that non-lawyers, employed by the CPS,
should be allowed to present cases in magistrates' courts. One of the things which
most struck me on visiting CPS offices was the amount of entirely straightforward
work being handled in the office and at court by lawyers. Much of this work must
be dispiriting. I am convinced that administrative staff, managed by lawyers and
dealing exclusively with uncontested cases, could successfully and efficiently
present cases at court, freeing lawyers to concentrate on contested cases.

There are a number of precedents at magistrates' courts . . . a number of statutes
give authority to specific individuals to prosecute . . . [including the Health and
Safety at Work etc. Act 1974 and the Social Security Administration Act 1992] . . .
even if he or she is not a solicitor or barrister. I recommend that the amendments
to the Prosecution of Offences Act should deal with this issue specifically as well
as providing for the more general delegation of file review.

In its response to the Narey Report, the Government accepted this recommendation
(and a number of others in Chapter 3) and what became s. 53 was added to the Bill
as a new clause (at the Committee stage in the Lords (*Hansard*, Lords, 24 February
1998, col. 557), designed to implement it by substituting a new s. 7A into the
Prosecution of Offences Act 1985. Although the new powers capable of being
designated under the new s. 7A will initially be introduced on a pilot basis from 30
September 1998, the section attracted quite a lot of critical comment in the Lords
which resulted in a number of modifications. In particular, the clause originally
explicitly enabled the DPP to designate lay staff to have 'the powers of a Crown
Prosecutor in relation to decisions whether to institute or continue legal proceedings'
but this was deleted at Third Reading and replaced by the delphic s. 7A(2)(b):

the powers of such a Prosecutor in relation to the conduct of criminal proceedings
not falling within paragraph (a)(ii) above'.

Lord Falconer explained this as follows (*Hansard*, Lords, 31 March 1998, col. 230):

[This] will exclude from clause 47 the powers of a Crown Prosecutor in relation to decisions whether to institute proceedings. The decision to institute proceedings is usually taken by the police and the sort of case in which it falls to the CPS to take that decision would certainly not be suitable for lay staff to deal with but should be reserved to a Crown Prosecutor.

Since Lord Falconer referred only to the decision to institute proceedings and since he continued to talk about lay staff having the power to review files, it appears that lay staff will, under s. 7A(2)(b), still be able to be given the power to decide whether to continue criminal proceedings which have already been instituted. That this is a sensitive matter is underlined by the fact that various other amendments were made by the Government to limit the types of cases in which the new powers for lay staff could be designated. These amendments are reflected in s. 7A(5) and(6), excluding the powers of lay staff in relation to proceedings for offences triable only on indictment (this exclusion will apply right from the outset of proceedings for the offence) or for offences which have been committed for trial or transferred for trial under the Criminal Justice Act 1987 or the Criminal Justice Act 1991 (since this criterion cannot be known in advance, this will only disenfranchise lay staff once this particular stage has been reached).

In addition to the power to review files (subject to the limitations discussed above), the new s. 7A also empowers the DPP through subsection (2)(a) to designate lay staff to have the powers and *rights of audience* of a Crown Prosecutor in relation to:

(i)   applications for, or relating to, bail in criminal proceedings;
(ii) the conduct of criminal proceedings in magistrates' courts other than trials.

Section 7A(2)(a)(i) does not provide any new power; these were matters which could already be delegated to lay staff under the previous s. 7A, and indeed the restrictions in s. 7A(5) and (6) relating to indictable offences in effect curtail powers which already existed but which were not in practice exercised. Section 7A(2)(a)(ii) though is new and implements the Narey Report's proposal that lay staff should be able to deal with straightforward guilty pleas. It will also enable lay staff to deal with other matters in the magistrates' courts other than contested trials; by s. 53(5)(c), 'a trial begins with the opening of the prosecution case after the entry of a plea of not guilty and ends with the conviction or acquittal of the accused'.

Because of the concerns expressed in the House of Lords about the effects of delegating powers to lay staff, subsection (7) was added, requiring the DPP to report each year the details of:

(a)   the criteria applied in determining whether to designate lay staff;
(b)   the training undergone by persons so designated; and
(c)   any general instructions given by the DPP under s. 7A(4) as to how the designated powers should be exercised.

Sections 54 to 56: New provisions relating to bail

Sections 54 and 55 are designed to reduce delay by reducing the need for unnecessary adjournments whereas s. 56 is more concerned to re-establish a matter of principle but will have little practical effect other than in the most exceptional circumstances. All three are already the subject of Home Office Circular 34/1998 issued on the 10 August 1998 and came into effect from 30 September 1998.

Increased powers to require security or impose conditions (s. 54)
These powers were proposed in the Home Office consultation paper, *Reducing Remand Delays*, published in October 1997. Section 54 (1) is designed to encourage the greater use of the practice of requiring a security to be given by the accused or someone on his behalf under s. 3(5) of the Bail Act 1976, the deposited security being liable to forfeiture in the event of failure to surrender to bail — thus providing a stronger incentive for the accused not to abscond. The use of s. 3(5) has in the past been restricted by the opening words of the subsection, 'If it appears that he is unlikely to remain in Great Britain until the time appointed for him to surrender to custody'. Section 54(1) repeals these words so that the courts can require a security in any case where it seems likely to be influential in encouraging the accused to answer to bail, whether or not he is likely to abscond within or without Great Britain. Home Office Circular 34/1998 notes (in para. 4(i)) that 'there may be cases where the court takes the view that an upfront payment, in the form of a security, of a relatively small amount would be more effective in securing the defendant's attendance than the availability of a surety with the means to enter into a recognizance for a more substantial sum'. Paragraph 7 then comments that the 'new power to take securities is likely to prove particularly useful in cases where the person to be bailed might not be able to provide a surety with the means to enter into a recognizance for a substantial amount. The means of the defendant, or of the person giving the security on his behalf, should continue to be a primary consideration'.

The power to require a security applies both to bail granted by a court and bail granted by the police.

Section 54(2) enables *a court* granting bail under s. 3(6) of the Bail Act 1976 to impose a requirement to attend an interview with a legal adviser; it has already been briefly mentioned above. Section 54(3) effectively means that the requirement is not one that can be attached to police bail. The point of the provision is to avoid time being wasted at the next appearance by the fact that the accused does not have legal representation and has not received advice about the charges. The accused still has a right to represent himself if he so wishes so it would not be right for the court to impose this condition if the accused made it clear he did not wish to have legal representation.

Home Office Circular 34/1998 (para. 11) emphasises that 'the defendant's solicitor should not be expected to report a breach if the defendant fails to attend an interview'. Paragraph 12 goes on to recognise that breach of the condition is normally only likely to come to light at the next hearing when the accused requests an adjournment to seek legal advice. It suggests that where there is no reasonable excuse, the court should 'adopt a robust approach' and insist that he seek a interview with the duty solicitor there and then as recommended by the Narey Report. However, the circular also notes that in some circumstances, including not guilty pleas and representation in committal proceedings, representation by the duty solicitor is prohibited by the Legal Aid Board Duty Solicitor Arrangements 1997. No suggestion is made as to how to deal with these circumstances and it is difficult to see how the court can avoid granting an adjournment in them.

Forfeiture of recognizances (s. 55)
This measure shifts the onus for establishing lack of culpability, where an accused fails to appear in accordance with the condition, firmly back on the surety whose responsibility it was to try to ensure that the accused did indeed appear. The provision was introduced into the Bill at Third Reading in the Lords (*Hansard*, Lords, 31 March 1998) where Lord Falconer described its aim as being 'to make sureties take their responsibilities more seriously. In too many cases delay is caused by adjournments due to the non-appearance of the defendant. . . .

Section 55 amends s. 120 of the Magistrates' Courts Act 1980 so that, where the accused fails to answer bail, the court is required to declare the automatic forfeiture of the surety's recognizance and then summons the surety to explain why he should not pay the sum. If the surety fails to answer the summons, the court can proceed in his absence and order the sum to be paid. The result should be that the process of collection is initiated at an earlier stage than under present arrangements.

Section 55 directly affects magistrates' courts only because forfeiture of recognizances is governed by statute (the Magistrates' Courts Act 1980) whereas in other courts, it is governed by secondary legislation. The relevant rules of court for the Crown Court (new r. 21A), the High Court (Order 79, r. 8) and the Court of Appeal (Criminal Appeal Rules, r. 6) are being drafted or amended to introduce a similar procedure for those courts.

Removal of absolute ban on bail for certain cases of homicide or rape (s. 56)
Section 25 of the Criminal Justice and Public Order Act 1994 placed an absolute prohibition on granting bail to a person awaiting trial or sentence for murder, attempted murder, manslaughter, rape or attempted rape who had a previous conviction for one of those offences or for culpable homicide (and who had been sentenced to either imprisonment or long-term detention in the case of manslaughter or culpable homicide). Section 56 of the 1998 Act amends s. 25 above so as to replace the absolute prohibition with a presumption against bail which can be rebutted only 'if the court or, as the case may be, the constable considering the grant of bail is satisfied that there are exceptional circumstances which justify it'.

Neither the original s. 25 nor this amendment to it are thought likely to affect any actual bail decisions in practice. A certain Tony Blair, as Shadow Home Secretary, described the original s. 25 as a 'gimmick' since, even before its passage, no-one who came within its terms would ever have been likely to be granted bail and it is most unlikely that anyone will be able to rebut the presumption under the new s. 25. Nevertheless, as a matter of principle, the possibility of establishing exceptional circumstances is preferable, particularly given the normal presumption in favour of bail, and the new provision is more compatible with the European Convention on Human Rights under which a number of cases were pending before the Commission e.g. (*C v UK* (C-32819/96). Even if exceptionally a magistrates' court was minded to grant bail in a case covered by s. 25, the prosecution would have a right of appeal to a Crown Court judge under the Bail (Amendment) Act 1993, pending which the accused would be kept in custody. There appears to be no direct right of appeal should the police grant bail in circumstances covered by s. 25 but such an event seems most unlikely and the Home Office circular calmly notes in this respect that 'the custody officer will wish to consult a more senior officer before authorising the release of the suspect on bail. It is also advisable to consult the Crown Prosecution Service before reaching a final decision to grant bail in exceptional circumstances and to make a record of the reasons for granting bail on the custody record'.

Section 57: Use of live television links at preliminary hearings

This provision to use TV links between prisons and the courts to avoid the necessity of the accused being present in court for preliminary hearings is to be piloted in two areas, Bristol and Manchester. It was originally canvassed on security grounds in the Learmont Report, *Review of Prison Service Security and the Escape from Parkhurst Prison on Tuesday 3rd January 1995* (Cm 3020), and was taken up as a means of reducing delays in the consultation paper, *Reducing Remand Delays*, in October 1997. Considerable reservations were expressed about it by the opposition in the Commons Committee stage (*Hansard*, Commons, Standing Committee B, 19 May 1998), where there were worries about confidential communications between lawyer and client, about the clause's potential use in mode of trial hearings and other significant pre-trial hearings and about the steer implicit in s. 57(3) requiring a magistrates' court to give reasons for not directing the use of a TV link where it has power to do so. Although the Government's response was that the pilots would be used to test out what was feasible and appropriate, one cannot help noticing that the proposal in the consultation paper talked about the use of TV links where the presence of the defendant is not required by statute. In contrast, s. 57(1) empowers the court to direct that 'the accused shall be treated as being present in the court' which is a potentially dangerous fiction particularly when its application is not dependent on the consent of the accused and can apply to 'any proceedings for an offence' qualified only by the fact that they must be 'before the start of the trial'. The experience from the pilots will require careful evaluation before the provision can be given any more widespread implementation.

TIME LIMITS

Section 22 of the Prosecution of Offences Act 1985 enabled the Secretary of State to set time limits for the prosecution to complete any preliminary stage of proceedings for an offence ('overall time limits') and/or for the maximum periods of time for which an accused should be in custody during such preliminary stages ('custody time limits'). No overall time limits have been set under the Act (exceeding such a time limit if set would result in an acquittal) and custody time limits have been set only for indictable offences (the expiration of a custody time limit entitles the accused to bail but not to an acquittal). In its consultation paper, *Reducing Remand Delays* of October 1997, the Government indicated its belief that the measures being introduced to reduce delays would enable it to set and bring into force overall time limits for all cases, adult and juvenile, summary or indictable:

> The new time limits will be set and introduced within twelve months of implementation of the Crime and Disorder Bill once the new procedures for ensuring more efficient case management are in place' [para. 10].
> There will be the power to set different limits for different classes of case, for example those in respect of indictable or summary offences, those initiated by charge or summons. Tougher limits will be set for juvenile cases, and even stricter limits for persistent young offender cases [para. 14].

Section 43(1) amends s. 22(2) to enable these varied and variable time limits to be set. The Government intends that the time limits will cover the same periods as the existing custody time limits (although their actual length will be determined after the pilot trials), so there will be time limits covering:

(a) first appearance to start of summary trial;
(b) first appearance to committal or transfer;
(c) committal or transfer to start of Crown Court trial

except that instead of first appearance the parameter shall be first listing.

Paragraph 15 of the consultation paper indicated that for juvenile cases, 'additional time limits will be introduced between arrest and first court listing and between conviction and sentence in both the magistrates' courts and the Crown Court'. This was in pursuance of the manifesto commitment to halve the time from arrest to sentence for persistent young offenders and further details of the proposals for young offenders were set out in a separate consultation paper, *Tackling Delays in the Youth Justice System* (October 1997). Section 44 inserts a new s. 22A into the 1985 Act to enable the Secretary of State to set these additional time limits.

The Government proposed to introduce tougher criteria for granting extensions to the new time limits and this is reflected in s. 43(2), which inserts a new subsection (3) into the 1985 Act. However, it is not clear that the criteria are in substance any different except that the new criteria include two specific examples of good and sufficient cause (in addition to which the prosecution must have acted with all due diligence and expedition).

Section 43(4) and (5) implements the proposal that where the accused escapes from custody or fails to answer to bail the court can effectively suspend the operation of the time limit rather than the time limit ceasing to operate as under the original s. 22(6).

Most importantly, the existing consequence of an overall time limit expiring, i.e. that the accused is treated for all purposes as acquitted (one of the reasons no overall time limits have been set), is changed by s. 43(3) amending s. 22(4) so that the consequence now is that the proceedings are stayed. Section 45 inserts a new s. 22B into the 1985 Act to deal with the effects of such a stay. The principal effect is that the proceedings for the offence can be reinstituted but only if the DPP or a Chief Crown Prosecutor (or other senior figure mentioned in s. 22B(2)) so directs within three months of the stay or such longer period as the court may allow (e.g., in circumstances where new evidence subsequently comes to light). This is also true where an initial stage time limit under the new s. 22A(1)(a) in relation to a juvenile expires, except that if such a limit expires *before* charge, 'he shall not be charged with it unless further evidence relating to it is obtained' (s. 22A(4)).

In furtherance of the achievement of the time limits to be set under the above provisions, s. 46 amends s. 47 of the Police and Criminal Evidence Act 1984, with the broad effect of requiring the custody officer, where a person is bailed by the police to appear before a magistrates' court, to set the earliest possible date for the accused's appearance rather than a date several weeks hence as is the normal current practice.

POWERS OF YOUTH COURTS

Sections 47 and 48 deal with a number of recommendations stemming from Chapter 8 of the Narey Report and the subsequent Government consultation paper, *Tackling Delays in the Youth System*.

The Narey Report found that older offenders were unsuitable for the youth court and recommended that 17-year-olds should be returned to the jurisdiction of the adult courts. The Government was not ready to accept this recommendation at this stage but did accept a related proposal that the youth court should have a discretion to transfer a case to the adult court where the defendant was a juvenile at the outset but becomes an adult in the course of the proceedings. Section 47(1) implements this proposal whereby the transfer may take place either before the start of the trial or after conviction and before sentence. The subsection confers a discretion and the Narey Report noted that 'where a case was well advanced or the court considered that in terms of maturity and attitude the [18]-year-old was suitable for the youth court, his case would be retained there'.

Section 47(5) is intended to reverse the effect of *Khan* (1994) *The Times*, 24 February 1994, which held that, save in exceptional circumstances, the youth court which sends a young person for trial at the Crown Court should postpone sentence in respect of other, ex hypothesi less serious, offences until after the more serious matter has been dealt with. The consultation paper noted that although *Khan* was 'concerned specifically with situations where one or more charges are transferred to the Crown Court for trial, in practice it has influenced the approach to multiple cases in the youth courts, whether proceedings are pending in the Crown Court or not' (para. 26).

Accordingly, s. 47(5) also implements the Government's proposal in para. 27 of the consultation paper to clarify 'that where the Youth Court is dealing with a defendant facing multiple charges (including those commonly referred to as 'spree offenders') there is no obligation to adjourn in order to tie up all outstanding cases'. This is done by means of subparagraph (b) of the new subsection 3A which is inserted into s. 10 of the Magistrates' Courts Act 1980, the new s. 10(3A)(a) dealing with the *Khan* point.

It is of course desirable that related charges should be dealt with together wherever possible, but this too has been difficult where a juvenile is committed for trial at the Crown Court for homicide or a grave offence listed in s. 53(2) of the Children and Young Persons Act 1933 since there was no power to commit for related indictable offences not falling within that category. Section 47(6) now enables this to happen, a related offence being one which 'could be joined in the same indictment (see the discussion in relation to indictable-only offences above).

Finally, s. 47(7) implements the Narey Report's recommendation that the out-dated 'inefficient' requirement in s. 47 of the Children and Young Persons Act 1933 that there should be an hour's interval between a youth court and a magistrates' court sitting in the same room should be repealed and s. 48 implements another Narey recommendation that stipendiaries should be able to sit alone in the youth court. The section is only necessary to deal with metropolitan stipendiaries; non-metropolitan stipendiaries will be given the same power by amendment of the Youth Courts (Constitution) Rules 1954.

Chapter 6
Sentencing: Young Offenders

Given the main focus of the Act upon young offenders, there are a number of important changes with respect to the sentencing of that key group of offenders. This chapter first deals with the planned introduction of a new custodial sentence for young offenders, the detention and training order. This sentence will, when brought into force, replace the sentence of detention in young offender institution for offenders aged 15, 16 and 17. It will also replace the secure training order, a custodial sentence appliable to offenders aged 12, 13 and 14, which was introduced by the Criminal Justice and Public Order Act 1994 but only brought into force in April 1998. These changes are expected to take place in Summer 1999. This chapter also describes the introduction of the action plan order, a new community sentence for young offenders, the reparation order, a new non-custodial sentence for young offenders, and various changes made by the Act to supervision orders and attendance centre orders.

DETENTION AND TRAINING ORDERS

The general scheme

Sections 73 to 79 of the Act will, when brought into force, create a new custodial sentence for young offenders — the detention and training order. The order will be available to youth courts and to the Crown Court in respect of offenders aged under 18 who have been convicted of an offence punishable with imprisonment in the case of an adult. The detention and training order will be a 'custodial sentence' for the purposes of s. 31 of the Criminal Justice Act 1991. This means that the general criteria apply for justifying the use of custodial sentences (see Criminal Justice Act 1991, s. 1(2)(a) (seriousness of offence/offences) and s. 1(2)(b) (violent or sexual offences)), and for fixing the length of such a sentence. They also permit the use of a detention and training order in circumstances where the offender has failed to express his willingness to comply with a requirement in a community order which requires such an expression of willingness (Criminal Justice Act 1991, s. 1(3)). The court is required to explain to the offender in open court why it has reached the view that either of the criteria in s. 1(2) are made out. The court will also normally be required to have obtained a pre-sentence report before imposing a detention and training order (Criminal Justice Act 1991, s. 3), unless in the opinion of the court such report is 'unnecessary'. The circumstances in which a court may sentence without a report are further limited when the offender is aged under 18 and not convicted of an offence triable only on indictment.

Section 73(1) states that, subject to s. 53 of the Children and Young Persons Act 1933 (detention during Her Majesty's pleasure and sentences of long-term detention in accordance with s. 53(2)), and to s. 8 of the Criminal Justice Act 1982 (custody for life), where an offender falling within this age group qualifies for a custodial sentence, the 'sentence *that the court is to pass*' (emphasis added) is the detention and training order. The effect of this is that when the powers to impose a detention and training order are brought into force, powers to impose a secure training order will be repealed, and the sentence of detention in a young offender institution will henceforth be available only to offenders aged 18, 19 or 20. At the time of writing it is expected that the detention and training order will not be introduced before the Summer of 1999, until which time the existing regime for the custodial sentencing of young offenders will remain in place. At present only one secure training centre is operational but it is likely that one or two more will be completed prior to the implementation of these further changes. The secure training centres will then be utilised as being one of the places in which a sentence of detention and training may be carried out.

Section 73(2)(b)(ii) envisages that, when the powers to pass a detention and training order are brought into force, they may be made available in respect of young offenders aged 10 or 11, but that a further order will be required from the Secretary of State to empower courts to impose the sentence on an offender aged under 12.

For young offenders aged 15, 16 and 17 the detention and training order will operate in a very similar fashion to the sentence of detention in a young offender institution, while for those aged 12, 13 and 14 the detention and training order will operate in a comparable manner to the secure training order. In reality, since the secure training order has only recently been brought into force, and since only one such centre is currently operational, at present the only custodial sentence available for those under 15 is detention under s. 53(2) of the Children and Young Persons Act 1933 provided that the various criteria for the use of that sentence are all made out. It will be noted that under s. 73(2)(a) power to pass a detention and training order on a young offender aged under 15 at the time of conviction is limited to cases in which the offender qualifies as a 'persistent' offender. This may be compared to the more precisely worded power to pass a secure training order which, in every case, requires proof that the young offender has been convicted of three or more imprisonable offences, has been in breach of a supervision order or has been convicted of an imprisonable offence while subject to a supervision order (Criminal Justice and Public Order Act 1994, s. 1(5)). Surprisingly, perhaps, the 1998 Act offers no definition of 'persistent' for the purposes of the detention and training order, it having been left to the courts to develop their own guidelines. In *Sheffield Youth Justices, ex parte M* (1998) *The Times*, 29 January 1998, Simon Brown LJ observed that, even though powers to pass a secure training order were not yet in force at the time of that case, counsel might wish to draw the attention of sentencers to the wording of s. 1(5) in any case in which the court was considering imposing a custodial sentence on an offender aged under 15. Section 74(1) states that, where the court makes a detention and training order on an offender aged under 15, it must state in open court that it is of the opinion mentioned in s. 73(2)(a) or s. 73(2)(a) and (b)(i). This is in addition to the normal obligations on the sentencer under s. 1(4) of the Criminal Justice Act 1991 to give reasons for imposing a custodial sentence.

Duration of detention and training order

The court will have the same powers to pass consecutive detention and training orders as if they were sentences of imprisonment (s. 74(2)), subject to the rule that the term, or aggregate term, must not exceed 24 months (s. 74(3)). If a longer term, or aggregate term, is imposed by the sentencer, the excess is automatically remitted (s. 74(4)). The period of 24 months is, of course, the maximum aggregate term of detention in a young offender institution which may currently be imposed on an offender aged 15, 16 or 17, where there is a similar rule relating to automatic remission of sentence length over 24 months (Criminal Justice Act 1982, s. 1B), and is also the maximum duration of a secure training order. There has been judicial criticism of the manner in which s. 1B automatically remits any term accidentally imposed in excess of 24 months, since there is no opportunity for a sentencer who has made such a mistake to rectify it. See, for example, *Smithyman* (1993) 14 Cr App R(S) 263. Section 74(4), nonetheless, adopts the same format.

By s. 73(5), the term of a detention and training order must be for one of the specific periods stated in that subsection, the minimum period being four months, through six, eight, 10, 12, and 18 months to the maximum of 24 months, with the period of supervision normally starting at the half-way point of the sentence and ending when the full term of the order expires (s. 75(2) and s. 76(1)). Supervision will be carried out by a probation officer, a social worker or a member of a youth offending team (s. 76(3)).

Specifying particular sentence lengths in this way is a novel sentencing development. Since all such orders will fall naturally into two parts, the periods selected clearly owe something to a desirable wish for ease of calculation. It may, however, cause problems when making the required allowance for the offender's timely guilty plea (see Criminal Justice and Public Order Act 1994, s. 48). Section 73(5) indicates that the sentence to be passed must be for one of the terms specified in that subsection. If the sentencer complies faithfully with s. 48, he or she will have to state what the sentence would have been if the case had been contested (say, 18 months) and that account has been taken of the timely guilty plea, thereby reducing the sentence. The next available term to which an 18-month sentence could be reduced is 12 months. Similar difficulties will arise where an appropriate reduction to sentence length is made to take account of a period spent by the defendent on remand in custody. A sentencer may feel that, in all the circumstances, this discount is too large but there is no other term of detention and training which is available to be imposed instead. The government resisted attempts in Parliament to make these sentencing arrangements more flexible, on the basis that selection from a menu such as that in s. 73(5) would help to make sentencing more consistent. It is hard to be against consistency, but here there seems little merit in the legislative method which has been chosen. Section 73(5) is expressed as being 'subject to' s. 73(6), which explains that when imposing such a sentence the court may not exceed the maximum term of imprisonment which the Crown Court could have imposed on an adult for that offence. It seems that s. 73(6) should have been expressed as being 'subject to' s. 73(5), since the legislative intention here must surely be to limit the maximum term of a detention and training order to the period specified in s. 73(5) or the maximum penalty, whichever is the shorter (as does the equivalent wording in CJA 1982, s. 1B(2)). Section 73 does not mention ss. 31 and 133 of the Magistrates' Courts Act

1980, which provide that magistrates' courts shall not normally have power to impose custodial sentences of more than six months, and not more than 12 months where consecutive sentences are being imposed for two either-way offences. As these provisions on the detention and training order currently stand, they empower youth courts to pass such a sentence for up to the maximum of 24 months. Dr David Thomas has argued (see *Sentencing News*, 27 May 1998, pp. 11–12) that this constitutes a dramatic extension to the powers of a youth court to impose custodial sentences, and that this result was intended by the Government, although introduced with minimal publicity. It is submitted, however, that this argument overlooks MCA 1980, s. 24(3), which limits the powers of a youth court to impose custodial sentences of no more than six months. The same point in fact applies to secure training orders which, on the face of it, empower the youth court to pass such a sentence for a term of up to 24 months. Again, the effect of s. 24(3) is to restrict the youth court powers to six months.

Regard should also be had, however, to the repeal by sch. 8, para. 41 of s. 37 of the MCA 1980. Section 37 is currently used in a case where the youth court, having dealt with the case of an offender aged 15, 16 or 17, concludes that a sentence of detention in a young offender institution is the appropriate sentence but that a term of more than six months is called for. They may then commit the young offender to the Crown Court to be sentenced, the Crown Court being able to pass a sentence of detention in a young offender institution of up to 24 months. The specific power provided by s. 37 will no longer be required when the 1998 Act provisions come into force and the power of youth courts to pass sentences of detention in a young offender institution is removed. Surely, however, s. 37, rather than being repealed by the 1998 Act, should have been amended by it, so as to give youth courts an equivalent power of committal in respect of the new detention and training order. As the legislation currently stands, there is no way in which the youth court may commit a young offender to the Crown Court with a view to the higher court imposing a term of detention and training for longer than six months. Of course, if a young offender fall to be sentenced after trial on indictment, the Crown Court will have power to impose a detention and training order of one of the periods specified in s. 73(5), up to the maximum of 24 months, and, where the relevant conditions are made out, for longer custodial terms under CYPA 1933, s. 53(2).

By s. 74 the court imposing a sentence of detention and training is required to take account of any period for which the offender was remanded in custody in connection with the offence. This includes any period during which he was held in police detention or remanded to local authority secure accommodation. Both 'police detention' and 'secure accommodation' are further defined in s. 74(7).

Section 79 deals with various complexities arising in a case where an offender who is already subject to a sentence of detention in a young offender institution then receives a detention and training order, or vice versa.

Breach of supervision and commission of further offence

Breach of the supervision requirement of a detention and training order may be dealt with by imposing a fine not exceeding £1,000, or by ordering the offender to be returned to custody for a period not exceeding the remainder of the full term of the order or for three months, whichever is the shorter period (s. 77(3)). Breach is constituted by the offender's failure to comply with the requirements of supervision, rather than the commission by him of a further offence.

If a person who is subject to a detention and training order commits during the supervision part of that order a further offence which is punishable with imprisonment in the case of an adult, the court dealing with him for the new offence may, whether or not it imposes any other sentence, order the offender to be detained for a period which begins with the date of the court's order and is equal in length to the period of the full order which remained unexpired at the time when the new offence was committed (s. 78(2)). This new period of detention must either be served before, or concurrently with, any sentence which is imposed for the new offence. These arrangements for returning an offender to custody in light of a further offence during the currency of a custodial sentence are very similar to those under s. 40 of the CJA 1991, which applies where the original sentence was one of imprisonment, detention in a young offender institution or a term of detention under s. 53(2) of the CYPA 1933. The Court of Appeal has issued general guidance on the exercise of the power under s. 40 in *Secretary of State for the Home Department, ex parte Probyn* [1998] 1 Cr App R(S) 312. Rose LJ there explained that the sentencer should first decide what was the proper sentence for the new offence. Then, in considering whether an order under s. 40 should also be made, the court should review the offender's progress since his release. If the new offence required a custodial sentence, and reinstatement of some period under s. 40 was also appropriate, regard should be had to the totality.

ACTION PLAN ORDERS

Action plan orders in general

Section 69 and 70 provide that the Crown Court or a youth court will have power to impose an action plan order on an offender aged under 18 who is convicted of any offence. Powers to impose an action plan order will initially be made available only to certain courts on a pilot basis, with the pilot schemes running for a period of 18 months from October 1998. In the White Paper *No More Excuses*, the Government describes the action plan order as 'a short intensive programme of community intervention combining punishment, rehabilitation and reparation to change offending behaviour and prevent further crime. [It] will be available for offenders aged between 10 and 17 inclusive and will impose requirements designed to address the specific causes of offending. Each order will last for three months'.

An action plan order is a 'community order' within the meaning of s. 6(4) of Criminal Justice Act 1991, so that the imposition of an action plan order requires justification in terms of the seriousness of the offence, or the offence and one or more offences associated with it. The community orders are now: probation order, community service order, combination order, curfew order, supervision order, attendance centre order, drug treatment and testing order (see Chapter 7) and action plan order. The action plan order is not one of the community sentences where the court is normally required to obtain a pre-sentence report.

The court may make an action plan order if it is of the opinion that it is desirable to do so in the interests of securing the young offender's rehabilitation, or of preventing the commission by him of further offences (s. 69(1)). The order will require the offender, for a period of three months beginning with the date of the order, to comply with an action plan, which is a series of requirements with respect to his action and whereabouts during that time, and which puts the young offender under supervision. Supervision is to be carried out by a probation officer, a social worker or a member of a youth offending team (s. 69(10)), and the order requires the young offender to comply with any directions given by that officer as well as requirements inserted into the order by the court. This appears to provide the responsible officer with a greater degree of discretion and control over the content of the order than is normally the case in a community order. By s. 69(5), requirements included in the order, or directions given by the responsible officer, may require the offender to do all or any of the following things (s. 69(5)):

(a)   to participate in activities specified in the requirements or directions at a time or times so specified;

(b)   to present himself to a person or persons specified in the requirements or directions at a place or places and at a time or times so specified;

(c)   to attend at an attendance centre specified in the requirements or directions for a number of hours so specified [this applies only if the offence which the young offender committed is punishable with imprisonment if committed by an adult];

(d)   to stay away from a place or places specified in the requirements or directions;

(e)   to comply with any arrangements for his education specified in the requirements or directions;

(f)   to make reparation specified in the requirements or directions to a person or persons so specified or to the community at large; and

(g)   to attend any hearing fixed by the court under section 70(3) below.

These requirements must, as far as practicable, avoid conflict with the offender's religious beliefs or with the requirements of any other community order to which he may be subject and must avoid interference with the times at which he normally works or is in education (s. 69(6)). The White Paper indicates that the requirements in the action plan order will be tailored to the individual young offender, reflecting consultation with the offender, his family, and perhaps with the victim and 'it may include elements such as motor projects, anger management courses, alcohol or drug treatment programmes or help with problems at home or at school or in finding accommodation, training or employment'.

The requirement to make reparation, indicated in s. 69(5)(f), must not be inserted in the order or required by the officer unless a person has been identified by the court or the officer as being 'a victim of the offence or a person otherwise affected by it' (s. 69(8)), and that the person consents to the reparation being made. The requirement to make reparation may be compared with the equivalent provision in relation to reparation orders (see below). The wording here indicates that the court may require reparation to be made to a person who is the victim of the offence or someone 'otherwise affected' by it. Thus, the court might require reparation to be made by the offender to the victim of an assault committed by him, and/or to be made to a bystander who suffered shock as a result of witnessing the assault. The language may also be compared to that applicable in relation to compensation orders, where the court may require the offender 'to pay compensation for any personal injury, loss or damage resulting from that offence . . .' (Powers of Criminal Courts Act 1973, s. 35(1)).

Although the court may pass an action plan order without first obtaining a pre-sentence report, s. 70(1) requires that before making such an order the court must obtain and consider a written report by a probation officer, a social worker or a member of a youth offending team which indicates the requirements proposed by that person to be included in the order, the benefits to the offender that the proposed requirements are designed to achieve and the attitude of a parent or guardian of the offender to the proposed requirements. If the offender is under 16 the report must also provide information as to the offender's family circumstances and the likely effect of the order on those circumstances. Before making an action plan order the court must explain to the offender in ordinary laguage the effect of the order and the requirements proposed to be included in it, the consequences which may follow if he fails to comply with any of those requirements and that the order may be reviewed by the court on the application either of the offender or of the responsible officer (s. 70(2)). Immediately after making the order the court may fix a further hearing for a date not more than 21 days ahead and direct the officer to make at that hearing a report as to the effectiveness of the order and the extent to which it has been implemented (s. 70(3)); s. 70(3) provides the court with a discretion as to whether to order a hearing or further hearings. This provision is in contrast to the specific requirement of periodic reviews where a drug treatment and testing order has been made by the court (see chapter 7). At such a hearing, the court may, after considering the officer's report and on the application of the officer or the offender, vary the order by cancelling any provision included in it or by inserting in it any provision which that the court could originally have included (s. 70(4)).

Combining action plan orders with other sentences or orders

Section 69(4) makes it clear that an action plan order cannot be imposed where the court also passes on the offender a custodial sentence or one of a range of other community orders. The subsection does not mention drug treatment and testing orders (see Chapter 7), so presumably an action plan order could be combined with such an order in the case of an offender aged 16 or 17. Nor does s. 69(4) mention curfew orders, so presumably an action plan order could be combined with a curfew order. Although s. 69(4) does not mention reparation orders, the relevant provision on reparation orders (s. 67(4)) states that reparation orders and action plan orders cannot be combined. There is nothing to prevent an action plan order being combined with a fine, or with ancillary orders such as a compensation order or an order for forfeiture under s. 43 of the Powers of Criminal Courts Act 1973.

Discharge, breach and revocation of action plan orders

Schedule 5 sets out provisions for the discharge or amendment of an action plan order (or reparation order: see below). Paragraph 2 states that, while the order is in force, the court may, on application of the responsible officer or the young offender, make an order discharging it or varying it, either by cancelling any existing provision or by inserting a fresh provision. If an application for discharge is dismissed by the court, no further application for discharge can be made without the consent of the court.

Arrangements for dealing with the offender's failure to comply with the terms of an action plan order (or reparation order) are also set out in sch. 5 to the Act. Where an action plan order or reparation order is in force and it is proved to the satisfaction of the appropriate youth court, on the application of the responsible officer, that the offender has failed to comply with any requirement in the order the court must, under para. 3 of sch. 5, proceed as follows. The court, whether or not it also makes an order under para. 2 (to discharge or vary the action plan order or reparation order), may order the offender to pay a fine of an amount not exceeding £1,000, or make an attendance centre order or curfew order in respect of him. Alternatively, if the reparation order or action plan order was made by a youth court, the youth court may discharge the order and deal with him for the offence in respect of which the order was made. In such a case, the court may deal with him in any manner in which he could have been dealt with for that offence by the court which made the order if the order had not been made; if the reparation order or action plan order was made by the Crown Court, the youth court may commit the young offender in custody or release him on bail until he can be brought or appear before the Crown Court.

If the youth court proceeds to commit the young offender to the Crown Court, it must send to the Crown Court a certificate detailing the offender's failure to comply, together with such other particulars as may be desirable. Once the young offender is before the Crown Court, and it is proved to the satisfaction of that court that he has failed to comply with the relevant order, that court may deal with him for the offence in respect of which the order was made in any manner in which it could have dealt with him for the offence if it had not made the order. Where the Crown Court so deals with the offender, it must revoke the action plan order or reparation order, if it is still in force.

Whether the offender is dealt with by the youth court or the Crown Court, when dealing with the failure to comply the court must take into account the extent to which the offender has complied with the terms of the order.

Paragraph 4 and 5 of sch. 5 deal with further procedural and supplemental matters, including the requirement that the offender must normally be present before the court which is dealing with his failure to comply with the order.

REPARATION ORDERS

Sections 67 and 68 of the Act provide that the Crown Court or a youth court will have power to impose a reparation order on an offender aged under 18 who is convicted of any offence. Powers to impose a reparation order will initially be made available only to certain courts on a pilot basis. These pilot schemes will run for a period of 18 months from October 1998. In the White Paper *No more Excuses* the Government describes the reparation order as:

> a new penalty ... which courts will have to consider imposing on young offenders in all cases where they do not impose a compensation order. The order will require reparation to be made in kind, up to a maximum of 24 hours' work within a period of three months. The reparation might involve writing a letter of apology, apologising to the victim in person, cleaning graffiti or repairing criminal damage. Of course not all victims would want reparation. The government's proposals will ensure that the victim's views will be sought before an order is made. Where a victim does not want direct reparation, the reparation may be made to the community at large.

Reparation orders in general

A reparation order is not a 'community order' within the meaning of s. 6(4) of Criminal Justice Act 1991, and therefore stands in contrast with the action plan order which is a community order. The order is available where a young offender under 18 is convicted of an offence other than one for which the sentence is fixed by law. The youth court or Crown Court may make a reparation order (s. 67(2)):

> which requires the offender to make reparation as specified in the order—
> (a)   to a person or persons so specified; or
> (b)   to the community at large;
> and any person so specified must be a person identified by the court as a victim of the offence or a person otherwise affected by it.

This wording indicates that the court may require reparation to be made to a person who is the victim of the offence or to someone 'otherwise affected' by it. In the case of an assault, this might include not just the person assaulted but also some other person who witnessed the incident and suffered shock as a result. The wording is the same as that used in relation to the reparation element which may be inserted into an action plan order under s. 69(8) (see above).

A reparation order must not require the young offender to work for more than 24 hours in aggregate. Any order for reparation must have the consent of the person to whom the reparation is to be made (s. 67(5)).

More generally, and subject to s. 67(5), requirements specified in a reparation order must be such as in the opinion of the court are 'commensurate with the seriousness of the offence, or the combination of the offence and one or more offences associated with it' (s. 67(6)). This means that, although the reparation order is not a community order, and hence its imposition does not require a finding by the court that the offence was 'serious enough' to justify such a response, the content of the order must be in proportion to the seriousness of the offence. This must surely apply to the nature of the work required as well as to the number of hours involved. It would be inappropriate for the court to require very onerous reparation, at least where that was not justified by the nature of the offence itself. Section 67(6) may provide a welcome legislative check on an overenthusiastic court inventing complex and onerous forms of reparation. It may perhaps be assumed that some forms of reparation would always be inappropriate for a court to require, such as where the work was of a dangerous, particularly unpleasant or demeaning character. The reparation required must be made under the supervision of a 'responsible officer', who will be a probation officer, a social worker or a member of a youth offending team (s. 67(8)). The responsible officer will, no doubt, draw upon the experience which has been gathered and the good practice which has been developed over the years from the various reparation-based schemes which have been in operation in the criminal justice system. The reparation requirements in a reparation order must, as far as practicable, avoid conflict with the young offender's religious beliefs or with the requirements of any community order to which he may be subject, and interference with the times at which he normally works or has educational commitments (s. 67(7)).

A reparation order may be imposed without the court first obtaining a pre-sentence report but, by s. 68(1), before making a reparation order the court must obtain and consider a report (from a probation officer, a social worker or a member of a youth offending team) indicating the type of work which is suitable for the young offender, and the attitude of the victim, or victims, to the requirements to be included in the order. Before making a reparation order, the court must explain to the young offender in ordinary language the effect of the order and of the requirements proposed to be included in it, the consequences which may follow if he fails to comply with any of those requirements, and that the order may be reviewed by the court on the application either of the offender or of the responsible officer (s. 68(2)).

Combining reparation orders with other sentences or orders

Section 67(4) makes it clear that a reparation order cannot be imposed where the court also passes on the offender a custodial sentence or one of the following community orders: a community service order, a combination order, a supervision order which includes requirements imposed under ss. 12 to 12C of the Children and Young Persons Act 1969 or an action plan order. This list does not include drug treatment and testing orders, so presumably a reparation order could be combined with such an order in the case of an offender aged 16 or 17. Nor does s. 67(4) mention probation orders, curfew orders or attendance centre orders so, again, presumably such orders could be combined with a reparation order. A reparation order may be combined with a supervision order which does not contain the particular requirements referred to, but it cannot be combined with an action plan order.

It is important to note that, in contrast to the Bill and to the passage from the White Paper set out above, s. 67(4) of the Act makes no mention of compensation orders. The Bill stated that the reparation order and the compensation order were alternative methods by which the court might order redress by the offender to the victim, and that both should not be ordered at the same time. The quotation taken from the White Paper indicates the Government's view that reparation should be an option for the court 'where they do not impose a compensation order'. To regard these measures as alternatives in this way was problematic, since the reparation order is clearly intended to be a form of punishment for the offence, while the compensation order is an ancillary order, not punishment at all (see further *Emmins on Sentencing*, 3rd ed., 1998, 7.4.2.). Dropping this approach in the Act is a sensible move. Section 67(11) requires the court to give reasons if it does not make a reparation order where it has power to do so. A similar provision, of course, exists in respect of compensation orders (Powers of Criminal Courts Act 1973, s. 35(1)) so, presumably, it might be sufficient reason for not making a reparation order that the court has made a compensation order instead, and vice versa.

Discharge, breach and revocation of reparation orders

Arrangements for dealing with applications to the court to discharge or vary a reparation order, or for the offender's failure to comply with the terms of a reparation order, are set out in sch. 5. The relevant provisions are the same as those applicable to action plan orders (see above).

SUPERVISION ORDERS

As the result of various provisions scattered around the Act and its schedules, the Act makes a number of changes to supervision orders. A supervision order may be made by a youth court or the Crown Court on a young offender aged under 18 who has been convicted of any offence. The supervision order is a community order within the meaning of the Criminal Justice Act 1991. A range of requirements may be inserted by the sentencing court into the supervision order. These may, for example, involve a requirement of residence (under Children and Young Persons Act 1969, s. 12), or of intermediate treatment (s. 12 or 12A), of treatment for a mental condition (s. 12B), or of specified arrangements for his education (s. 12C). The changes made by the 1998 Act to the regime of supervision orders are dealt with in turn below.

Reparation requirement in supervision order

By s. 12A of the Children and Young Persons Act 1969, the court has power to insert a range of requirements into a supervision order (sometimes known as stipulated intermediate treatment), such as a requirement to remain at a specified place for specified periods between 6 p.m. and 6 a.m., or to participate in designated activities, or to refrain from particular activities. Section 71 of the 1998 Act amends s. 12A(3) by inserting a new paragraph (aa), by which the court may require the young offender 'to make reparation specified in the order to a person or persons so specified or to the community at large'. The person identified in the order must be a victim of the offence committed by the young offender, or a person 'otherwise affected by it'. The wording here is identical to that described above in relation to action plan orders and reparation orders. As is the case with the other orders, the order cannot be made unless the victim consents to the arrangement being made.

Local authority accommodation: changed criteria

By s. 12AA of the Children and Young Persons Act 1969 the court has power to insert a requirement into a supervision order that the young offender shall for a specified period reside in local authority accommodation for a maximum period of six months. Such an order can be made only where the young offender has already had one supervision order imposed upon him and fulfils one of a number of other specified criteria. It is these criteria which s. 71(4) of the 1998 Act has changed.

Formerly, such an order could be made only where the previous supervision order contained a residence requirement under s. 12A, the young offender had committed an offence during its operational period which was an offence punishable with imprisonment in the case of an adult, the offence was serious, and its commission was, in the opinion of the court, due to a significant extent to the circumstances in which the young offender was living. This rather complex formula is relaxed somewhat in the new version; a requirement to reside in local authority accommodation may henceforth be imposed where:

(a)   the previous supervision order contained *any* requirement under s. 12, s. 12A or s. 12C or a residence requirement;

(b)   the young offender *failed to comply* with the requirement or had committed an offence within its operational period;

(c)   the court is satisfied that the commission of the offence was due to a significant extent to the circumstances in which he was living, and that a residence requirement would assist in the young offender's rehabilitation.

Custodial sentence on breach of supervision order

By s. 12D of the Children and Young Persons Act 1969, as it stood before the 1998 Act, the Court when making an order of stipulated intermediate treatment under s. 12A, may state that the circumstances of the offence were such that, had the court not made a supervision order, it would have passed a custodial sentence. The court must in such a case state that the supervision order is being made instead of custody, and confirm that the offence qualified the offender for custody under one or other of the standard criteria specified in s. 1 of the CJA 1991. The 1998 Act, by para. 18 of sch. 8, repeals s. 12D. The repeal of this provision has to be seen alongside general changes to the powers of enforcement for supervision orders, set out in s. 15 of the 1969 Act. These changes, brought about by s. 72 of the 1998 Act, mean that a young offender's failure to comply with the terms of a supervision order may now more readily attract a custodial sentence. The court need no longer specify in advance, at the time of making that order, that it was made in lieu of a custodial sentence. Whether it is the youth court that deals with the breach (under the new s. 15(3)(b)), or the Crown Court where the matter is remitted to them by the youth court (under the new s. 15(4)), the court may revoke the order and re-sentence in any manner in which it could have dealt with the young offender for that offence. This of course includes where appropriate, a custodial sentence. As before, by s. 15(8), the breach court is bound to take into account the extent to which the young offender had complied with the requirements of the supervision order before it was breached.

Miscellaneous changes

Further minor changes are made to supervision orders:

(a) by sch. 7, para. 4 (inserting a provision now standard to community orders, that directions given by the supervisor to the young offender should not conflict with the young offender's religious beliefs, the requirements of any other community orders to which he may be subject, or the times at which he works or has educational commitments);

(b) by sch. 7, para. 5 (replacing the term 'medical practitioner' in s. 12B of the Children and Young Persons Act 1969 with 'registered medical practitioner' and providing a definition of the latter term);

(c) by s. 72(5) and sch. 10, in line with various other amendments relating to 'supervision' by probation officers it repeals s. 13(2) of the 1969 Act, which provided that, where a young offender is under 13 years of age, supervision under a supervision order should be carried out by a social worker unless the probation service had already been involved with the offender's family.

ATTENDANCE CENTRE ORDERS

Imposition of attendance centre orders

Schedule 7 to the Act (paras 33 to 38) re-shapes the main statutory provisions on attendance centre orders, in particular s. 17 of the Criminal Justice Act 1982. This is in part a matter of clarification, but there are some changes of substance. Attendance centre orders may now be imposed in several rather different circumstances, as a result of changes made in recent criminal justice legislation. The 1998 Act performs a useful service by re-casting s. 17 so as to clarify the different routes by which such an order may be imposed.

The first route, as expressed by a newly substituted s. 17(1), is where a youth court or the Crown Court imposes an attendance centre order as a community order on an offender aged under 21 convicted of an offence punishable with imprisonment. The second route, by s. 17(1)(a), is where a person receives an attendance centre order in default of payment of a fine, etc., and where imprisonment is not available because they are aged under 21. The third route, by s. 17(1)(b), refers to the court's power to employ an attendance centre order in response to an offender's failure to comply with the requirements of a probation order or a curfew order (see CJA 1991, sch. 2). The former option is available only where the probationer is aged under 21 and the latter option is available only where the offender under curfew is aged under 16. The fourth route, by s. 17(1)(c), is where person in default of payment of a fine, etc. who is aged at least 21 but is under 25 receives an attendance centre order as an alternative to commitment to prison.

Miscellaneous changes

Various minor changes are made to attendance centre orders by sch. 7:

(a)   a new s. 17(1A) of the Criminal Justice Act 1982 helps to clarify the alternative routes to the imposition of an attendance centre order, described above (para. 36(4));

(b)   a provision now standard to community orders is inserted into s. 17(8), namely that the times at which a young offender is required to attend at an attendance centre order must, as far as possible, not conflict with the young offender's religious beliefs, the requirements of any other community orders to which he may be subject, or the times at which he works or has educational commitments (para. 36(5));

(c)   paras 37 and 38 re-cast and tidy up the provisions on breach of attendance centre orders, changing the wording as appropriate to allow for the fact that on some occasions the breach court will be dealing with an attendance centre order imposed for an offence, while on other occasions it will have been imposed as a method of fine enforcement.

Chapter 7
Sentencing: General

In Chapter 6 we considered a range of sentencing changes introduced by the Act which address the general theme of disposal of young offenders. In common with all other recent Criminal Justice Acts, the 1998 Act also contains a number of more general sentencing changes. In this chapter we examine the introduction of a new community sentence, the drug treatment and testing order, and consider a range of amendments to the operation of other community orders and to discharges. The new regime for the imposition of extended sentences for sexual or violent offences is explained. Reference is also made to the new machinery for the provision of authoritative sentencing guidelines and the establishment of the Sentencing Advisory Panel. Finally, a number of miscellaneous items are discussed. These include changes to arrangements for release and recall of prisoners, further consideration of the issue of racial aggravation in sentencing, and a reference to the abolition of the death penalty for treason and piracy, which is of symbolic importance but clearly of very little practical relevance.

DRUG TREATMENT AND TESTING ORDERS

Powers to impose a drug treatment and testing order

Sections 61 to 64 provide a new power for the Crown Court and magistrates' courts to impose a drug treatment and testing order on an offender aged 16 or over who is convicted of any offence apart from murder or one to which the provisions of ss. 2, 3 and 4 of the Crime (Sentences) Act 1997 apply. Those sections provide, respectively, for an automatic life sentence for the second serious offence and a mandatory sentence of seven years for the third Class A drug trafficking offence. Section 4 of the 1997 Act, on sentencing for domestic burglary, is not in force. Powers to impose a drug treatment and testing order will initially be made available only to certain courts on a pilot basis from 30 September 1998.

A drug treatment and testing order is a 'community order' within the meaning of s. 6(4) of the Criminal Justice Act 1991, so that the imposition of a drug treatment and testing order requires justification in terms of the seriousness of the offence, or the offence and one or more offences associated with it. The offence must be 'serious enough' to justify the use of a community sentence. The Criminal Justice Act 1991 also contains procedural requirements relating to community sentences, in particular that the court should normally obtain a pre-sentence report before imposing a drug treatment and testing order (CJA 1991, s. 7(3), as amended by the 1998 Act, sch. 8, para. 56) unless the court is of the opinion that it is unnecessary to obtain one.

The drug treatment and testing order may usefully be compared with the requirement as to treatment for drug or alcohol dependency which may be inserted by the court as a requirement of a probation order (see Powers of Criminal Courts Act 1973, sch. 1A, para. 6(1)). The obvious differences between the orders are that the probation requirement also extends to alcohol dependency or misuse, and it lacks the 'testing requirement' integral to the drug treatment and testing order. The 1998 Act provides that, when local arrangements are in place for implementing drug treatment and testing orders, the probation order requirement shall be limited to offenders who are dependent on alcohol, but not on drugs. Another difference between the orders, which may or may not be significant, is that the probation requirement states that the offender's dependency should have 'caused or contributed to the offence', while no such causal link is specified for the drug treatment and testing order.

The drug treatment and testing order has effect for a period specified in the order, of not less than six months nor more than three years ('the treatment and testing period'). The Secretary of State retains power to vary these periods subsequently by order.

The court must be satisfied that the offender is dependent on, or has a propensity to misuse, drugs and that his dependency or propensity is such as requires and may be susceptible to treatment (s. 61(2) and (5)). In order to ascertain for these purposes whether the offender has any drug in his body, the court may by order require him to provide samples of such description as it may specify, but the court cannot make such an order unless the offender expresses his willingness to comply (s. 61(6)). Since the general requirements of consent to community sentences were abolished by the Crime (Sentences) Act 1997, the requirement in s. 61(6) is one of only a few occasions on which the court must still secure the offender's willingness to comply with the order before it can be imposed. The others relate to the imposition of requirements of treatment for a mental condition inserted into a probation order or a supervision order and the probation order requirement of treatment for drug or alcohol dependency, mentioned above. Section 1(3) of the CJA 1991 (as amended by the 1998 Act) states that 'Nothing ... shall prevent the court from passing a custodial sentence on the offender if he fails to express his willingness to comply ...' with any such requirement.

By s. 62 of the 1998 Act, a drug treatment and testing order shall include a requirement ('the treatment requirement') that the offender shall submit, during the whole of the treatment and testing period, to treatment by or under the direction of a specified person having the necessary qualifications or experience ('the treatment provider') with a view to the reduction or elimination of the offender's dependency on or propensity to misuse drugs. The required treatment for any period shall be treatment as a resident in such institution or place as may be specified in the order, or treatment as a non-resident in or at such institution or place, and at such intervals, as may be so specified. The nature of the treatment shall not otherwise be specified in the order (s. 62(2)). The court cannot make a drug treatment and testing order unless it is satisfied that arrangements have been, or can be, made for that treatment and for the reception of the offender in the place where he is to be treated (s. 62(3)).

Also by s. 62, the drug treatment and testing order must include a 'testing requirement', which requires the offender to provide samples during the treatment and testing period at such times or in such circumstances as may be determined by the treatment provider. The testing requirement shall specify, for each month, the minimum number of occasions on which samples are to be provided (s. 62(5)). The drug treatment and testing order must also provide that, for the treatment and testing period, the offender shall be under the supervision of a probation officer ('the responsible officer'). The offender must keep in touch with the responsible officer and notify him or her of any change of address. The results of the tests carried out on the samples must be communicated to the responsible officer. Supervision is limited to enabling the officer to report on the offender's progress to the court, to report to the court any failure by the offender to comply with the requirements of the order, and matters relating to revocation or amendment of the order.

Before making a drug treatment and testing order, the court must explain to the offender in ordinary language the effect of the order and the requirements proposed to be inserted in it, the consequences which may follow if he fails to comply with any of those requirements, that the order may be reviewed on the application either of the offender or of the responsible officer and that the order will be reviewed periodically by the court making the order (s. 64(1)). The court shall forthwith give copies of the order to a probation officer assigned to the court, and he shall give copies to the offender, to the treatment provider, and to the responsible officer (s. 64(3)). It is unlikely that non-compliance with the provision of the copies of the order would render the drug treatment and testing order invalid, by analogy with *Walsh* v *Barlow* [1985] 1 WLR 90 (see *Blackstone's Criminal Practice*, **E4.2**).

Review hearings

An essential part of the arrangements for the drug treatment and testing order is that allowance is made for periodic reviews to be made of the offender's progress under the terms of the order by the court which made it, at regular intervals of not less than one month. These reviews, at least initially, will require the offender's attendance at each 'review hearing' in court, at which the offender's test results, the responsible officer's written report on his progress under the order, and the views of the person providing the treatment will all be considered by the court (s. 63(1)). At a review hearing the court, after considering the report of the responsible officer, may amend any requirement or provision of the order (s. 63(2)), except that the court shall not amend the treatment or testing requirement in the order unless the offender expresses his willingness to comply with the amendment, and the court shall not reduce the treatment and testing period below the minimum or increase it above the maximum. If the offender fails to express his willingness to comply with the amendment, the court may revoke the order and re-sentence for the offence (s. 63(4)), including where appropriate the passing of a custodial sentence, but in re-sentencing the court must take into account the extent to which the offender has complied with the order's requirements. If at a review hearing it appears that the offender's progress under the order is continuing satisfactorily, subsequent reviews may be carried out by the court without a full review hearing (in the case of the Crown Court, by a judge, and in the case of a magistrates' court, by a justice of the peace acting for the relevant commission area) but, if progress subsequently becomes unsatisfactory, a further review hearing in court must be convened (s. 63(8)).

Breach and revocation of drug treatment and testing orders

A drug treatment and testing order is a 'community order' within the meaning of s. 6(4) of the Criminal Justice Act 1991. The provisions relating to breach and revocation of community orders are set out in sch. 2 to the Criminal Justice Act 1991, as amended by the 1998 Act.

COMMUNITY ORDERS AND DISCHARGES

Changes to probation orders and combination orders

There are a number of such changes, occasioned by various provisions scattered throughout the 1998 Act.

Supervision by youth offending team
Section 2 of the Powers of Criminal Courts Act 1973, which is the main enabling provision in relation to probation orders, is amended by the 1998 Act in the following way. Prior to the Act, supervision under a probation order was always carried out by a probation officer assigned to the relevant area. This is now changed so that, where the offender is under the age of 18, supervision will be carried out by a member of a youth offending team established by the local authority within whose area the offender lives. This change is also relevant to the probation part of a combination order, and s. 11 of the Criminal Justice Act 1991 is amended so that 'supervision of a probation officer' now simply reads 'supervision'.

Requirements to avoid conflicts
Schedule 1A to the 1973 Act deals with the various requirements which may be inserted by a sentencing court into a probation order. In respect of certain of these requirements, the requirement that the probationer shall engage in specified (under para. 2) and the requirement of attendance at a probation centre (under para. 3) are both made subject to the now standard provision that such requirements shall be such as to avoid conflict with the offender's religious beliefs, the requirements of any other community order to which he may also be subject, and the times at which he works or has eductional commitments. These changes are also applicable to the probation part of a combination order.

Treatment for drug or alcohol dependency
Still on the subject of requirements which may be inserted into probation orders, para. 6 of sch. 1A allows for the insertion of a requirement as to treatment for drug or alcohol dependency. On the relationship between this requirement and the introduction by the 1998 Act of the new drug treatment and testing order, see above. The Act provides that when local arrangements are in place for implementing drug treatment and testing orders, the requirement as to treatment under para. 6 shall be confined to offenders dependent on *alcohol*, but not on drugs.

Prior to the 1998 Act, the court which proposed to insert such a requirement into a probation order had to ensure that arrangements had been made for the relevant treatment to be carried out. This obligation on the court has been relaxed slightly, the new formulation being that the court must be satisfied that the relevant arrangements 'have been *or can be* made' for the treatment to be carried out. This change is also relevant to the probation part of a combination order.

Substitution of order

Section 11 of the Powers of Criminal Courts Act 1973, which allowed for application to be made to the court, by the probation officer or by the probationer, for the substitution of a conditional discharge for an existing probation order, has been repealed by para. 17 of sch. 7 to the 1998 Act. In practice s. 11 was used in cases where the probationer's circumstances having changed, the probation officer felt that continuing with the order would serve no useful purpose, but it was perhaps too early in the term to seek revocation of the order. Section 11 was something of an anachronism. The Criminal Justice Act 1991 re-cast the arrangements for variation, breach and revocation of community orders and, in that light, the continuing relevance of s. 11 was unclear. See further *Emmins on Sentencing*, 3rd ed., 5.2.10.

Combination with ancillary order

Section 12(4) of the Powers of Criminal Courts Act 1973 is substituted by the 1998 Act. This subsection, as far as probation orders is concerned, merely confirmed that such an order might properly be combined with an order for costs, a compensation order, or an order for forfeiture of property under s. 43 of the 1973 Act. The position in relation to probation orders is unaffected by the substitution of the subsection. The new wording does, however, affect the law relating to discharges, as to which see below.

Combining community order with suspended sentence

Section 22(3) of the Powers of Criminal Courts Act 1973 prevented a court from passing a suspended sentence of imprisonment and a probation order on the same sentencing occasion, whether the offences were charged in the same or different indictments. The subsection is amended by para. 22 of sch. 7 to the 1998 Act so as to extend this prohibition to the mixing of a suspended sentence with *any* community sentence. This is a useful clarification to the law.

It may be noted in passing that, despite all the sentencing changes which have taken place in recent years, the suspended sentence supervision order remains available (in effect, just to the Crown Court since it applies only where a prison sentence of more than six months has been suspended) by virtue of s. 26 of the 1973 Act. Such an order does provide a means of adding a supervision element to a suspended prison sentence.

Changes to community service orders

There are few changes, and these are minor and essentially classificatory in character.

Restricting imposition of orders

Section 14 of the Powers of Criminal Courts Act 1973, which is the main enabling provision for community service orders, is amended by the 1998 Act so as to make it clear that such an order cannot be imposed where the offence committed is murder, or is one which falls within s. 2(2) of the Crime (Sentences) Act 1997 (automatic life sentence for a second serious offence), s. 3(2) of that Act (minimum custodial sentence of seven years for the third Class A drug trafficking offence) or s. 4(2) (minimum custodial sentence of three years for the third domestic burglary: *not* in force). It is likely that everyone assumed that this was the case anyway. Under either of the two subsections of the 1997 Act which are in force the sentencing court has a discretion not to impose the prescribed sentence. In such a case, the court could in principle select any other sentence, including a community service order. For changes made by the 1998 Act to these sections of the 1997 Act, see below.

Role of youth offending team
In line with other changes involving the transfer of functions from the probation service to youth offending teams, the 1998 Act states that references in s. 14(2), (4), (5) and (6) of the Powers of Criminal Courts Act 1973 to the role of a 'probation officer' shall be construed, where the offender is aged under 18, to include reference to a member of a local youth offending team.

Combination with ancillary orders
Section 14(8) of the Powers of Criminal Courts Act 1973 is repealed by the 1998 Act. This subsection merely confirmed that a community service order could be made at the same time as an order for costs, a disqualification of any kind imposed on the offender, a compensation order, or an order for the forfeiture of property under s. 43 of the 1973 Act. This provision was superfluous, and its repeal does not affect the position in practice.

Instruction to avoid conflicts
Section 15(3) of the Powers of Criminal Courts Act 1973 is also subject to minor amendment so as to include the now standard requirement that the instructions given to the offender in respect of whom a community service is in force shall be such as, so far as possible, to avoid conflict with the offender's religious beliefs, the requirements of any other community order to which he may be subject, and the times at which he works or has educational commitments.

Changes to provisions on absolute and conditional discharge

Several of the changes made by the 1998 Act impinge upon the use by sentencing courts of the absolute and conditional discharge. Taken together, these are quite significant for future practice.

Section 1A of the Powers of Criminal Courts Act 1973, which is the enabling provision with respect to the absolute and conditional discharge, states that such disposal shall be used where the court 'is of opinion, having regard to the circumstances including the nature of the offence and the character of the offender, that it is inexpedient to inflict punishment'. An important effect of this wording is that a discharge cannot be combined on sentence with a punitive measure for the same offence, except where this has been specifically permitted by statute. Thus, a discharge cannot be combined with a custodial sentence, a community sentence, or a fine (on the last of these, see *Sanck* (1990) 12 Cr App R(S) 155). These restrictions apply to combining the measures when sentencing for a *single offence*. The court is free to impose a punishment in respect of one offence and a discharge in respect of another offence where the offences are sentenced on the same occasion. Section 12(4) of the 1973 Act, before its substitution by the 1998 Act, stated that nothing in s. 1A

should be construed as taking away the court's power to combine a discharge with
an order for costs, a compensation order, or an order for forfeiture of property under
s. 43 of the 1973 Act. The new version of s. 12(4), as substituted by para. 18 of sch.
7 to the 1998 Act, now reads:

> (4)   Nothing in section 1A of the Act shall be construed as preventing a court,
> on discharging an offender absolutely or conditionally in respect of any offence,
> from making in order for costs against the offender or imposing any disqualifica-
> tion on him or from making in respect of the offence an order under section 35 or
> 43 of this Act or section 28 of the Theft Act 1968.

Section 35 relates to compensation orders. Section 28 of the Theft Act relates to
restitution orders. There was little doubt that a restitution order could be combined
with a discharge, but this new provision makes the matter clear beyond question. The
main change here is with respect to orders for disqualification. The new wording
permits the combination of a discharge with 'any disqualification'. Prior to the 1998
Act, disqualification from driving under the Road Traffic Offenders Act 1988 could be
imposed on a discharged offender because there was specific provision to that effect
(s. 46 of the 1988 Act), but not where the driving disqualification was imposed by the
Crown Court under s. 44 of the 1973 Act, or by the magistrates' court or Crown Court
under powers introduced on a pilot basis by s. 39 of the Crime (Sentences) Act 1997. It
is now clear that these combinations are permitted. It also follows from the re-wording
of s. 12(4) that a discharge may now be combined with an order to disqualify a person
from acting as a company director (thereby reversing the effect of the decision in
Young (1990) 12 Cr App R(S) 262) and, presumably, with any one of a whole range of
existing powers to disqualify offenders, e.g., from keeping animals where the offender
has been found guilty of an offence involving animal cruelty (Pet Animals Act 1951,
s. 5; Animal Boarding Establishments Act 1963, s. 3; Protection of Animals Act
1911).

The 1998 Act contains three provisions, novel in their form and effect, to restrict the
sentencing court from using the conditional discharge on particular occasions. The
first is by s. 1(11), where a person is convicted of without reasonable excuse doing
something which he is prohibited from doing by an anti-social behaviour order, 'it
shall not be open to the court . . . to make an order under subsection (1)(b) (conditional
discharge) of section 1A [of the 1973 Act]'. The second is by s. 2(9), the parallel
offence with respect to the sex offender order. The third is by s. 66(4), where a young
person is convicted within two years of receiving a 'warning' from a police officer,
although in this last case the court may identify, and explain in open court, 'exceptional
circumstances relating to the offence or the offender' which justify the disposal of the
case by way of a conditional discharge. The legislative message here seems to be that
breach of either of the first two orders and nearly every contravention of the third will
be sufficiently serious that an order under s. 1A (where it is 'inexpedient to inflict
punishment') is inappropriate. It is rather curious that the restriction upon use of the
discharge is confined to the *conditional* discharge. The absolute discharge could still
be used in these cases. So might an alternative lenient disposal, such as a small fine, or
an order binding the offender over to keep the peace and to be of good behaviour.

Section 1C of the Powers of Criminal Courts Act 1973 states that where an order
for absolute or conditional discharge is made by the sentencing court such order shall

count as a 'conviction' for limited purposes only (for detailed discussion of this provision see the article by Wasik, M. at (1997) 113 *Law Quarterly Review* 637). Section 1C is tidied up by the 1998 Act in two respects. The first is to delete a reference to s. 1(2)(bb) of the Children and Young Persons Act 1969, which appears to have been redundant anyway. The second is to give legislative effect to the decision in *Moore* [1995] QB 353. In that case the Court of Appeal noted that there was a drafting error in s. 1C, and managed to construe 'the following provisions' in s. 1C(1)(a) to mean 'the preceding provisions'. The 1998 Act substitutes a reference to 'section 1B' for the phrase 'the following provisions'.

SEXUAL AND VIOLENT OFFENCES: EXTENDED SENTENCES

The Criminal Justice Act 1991, by s. 44, allowed the sentencing court, when sentencing an offender for a 'sexual offence', to make an order that the offender shall, upon his release from a custodial sentence, be required to serve out the full term of his sentence under supervision rather than, as would otherwise be the case, receiving unconditional release at the three-quarter point of the sentence. Lord Bingham CJ, in *A-G's Reference (No. 7 of 1996)* [1997] 1 Cr App R(S) 399, commended the use of s. 44 to sentencers. He noted that the section provided the court with additional control over the offender.

From 30 September 1998 when ss. 58 and 59 of the 1998 Act were brought into force, s. 44 of the 1991 Act will be substituted, replaced by new powers to impose 'extended' custodial sentences on offenders convicted of violent or sexual offences. The ambit of these new provisions is broader than that of the existing s. 44, in that it will apply to *violent* offences as well as to sexual offences. An extended sentence will be imposed by the court in accordance with the provisions of s. 58 of the 1998 Act, and the new s. 44 of the 1991 Act (inserted by s. 59) sets out what the effect of such an order will be upon the offender's licence arrangements. The terms 'violent offence' and 'sexual offence' have the same meanings as in s. 31 of the 1991 Act, as amended. These definitions are as follows:

According to s. 31(1) of the Criminal Justice Act 1991, a 'violent offence' is one:

which leads, or is intended or likely to lead, to a person's death or to physical injury to a person, and includes an offence which is required to be charged as arson (whether or not it would otherwise fall within this definition).

According to s. 31(1), as amended by the Criminal Justice and Public Order Act 1994, a sexual offence is:

(a)   an offence under the Sexual Offences Act 1956, other than an offence under section 30, 31 or 33 to 36 of that Act;

(b)   an offence under section 128 of the Mental Health Act 1959;

(c)   an offence under the Indecency with Children Act 1960;

(d)   an offence under section 9 of the Theft Act 1968 of burglary with intent to commit rape;

(e)   an offence under section 54 of the Criminal Law Act 1977;

(f)   an offence under the Protection of Children Act 1978;

(g)   an offence under section 1 of the Criminal Law Act 1977 of conspiracy to commit any of the offences in paragraphs (a) to (f) above;

(h)   an offence under section 1 of the Criminal Attempts Act 1981 of attempting to commit any of those offences;

(i)   an offence of inciting another to commit any of those offences.

Power to pass an extended sentence

By s. 58(1), the court may pass an extended sentence in a case in which it considers that the offender would otherwise be subject to a licence period which is inadequate for the purposes of preventing the commission by him of further offences and of securing his rehabilitation. The 'extended sentence' will be the sum of the custodial sentence which the court would otherwise have passed for the offence ('the custodial term') and a further period ('the extension period') during which the offender will be subject to a licence and which, subject to certain limitations explained below, is itself of a length the court considers necessary to achieve the purposes indicated in s. 58(1).

The general rule derived from the Criminal Justice Act 1991 is that sentence length should be commensurate with the seriousness of the offence, or the combination of the offence and other offences associated with it (s. 2(2)(a)). Exceptionally, the court may impose a longer than normal sentence where a violent or sexual offence has been committed and where it is necessary to protect the public from serious harm and the passing of a proportionate sentence would not provide adequate protection (s. 2(2)(b)). It is clear that the power to impose an extended sentence under s. 58 is available whether the offender would otherwise have received a sentence under s. 2(2)(a) or (b) of the 1991 Act. Section 58(6) states that s. 2(2) of the 1991 Act 'shall apply as if the term of an extended sentence did not include the extension period', which seems to mean that whether the court is fixing the custodial term in accordance with s. 2(2)(a) or (b) it should continue to do so in accordance with that subsection and the relevant case law. Only then, if the court considers that the licence period applicable to that custodial term would be inadequate, should it add an extension period to the custodial term, to take account of the purposes referred to in s. 58(1).

By s. 58(3) and (4), if the offence is a violent offence, the court shall not pass an extended sentence the custodial term of which is less than four years, and the extension period must not exceed five years. If the offence is a sexual offence there is no specified minimum for the length of the custodial term, but the extension period must not exceed 10 years. In no case can the extended sentence exceed the maximum sentence for the offence committed (s. 58(5)). This Act does not say which subsection applies when the crime is both violent *and* a sexual offence.

The impact on licence arrangements

Section 59 of the 1998 Act substitutes a new s. 44 into the Criminal Justice Act 1991, and this provision explains the effect which the imposition of an extended sentence will have on the offender's licence arrangements. The question whether the offender qualifies as a short-term or a long-term prisoner is determined by the overall length of the extended sentence (s. 44(7)). If the offender would otherwise have been released unconditionally (i.e., the extended sentence is for less than 12 months), the effect of an order will be that his release will be on licence until the end of the extension period (s. 44(4)). If the offender would otherwise have been released on licence (i.e., the extended period is for 12 months or more), the effect of an order is that the licence period, rather than ending at the three-quarter point of the sentence, will last from the date of his release until the end of the extension period (s. 44(3)).

Commission of further offence

If the offender commits a new offence while on licence and the court, in addition to dealing with him for the new offence, decides to order the offender's return to custody under s. 40 of the Criminal Justice Act 1991, for the whole or part of the period outstanding, it seems from s. 44(2) that the extension period must be included when determining the duration of the period to be reinstated. This means that an order under s. 40 can be made if the new offence is committed at any time within the entire licence period including the extension period.

RELEASE AND RECALL OF PRISONERS

Sections 99 to 105 contain provisions affecting in various ways the existing laws on early release and also contain a power to introduce a completely new basis for early release.

Electronically monitored home detention curfew

Curfews enforced by electronic monitoring (or tagging as it is known) have been trialled with varying degrees of success ever since they were first canvassed ten years ago in the Green Paper, *Punishment Custody and the Community* (Cm 424, 1998). The initial pilot project did not require primary legislation; it was in respect of electronic monitoring of defendants remanded on bail awaiting trial and had mixed results (see *Electronic Monitoring: The Trials and their Results*, Home Office Research Study 120, 1990).

Nevertheless powers were conferred by ss. 12 and 13 of the Criminal Justice Act 1991 to impose an electronically monitored curfew order as a sentence in its own right on a convicted defendant aged 16 or over rather than as a condition of bail prior to trial and these sections also provided for the electronic monitoring to be contracted out. Trials in Berkshire, Manchester and Norfolk were begun in 1995 and were twice extended, to March 1997 and then to March 1998. Section 41 of the Crime (Sentences) Act 1991 amended s. 12 of the 1991 Act *inter alia* so as to make it possible to make an electronically monitored curfew order on a child below the age of 16; s. 41 was brought into effect on 1 January 1998 and separate trials are currently being undertaken in relation to offenders aged under 16.

The Government clearly has begun to feel more confident about the viability and feasibility of electronic tagging and, although the Labour Party was initially opposed to tagging back in 1991, the Home Secretary announced in November 1997 (*Hansard*, Commons, 20 November 1997, col. 457) that tagging was to be extended to those who have been in prison and are nearing the end of their sentences. Thus, having started as a condition of bail before trial and then become a sentence in its own right following conviction, electronic tagging is now going to be found in a third form, as a means of serving part of a custodial sentence already passed.

The justification for the proposal was expressed by the Home Secretary in the following way:

Those who are sentenced to prison typically have lived disordered, irresponsible lives. They are poor at making sensible decisions about their own futures or those of their families. In prison of course they do not have to. However, the moment prisoners come out of prison, they have to make critical decisions about what they do with every moment of the day ... If prisoners who are serving short-term sentences are tagged towards the end of the custodial period of their nominal sentence, they can be given the opportunity to structure their lives more effectively and be swiftly brought back to prison if they breach the tagging conditions.

He then went on to say more pragmatically:

The case for introducing an element of tagging into the last part of a short-term prison sentence is very strong in any event, but it has been reinforced by the recent rise in the prison population. No-one wants to see an unnecessarily overcrowded prison system, and it would be the height of irresponsibility not to take advantage of modern technology to help prevent that. The alternatives are bound to be at the expense of constructive prison regimes, and at the expense of improving the prisoner's prospects for resettlement — in other words, at the expense of the law-abiding public.

The way in which the new provision would work was then described by the Home Secretary:

Home detention curfews will be available for prisoners who have received sentences of more than three months but less than four years' imprisonment. They will be tagged for between two weeks and two months according to the length of their original sentence. Currently, under the Criminal Justice Act 1991, such prisoners are automatically released at the half-way point of their sentence. All these prisoners will in any event shortly be back in the community.

There will be no automatic entitlement to tagging. The Prison Service will in each case conduct a risk assessment. If the prisoner fails it, he or she will continue to serve the sentence in prison until its half-way point, as now. The prison governor will set the place and times of curfew, in consultation, where needed, with the probation service. It will usually be twelve hours a day and could be more but will in no case be less than nine hours a day.

The above proposals are now provided for by ss. 99 and 100 of the 1998 Act, which insert new ss. 34A, 37A and 38A into Part II of the Criminal Justice Act 1991 (early release). The new section 34A provides the power to release on licence short-term prisoners (i.e., those serving less than four years), who are serving a term of three months or more, once they have served the 'requisite period'. The requisite period which is to be served before early release is set out in s. 34A(4) in effect as:

    (a)   (a minimum of) 30 days (for sentences between three and four months), or
    (b)   one quarter of the sentence (for sentences between four months and eight months), or
    (c)   half of the sentence less 60 days (for sentences between eight months and four years).

Since the prisoner would have been released at the half-way point of the sentence anyway and this is the point at which the curfew condition is to end (s. 37A(3)), the effect is that the period of early release on curfew will be for the period of 15 days for a person serving three months (30 days in prison followed by 15 days curfew up to the half-way point in the sentence) rising to a month for someone serving four months (one month in prison followed by one month curfew up to the half-way point in the sentence) rising to the maximum of two months (60 days) curfew for someone serving eight months or more.

The decision to restrict the provision to sentences of a minimum of three months, on the grounds that 14 days is the minimum period for which tagging can have any effect in terms of inculcating disciplined behaviour and that 30 days is the minimum period to which the actual time served in prison should be reduced, does lead to some odd effects. A convicted person sentenced to three months will spend exactly the same time in prison (30 days) as the person sentenced to four months (assuming each of them is given a favourable risk assessment after serving the minimum period of 30 days), although the latter will be subject to the curfew for a full month rather than just 15 days. More anomalous, however, is the fact that a person sentenced to less than three months (e.g., 10 weeks) may spend more time in prison (five weeks) than the person given three or four months who may actually spend only 30 days in prison.

Early release under these provisions is not available in a number of situations listed in s. 34A(2), including the case of an extended sentence under s. 58 of the 1998 Act and situations where the prisoner has been released on licence previously and failed to comply with the licence. The power to release on licence for home detention curfew is currently limited to prisoners aged 18 or over but s. 34A(5) enables this limitation to be removed by statutory instrument (in the light it would seem of the trials of curfew orders under ss. 12 and 13 of the Criminal Justice Act 1991 relating to younger offenders). The requisite period which has to be served in prison before early release can be allowed may also be amended by statutory instrument, so it is conceivable that in the future a much higher proportion of a prison sentence might be served in the form of a home detention curfew. There is obviously much more scope for this in relation to longer sentences within the overall limitation that they must be under four years. There is no power to extend the provisions so as to apply to long-term prisoners serving four years or more.

Under s. 38A(1) of the Criminal Justice Act 1991, the prisoner's licence may be revoked and the prisoner recalled to prison if it appears to the Secretary of State:

(a)   that he had failed to comply with the curfew condition;

(b)   that his whereabouts can no longer be electronically monitored at the place for the time being specified in that condition; or

(c)   that it is necessary to do so in order to protect the public from serious harm from him.

It will be noticed that s. 38(1)(b) may apply without any fault on the part of the prisoner (e.g., where monitoring equipment breaks down) and it is only s. 38A(1)(a) that renders a prisoner ineligible for home detention curfew release (at any time) in the future (see s. 34A(1)(f)).

The provisions are expected to be brought into force in early 1999 and the electronic monitoring will be contracted out. It is likely that it will be introduced area by area and s. 37A(6) makes it clear that the Secretary of State is not under any duty to ensure that electronic monitoring is introduced or available in any particular area.

Early release: two or more sentences

The Criminal Justice Act 1991 makes a sharp division between long-term and short-term prisoners which turns on whether the prisoner has been sentenced to a term of four years or less. This is important for a variety of reasons — not least that a short-term prisoner is entitled to release after serving half the sentence whereas a long-term prisoner only becomes eligible for consideration for release at that stage and only becomes entitled to release at the two-thirds point. (There are also important differences between single terms of less than 12 months and short-term sentences above that length.) Where a number of sentences are imposed, it can be vital to know whether they should be aggregated together to constitute one term (which may be over four years) or whether they are separate terms (which means that the offender may still be a short-term prisoner). As originally enacted s. 51(2) of the Criminal Justice Act 1991 simply stated that concurrent or consecutive terms 'shall be treated as a single term' but s. 101 of the 1998 Act qualifies this by adding to s. 51(2) the following condition:

... if—
    (a) the sentences were passed on the same occasion; or
    (b) where they were passed on different occasions, the person has not been released under this Part at any time during the period beginning with the first and ending with the last of those occasions.

A new s. 51(2A) makes it clear that the activation of a suspended sentence counts as the passing of the sentence for these purposes.

The effect of the new provisions is that, if the prisoner has been released before the second or subsequent sentence, even if the first sentence has still not expired in the sense that the offender is still liable to recall for breach of his licence or for further offending, the second sentence will not be aggregated with the first to form a single term. This is designed to confirm current practice, except that it appears that it differs from current practice in that the new s. 51(2) would not aggregate the terms even if by the time of the second sentence the offender has actually been recalled to prison for breach of his first licence. In this situation too, the prisoner will not have the seocnd sentence aggregated with the first to form a single term.

Section 101 of the 1998 Act also makes a number of other amendments to s. 51 of the 1991 Act to make it clear that, where terms are not treated as a single term but as separate terms, each term has to be looked at separately in terms of, e.g., early release date, licence expiry date etc., and it is the latest date of any of the sentences which is the relevant and applicable date.

Section 102 deals further with the situation where the second sentence is imposed after the offender has been given early release from his first sentence (but that sentence has not yet expired). It provides that the second sentence must not be made to commence after the expiry of the first sentence. This will certainly apply where the second sentence relates to offences committed before the early release from the first sentence. However, it seems that the position is different where the second sentence is for an offence committed after the original early release on account of which the offender is returned to prison to serve all or part of the unexpired term of the original sentence. Section 41(4) of the Criminal Justice Act 1991 still applies in this situation and the period for which the offender is ordered to be returned to prison may be ordered to be 'served before, and followed by, the sentence imposed for the new offence'. This has to be read subject to *Johnson* [1998] 1 Cr App R (S) 126, where it was held that, if the new sentence is a longer than normal sentence passed under s. 2(2) of the Criminal Justice Act 1991 for the protection of the public, it would be illogical to order the new term to start in the future when its length has been determined by reference to the period necessary to protect the public. In such a case the new sentence would have to be concurrent with the period of return to prison under the original sentence.

It should also be noted that, where a custodial sentence for a new offence is passed and made partially consecutive to the period of return to prison under the original sentence, the period of return is treated as a sentence of imprisonment and forms a single term with the new custodial sentence for the purposes of calculating whether it is a short-term or long-term sentence. However, it is only the period of return which can be aggregated with the new sentence, not the full period of the earlier sentence since that is what is prohibited by the new s. 51(2)(b) of the 1991 Act, as substituted by s. 101 of the 1998 Act.

The operation of these provisions is discussed further in Home Office Circular 44/1998 (issued on 17 September 1998) which has some extremely complex examples in appendix A. The changes came into force on 30 September 1998 and are applicable where one or more of the sentences concerned was passed on or after that date.

Recall of short-term prisoners

Section 103 repeals s. 38 of the Criminal Justice Act 1991 which provided for breach of licence by short-term prisoners to be dealt with by magistrates' courts. Instead, breach of licence will be dealt with by the Home Secretary on the recommendation of the Parole Board under s. 39 of the 1991 Act as with long-term prisoners. This provision is not intended to come into force until the year 2000.

Release on licence following recall or return to prison

Section 104 and 105 form part of a recurring theme of the Act: to ensure that people are not released from prison without some sort of supervision for the first few weeks or months.

Section 104 deals with prisoners who have been recalled to prison for breach of their licence who, under the original s. 33(3) of the Criminal Justice Act 1991, were entitled to be released unconditionally on reaching the three-quarter point of their sentence. Thus, those who had perhaps shown themselves to be most in need of supervision would be the ones who might be released without any supervision (having served a longer proportion of the sentence in prison). Section 33(3) is amended, as is s. 37(1) of the 1991 Act, so that the ultimate release following recall is on licence and so that the licence does not expire until the end of the whole sentence.

Section 105 deals with the position where rather than a recall for breach of licence there is an order to return to prison upon committing a further offence before the expiry of the original sentence. Here there is normally no problem over the licence period, since the order under s. 40 and any new sentence passed at the same time constitute another single term of imprisonment to which the provisions as to early release on licence apply. However, if the period of return plus any new sentence is less than 12 months the release at the half-way point would normally be unconditional so a new s. 40A is inserted into the 1991 Act, imposing a licence period of three months in this situation.

These provisions came into force on 30 September 1998 but only in respect of sentences for offences committed after that date.

MISCELLANEOUS SENTENCING CHANGES

Sentencing guidelines and Sentencing Advisory Panel

There is now a substantial tradition of the Court of Appeal, under the guidance of the Lord Chief Justice, of issuing sentencing guidelines for various offence categories for the assistance of the Crown Court and, to a lesser extent, magistrates' courts. Such guidelines are issued to try to address disparity in sentencing practice, and to update advice to sentencers. Recent examples include *Brewster* [1998] 1 Cr App R 220 on sentencing for domestic burglary, *Clark* [1998] 1 Cr App R(S) 95, which updates the sentencing guidelines on theft in breach of trust which were originally issued in *Barrick* (1985) 81 Cr App R 78, and *Hurley* [1998] 1 Cr App R(S) 299 on sentence levels for importation of LSD, one of a series of decisions regarding offences in relation to drugs in which the Court of Appeal has built on the guideline case of *Aramah* (1982) 76 Cr App R 190.

The provision of guidance has been an important element in the development of sentencing jurisprudence, but there are limits to what can be achieved by guideline judgments. It has often been pointed out that existing guideline judgments tend to be focused around the very serious end of the offending spectrum, since these are the cases which tend to come before the Court of Appeal most often on appeal against sentence. There is, therefore, very little guidance on some of the more middle-of-the-road offences, such as handling stolen goods and the deception offences. Again, in the nature of things, most of the guideline judgments concentrate on identifying sentencing brackets which involve lengthy terms of imprisonment. There is little appellate guidance available on community sentences, and little which provides direct assistance to the summary courts. It is perhaps not unfair to say that the Court of Appeal's guidance on the community sentence and custodial sentence thresholds established by the Criminal Justice Act 1991 has been very disappointing. A further weakness is that since each guideline judgment focuses on the sentencing pattern for an individual offence, little sense can be developed of overall sentencing patterns, and the relationship between different offences.

Section 80 of the 1998 Act, which is expected to be brought into force in Spring 1999, places the provision of guideline judgments by the Court of Appeal for the first time on a statutory footing. By s. 80(1) and (2), whenever the Court of Appeal has before it an appeal against sentence, or an Attorney-General's Reference (unduly lenient sentence), or receives a proposal from the Sentencing Advisory Panel established under s. 81 in relation to a 'category of offence', the Court must consider:

(a) whether to frame guidelines as to the sentencing of offenders for offences of the relevant category, or

(b) where such guidelines already exist, whether it would be appropriate to review them.

If the Court decides to frame or revise the guidelines, it must have regard to the need to promote consistency in sentencing, current sentence levels for the offence, the relative costs and efficacy of different sentences, the need to promote public confidence in the criminal justice system, and the views of the Sentencing Advisory Panel as communicated to the Court (s. 80(3)). The guidelines must include criteria for determining offence seriousness, including the weight to be given to previous convictions, and they must be issued either as part of the Court's judgment in the appeal which was before it or, if the guidelines are issued pursuant to a proposal from the Sentencing Advisory Panel, at the next appropriate opportunity (s. 80(6)).

Much of s. 80 (apart from the references to the Sentencing Advisory Panel) reflect existing practice. One possible criticism of the provisions as they stand is that they focus entirely on the sentencing of offenders for particular offence categories. That leaves out of account the possibility of issuing a guideline judgment on, say, the use of a particular sentencing option (the case of *George* [1984] 1 WLR 1082 on deferment of sentence would be such an example), or guidance on the meaning of s. 29(1) of the Criminal Justice Act 1991 (on the relevance of previous convictions to offence seriousness) generally, rather than just in the context of a particular offence category. The relationship between the seriousness of different offence categories, identified above as a weakness of the existing system, also cannot easily be addressed under the statutory arrangement. Presumably, however, the Court of Appeal may still issue authoratative advice and guidance on sentencing in respect of matters strictly falling outside the wording of s. 80. Section 80 places a *duty* on the Court of Appeal to issue guidance in the cases so specified, but does not prevent the Court from issuing guidance in other types of case.

As mentioned above, s. 81 establishes a Sentencing Advisory Panel, the membership of which is to be determined by the Lord Chancellor after consultation with the Home Secretary and the Lord Chief Justice. If the Court of Appeal decides to issue or revise guidelines in respect of a case which is before it, s. 81(2) provides that it shall notify the Panel accordingly. The Panel may then obtain and consider views and communicate its views to the Court. There will be pressure of time for this to be done. Appeals against sentence cause considerable anxiety for those concerned, particularly where the offender is serving a custodial sentence. Otherwise, the Panel may on its own initiative, or at the request of the Home Secretary, propose to the Court of Appeal that guidelines be formulated, and indicate its views (s. 81(3)). Again, s. 81(3) is confined to proffering views on sentencing guidelines 'for a particular category of offence', and this wording may prevent the Panel from developing guidelines on a matter such as the relevance of previous record, referred to above.

It is clear that the setting up of the Sentencing Advisory Panel owes much to the proposal for a Sentencing Council put forward by Professor Ashworth in 1983 and most fully developed in his book *Sentencing and Criminal Justice*, 2nd ed. 1995, pp. 343–51. The idea was rejected by the Conservative Government in its White Paper *Crime, Justice and Protecting the Public* in 1990. The Labour Party has always been more receptive to it, but attempts to establish a Sentencing Council at the time of passage of the Criminal Justice and Public Order Act 1994 were unsuccessful. The eventual legislative provisions in the 1998 Act seem to provide for the Panel to act as assistant and consultant to the Court of Appeal, whereas Professor Ashworth's proposal would have gone much further in charging the Council, or Panel, 'with the task of developing and keeping under review a corpus of coherent sentencing guidance for the Crown Courts and magistrates' courts' (p. 343). The usefulness of such a body in the longer term will, of course depend very much upon who is appointed to it, and the extent to which it is able to play a developmental role from out of the dominant shadow of the Court of Appeal. Nonetheless, a development which allows reference to a wider range of informed opinion in the formulation of sentencing guidelines can only be welcomed.

Parenting orders

Parenting orders have been considered in detail in Chapter 2. Such orders may be imposed, *inter alia*, on the parent or guardian of a child or young person where that child or young person has been convicted of any offence (s. 8(1)(c)). Powers to impose parenting orders will initially be made available only to certain courts on a pilot basis, from 30 September 1998.

Racial aggravation as a factor in sentencing

The provisions in the 1998 Act which create a number of racially aggravated offences have already been described and assessed in Chapter 3. In addition, s. 82 of the Act states that if the offence was racially aggravated, the court shall treat that as a factor which increases the seriousness of the offence. The section also requires that the court shall state in open court that the offence was so aggravated. It has often been stated by the Court of Appeal that racial motivation is an important aggravating factor in sentencing. One example is *Ribbans* (1995) 16 Cr App R(S) 698, where Lord Taylor CJ said that 'it cannot be too strongly emphasised by this court that where there is a racial element in a crime of violence, that is a gravely aggravating feature'. The Magistrates' Association's *Sentencing Guidelines* list racial motivation as an aggravating factor in a range of offence guidelines. It will be argued by some, therefore, that s. 82 is unnecessary. On the other hand, if the matter of racial motivation is of such importance, it may be appropriate that it should be spelled out in statutory form.

The wording of s. 82 is mandatory. It may be compared with the requirement under s. 29(2) of the Criminal Justice Act 1991 that the court 'shall' treat the fact that an offence was committed on bail as an aggravating factor, and contrasted with the provision under s. 29(1) of the 1991 Act, that the court 'may' take account of any previous convictions of the offender when determining the seriousness of the offence. Section 82 also requires that the court shall state in open court that the offence was so aggravated. This may be compared with s. 48 of the Criminal Justice and Public Order Act 1994, which requires sentencers to state in open court the fact that it has imposed a lesser punishment on the offender by virtue of the stage in the criminal proceedings at which he indicated his intention to plead guilty and the circumstances in which that indication was given.

The racial aggravation provision in s. 82 is of general application in sentencing, and came into force on 30 September 1998. It is important to note, however, that s. 82 does not apply where the court is imposing a sentence for one of the racially aggravated offences under ss. 28 to 32 of the Act. For the purposes of s. 82, the offence is 'racially aggravated' if (s. 28(1)):

(a)   at the time of committing the offence, or immediately before or after doing so, the offender demonstrates towards the victim of the offence hostility based upon the victim's membership (or presumed membership) or a racial group; or
(b)   the offence is motivated (wholly or partly) by hostility towards members of a racial group based on their membership of that group.

The term 'racial group' means a group of citizens defined by reference to race, colour, nationality (including citizenship) or ethnic or national origins (s. 28(4)).

Abolition of death penalty for treason and piracy

Until the change initiated by s. 36 of the 1998 Act, the death penalty was, at least in theory, still in existence for offences of piracy and treason. The Piracy Act 1837 provided for use of the death penalty for offences of piracy involving 'assault with intent to murder' but the Act has not been used since 1860 and it is more than 150 years since anyone has hanged for piracy. The death penalty was also available for an offence of high treason (Treason Act 1814, s. 1). It is more than 50 years since the last person was hanged for treason. Section 36 gives effect to a commitment made by the Prime Minister at a Council of Europe summit in October 1997, when the heads of government of 40 European countries agreed to work for the abolition of the death penalty across Europe. It would now appear that the UK would be in a position to ratify Protocol 6 of the European Convention on Human Rights.

Section 36 took effect from 30 September 1998.

Football spectators

Section 84 of the 1998 Act increases the penalty for the offence of failing to comply with a duty to report to a police station, imposed by a restriction order made under s. 16(4) of the Football Spectators Act 1989, from one month to six months' imprisonment, and increases the available fine from level 3 to 5. The offence of failing to comply is also made an arrestable offence. It is perhaps surprising that the government, which tabled this provision at a late stage in the passage of the Bill through Parliament, did not also seek to increase the penalties available under s. 32(3) of the Public Order Act 1986, which relates to a person subject to a football exclusion order entering premises (i.e., a football ground) in breach of that order.

Section 84 took effect from 1 August 1998.

Confiscation orders on committal for sentence

Section 83 of the 1998 Act makes a significant addition to the powers of the criminal courts to impose a confiscation order, under the CJA 1988, on an offender who has been convicted of a lucrative offence (an 'offence of a relevant description', as the

Act rather unhelpfully puts it). These powers to confiscate the offender's profits of his offending are available to the Crown Court where the offender has been convicted of any indictable offence, but to the magistrates' court only where one of a rather limited range of summary offences (listed in sch. 4 to the 1988 Act) has been committed. The effect of s. 83 is that where the offender has been dealt with in the magistrates' court, but after conviction is committed for sentence to the Crown Court, the confiscation order powers shall apply as if the offender had been convicted on indictment rather than summarily. Thus, in principle, confiscation may now be ordered in respect of any indictable offence, whether tried on indictment or summarily. Committal for sentence from the magistrates' court usually takes place in accordance with MCA 1980, s. 38. It is applicable in respect of offenders aged 18 or over in circumstances where the magistrates are of the opinion that the offence is so serious that greater punishment should be inflicted for the offence than the court has power to impose. It would appear from this that a magistrates' court may not commit under s. 38 *merely* for the purpose of allowing the Crown Court to investigate the offender's assets and, where appropriate, to make a confiscation order. Confiscation of assets is a form of ancilliary order and is clearly not a punishment. However, provided that committal for sentence is itself justified on the basis of seriousness, as s. 38 requires, the Crown Court may, in addition to imposing a sentence commensurate with the seriousness of that offence, undertake the necessary enquiries as specified in the 1988 Act and impose a confiscation order as well.

Crime and Disorder Act 1998

CHAPTER 37

ARRANGEMENT OF SECTIONS

PART I
PREVENTION OF CRIME AND DISORDER

CHAPTER I
ENGLAND AND WALES

Crime and disorder: general

PART IV
DEALING WITH OFFENDERS

CHAPTER I
ENGLAND AND WALES

Sexual or violent offenders

Offenders dependent etc. on drugs

Young offenders: reprimands and warnings

Young offenders: non-custodial orders

CHAPTER II
SCOTLAND

PART V
MISCELLANEOUS AND SUPPLEMENTAL

Crime and Disorder Act 1998

1998 CHAPTER 37

An Act to make provision for preventing crime and disorder; to create certain racially-aggravated offences; to abolish the rebuttable presumption that a child is doli incapax and to make provision as to the effect of a child's failure to give evidence at his trial; to abolish the death penalty for treason and piracy; to make changes to the criminal justice system; to make further provision for dealing with offenders; to make further provision with respect to remands and committals for trial and the release and recall of prisoners; to amend Chapter I of Part II of the Crime (Sentences) Act 1997 and to repeal Chapter I of Part III of the Crime and Punishment (Scotland) Act 1997; to make amendments designed to facilitate, or otherwise desirable in connection with, the consolidation of certain enactments; and for connected purposes. [31st July 1998]

BE IT ENACTED by the Queen's most Excellent Majesty, by and with the advice and consent of the Lords Spiritual and Temporal, and Commons, in this present Parliament assembled, and by the authority of the same, as follows:

PART I
PREVENTION OF CRIME AND DISORDER

CHAPTER I
ENGLAND AND WALES

Crime and disorder: general

1. Anti-social behaviour orders

(1) An application for an order under this section may be made by a relevant authority if it appears to the authority that the following conditions are fulfilled with respect to any person aged 10 or over, namely—

(a) that the person has acted, since the commencement date, in an anti-social manner, that is to say, in a manner that caused or was likely to cause harassment, alarm or distress to one or more persons not of the same household as himself; and

(b) that such an order is necessary to protect persons in the local government area in which the harassment, alarm or distress was caused or was likely to be caused from further anti-social acts by him;

and in this section 'relevant authority' means the council for the local government area or any chief officer of police any part of whose police area lies within that area.

(2)   A relevant authority shall not make such an application without consulting each other relevant authority.

(3)   Such an application shall be made by complaint to the magistrates' court whose commission area includes the place where it is alleged that the harassment, alarm or distress was caused or was likely to be caused.

(4)   If, on such an application, it is proved that the conditions mentioned in subsection (1) above are fulfilled, the magistrates' court may make an order under this section (an 'anti-social behaviour order') which prohibits the defendant from doing anything described in the order.

(5)   For the purpose of determining whether the condition mentioned in subsection (1)(a) above is fulfilled, the court shall disregard any act of the defendant which he shows was reasonable in the circumstances.

(6)   The prohibitions that may be imposed by an anti-social behaviour order are those necessary for the purpose of protecting from further antisocial acts by the defendant—

(a)   persons in the local government area; and

(b)   persons in any adjoining local government area specified in the application for the order;

and a relevant authority shall not specify an adjoining local government area in the application without consulting the council for that area and each chief officer of police any part of whose police area lies within that area.

(7)   An anti-social behaviour order shall have effect for a period (not less than two years) specified in the order or until further order.

(8)   Subject to subsection (9) below, the applicant or the defendant may apply by complaint to the court which made an anti-social behaviour order for it to be varied or discharged by a further order.

(9)   Except with the consent of both parties, no anti-social behaviour order shall be discharged before the end of the period of two years beginning with the date of service of the order.

(10)   If without reasonable excuse a person does anything which he is prohibited from doing by an anti-social behaviour order, he shall be liable—

(a)   on summary conviction, to imprisonment for a term not exceeding six months or to a fine not exceeding the statutory maximum, or to both; or

(b)   on conviction on indictment, to imprisonment for a term not exceeding five years or to a fine, or to both.

(11)   Where a person is convicted of an offence under subsection (10) above, it shall not be open to the court by or before which he is so convicted to make an order under subsection (1)(b) (conditional discharge) of section 1A of the Powers of Criminal Courts Act 1973 ('the 1973 Act') in respect of the offence.

(12)   In this section—

'the commencement date' means the date of the commencement of this section;

'local government area' means—

(a)   in relation to England, a district or London borough, the City of London, the Isle of Wight and the Isles of Scilly;

(b)   in relation to Wales, a county or county borough.

2. Sex offender orders

(1) If it appears to a chief officer of police that the following conditions are fulfilled with respect to any person in his police area, namely—

    (a)   that the person is a sex offender; and

    (b)   that the person has acted, since the relevant date, in such a way as to give reasonable cause to believe that an order under this section is necessary to protect the public from serious harm from him,

the chief officer may apply for an order under this section to be made in respect of the person.

(2) Such an application shall be made by complaint to the magistrates' court whose commission area includes any place where it is alleged that the defendant acted in such a way as is mentioned in subsection (1)(b) above.

(3) If, on such an application, it is proved that the conditions mentioned in subsection (1) above are fulfilled, the magistrates' court may make an order under this section (a 'sex offender order') which prohibits the defendant from doing anything described in the order.

(4) The prohibitions that may be imposed by a sex offender order are those necessary for the purpose of protecting the public from serious harm from the defendant.

(5) A sex offender order shall have effect for a period (not less than five years) specified in the order or until further order; and while such an order has effect, Part I of the Sex Offenders Act 1997 shall have effect as if—

    (a)   the defendant were subject to the notification requirements of that Part; and

    (b)   in relation to the defendant, the relevant date (within the meaning of that Part) were the date of service of the order.

(6) Subject to subsection (7) below, the applicant or the defendant may apply by complaint to the court which made a sex offender order for it to be varied or discharged by a further order.

(7) Except with the consent of both parties, no sex offender order shall be discharged before the end of the period of five years beginning with the date of service of the order.

(8) If without reasonable excuse a person does anything which he is prohibited from doing by a sex offender order, he shall be liable—

    (a)   on summary conviction, to imprisonment for a term not exceeding six months or to a fine not exceeding the statutory maximum, or to both; or

    (b)   on conviction on indictment, to imprisonment for a term not exceeding five years or to a fine, or to both.

(9) Where a person is convicted of an offence under subsection (8) above, it shall not be open to the court by or before which he is so convicted to make an order under subsection (1)(b) (conditional discharge) of section 1A of the 1973 Act in respect of the offence.

3. Sex offender orders: supplemental

(1) In section 2 above and this section 'sex offender' means a person who—

    (a)   has been convicted of a sexual offence to which Part I of the Sex Offenders Act 1997 applies;

(b)   has been found not guilty of such an offence by reason of insanity, or found to be under a disability and to have done the act charged against him in respect of such an offence;

(c)   has been cautioned by a constable, in England and Wales or Northern Ireland, in respect of such an offence which, at the time when the caution was given, he had admitted; or

(d)   has been punished under the law in force in a country or territory outside the United Kingdom for an act which—

(i)   constituted an offence under that law; and

(ii)   would have constituted a sexual offence to which that Part applies if it had been done in any part of the United Kingdom.

(2)   In subsection (1) of section 2 above 'the relevant date', in relation to a sex offender, means—

(a)   the date or, as the case may be, the latest date on which he has been convicted, found, cautioned or punished as mentioned in subsection (1) above; or

(b)   if later, the date of the commencement of that section.

(3)   Subsections (2) and (3) of section 6 of the Sex Offenders Act 1997 apply for the construction of references in subsections (1) and (2) above as they apply for the construction of references in Part I of that Act.

(4)   In subsections (1) and (2) above, any reference to a person having been cautioned shall be construed as including a reference to his having been reprimanded or warned (under section 65 below) as a child or young person.

(5)   An act punishable under the law in force in any country or territory outside the United Kingdom constitutes an offence under that law for the purposes of subsection (1) above, however it is described in that law.

(6)   Subject to subsection (7) below, the condition in subsection (1)(d)(i) above shall be taken to be satisfied unless, not later than rules of court may provide, the defendant serves on the applicant a notice—

(a)   stating that, on the facts as alleged with respect to the act in question, the condition is not in his opinion satisfied;

(b)   showing his grounds for that opinion; and

(c)   requiring the applicant to show that it is satisfied.

(7)   The court, if it thinks fit, may permit the defendant to require the applicant to show that the condition is satisfied without the prior service of a notice under subsection (6) above.

4. Appeals against orders

(1)   An appeal shall lie to the Crown Court against the making by a magistrates' court of an anti-social behaviour order or sex offender order.

(2)   On such an appeal the Crown Court—

(a)   may make such orders as may be necessary to give effect to its determination of the appeal; and

(b)   may also make such incidental or consequential orders as appear to it to be just.

(3)   Any order of the Crown Court made on an appeal under this section (other than one directing that an application be re-heard by a magistrates' court) shall, for the purposes of section 1(8) or 2(6) above, be treated as if it were an order of the magistrates' court from which the appeal was brought and not an order of the Crown Court.

Crime and disorder strategies

5. Authorities responsible for strategies

(1) Subject to the provisions of this section, the functions conferred by section 6 below shall be exercisable in relation to each local government area by the responsible authorities, that is to say—

(a) the council for the area and, where the area is a district and the council is not a unitary authority, the council for the county which includes the district; and

(b) every chief officer of police any part of whose police area lies within the area.

(2) In exercising those functions, the responsible authorities shall act in co-operation with the following persons and bodies, namely—

(a) every police authority any part of whose police area lies within the area;

(b) every probation committee or health authority any part of whose area lies within the area; and

(c) every person or body of a description which is for the time being prescribed by order of the Secretary of State under this subsection;

and it shall be the duty of those persons and bodies to co-operate in the exercise by the responsible authorities of those functions.

(3) The responsible authorities shall also invite the participation in their exercise of those functions of at least one person or body of each description which is for the time being prescribed by order of the Secretary of State under this subsection.

(4) In this section and sections 6 and 7 below 'local government area' means—

(a) in relation to England, each district or London borough, the City of London, the Isle of Wight and the Isles of Scilly;

(b) in relation to Wales, each county or county borough.

6. Formulation and implementation of strategies

(1) The responsible authorities for a local government area shall, in accordance with the provisions of section 5 above and this section, formulate and implement, for each relevant period, a strategy for the reduction of crime and disorder in the area.

(2) Before formulating a strategy, the responsible authorities shall—

(a) carry out a review of the levels and patterns of crime and disorder in the area (taking due account of the knowledge and experience of persons in the area);

(b) prepare an analysis of the results of that review;

(c) publish in the area a report of that analysis; and

(d) obtain the views on that report of persons or bodies in the area (including those of a description prescribed by order under section 5(3) above), whether by holding public meetings or otherwise.

(3) In formulating a strategy, the responsible authorities shall have regard to the analysis prepared under subsection (2)(b) above and the views obtained under subsection (2)(d) above.

(4) A strategy shall include—

(a) objectives to be pursued by the responsible authorities, by co-operating persons or bodies or, under agreements with the responsible authorities, by other persons or bodies; and

(b) long-term and short-term performance targets for measuring the extent to which such objectives are achieved.

(5) After formulating a strategy, the responsible authorities shall publish in the area a document which includes details of—

(a) co-operating persons and bodies;

(b) the review carried out under subsection (2)(a) above;

(c) the report published under subsection (2)(c) above; and

(d) the strategy, including in particular—

(i) the objectives mentioned in subsection (4)(a) above and, in each case, the authorities, persons or bodies by whom they are to be pursued; and

(ii) the performance targets mentioned in subsection (4)(b) above.

(6) While implementing a strategy, the responsible authorities shall keep it under review with a view to monitoring its effectiveness and making any changes to it that appear necessary or expedient.

(7) In this section—

'co-operating persons or bodies' means persons or bodies co-operating in the exercise of the responsible authorities' functions under this section;

'relevant period' means—

(a) the period of three years beginning with such day as the Secretary of State may by order appoint; and

(b) each subsequent period of three years.

7. Supplemental

(1) The responsible authorities for a local government area shall, whenever so required by the Secretary of State, submit to the Secretary of State a report on such matters connected with the exercise of their functions under section 6 above as may be specified in the requirement.

(2) A requirement under subsection (1) above may specify the form in which a report is to be given.

(3) The Secretary of State may arrange, or require the responsible authorities to arrange, for a report under subsection (1) above to be published in such manner as appears to him to be appropriate.

Youth crime and disorder

8. Parenting orders

(1) This section applies where, in any court proceedings—

(a) a child safety order is made in respect of a child;

(b) an anti-social behaviour order or sex offender order is made in respect of a child or young person;

(c) a child or young person is convicted of an offence; or

(d) a person is convicted of an offence under section 443 (failure to comply with school attendance order) or section 444 (failure to secure regular attendance at school of registered pupil) of the Education Act 1996.

(2) Subject to subsection (3) and section 9(1) below, if in the proceedings the court is satisfied that the relevant condition is fulfilled, it may make a parenting order in respect of a person who is a parent or guardian of the child or young person or, as the case may be, the person convicted of the offence under section 443 or 444 ('the parent').

(3) A court shall not make a parenting order unless it has been notified by the Secretary of State that arrangements for implementing such orders are available in

the area in which it appears to the court that the parent resides or will reside and the notice has not been withdrawn.

(4)   A parenting order is an order which requires the parent—

(a)   to comply, for a period not exceeding twelve months, with such requirements as are specified in the order; and

(b)   subject to subsection (5) below, to attend, for a concurrent period not exceeding three months and not more than once in any week, such counselling or guidance sessions as may be specified in directions given by the responsible officer;

and in this subsection 'week' means a period of seven days beginning with a Sunday.

(5)   A parenting order may, but need not, include such a requirement as is mentioned in subsection (4)(b) above in any case where such an order has been made in respect of the parent on a previous occasion.

(6)   The relevant condition is that the parenting order would be desirable in the interests of preventing—

(a)   in a case falling within paragraph (a) or (b) of subsection (1) above, any repetition of the kind of behaviour which led to the child safety order, anti-social behaviour order or sex offender order being made;

(b)   in a case falling within paragraph (c) of that subsection, the commission of any further offence by the child or young person;

(c)   in a case falling within paragraph (d) of that subsection, the commission of any further offence under section 443 or 444 of the Education Act 1996.

(7)   The requirements that may be specified under subsection (4)(a) above are those which the court considers desirable in the interests of preventing any such repetition or, as the case may be, the commission of any such further offence.

(8)   In this section and section 9 below 'responsible officer', in relation to a parenting order, means one of the following who is specified in the order, namely—

(a)   a probation officer;

(b)   a social worker of a local authority social services department; and

(c)   a member of a youth offending team.

9.   Parenting orders: supplemental

(1)   Where a person under the age of 16 is convicted of an offence, the court by or before which he is so convicted—

(a)   if it is satisfied that the relevant condition is fulfilled, shall make a parenting order; and

(b)   if it is not so satisfied, shall state in open court that it is not and why it is not.

(2)   Before making a parenting order—

(a)   in a case falling within paragraph (a) of subsection (1) of section 8 above;

(b)   in a case falling within paragraph (b) or (c) of that subsection, where the person concerned is under the age of 16; or

(c)   in a case falling within paragraph (d) of that subsection, where the person to whom the offence related is under that age,

a court shall obtain and consider information about the person's family circumstances and the likely effect of the order on those circumstances.

(3)   Before making a parenting order, a court shall explain to the parent in ordinary language—

(a)   the effect of the order and of the requirements proposed to be included in it;

(b)   the consequences which may follow (under subsection (7) below) if he fails to comply with any of those requirements; and

(c)   that the court has power (under subsection (5) below) to review the order on the application either of the parent or of the responsible officer.

(4)   Requirements specified in, and directions given under, a parenting order shall, as far as practicable, be such as to avoid—

(a)   any conflict with the parent's religious beliefs; and

(b)   any interference with the times, if any, at which he normally works or attends an educational establishment.

(5)   If while a parenting order is in force it appears to the court which made it, on the application of the responsible officer or the parent, that it is appropriate to make an order under this subsection, the court may make an order discharging the parenting order or varying it—

(a)   by cancelling any provision included in it; or

(b)   by inserting in it (either in addition to or in substitution for any of its provisions) any provision that could have been included in the order if the court had then had power to make it and were exercising the power.

(6)   Where an application under subsection (5) above for the discharge of a parenting order is dismissed, no further application for its discharge shall be made under that subsection by any person except with the consent of the court which made the order.

(7)   If while a parenting order is in force the parent without reasonable excuse fails to comply with any requirement included in the order, or specified in directions given by the responsible officer, he shall be liable on summary conviction to a fine not exceeding level 3 on the standard scale.

10.   Appeals against parenting orders

(1)   An appeal shall lie—

(a)   to the High Court against the making of a parenting order by virtue of paragraph (a) of subsection (1) of section 8 above; and

(b)   to the Crown Court against the making of a parenting order by virtue of paragraph (b) of that subsection.

(2)   On an appeal under subsection (1) above the High Court or the Crown Court—

(a)   may make such orders as may be necessary to give effect to its determination of the appeal; and

(b)   may also make such incidental or consequential orders as appear to it to be just.

(3)   Any order of the High Court or the Crown Court made on an appeal under subsection (1) above (other than one directing that an application be re-heard by a magistrates' court) shall, for the purposes of subsections (5) to (7) of section 9 above, be treated as if it were an order of the court from which the appeal was brought and not an order of the High Court or the Crown Court.

(4)   A person in respect of whom a parenting order is made by virtue of section 8(1)(c) above shall have the same right of appeal against the making of the order as if—

(a)   the offence that led to the making of the order were an offence committed by him; and

(b)   the order were a sentence passed on him for the offence.

(5)   A person in respect of whom a parenting order is made by virtue of section 8(1)(d) above shall have the same right of appeal against the making of the order as if the order were a sentence passed on him for the offence that led to the making of the order.

(6)   The Lord Chancellor may by order make provision as to the circumstances in which appeals under subsection (1)(a) above may be made against decisions taken by courts on questions arising in connection with the transfer, or proposed transfer, of proceedings by virtue of any order under paragraph 2 of Schedule 11 (jurisdiction) to the Children Act 1989 ('the 1989 Act').

(7)   Except to the extent provided for in any order made under subsection (6) above, no appeal may be made against any decision of a kind mentioned in that subsection.

11.   Child safety orders

(1)   Subject to subsection (2) below, if a magistrates' court, on the application of a local authority, is satisfied that one or more of the conditions specified in subsection (3) below are fulfilled with respect to a child under the age of 10, it may make an order (a 'child safety order') which—

(a)   places the child, for a period (not exceeding the permitted maximum) specified in the order, under the supervision of the responsible officer; and

(b)   requires the child to comply with such requirements as are so specified.

(2)   A court shall not make a child safety order unless it has been notified by the Secretary of State that arrangements for implementing such orders are available in the area in which it appears that the child resides or will reside and the notice has not been withdrawn.

(3)   The conditions are—

(a)   that the child has committed an act which, if he had been aged 10 or over, would have constituted an offence;

(b)   that a child safety order is necessary for the purpose of preventing the commission by the child of such an act as is mentioned in paragraph (a) above;

(c)   that the child has contravened a ban imposed by a curfew notice; and

(d)   that the child has acted in a manner that caused or was likely to cause harassment, alarm or distress to one or more persons not of the same household as himself.

(4)   The maximum period permitted for the purposes of subsection (1)(a) above is three months or, where the court is satisfied that the circumstances of the case are exceptional, 12 months.

(5)   The requirements that may be specified under subsection (1)(b) above are those which the court considers desirable in the interests of—

(a)   securing that the child receives appropriate care, protection and support and is subject to proper control; or

(b)   preventing any repetition of the kind of behaviour which led to the child safety order being made.

(6)   Proceedings under this section or section 12 below shall be family proceedings for the purposes of the 1989 Act or section 65 of the Magistrates' Courts Act 1980 ('the 1980 Act'); and the standard of proof applicable to such proceedings shall be that applicable to civil proceedings.

(7) In this section 'local authority' has the same meaning as in the 1989 Act.

(8) In this section and section 12 below, 'responsible officer', in relation to a child safety order, means one of the following who is specified in the order, namely—

(a) a social worker of a local authority social services department; and

(b) a member of a youth offending team.

12. Child safety orders: supplemental

(1) Before making a child safety order, a magistrates' court shall obtain and consider information about the child's family circumstances and the likely effect of the order on those circumstances.

(2) Before making a child safety order, a magistrates' court shall explain to the parent or guardian of the child in ordinary language—

(a) the effect of the order and of the requirements proposed to be included in it;

(b) the consequences which may follow (under subsection (6) below) if the child fails to comply with any of those requirements; and

(c) that the court has power (under subsection (4) below) to review the order on the application either of the parent or guardian or of the responsible officer.

(3) Requirements included in a child safety order shall, as far as practicable, be such as to avoid—

(a) any conflict with the parent's religious beliefs; and

(b) any interference with the times, if any, at which the child normally attends school.

(4) If while a child safety order is in force in respect of a child it appears to the court which made it, on the application of the responsible officer or a parent or guardian of the child, that it is appropriate to make an order under this subsection, the court may make an order discharging the child safety order or varying it—

(a) by cancelling any provision included in it; or

(b) by inserting in it (either in addition to or in substitution for any of its provisions) any provision that could have been included in the order if the court had then had power to make it and were exercising the power.

(5) Where an application under subsection (4) above for the discharge of a child safety order is dismissed, no further application for its discharge shall be made under that subsection by any person except with the consent of the court which made the order.

(6) Where a child safety order is in force and it is proved to the satisfaction of the court which made it or another magistrates' court acting for the same petty sessions area, on the application of the responsible officer, that the child has failed to comply with any requirement included in the order, the court—

(a) may discharge the order and make in respect of him a care order under subsection (1)(a) of section 31 of the 1989 Act; or

(b) may make an order varying the order

(i) by cancelling any provision included in it; or

(ii) by inserting in it (either in addition to or in substitution for any of its provisions) any provision that could have been included in the order if the court had then had power to make it and were exercising the power.

(7) Subsection (6)(a) above applies whether or not the court is satisfied that the conditions mentioned in section 31(2) of the 1989 Act are fulfilled.

13. Appeals against child safety orders

(1) An appeal shall lie to the High Court against the making by a magistrates' court of a child safety order; and on such an appeal the High Court—

(a) may make such orders as may be necessary to give effect to its determination of the appeal; and

(b) may also make such incidental or consequential orders as appear to it to be just.

(2) Any order of the High Court made on an appeal under this section (other than one directing that an application be re-heard by a magistrates' court) shall, for the purposes of subsections (4) to (6) of section 12 above, be treated as if it were an order of the magistrates' court from which the appeal was brought and not an order of the High Court.

(3) Subsections (6) and (7) of section 10 above shall apply for the purposes of subsection (1) above as they apply for the purposes of subsection (1)(a) of that section.

14. Local child curfew schemes

(1) A local authority may make a scheme (a 'local child curfew scheme') for enabling the authority—

(a) subject to and in accordance with the provisions of the scheme; and

(b) if, after such consultation as is required by the scheme, the authority considers it necessary to do so for the purpose of maintaining order,

to give a notice imposing, for a specified period (not exceeding 90 days), a ban to which subsection (2) below applies.

(2) This subsection applies to a ban on children of specified ages (under 10) being in a public place within a specified area—

(a) during specified hours (between 9 pm and 6 am); and

(b) otherwise than under the effective control of a parent or a responsible person aged 18 or over.

(3) Before making a local child curfew scheme, a local authority shall consult—

(a) every chief officer of police any part of whose police area lies within its area; and

(b) such other persons or bodies as it considers appropriate.

(4) A local child curfew scheme shall be made under the common seal of the local authority and shall not have effect until it is confirmed by the Secretary of State.

(5) The Secretary of State—

(a) may confirm, or refuse to confirm, a local child curfew scheme submitted under this section for confirmation; and

(b) may fix the date on which such a scheme is to come into operation;

and if no date is so fixed, the scheme shall come into operation at the end of the period of one month beginning with the date of its confirmation.

(6) A notice given under a local child curfew scheme (a 'curfew notice') may specify different hours in relation to children of different ages.

(7) A curfew notice shall be given—

(a) by posting the notice in some conspicuous place or places within the specified area; and

(b) in such other manner, if any, as appears to the local authority to be desirable for giving publicity to the notice.

(8) In this section—

'local authority' means—

(a) in relation to England, the council of a district or London borough, the Common Council of the City of London, the Council of the Isle of Wight and the Council of the Isles of Scilly;

(b) in relation to Wales, the council of a county or county borough;

'public place' has the same meaning as in Part II of the Public Order Act 1986.

15. Contravention of curfew notices

(1) Subsections (2) and (3) below apply where a constable has reasonable cause to believe that a child is in contravention of a ban imposed by a curfew notice.

(2) The constable shall, as soon as practicable, inform the local authority for the area that the child has contravened the ban.

(3) The constable may remove the child to the child's place of residence unless he has reasonable cause to believe that the child would, if removed to that place, be likely to suffer significant harm.

(4) In subsection (1) of section 47 of the 1989 Act (local authority's duty to investigate)—

(a) in paragraph (a), after sub-paragraph (ii) there shall be inserted the following sub-paragraph—

'(iii) has contravened a ban imposed by a curfew notice within the meaning of Chapter I of Part I of the Crime and Disorder Act 1998; or'; and

(b) at the end there shall be inserted the following paragraph—

'In the case of a child falling within paragraph (a)(iii) above, the enquiries shall be commenced as soon as practicable and, in any event, within 48 hours of the authority receiving the information.'

16. Removal of truants to designated premises etc.

(1) This section applies where a local authority—

(a) designates premises in a police area ('designated premises') as premises to which children and young persons of compulsory school age may be removed under this section; and

(b) notifies the chief officer of police for that area of the designation.

(2) A police officer of or above the rank of superintendent may direct that the powers conferred on a constable by subsection (3) below—

(a) shall be exercisable as respects any area falling within the police area and specified in the direction; and

(b) shall be so exercisable during a period so specified;

and references in that subsection to a specified area and a specified period shall be construed accordingly.

(3) If a constable has reasonable cause to believe that a child or young person found by him in a public place in a specified area during a specified period—

(a) is of compulsory school age; and

(b) is absent from a school without lawful authority,

the constable may remove the child or young person to designated premises, or to the school from which he is so absent.

(4) A child's or young person's absence from a school shall be taken to be without lawful authority unless it falls within subsection (3) (leave, sickness,

unavoidable cause or day set apart for religious observance) of section 444 of the Education Act 1996.

(5) In this section—
'local authority' means—

(a) in relation to England, a county council, a district council whose district does not form part of an area that has a county council, a London borough council or the Common Council of the City of London;

(b) in relation to Wales, a county council or a county borough council;

'public place' has the same meaning as in section 14 above;

'school' has the same meaning as in the Education Act 1996.

Miscellaneous and supplemental

17. Duty to consider crime and disorder implications

(1) Without prejudice to any other obligation imposed on it, it shall be the duty of each authority to which this section applies to exercise its various functions with due regard to the likely effect of the exercise of those functions on, and the need to do all that it reasonably can to prevent, crime and disorder in its area.

(2) This section applies to a local authority, a joint authority, a police authority, a National Park authority and the Broads Authority.

(3) In this section—
'local authority' means a local authority within the meaning given by section 270(1) of the Local Government Act 1972 or the Common Council of the City of London;

'joint authority' has the same meaning as in the Local Government Act 1985;

'National Park authority' means an authority established under section 63 of the Environment Act 1995.

18. Interpretation etc. of Chapter I

(1) In this Chapter—
'anti-social behaviour order' has the meaning given by section 1(4) above;

'chief officer of police' has the meaning given by section 101(1) of the Police Act 1996;

'child safety order' has the meaning given by section 11(1) above;

'curfew notice' has the meaning given by section 14(6) above;

'local child curfew scheme' has the meaning given by section 14(1) above;

'parenting order' has the meaning given by section 8(4) above;

'police area' has the meaning given by section 1(2) of the Police Act 1996;

'police authority' has the meaning given by section 101(1) of that Act;

'responsible officer'—

(a) in relation to a parenting order, has the meaning given by section 8(8) above;

(b) in relation to a child safety order, has the meaning given by section 11(8) above;

'sex offender order' has the meaning given by section 2(3) above.

(2) In this Chapter, unless the contrary intention appears, expressions which are also used in Part I of the Criminal Justice Act 1991 ('the 1991 Act') have the same meanings as in that Part.

(3)   Where directions under a parenting order are to be given by a probation officer, the probation officer shall be an officer appointed for or assigned to the petty sessions area within which it appears to the court that the child or, as the case may be, the parent resides or will reside.

(4)   Where the supervision under a child safety order is to be provided, or directions under a parenting order are to be given, by—

(a)   a social worker of a local authority social services department; or

(b)   a member of a youth offending team,

the social worker or member shall be a social worker of, or a member of a youth offending team established by, the local authority within whose area it appears to the court that the child or, as the case may be, the parent resides or will reside.

(5)   For the purposes of this Chapter the Inner Temple and the Middle Temple form part of the City of London.

CHAPTER II
SCOTLAND

19.   Anti-social behaviour orders

(1)   A local authority may make an application for an order under this section if it appears to the authority that the following conditions are fulfilled with respect to any person of or over the age of 16, namely—

(a)   that the person has—

(i)   acted in an anti-social manner, that is to say, in a manner that caused or was likely to cause alarm or distress; or

(ii)   pursued a course of anti-social conduct, that is to say, pursued a course of conduct that caused or was likely to cause alarm or distress,

to one or more persons not of the same household as himself in the authority's area (and in this section 'anti-social acts' and 'anti-social conduct' shall be construed accordingly); and

(b)   that such an order is necessary to protect persons in the authority's area from further anti-social acts or conduct by him.

(2)   An application under subsection (1) above shall be made by summary application to the sheriff within whose sheriffdom the alarm or distress was alleged to have been caused or to have been likely to be caused.

(3)   On an application under subsection (1) above, the sheriff may, if he is satisfied that the conditions mentioned in that subsection are fulfilled, make an order under this section (an 'anti-social behaviour order') which, for the purpose of protecting persons in the area of the local authority from further anti-social acts or conduct by the person against whom the order is sought, prohibits him from doing anything described in the order.

(4)   For the purpose of determining whether the condition mentioned in subsection (1)(a) is fulfilled, the sheriff shall disregard any act of the person in respect of whom the application is made which that person shows was reasonable in the circumstances.

(5)   This section does not apply in relation to anything done before the commencement of this section.

(6)   Nothing in this section shall prevent a local authority from instituting any legal proceedings otherwise than under this section against any person in relation to any anti-social act or conduct.

(7)　In this section 'conduct' includes speech and a course of conduct must involve conduct on at least two occasions.

(8)　In this section and section 21 below 'local authority' means a council constituted under section 2 of the Local Government etc. (Scotland) Act 1994 and any reference to the area of such an authority is a reference to the local government area within the meaning of that Act for which it is so constituted.

20.　Sex offender orders

(1)　An application for an order under this section may be made by a chief constable if it appears to him that the conditions mentioned in subsection (2) below are fulfilled with respect to any person in the area of his police force.

(2)　The conditions are—

    (a)　that the person in respect of whom the application for the order is made is—

        (i)　of or over the age of 16 years; and

        (ii)　a sex offender; and

    (b)　that the person has acted, since the relevant date, in such a way as to give reasonable cause to believe that an order under this section is necessary to protect the public from serious harm from him.

(3)　An application under subsection (1) above shall be made by summary application to the sheriff within whose sheriffdom the person is alleged to have acted as mentioned in subsection (2)(b) above.

(4)　On an application under subsection (1) above the sheriff may—

    (a)　pending the determination of the application, make any such interim order as he considers appropriate; and

    (b)　if he is satisfied that the conditions mentioned in subsection (2) above are fulfilled, make an order under this section ('a sex offender order') which prohibits the person in respect of whom it is made from doing anything described in the order.

(5)　The prohibitions that may be imposed by an order made under subsection (4) above are those necessary for the purpose of protecting the public from serious harm from the person in respect of whom the order is made.

(6)　While a sex offender order has effect, Part I of the Sex Offenders Act 1997 shall have effect as if—

    (a)　the person in respect of whom the order has been obtained were subject to the notification requirements of that Part; and

    (b)　in relation to that person, the relevant date (within the meaning of that Part) were the date on which the copy of the order was given or delivered to that person in accordance with subsections (8) and (9) of section 21 below.

(7)　Section 3 above applies for the purposes of this section as it applies for the purposes of section 2 above with the following modifications—

    (a)　any reference in that section to the defendant shall be construed as a reference to the person in respect of whom the order is sought; and

    (b)　in subsection (2) of that section, the reference to subsection (1) of the said section 2 shall be construed as a reference to subsection (2)(b) of this section.

(8)　A constable may arrest without warrant a person whom he reasonably suspects of doing, or having done, anything prohibited by an order under subsection (4)(a) above or a sex offender order.

21.　Procedural provisions with respect to orders

(1)　Before making an application under—

(a)   section 19(1) above;

(b)   subsection (7)(b)(i) below,

the local authority shall consult the relevant chief constable.

(2)   Before making an application under section 20(1) above or subsection (7)(b)(i) below, the chief constable shall consult the local authority within whose area the person in respect of whom the order is sought is for the time being.

(3)   In subsection (1) above 'relevant chief constable' means the chief constable of the police force maintained under the Police (Scotland) Act 1967 the area of which includes the area of the local authority making the application.

(4)   A failure to comply with subsection (1) or (2) above shall not affect ,the validity of an order made on any application to which either of those subsections applies.

(5)   A record of evidence shall be kept on any summary application under section 19 or 20 above or subsection (7)(b) below.

(6)   Subsections (7) to (9) below apply to anti-social behaviour orders and sex offender orders and subsections (8) and (9) below apply to an order made under section 20(4)(a) above.

(7)   An order to which this subsection applies—

(a)   shall have effect for a period specified in the order or indefinitely; and

(b)   may at any time be varied or revoked on a summary application by—

(i)   the local authority or, as the case may be, chief constable who obtained the order; or

(ii)   the person subject to the order.

(8)   The clerk of the court by which an order to which this subsection applies is made or varied shall cause a copy of the order as so made or varied to be—

(a)   given to the person named in the order; or

(b)   sent to the person so named by registered post or by the recorded delivery service.

(9)   An acknowledgement or certificate of delivery of a letter sent under subsection (8)(b) above issued by the Post Office shall be sufficient evidence of the delivery of the letter on the day specified in such acknowledgement or certificate.

(10)   Where an appeal is lodged against the determination of an application under section 19 or 20 above or subsection (7)(b) above, any order made on the application shall, without prejudice to the determination of an application under subsection (7)(b) above made after the lodging of the appeal, continue to have effect pending the disposal of the appeal.

22.   Offences in connection with breach of orders

(1)   Subject to subsection (3) below, if without reasonable excuse a person breaches an anti-social behaviour order by doing anything which he is prohibited from doing by the order, he shall be guilty of an offence and shall be liable—

(a)   on summary conviction, to a term of imprisonment not exceeding six months or to a fine not exceeding the statutory maximum or to both; or

(b)   on conviction on indictment, to imprisonment for a term not exceeding five years or to a fine or to both.

(2)   Subsection (3) applies where—

(a)   the breach of the anti-social behaviour order referred to in subsection (1) above consists in the accused having acted in a manner prohibited by the order which constitutes a separate offence (in this section referred to as the 'separate offence'); and

(b) the accused has been charged with that separate offence.

(3) Where this subsection applies, the accused shall not be liable to be proceeded against for an offence under subsection (1) above but, subject to subsection (4) below, the court which sentences him for that separate offence shall, in determining the appropriate sentence or disposal for that offence, have regard to—

(a) the fact that the offence was committed by him while subject to an anti-social behaviour order;

(b) the number of such orders to which he was subject at the time of the commission of the offence;

(c) any previous conviction of the accused of an offence under subsection (1) above; and

(d) the extent to which the sentence or disposal in respect of any such previous conviction of the accused differed, by virtue of this subsection, from that which the court would have imposed but for this subsection.

(4) The court shall not, under subsection (3) above, have regard to the fact that the separate offence was committed while the accused was subject to an anti-social behaviour order unless that fact is libelled in the indictment or, as the case may be, specified in the complaint.

(5) The fact that the separate offence was committed while the accused was subject to an anti-social behaviour order shall, unless challenged—

(a) in the case of proceedings on indictment, by giving notice of a preliminary objection under paragraph (b) of section 72 of the Criminal Procedure (Scotland) Act 1995 ('the 1995 Act') or under that paragraph as applied by section 71(2) of that Act; or

(b) in summary proceedings, by preliminary objection before his plea is recorded,
be held as admitted.

(6) Subject to subsection (7) below, subsections (1) to (5) above apply in relation to an order under section 20(4)(a) above and to a sex offender order as they apply in relation to an anti-social behaviour order.

(7) Subsection (2) above as applied for the purposes of subsection (6) above shall have effect with the substitution of the words 'at the time at which he committed' for the words 'which constitutes'.

23. Anti-social behaviour as ground of eviction

(1) Schedule 3 to the Housing (Scotland) Act 1987 (grounds of eviction in relation to secure tenancies) shall be amended in accordance with subsections (2) and (3) below.

(2) For paragraph 2 there shall be substituted the following paragraph—

'2.—(1) The tenant, a person residing or lodging in the house with the tenant or a person visiting the house has been convicted of—

(a) using or allowing the house to be used for immoral or illegal purposes; or

(b) an offence punishable by imprisonment committed in, or in the locality of, the house.

(2) In sub-paragraph (1) above "tenant" includes any one of joint tenants and any sub-tenant.'

(3) For paragraph 7 there shall be substituted the following paragraph—

'7.—(1) The tenant, a person residing or lodging in the house with the tenant or a person visiting the house has—

(a)   acted in an anti-social manner in relation to a person residing, visiting or otherwise engaging in lawful activity in the locality; or
(b)   pursued a course of anti-social conduct in relation to such a person as is mentioned in head (a) above,
and it is not reasonable in all the circumstances that the landlord should be required to make other accommodation available to him.
(2)   In sub-paragraph (1) above—
"anti-social", in relation to an action or course of conduct, means causing or likely to cause alarm, distress, nuisance or annoyance;
"conduct" includes speech and a course of conduct must involve conduct on at least two occasions; and
"tenant" includes any one of joint tenants and any sub-tenant.'
(4)   For Ground 15 in Schedule 5 to the Housing (Scotland) Act 1988 (eviction on ground of use of premises for immoral or illegal purposes etc.) there shall be substituted the following—

'*Ground 15*

The tenant, a person residing or lodging in the house with the tenant or a person visiting the house has—
(a)   been convicted of—
(i)   using or allowing the house to be used for immoral or illegal purposes; or
(ii)   an offence punishable by imprisonment committed in, or in the locality of, the house; or
(b)   acted in an anti-social manner in relation to a person residing, visiting or otherwise engaging in lawful activity in the locality; or
(c)   pursued a course of anti-social conduct in relation to such a person as is mentioned in head (b) above.
In this Ground "anti-social", in relation to an action or course of conduct, means causing or likely to cause alarm, distress, nuisance or annoyance, "conduct" includes speech and a course of conduct must involve conduct on at least two occasions and "tenant" includes any one of joint tenants.'
(5)   No person shall be liable to eviction under paragraph 2 or 7 of Schedule 3 to the Housing (Scotland) Act 1987 or Ground 15 in Schedule 5 to the Housing (Scotland) Act 1988 as substituted respectively by subsection (2), (3) and (4) above in respect of any act or conduct before the commencement of this section unless he would have been liable to be evicted under those paragraphs or, as the case may be, that Ground as they had effect before that substitution.

24.   Noise-making equipment: police power of seizure
(1)   The Civic Government (Scotland) Act 1982 shall be amended in accordance with this section.
(2)   In section 54 (offence of playing instruments, etc.), after subsection (2) there shall be inserted the following subsections—
'(2A)   Where a constable reasonably suspects that an offence under subsection (1) above has been committed in relation to a musical instrument or in relation to such a device as is mentioned in paragraph (c) of that subsection, he may enter any

premises on which he reasonably suspects that instrument or device to be and seize any such instrument or device he finds there.

(2B)   A constable may use reasonable force in the exercise of the power conferred by subsection (2A) above.

(2C)   Schedule 2A to this Act (which makes provision in relation to the retention and disposal of property seized under subsection (2A) above) shall have effect.'

(3)   In section 60 (powers of search and seizure)—

(a)   in subsection (5)—

(i)   after the words 'Nothing in' there shall be inserted the words 'section 54(2A) of this Act or'; and

(ii)   for the words from 'which' to the end there shall be substituted the words 'which is otherwise exercisable by a constable'; and

(b)   in subsection (6)—

(i)   in paragraph (a), for the words from 'in pursuance' to the word 'vessel' there shall be substituted the words—

'to enter and search—

(i)   any premises in pursuance of section 54(2A) of this Act or of subsection (1) above; or

(i)   any vehicle or vessel in pursuance of the said subsection (1),'; and

(ii)   in paragraph (c), after 'under' there shall be inserted the words 'section 54(2A) of this Act or'.

(4)   After Schedule 2 there shall be inserted the Schedule set out in Schedule 1 to this Act.

CHAPTER III
GREAT BRITAIN

25.   Powers to require removal of masks etc.

(1)   After subsection (4) of section 60 (powers to stop and search in anticipation of violence) of the Criminal Justice and Public Order Act 1994 ('the 1994 Act') there shall be inserted the following subsection—

'(4A)   This section also confers on any constable in uniform power—

(a)   to require any person to remove any item which the constable reasonably believes that person is wearing wholly or mainly for the purpose of concealing his identity;

(b)   to seize any item which the constable reasonably believes any person intends to wear wholly or mainly for that purpose.'

(2)   In subsection (5) of that section, for the words 'those powers' there shall be substituted the words 'the powers conferred by subsection (4) above'.

(3)   In subsection (8) of that section, for the words 'to stop or (as the case may be) to stop the vehicle' there shall be substituted the following paragraphs—

'(a)   to stop, or to stop a vehicle; or

(b)   to remove an item worn by him,'.

26.   Retention and disposal of things seized

After section 60 of the 1994 Act there shall be inserted the following section—

'60A. Retention and disposal of things seized under section 60

(1) Any things seized by a constable under section 60 may be retained in accordance with regulations made by the Secretary of State under this section.

(2) The Secretary of State may make regulations regulating the retention and safe keeping, and the disposal and destruction in prescribed circumstances, of such things.

(3) Regulations under this section may make different provisions for different classes of things or for different circumstances.

(4) The power to make regulations under this section shall be exercisable by statutory instrument which shall be subject to annulment in pursuance of a resolution of either House of Parliament.'

27. Power of arrest for failure to comply with requirement.

(1) In section 24(2) (arrestable offences) of the Police and Criminal Evidence Act 1984 ('the 1984 Act'), after paragraph (n) there shall be inserted—

'(o) an offence under section 60(8)(b) of the Criminal Justice and Public Order Act 1994 (failing to comply with requirement to remove mask etc.);'.

(2) After section 60A of the 1994 Act there shall be inserted the following section—

'60B. Arrest without warrant for offences under section 60: Scotland

In Scotland, where a constable reasonably believes that a person has committed or is committing an offence under section 60(8) he may arrest that person without warrant.'

PART II
CRIMINAL LAW

Racially-aggravated offences: England and Wales

28. Meaning of 'racially aggravated'

(1) An offence is racially aggravated for the purposes of sections 29 to 32 below if—

(a) at the time of committing the offence, or immediately before or after doing so, the offender demonstrates towards the victim of the offence hostility based on the victim's membership (or presumed membership) of a racial group; or

(b) the offence is motivated (wholly or partly) by hostility towards members of a racial group based on their membership of that group.

(2) In subsection (1)(a) above—

'membership', in relation to a racial group, includes association with members of that group;

'presumed' means presumed by the offender.

(3) It is immaterial for the purposes of paragraph (a) or (b) of subsection (1) above whether or not the offender's hostility is also based, to any extent, on—

(a) the fact or presumption that any person or group of persons belongs to any religious group; or

(b) any other factor not mentioned in that paragraph.

(4) In this section 'racial group' means a group of persons defined by reference to race, colour, nationality (including citizenship) or ethnic or national origins.

29. Racially-aggravated assaults
   (1)   A person is guilty of an offence under this section if he commits—
      (a)   an offence under section 20 of the Offences Against the Person Act 1861 (malicious wounding or grievous bodily harm);
      (b)   an offence under section 47 of that Act (actual bodily harm); or
      (c)   common assault,
which is racially aggravated for the purposes of this section.
   (2)   A person guilty of an offence falling within subsection (1)(a) or (b) above shall be liable—
      (a)   on summary conviction, to imprisonment for a term not exceeding six months or to a fine not exceeding the statutory maximum, or to both;
      (b)   on conviction on indictment, to imprisonment for a term not exceeding seven years or to a fine, or to both.
   (3)   A person guilty of an offence falling within subsection (1)(c) above shall be liable—
      (a)   on summary conviction, to imprisonment for a term not exceeding six months or to a fine not exceeding the statutory maximum,, or to both;
      (b)   on conviction on indictment, to imprisonment for a term not exceeding two years or to a fine, or to both.

30. Racially-aggravated criminal damage
   (1)   A person is guilty of an offence under this section if he commits an offence under section 1(1) of the Criminal Damage Act 1971 (destroying or damaging property belonging to another) which is racially aggravated for the purposes of this section.
   (2)   A person guilty of an offence under this section shall be liable—
      (a)   on summary conviction, to imprisonment for a term not exceeding six months or to a fine not exceeding the statutory maximum, or to both;
      (b)   on conviction on indictment, to imprisonment for a term not exceeding fourteen years or to a fine, or to both.
   (3)   For the purposes of this section, section 28(1)(a) above shall have effect as if the person to whom the property belongs or is treated as belonging for the purposes of that Act were the victim of the offence.

31. Racially-aggravated public order offences
   (1)   A person is guilty of an offence under this section if he commits—
      (a)   an offence under section 4 of the Public Order Act 1986 (fear or provocation of violence);
      (b)   an offence under section 4A of that Act (intentional harassment, alarm or distress); or
      (c)   an offence under section 5 of that Act (harassment, alarm or distress),
which is racially aggravated for the purposes of this section.
   (2)   A constable may arrest without warrant anyone whom he reasonably suspects to be committing an offence falling within subsection (1)(a) or (b) above.
   (3)   A constable may arrest a person without warrant if—
      (a)   he engages in conduct which a constable reasonably suspects to constitute an offence falling within subsection (1)(c) above;

(b) he is warned by that constable to stop; and

(c) he engages in further such conduct immediately or shortly after the warning.

The conduct mentioned in paragraph (a) above and the further conduct need not be of the same nature.

(4) A person guilty of an offence falling within subsection (1)(a) or (b) above shall be liable—

(a) on summary conviction, to imprisonment for a term not exceeding six months or to a fine not exceeding the statutory maximum, or to both;

(b) on conviction on indictment, to imprisonment for a term not exceeding two years or to a fine, or to both.

(5) A person guilty of an offence falling within subsection (1)(c) above shall be liable on summary conviction to a fine not exceeding level 4 on the standard scale.

(6) If, on the trial on indictment of a person charged with an offence falling within subsection (1)(a) or (b) above, the jury find him not guilty of the offence charged, they may find him guilty of the basic offence mentioned in that provision.

(7) For the purposes of subsection (1)(c) above, section 28(1)(a) above shall have effect as if the person likely to be caused harassment, alarm or distress were the victim of the offence.

32. Racially-aggravated harassment etc.

(1) A person is guilty of an offence under this section if he commits—

(a) an offence under section 2 of the Protection from Harassment Act 1997 (offence of harassment); or

(b) an offence under section 4 of that Act (putting people in fear of violence), which is racially aggravated for the purposes of this section.

(2) In section 24(2) of the 1984 Act (arrestable offences), after paragraph (o) there shall be inserted—

'(p) an offence falling within section 32(1)(a) of the Crime and Disorder Act 1998 (racially-aggravated harassment);'.

(3) A person guilty of an offence falling within subsection (1)(a) above shall be liable—

(a) on summary conviction, to imprisonment for a term not exceeding six months or to a fine not exceeding the statutory maximum, or to both;

(b) on conviction on indictment, to imprisonment for a term not exceeding two years or to a fine, or to both.

(4) A person guilty of an offence falling within subsection (1)(b) above shall be liable—

(a) on summary conviction, to imprisonment for a term not exceeding six months or to a fine not exceeding the statutory maximum, or to both;

(b) on conviction on indictment, to imprisonment for a term not exceeding seven years or to a fine, or to both.

(5) If, on the trial on indictment of a person charged with an offence falling within subsection (1)(a) above, the jury find him not guilty of the offence charged, they may find him guilty of the basic offence mentioned in that provision.

(6) If, on the trial on indictment of a person charged with an offence falling within subsection (1)(b) above, the jury find him not guilty of the offence charged, they may find him guilty of an offence falling within subsection (1)(a) above.

(7) Section 5 of the Protection from Harassment Act 1997 (restraining orders) shall have effect in relation to a person convicted of an offence under this section as if the reference in subsection (1) of that section to an offence under section 2 or 4 included a reference to an offence under this section.

Racially-aggravated offences: Scotland

33. Racially-aggravated offences

After section 50 of the Criminal Law (Consolidation) (Scotland) Act 1995 there shall be inserted the following section—

'Racially-aggravated harassment

50A. Racially-aggravated harassment

(1) A person is guilty of an offence under this section if he—

(a) pursues a racially-aggravated course of conduct which amounts to harassment of a person and—

(i) is intended to amount to harassment of that person; or

(ii) occurs in circumstances where it would appear to a reasonable person that it would amount to harassment of that person; or

(b) acts in a manner which is racially aggravated and which causes, or is intended to cause, a person alarm or distress.

(2) For the purposes of this section a course of conduct or an action is racially aggravated if—

(a) immediately before, during or immediately after carrying out the course of conduct or action the offender evinces towards the person affected malice and ill-will based on that person's membership (or presumed membership) of a racial group; or

(b) the course of conduct or action is motivated (wholly or partly) by malice and ill-will towards members of a racial group based on their membership of that group.

(3) In subsection (2)(a) above—

"membership", in relation to a racial group, includes association with members of that group;

"presumed" means presumed by the offender.

(4) It is immaterial for the purposes of paragraph (a) or (b) of subsection (2) above whether or not the offender's malice and ill-will is also based, to any extent, on—

(a) the fact or presumption that any person or group of persons belongs to any religious group; or

(b) any other factor not mentioned in that paragraph.

(5) A person who is guilty of an offence under this section shall—

(a) on summary conviction, be liable to a fine not exceeding the statutory maximum, or imprisonment for a period not exceeding six months, or both such fine and such imprisonment; and

(b) on conviction on indictment, be liable to a fine or to imprisonment for a period not exceeding seven years, or both such fine and such imprisonment.

(6) In this section—

"conduct" includes speech;

"harassment" of a person includes causing the person alarm or distress;
"racial group" means a group of persons defined by reference to race, colour, nationality (including citizenship) or ethnic or national origins,
and a course of conduct must involve conduct on at least two occasions.'

Miscellaneous

34.   Abolition of rebuttable presumption that a child is doli incapax
The rebuttable presumption of criminal law that a child aged 10 or over is incapable of committing an offence is hereby abolished.

35.   Effect of child's silence at trial
In section 35 of the 1994 Act (effect of accused's silence at trial), the following provisions shall cease to have effect, namely—
(a)   in subsection (1), the words 'who has attained the age of fourteen years'; and
(b)   subsection (6).

36.   Abolition of death penalty for treason and piracy
(1)   In section I of the Treason Act (Ireland) 1537 (practising any harm etc. to, or slandering, the King, Queen or heirs apparent punishable as high treason), for the words 'have and suffer such pains of death and' there shall be substituted the words 'be liable to imprisonment for life and to such'.
(2)   In the following enactments, namely—
(a)   section II of the Crown of Ireland Act 1542 (occasioning disturbance etc. to the crown of Ireland punishable as high treason);
(b)   section XII of the Act of Supremacy (Ireland) 1560 (penalties for maintaining or defending foreign authority);
(c)   section 3 of the Treason Act 1702 (endeavouring to hinder the succession to the Crown etc. punishable as high treason);
(d)   section I of the Treason Act (Ireland) 1703 (which makes corresponding provision),
for the words 'suffer pains of death' there shall be substituted the words 'be liable to imprisonment for life'.
(3)   The following enactments shall cease to have effect, namely—
(a)   the Treason Act 1790;
(b)   the Treason Act 1795.
(4)   In section 1 of the Treason Act 1814 (form of sentence in case of high treason), for the words 'such person shall be hanged by the neck until such person be dead', there shall be substituted the words 'such person shall be liable to imprisonment for life'.
(5)   In section 2 of the Piracy Act 1837 (punishment of piracy when murder is attempted), for the words 'and being convicted thereof shall suffer death' there shall be substituted the words 'and being convicted thereof shall be liable to imprisonment for life'.
(6)   The following enactments shall cease to have effect, namely—
(a)   the Sentence of Death (Expectant Mothers) Act 1931; and
(b)   sections 32 and 33 of the Criminal Justice Act (Northern Ireland) 1945 (which make corresponding provision).

PART III
CRIMINAL JUSTICE SYSTEM

Youth justice

37. Aim of the youth justice system

(1) It shall be the principal aim of the youth justice system to prevent offending by children and young persons.

(2) In addition to any other duty to which they are subject, it shall be the duty of all persons and bodies carrying out functions in relation to the youth justice system to have regard to that aim.

38. Local provision of youth justice services

(1) It shall be the duty of each local authority, acting in co-operation with the persons and bodies mentioned in subsection (2) below, to secure that, to such extent as is appropriate for their area, all youth justice services are available there.

(2) It shall be the duty of—

(a) every chief officer of police or police authority any part of whose police area lies within the local authority's area; and

(b) every probation committee or health authority any part of whose area lies within that area,

to co-operate in the discharge by the local authority of their duty under subsection (1) above.

(3) The local authority and every person or body mentioned in subsection (2) above shall have power to make payments towards expenditure incurred in the provision of youth justice services—

(a) by making the payments directly; or

(b) by contributing to a fund, established and maintained by the local authority, out of which the payments may be made.

(4) In this section and sections 39 to 41 below 'youth justice services' means any of the following, namely—

(a) the provision of persons to act as appropriate adults to safeguard the interests of children and young persons detained or questioned by police officers;

(b) the assessment of children and young persons, and the provision for them of rehabilitation programmes, for the purposes of section 66(2) below;

(c) the provision of support for children and young persons remanded or committed on bail while awaiting trial or sentence;

(d) the placement in local authority accommodation of children and young persons remanded or committed to such accommodation under section 23 of the Children and Young Persons Act 1969 ('the 1969 Act');

(e) the provision of reports or other information required by courts in criminal proceedings against children and young persons;

(f) the provision of persons to act as responsible officers in relation to parenting orders, child safety orders, reparation orders and action plan orders;

(g) the supervision of young persons sentenced to a probation order, a community service order or a combination order;

(h) the supervision of children and young persons sentenced to a detention and training order or a supervision order;

(i)   the post-release supervision of children and young persons under section 37(4A) or 65 of the 1991 Act or section 31 of the Crime (Sentences) Act 1997 ('the 1997 Act');

(j)   the performance of functions under subsection (1) of section 75 below by such persons as may be authorised by the Secretary of State under that subsection.

(5)   The Secretary of State may by order amend subsection (4) above so as to extend, restrict or otherwise alter the definition of 'youth justice services' for the time being specified in that subsection.

39.   Youth offending teams

(1)   Subject to subsection (2) below, it shall be the duty of each local authority, acting in co-operation with the persons and bodies mentioned in subsection (3) below, to establish for their area one or more youth offending teams.

(2)   Two (or more) local authorities acting together may establish one or more youth offending teams for both (or all) their areas; and where they do so—

(a)   any reference in the following provisions of this section (except subsection (4)(b)) to, or to the area of, the local authority or a particular local authority shall be construed accordingly, and

(b)   the reference in subsection (4)(b) to the local authority shall be construed as a reference to one of the authorities.

(3)   It shall be the duty of—

(a)   every chief officer of police any part of whose police area lies within the local authority's area; and

(b)   every probation committee or health authority any part of whose area lies within that area,

to co-operate in the discharge by the local authority of their duty under subsection (1) above.

(4)   The local authority and every person or body mentioned in subsection (3) above shall have power to make payments towards expenditure incurred by, or for purposes connected with, youth offending teams—

(a)   by making the payments directly; or

(b)   by contributing to a fund, established and maintained by the local authority, out of which the payments may be made.

(5)   A youth offending team shall include at least one of each of the following, namely—

(a)   a probation officer;

(b)   a social worker of a local authority social services department;

(c)   a police officer;

(d)   a person nominated by a health authority any part of whose area lies within the local authority's area;

(e)   a person nominated by the chief education officer appointed by the local authority under section 532 of the Education Act 1996.

(6)   A youth offending team may also include such other persons as the local authority thinks appropriate after consulting the persons and bodies mentioned in subsection (3) above.

(7)   It shall be the duty of the youth offending team or teams established by a particular local authority—

(a) to co-ordinate the provision of youth justice services for all those in the authority's area who need them; and

(b) to carry out such functions as are assigned to the team or teams in the youth justice plan formulated by the authority under section 40(1) below.

40. Youth justice plans

(1) It shall be the duty of each local authority, after consultation with the relevant persons and bodies, to formulate and implement for each year a plan (a 'youth justice plan') setting out—

(a) how youth justice services in their area are to be provided and funded; and

(b) how the youth offending team or teams established by them (whether alone or jointly with one or more other local authorities) are to be composed and funded, how they are to operate, and what functions they are to carry out.

(2) In subsection (1) above 'the relevant persons and bodies' means the persons and bodies mentioned in section 38(2) above and, where the local authority is a county council, any district councils whose districts form part of its area.

(3) The functions assigned to a youth offending team under subsection (1)(b) above may include, in particular, functions under paragraph 7(b) of Schedule 2 to the 1989 Act (local authority's duty to take reasonable steps designed to encourage children and young persons not to commit offences).

(4) A local authority shall submit their youth justice plan to the Board established under section 41 below, and shall publish it in such manner and by such date as the Secretary of State may direct.

41. The Youth Justice Board

(1) There shall be a body corporate to be known as the Youth Justice Board for England and Wales ('the Board').

(2) The Board shall not be regarded as the servant or agent of the Crown or as enjoying any status, immunity or privilege of the Crown; and the Board's property shall not be regarded as property of, or held on behalf of, the Crown.

(3) The Board shall consist of 10, 11 or 12 members appointed by the Secretary of State.

(4) The members of the Board shall include persons who appear to the Secretary of State to have extensive recent experience of the youth justice system.

(5) The Board shall have the following functions, namely—

(a) to monitor the operation of the youth justice system and the provision of youth justice services;

(b) to advise the Secretary of State on the following matters, namely—

(i) the operation of that system and the provision of such services;

(ii) how the principal aim of that system might most effectively be pursued;

(iii) the content of any national standards he may see fit to set with respect to the provision of such services, or the accommodation in which children and young persons are kept in custody; and

(iv) the steps that might be taken to prevent offending by children and young persons;

(c) to monitor the extent to which that aim is being achieved and any such standards met;

(d) for the purposes of paragraphs (a), (b) and (c) above, to obtain information from relevant authorities;

(e) to publish information so obtained;

(f) to identify, to make known and to promote good practice in the following matters, namely—

(i) the operation of the youth justice system and the provision of youth justice services;

(ii) the prevention of offending by children and young persons; and

(iii) working with children and young persons who are or are at risk of becoming offenders;

(g) to make grants, with the approval of the Secretary of State, to local authorities or other bodies for them to develop such practice, or to commission research in connection with such practice; and

(h) themselves to commission research in connection with such practice.

(6) The Secretary of State may by order—

(a) amend subsection (5) above so as to add to, subtract from or alter any of the functions of the Board for the time being specified in that subsection; or

(b) provide that any function of his which is exercisable in relation to the youth justice system shall be exercisable concurrently with the Board.

(7) In carrying out their functions, the Board shall comply with any directions given by the Secretary of State and act in accordance with any guidance given by him.

(8) A relevant authority—

(a) shall furnish to the Board any information required for the purposes of subsection (5)(a), (b) or (c) above; and

(b) whenever so required by the Board, shall submit to the Board a report on such matters connected with the discharge of their duties under the foregoing provisions of this Part as may be specified in the requirement.

A requirement under paragraph (b) above may specify the form in which a report is to be given.

(9) The Board may arrange, or require the relevant authority to arrange, for a report under subsection (8)(b) above to be published in such manner as appears to the Board to be appropriate.

(10) In this section 'relevant authority' means a local authority, a chief officer of police, a police authority, a probation committee and a health authority.

(11) Schedule 2 to this Act (which makes further provision with respect to the Board) shall have effect.

42. Supplementary provisions

(1) In the foregoing provisions of this Part and this section—

'chief officer of police' has the meaning given by section 101(1) of the Police Act 1996;

'local authority' means—

(a) in relation to England, a county council, a district council whose district does not form part of an area that has a county council, a London borough council or the Common Council of the City of London;

(b) in relation to Wales, a county council or a county borough council;

'police authority' has the meaning given by section 101(1) of the Police Act 1996;

'youth justice system' means the system of criminal justice in so far as it relates to children and young persons.

(2)   For the purposes of those provisions, the Isles of Scilly form part of the county of Cornwall and the Inner Temple and the Middle Temple form part of the City of London.

(3)   In carrying out any of their duties under those provisions, a local authority, a police authority, a probation committee or a health authority shall act in accordance with any guidance given by the Secretary of State.

Time limits etc.

43. Time limits

(1)   In subsection (2) of section 22 (time limits in relation to criminal proceedings) of the Prosecution of Offences Act 1985 ('the 1985 Act'), for paragraphs (a) and (b) there shall be substituted the following paragraphs—

'(a)   be made so as to apply only in relation to proceedings instituted in specified areas, or proceedings of, or against persons of, specified classes or descriptions;

(b)   make different provision with respect to proceedings instituted in different areas, or different provision with respect to proceedings of, or against persons of, different classes or descriptions;'.

(2)   For subsection (3) of that section there shall be substituted the following subsection—

'(3)   The appropriate court may, at any time before the expiry of a time limit imposed by the regulations, extend, or further extend, that limit; but the court shall not do so unless it is satisfied—

(a)   that the need for the extension is due to—

(i)   the illness or absence of the accused, a necessary witness, a judge or a magistrate;

(ii)   a postponement which is occasioned by the ordering by the court of separate trials in the case of two or more accused or two or more offences; or

(iii)   some other good and sufficient cause; and

(b)   that the prosecution has acted with all due diligence and expedition.'

(3)   In subsection (4) of that section, for the words from 'the accused' to the end there shall be substituted the words 'the appropriate court shall stay the proceedings'.

(4)   In subsection (6) of that section—

(a)   for the word 'Where' there shall be substituted the words 'Subsection (6A) below applies where'; and

(b)   for the words from 'the overall time limit' to the end there shall be substituted the words 'and is accordingly unlawfully at large for any period.'

(5)   After that subsection there shall be inserted the following subsection—

'(6A)   The following, namely—

(a)   the period for which the person is unlawfully at large; and

(b)   such additional period (if any) as the appropriate court may direct, having regard to the disruption of the prosecution occasioned by—

(i)   the person's escape or failure to surrender; and

(ii)   the length of the period mentioned in paragraph (a) above,

shall be disregarded, so far as the offence in question is concerned, for the purposes of the overall time limit which applies in his case in relation to the stage which the proceedings have reached at the time of the escape or, as the case may be, at the appointed time.'

(6) In subsection (7) of that section, after the words 'time limit,' there shall be inserted the words 'or to give a direction under subsection (6A) above,'.

(7) In subsection (8) of that section, after the words 'time limit' there shall be inserted the words 'or to give a direction under subsection (6A) above,'.

(8) After subsection (11) of that section there shall be inserted the following subsection—

'(11ZA) For the purposes of this section, proceedings for an offence shall be taken to begin when the accused is charged with the offence or, as the case may be, an information is laid charging him with the offence.'

44. Additional time limits for persons under 18

After section 22 of the 1985 Act there shall be inserted the following section—

'22A. Additional time limits for persons under 18

(1) The Secretary of State may by regulations make provision—

(a) with respect to a person under the age of 18 at the time of his arrest in connection with an offence, as to the maximum period to be allowed for the completion of the stage beginning with his arrest and ending with the date fixed for his first appearance in court in connection with the offence ("the initial stage");

(b) with respect to a person convicted of an offence who was under that age at the time of his arrest for the offence or (where he was not arrested for it) the laying of the information charging him with it, as to the period within which the stage between his conviction and his being sentenced for the offence should be completed.

(2) Subsection (2) of section 22 above applies for the purposes of regulations under subsection (1) above as if—

(a) the reference in paragraph (d) to custody or overall time limits were a reference to time limits imposed by the regulations; and

(b) the reference in paragraph (e) to proceedings instituted before the commencement of any provisions of the regulations were a reference to a stage begun before that commencement.

(3) A magistrates' court may, at any time before the expiry of the time limit imposed by the regulations under subsection (1)(a) above ("the initial stage time limit"), extend, or further extend, that limit; but the court shall not do so unless it is satisfied—

(a) that the need for the extension is due to some good and sufficient cause; and

(b) that the investigation has been conducted, and (where applicable) the prosecution has acted, with all due diligence and expedition.

(4) Where the initial stage time limit (whether as originally imposed or as extended or further extended under subsection (3) above) expires before the person arrested is charged with the offence, he shall not be charged with it unless further evidence relating to it is obtained, and—

(a) if he is then under arrest, he shall be released;

(b) if he is then on bail under Part IV of the Police and Criminal Evidence Act 1984, his bail (and any duty or conditions to which it is subject) shall be discharged.

(5) Where the initial stage time limit (whether as originally imposed or as extended or further extended under subsection (3) above) expires after the person arrested is charged with the offence but before the date fixed for his first appearance in court in connection with it, the court shall stay the proceedings.

(6) Where—

(a) a person escapes from arrest; or

(b) a person who has been released on bail under Part IV of the Police and Criminal Evidence Act 1984 fails to surrender himself at the appointed time,

and is accordingly unlawfully at large for any period, that period shall be disregarded, so far as the offence in question is concerned, for the purposes of the initial stage time limit.

(7) Subsections (7) to (9) of section 22 above apply for the purposes of this section, at any time after the person arrested has been charged with the offence in question, as if any reference (however expressed) to a custody or overall time limit were a reference to the initial stage time limit.

(8) Where a person is convicted of an offence in any proceedings, the exercise of the power conferred by subsection (3) above shall not be called into question in any appeal against that conviction.

(9) Any reference in this section (however expressed) to a person being charged with an offence includes a reference to the laying of an information charging him with it.'

45. Re-institution of stayed proceedings

After section 22A of the 1985 Act there shall be inserted the following section—

'**22B. Re-institution of proceedings stayed under section 22(4) or 22A(5)**

(1) This section applies where proceedings for an offence ("the original proceedings") are stayed by a court under section 22(4) or 22A(5) of this Act.

(2) If—

(a) in the case of proceedings conducted by the Director, the Director or a Chief Crown Prosecutor so directs;

(b) in the case of proceedings conducted by the Director of the Serious Fraud Office, the Commissioners of Inland Revenue or the Commissioners of Customs and Excise, that Director or those Commissioners so direct; or

(c) in the case of proceedings not conducted as mentioned in paragraph (a) or (b) above, a person designated for the purpose by the Secretary of State so directs,

fresh proceedings for the offence may be instituted within a period of three months (or such longer period as the court may allow) after the date on which the original proceedings were stayed by the court.

(3) Fresh proceedings shall be instituted as follows—

(a) where the original proceedings were stayed by the Crown Court, by preferring a bill of indictment;

(b) where the original proceedings were stayed by a magistrates' court, by laying an information.

(4) Fresh proceedings may be instituted in accordance with subsections (2) and (3)(b) above notwithstanding anything in section 127(1) of the Magistrates' Courts Act 1980 (limitation of time).

(5)   Where fresh proceedings are instituted, anything done in relation to the original proceedings shall be treated as done in relation to the fresh proceedings if the court so directs or it was done—

(a)   by the prosecutor in compliance or purported compliance with section 3, 4, 7 or 9 of the Criminal Procedure and Investigations Act 1996; or

(b)   by the accused in compliance or purported compliance with section 5 or 6 of that Act.

(6)   Where a person is convicted of an offence in fresh proceedings under this section, the institution of those proceedings shall not be called into question in any appeal against that conviction.'

46.   Date of first court appearance in bail cases

(1)   In subsection (3) of section 47 of the 1984 Act (bail after arrest), for the words 'subsection (4)' there shall be substituted the words 'subsections (3A) and (4)'.

(2)   After that subsection there shall be inserted the following subsection—

'(3A)   Where a custody officer grants bail to a person subject to a duty to appear before a magistrates' court, he shall appoint for the appearance—

(a)   a date which is not later than the first sitting of the court after the person is charged with the offence; or

(b)   where he is informed by the clerk to the justices for the relevant petty sessions area that the appearance cannot be accommodated until a later date, that later date.'

Functions of courts etc.

47.   Powers of youth courts

(1)   Where a person who appears or is brought before a youth court charged with an offence subsequently attains the age of 18, the youth court may, at any time—

(a)   before the start of the trial; or

(b)   after conviction and before sentence,

remit the person for trial or, as the case may be, for sentence to a magistrates' court (other than a youth court) acting for the same petty sessions area as the youth court.

In this subsection 'the start of the trial' shall be construed in accordance with section 22(11B) of the 1985 Act.

(2)   Where a person is remitted under subsection (1) above—

(a)   he shall have no right of appeal against the order of remission;

(b)   the remitting court shall adjourn proceedings in relation to the offence; and

(c)   subsections (3) and (4) below shall apply.

(3)   The following, namely—

(a)   section 128 of the 1980 Act; and

(b)   all other enactments (whenever passed) relating to remand or the granting of bail in criminal proceedings,

shall have effect in relation to the remitting court's power or duty to remand the person on the adjournment as if any reference to the court to or before which the person remanded is to be brought or appear after remand were a reference to the court to which he is being remitted ('the other court').

(4)   The other court may deal with the case in any way in which it would have power to deal with it if all proceedings relating to the offence which took place before the remitting court had taken place before the other court.

(5)   After subsection (3) of section 10 of the 1980 Act (adjournment of trial) there shall be inserted the following subsection—

'(3A)   A youth court shall not be required to adjourn any proceedings for an offence at any stage by reason only of the fact—

(a)   that the court commits the accused for trial for another offence; or

(b)   that the accused is charged with another offence.'

(6)   After subsection (1) of section 24 of the 1980 Act (summary trial of information against child or young person for indictable offence) there shall be inserted the following subsection—

'(1A)   Where a magistrates' court—

(a)   commits a person under the age of 18 for trial for an offence of homicide; or

(b)   in a case failing within subsection (1)(a) above, commits such a person for trial for an offence,

the court may also commit him for trial for any other indictable offence with which he is charged at the same time if the charges for both offences could be joined in the same indictment.'

(7)   In subsection (2) of section 47 (procedure in youth courts) of the Children and Young Persons Act 1933 ('the 1933 Act'), the words from the beginning to 'court; and' shall cease to have effect.

48.   Youth courts: power of stipendiary magistrates to sit alone

(1)   In paragraph 15 of Schedule 2 to the 1933 Act (constitution of youth courts)—

(a)   in paragraph (a), after the word 'shall', in the first place where it occurs, there shall be inserted the words 'either consist of a metropolitan stipendiary magistrate sitting alone or' and the word 'shall', in the other place where it occurs, shall cease to have effect;

(b)   in paragraph (b), after the words 'the chairman' there shall be inserted the words '(where applicable)'; and

(c)   in paragraph (c), after the words 'the other members' there shall be inserted the words '(where applicable)'.

(2)   In paragraph 17 of that Schedule, the words 'or, if a metropolitan stipendiary magistrate, may sit alone' shall cease to have effect.

49.   Powers of magistrates' courts exercisable by single justice etc.

(1)   The following powers of a magistrates' court for any area may be exercised by a single justice of the peace for that area, namely—

(a)   to extend bail or to impose or vary conditions of bail;

(b)   to mark an information as withdrawn;

(c)   to dismiss an information, or to discharge an accused in respect of an information, where no evidence is offered by the prosecution;

(d)   to make an order for the payment of defence costs out of central funds;

(e)   to request a pre-sentence report following a plea of guilty and, for that purpose, to give an indication of the seriousness of the offence;

(f)   to request a medical report and, for that purpose, to remand the accused in custody or on bail;

(g)   to remit an offender to another court for sentence;

(h)   where a person has been granted police bail to appear at a magistrates' court, to appoint an earlier time for his appearance;

(i)   to extend, with the consent of the accused, a custody time limit or an overall time limit;

(j) ˙ where a case is to be tried on indictment, to grant representation under Part V of the Legal Aid Act 1988 for purposes of the proceedings in the Crown Court;

(k)   where an accused has been convicted of an offence, to order him to produce his driving licence;

(l)   to give a direction prohibiting the publication of matters disclosed or exempted from disclosure in court;

(m)   to give, vary or revoke directions for the conduct of a trial, including directions as to the following matters, namely—

(i)   the timetable for the proceedings;

(ii)   the attendance of the parties;

(iii)   the service of documents (including summaries of any legal arguments relied on by the parties);

(iv)   the manner in which evidence is to be given; and

(n)   to give, vary or revoke orders for separate or joint trials in the case of two or more accused or two or more informations.

(2)   Without prejudice to the generality of subsection (1) of section 144 of the 1980 Act (rules of procedure)—

(a)   rules under that section may, subject to subsection (3) below, provide that any of the things which, by virtue of subsection (1) above, are authorised to be done by a single justice of the peace for any area may, subject to any specified restrictions or conditions, be done by a justices' clerk for that area; and

(b)   rules under that section which make such provision as is mentioned in paragraph (a) above may make different provision for different areas.

(3)   Rules under that section which make such provision as is mentioned in subsection (2) above shall not authorise a justices' clerk—

(a)   without the consent of the prosecutor and the accused, to extend bail on conditions other than those (if any) previously imposed, or to impose or vary conditions of bail;

(b)   to give an indication of the seriousness of an offence for the purposes of a pre-sentence report;

(c)   to remand the accused in custody for the purposes of a medical report or, without the consent of the prosecutor and the accused, to remand the accused on bail for those purposes on conditions other than those (if any) previously imposed;

(d)   to give a direction prohibiting the publication of matters disclosed or exempted from disclosure in court; or

(e)   without the consent of the parties, to give, vary or revoke orders for separate or joint trials in the case of two or more accused or two or more informations.

(4)   Before making any rules under that section which make such provision as is mentioned in subsection (2) above in relation to any area, the Lord Chancellor shall consult justices of the peace and justices' clerks for that area.

(5)   In this section and section 50 below 'justices' clerk' has the same meaning as in section 144 of the 1980 Act.

50. Early administrative hearings

(1) Where a person ('the accused') has been charged with an offence at a police station, the magistrates' court before whom he appears or is brought for the first time in relation to the charge may, unless the accused falls to be dealt with under section 51 below, consist of a single justice.

(2) At a hearing conducted by a single justice under this section—

    (a) the accused shall be asked whether he wishes to receive legal aid; and

    (b) if he indicates that he does, his eligibility for it shall be determined; and

    (c) if it is determined that he is eligible for it, the necessary arrangements or grant shall be made for him to obtain it.

(3) At such a hearing the single justice—

    (a) may exercise, subject to subsection (2) above, such of his powers as a single justice as he thinks fit; and

    (b) on adjourning the hearing, may remand the accused in custody or on bail.

(4) This section applies in relation to a justices' clerk as it applies in relation to a single justice; but nothing in subsection (3)(b) above authorises such a clerk to remand the accused in custody or, without the consent of the prosecutor and the accused, to remand the accused on bail on conditions other than those (if any) previously imposed.

(5) In this section 'legal aid' means representation under Part V of the Legal Aid Act 1988.

51. No committal proceedings for indictable-only offences

(1) Where an adult appears or is brought before a magistrates' court ('the court') charged with an offence triable only on indictment ('the indictable-only offence'), the court shall send him forthwith to the Crown Court for trial—

    (a) for that offence, and

    (b) for any either-way or summary offence with which he is charged which fulfils the requisite conditions (as set out in subsection (11) below).

(2) Where an adult who has been sent for trial under subsection (1) above subsequently appears or is brought before a magistrates' court charged with an either-way or summary offence which fulfils the requisite conditions, the court may send him forthwith to the Crown Court for trial for the either-way or summary offence.

(3) Where—

    (a) the court sends an adult for trial under subsection (1) above;

    (b) another adult appears or is brought before the court on the same or a subsequent occasion charged jointly with him with an either-way offence; and

    (c) that offence appears to the court to be related to the indictable-only offence,

the court shall where it is the same occasion, and may where it is a subsequent occasion, send the other adult forthwith to the Crown Court for trial for the either-way offence.

(4) Where a court sends an adult for trial under subsection (3) above, it shall at the same time send him to the Crown Court for trial for any either-way or summary offence with which he is charged which fulfils the requisite conditions.

(5) Where—

    (a) the court sends an adult for trial under subsection (1) or (3) above;and

(b)   a child or young person appears or is brought before the court on the same or a subsequent occasion charged jointly with the adult with an indictable offence for which the adult is sent for trial,

the court shall, if it considers it necessary in the interests of justice to do so, send the child or young person forthwith to the Crown Court for trial for the indictable offence.

(6)   Where a court sends a child or young person for trial under subsection (5) above, it may at the same time send him to the Crown Court for trial for any either-way or summary offence with which he is charged which fulfils the requisite conditions.

(7)   The court shall specify in a notice the offence or offences for which a person is sent for trial under this section and the place at which he is to be tried; and a copy of the notice shall be served on the accused and given to the Crown Court sitting at that place.

(8)   In a case where there is more than one indictable-only offence and the court includes an either-way or a summary offence in the notice under subsection (7) above, the court shall specify in that notice the indictable-only offence to which the either-way offence or, as the case may be, the summary offence appears to the court to be related.

(9)   The trial of the information charging any summary offence for which a person is sent for trial under this section shall be treated as if the court had adjourned it under section 10 of the 1980 Act and had not fixed the time and place for its resumption.

(10)   In selecting the place of trial for the purpose of subsection (7) above, the court shall have regard to—

(a)   the convenience of the defence, the prosecution and the witnesses;

(b)   the desirability of expediting the trial; and

(c)   any direction given by or on behalf of the Lord Chief Justice with the concurrence of the Lord Chancellor under section 75(1) of the Supreme Court Act 1981.

(11)   An offence fulfils the requisite conditions if—

(a)   it appears to the court to be related to the indictable-only offence; and

(b)   in the case of a summary offence, it is punishable with imprisonment or involves obligatory or discretionary disqualification from driving.

(12)   For the purposes of this section—

(a)   'adult' means a person aged 18 or over, and references to an adult include references to a corporation;

(b)   'either-way offence' means an offence which, if committed by an adult, is triable either on indictment or summarily;

(c)   an either-way offence is related to an indictable-only offence if the charge for the either-way offence could be joined in the same indictment as the charge for the indictable-only offence;

(d)   a summary offence is related to an indictable-only offence if it arises out of circumstances which are the same as or connected with those giving rise to the indictable-only offence.

52.   Provisions supplementing section 51

(1)   Subject to section 4 of the Bail Act 1976, section 41 of the 1980 Act, regulations under section 22 of the 1985 Act and section 25 of the 1994 Act, the court may send a person for trial under section 51 above—

(a)   in custody, that is to say, by committing him to custody there to be safely kept until delivered in due course of law; or

(b)   on bail in accordance with the Bail Act 1976, that is to say, by directing him to appear before the Crown Court for trial.

(2)   Where—

(a)   the person's release on bail under subsection (1)(b) above is conditional on his providing one or more sureties; and

(b)   in accordance with subsection (3) of section 8 of the Bail Act 1976, the court fixes the amount in which a surety is to be bound with a view to his entering into his recognisance subsequently in accordance with subsections (4) and (5) or (6) of that section,

the court shall in the meantime make an order such as is mentioned in subsection (1)(a) above.

(3)   The court shall treat as an indictable offence for the purposes of section 51 above an offence which is mentioned in the first column of Schedule 2 to the 1980 Act (offences for which the value involved is relevant to the mode of trial) unless it is clear to the court, having regard to any representations made by the prosecutor or the accused, that the value involved does not exceed the relevant sum.

(4)   In subsection (3) above 'the value involved' and 'the relevant sum' have the same meanings as in section 22 of the 1980 Act (certain offences triable either way to be tried summarily if value involved is small).

(5)   A magistrates' court may adjourn any proceedings under section 51 above, and if it does so shall remand the accused.

(6)   Schedule 3 to this Act (which makes further provision in relation to persons sent to the Crown Court for trial under section 51 above) shall have effect.

Miscellaneous

53.   Crown Prosecution Service: powers of non-legal staff

For section 7A of the 1985 Act there shall be substituted the following section—

'7A.   Powers of non-legal staff

(1)   The Director may designate, for the purposes of this section, members of the staff of the Crown Prosecution Service who are not Crown Prosecutors.

(2)   Subject to such exceptions (if any) as may be specified in the designation, a person so designated shall have such of the following as may be so specified, namely—

(a)   the powers and rights of audience of a Crown Prosecutor in relation to—

(i)   applications for, or relating to, bail in criminal proceedings;

(ii)   the conduct of criminal proceedings in magistrates' courts other than trials;

(b)   the powers of such a Prosecutor in relation to the conduct of criminal proceedings not falling within paragraph (a)(ii) above.

(3)   A person so designated shall exercise any such powers subject to instructions given to him by the Director.

(4)   Any such instructions may be given so as to apply generally.

(5)   For the purposes of this section—

(a) "bail in criminal proceedings" has the same meaning as it would have in the Bail Act 1976 by virtue of the definition in section 1 of that Act if in that section "offence" did not include an offence to which subsection (6) below applies;

(b) "criminal proceedings" does not include proceedings for an offence to which subsection (6) below applies; and

(c) a trial begins with the opening of the prosecution case after the entry of a plea of not guilty and ends with the conviction or acquittal of the accused.

(6) This subsection applies to an offence if it is triable only on indictment, or is an offence—

(a) for which the accused has elected to be tried by a jury;

(b) which a magistrates' court has decided is more suitable to be so tried; or

(c) in respect of which a notice of transfer has been given under section 4 of the Criminal Justice Act 1987 or section 53 of the Criminal Justice Act 1991.

(7) Details of the following for any year, namely—

(a) the criteria applied by the Director in determining whether to designate persons under this section;

(b) the training undergone by persons so designated; and

(c) any general instructions given by the Director under subsection (4) above,

shall be set out in the Director's report under section 9 of this Act for that year.'

54. Bail: increased powers to require security or impose conditions

(1) In subsection (5) of section 3 of the Bail Act 1976 (general provisions as to bail), the words 'If it appears that he is unlikely to remain in Great Britain until the time appointed for him to surrender to custody' shall cease to have effect.

(2) In subsection (6) of that section, after paragraph (d) there shall be inserted the following paragraph—

'(e) before the time appointed for him to surrender to custody, he attends an interview with an authorised advocate or authorised litigator, as defined by section 119(1) of the Courts and Legal Services Act 1990;'.

(3) In subsection (2) of section 3A of that Act (conditions of bail in the case of police bail), for the words 'paragraph (d)' there shall be substituted the words 'paragraph (d) or (e)'.

55. Forfeiture of recognizances

For subsections (1) and (2) of section 120 of the 1980 Act (forfeiture of recognizances) there shall be substituted the following subsections—

'(1) This section applies where—

(a) a recognizance to keep the peace or to be of good behaviour has been entered into before a magistrates' court; or

(b) any recognizance is conditioned for the appearance of a person before a magistrates' court, or for his doing any other thing connected with a proceeding before a magistrates' court.

(1A) If, in the case of a recognizance which is conditioned for the appearance of an accused before a magistrates' court, the accused fails to appear in accordance with the condition, the court shall—

(a) declare the recognizance to be forfeited;

(b)   issue a summons directed to each person bound by the recognizance as surety, requiring him to appear before the court on a date specified in the summons to show cause why he should not be adjudged to pay the sum in which he is bound; and on that date the court may proceed in the absence of any surety if it is satisfied that he has been served with the summons.

(2)   If, in any other case falling within subsection (1) above, the recognizance appears to the magistrates' court to be forfeited, the court may—

(a)   declare the recognizance to be forfeited; and

(b)   adjudge each person bound by it, whether as principal or surety, to pay the sum in which he is bound;

but in a case falling within subsection (1)(a) above, the court shall not declare the recognizance to be forfeited except by order made on complaint.'

56.   Bail: restrictions in certain cases of homicide or rape

In subsection (1) of section 25 of the 1994 Act (no bail for defendants charged with or convicted of homicide or rape after previous conviction of such offences), for the words 'shall not be granted bail in those proceedings' there shall be substituted the words 'shall be granted bail in those proceedings only if the court or, as the case may be, the constable considering the grant of bail is satisfied that there are exceptional circumstances which justify it'.

57.   Use of live television links at preliminary hearings

(1)   In any proceedings for an offence, a court may, after hearing representations from the parties, direct that the accused shall be treated as being present in the court for any particular hearing before the start of the trial if, during that hearing—

(a)   he is held in custody in a prison or other institution; and

(b)   whether by means of a live television link or otherwise, he is able to see and hear the court and to be seen and heard by it.

(2)   A court shall not give a direction under subsection (1) above unless—

(a)   it has been notified by the Secretary of State that facilities are available for enabling persons held in custody in the institution in which the accused is or is to be so held to see and hear the court and to be seen and heard by it; and

(b)   the notice has not been withdrawn.

(3)   If in a case where it has power to do so a magistrates' court decides not to give a direction under subsection (1) above, it shall give its reasons for not doing so.

(4)   In this section 'the start of the trial' has the meaning given by subsection (11A) or (11B) of section 22 of the 1985 Act.

PART IV
DEALING WITH OFFENDERS

CHAPTER I
ENGLAND AND WALES

Sexual or violent offenders

58.   Sentences extended for licence purposes

(1)   This section applies where a court which proposes to impose a custodial sentence for a sexual or violent offence considers that the period (if any) for which the offender would, apart from this section, be subject to a licence would not be

adequate for the purpose of preventing the commission by him of further offences and securing his rehabilitation.

(2)   Subject to subsections (3) to (5) below, the court may pass on the offender an extended sentence, that is to say, a custodial sentence the term of which is equal to the aggregate of—

(a)   the term of the custodial sentence that the court would have imposed if it had passed a custodial sentence otherwise than under this section ('the custodial term'); and

(b)   a further period ('the extension period') for which the offender is to be subject to a licence and which is of such length as the court considers necessary for the purpose mentioned in subsection (1) above.

(3)   Where the offence is a violent offence, the court shall not pass an extended sentence the custodial term of which is less than four years.

(4)   The extension period shall not exceed—

(a)   ten years in the case of a sexual offence; and

(b)   five years in the case of a violent offence.

(5)   The term of an extended sentence passed in respect of an offence shall not exceed the maximum term permitted for that offence.

(6)   Subsection (2) of section 2 of the 1991 Act (length of custodial sentences) shall apply as if the term of an extended sentence did not include the extension period.

(7)   The Secretary of State may by order amend paragraph (b) of subsection (4) above by substituting a different period, not exceeding ten years, for the period for the time being specified in that paragraph.

(8)   In this section—

'licence' means a licence under Part II of the 1991 Act;

'sexual offence' and 'violent offence' have the same meanings as in Part I of that Act.

59.   Effect of extended sentences

For section 44 of the 1991 Act there shall be substituted the following section—

'44.   Extended sentences for sexual or violent offenders

(1)   This section applies to a prisoner serving an extended sentence within the meaning of section 58 of the Crime and Disorder Act 1998.

(2)   Subject to the provisions of this section and section 51(2D) below, this Part, except sections 40 and 40A, shall have effect as if the term of the extended sentence did not include the extension period.

(3)   Where the prisoner is released on licence under this Part, the licence shall, subject to any revocation under section 39(1) or (2) above, remain in force until the end of the extension period.

(4)   Where, apart from this subsection, the prisoner would be released unconditionally—

(a)   he shall be released on licence; and

(b)   the licence shall, subject to any revocation under section 39(1) or (2) above, remain in force until the end of the extension period.

(5)   The extension period shall be taken to begin as follows—

(a)   for the purposes of subsection (3) above, on the date given by section 37(1) above;

(b)   for the purposes of subsection (4) above, on the date on which, apart from that subsection, the prisoner would have been released unconditionally.

(6)   Sections 33(3) and 33A(1) above and section 46 below shall not apply in relation to the prisoner.

(7)   For the purposes of sections 37(5) and 39(1) and (2) above the question whether the prisoner is a long-term or short-term prisoner shall be determined by reference to the term of the extended sentence.

(8)   In this section "extension period" has the same meaning as in section 58 of the Crime and Disorder Act 1998.'

60.   Re-release of prisoners serving extended sentences
After section 44 of the 1991 Act there shall be inserted the following section—

'**44.   Re-release of prisoners serving extended sentences**
(1)   This section applies to a prisoner serving an extended sentence within the meaning of section 58 of the Crime and Disorder Act 1998 who is recalled to prison under section 39(1) or (2) above.

(2)   Subject to subsection (3) below, the prisoner may require the Secretary of State to refer his case to the Board at any time.

(3)   Where there has been a previous reference of the prisoner's case to the Board (whether under this section or section 39(4) above), the Secretary of State shall not be required to refer the case until after the end of the period of one year beginning with the disposal of that reference.

(4)   On a reference—
    (a)   under this section; or
    (b)   under section 39(4) above,
the Board shall direct the prisoner's release if satisfied that it is no longer necessary for the protection of the public that he should be confined (but not otherwise).

(5)   If the Board gives a direction under subsection (4) above it shall be the duty of the Secretary of State to release the prisoner on licence.'

Offenders dependent etc. on drugs

61.   Drug treatment and testing orders
(1)   This section applies where a person aged 16 or over is convicted of an offence other than one for which the sentence—
    (a)   is fixed by law; or
    (b)   falls to be imposed under section 2(2), 3(2) or 4(2) of the 1997 Act.

(2)   Subject to the provisions of this section, the court by or before which the offender is convicted may make an order (a 'drug treatment and testing order') which—
    (a)   has effect for a period specified in the order of not less than six months nor more than three years ('the treatment and testing period'); and
    (b)   includes the requirements and provisions mentioned in section 62 below.

(3)   A court shall not make a drug treatment and testing order unless it has been notified by the Secretary of State that arrangements for implementing such orders are available in the area proposed to be specified in the order and the notice has not been withdrawn.

(4) A drug treatment and testing order shall be a community order for the purposes of Part I of the 1991 Act; and the provisions of that Part, which include provisions with respect to restrictions on imposing, and procedural requirements for, community sentences (sections 6 and 7), shall apply accordingly.

(5) The court shall not make a drug treatment and testing order in respect of the offender unless it is satisfied—

(a) that he is dependent on or has a propensity to misuse drugs; and

(b) that his dependency or propensity is such as requires and may be susceptible to treatment.

(6) For the purpose of ascertaining for the purposes of subsection (5) above whether the offender has any drug in his body, the court may by order require him to provide samples of such description as it may specify; but the court shall not make such an order unless the offender expresses his willingness to comply with its requirements.

(7) The Secretary of State may by order amend subsection (2) above by substituting a different period for the minimum or maximum period for the time being specified in that subsection.

62. Requirements and provisions to be included in orders

(1) A drug treatment and testing order shall include a requirement ('the treatment requirement') that the offender shall submit, during the whole of the treatment and testing period, to treatment by or under the direction of a specified person having the necessary qualifications or experience ('the treatment provider') with a view to the reduction or elimination of the offender's dependency on or propensity to misuse drugs.

(2) The required treatment for any particular period shall be—

(a) treatment as a resident in such institution or place as may be specified in the order; or

(b) treatment as a non-resident in or at such institution or place, and at such intervals, as may be so specified;

but the nature of the treatment shall not be specified in the order except as mentioned in paragraph (a) or (b) above.

(3) A court shall not make a drug treatment and testing order unless it is satisfied that arrangements have been or can be made for the treatment intended to be specified in the order (including arrangements for the reception of the offender where he is to be required to submit to treatment as a resident).

(4) A drug treatment and testing order shall include a requirement ('the testing requirement') that, for the purpose of ascertaining whether he has any drug in his body during the treatment and testing period, the offender shall provide during that period, at such times or in such circumstances as may (subject to the provisions of the order) be determined by the treatment provider, samples of such description as may be so determined.

(5) The testing requirement shall specify for each month the minimum number of occasions on which samples are to be provided.

(6) A drug treatment and testing order shall include a provision specifying the petty sessions area in which it appears to the court making the order that the offender resides or will reside.

(7) A drug treatment and testing order shall—

(a)　provide that, for the treatment and testing period, the offender shall be under the supervision of a responsible officer, that is to say, a probation officer appointed for or assigned to the petty sessions area specified in the order;

(b)　require the offender to keep in touch with the responsible officer in accordance with such instructions as he may from time to time be given by that officer, and to notify him of any change of address; and

(c)　provide that the results of the tests carried out on the samples provided by the offender in pursuance of the testing requirement shall be communicated to the responsible officer.

(8)　Supervision by the responsible officer shall be carried out to such extent only as may be necessary for the purpose of enabling him—

(a)　to report on the offender's progress to the court responsible for the order;

(b)　to report to that court any failure by the offender to comply with the requirements of the order; and

(c)　to determine whether the circumstances are such that he should apply to that court for the revocation or amendment of the order.

(9)　In this section and sections 63 and 64 below, references to the court responsible for a drug treatment and testing order are references to—

(a)　the court by which the order is made; or

(b)　where another court is specified in the order in accordance with subsection (10) below, that court.

(10)　Where the area specified in a drug treatment and testing order made by a magistrates' court is not the area for which the court acts, the court may, if it thinks fit, include in the order provision specifying for the purposes of subsection (9) above a magistrates' court which acts for that area.

63.　Periodic reviews

(1)　A drug treatment and testing order shall—

(a)　provide for the order to be reviewed periodically at intervals of not less than one month;

(b)　provide for each review of the order to be made, subject to subsection (7) below, at a hearing held for the purpose by the court responsible for the order (a 'review hearing');

(c)　require the offender to attend each review hearing;

(d)　provide for the responsible officer to make to the court, before each review, a report in writing on the offender's progress under the order; and

(e)　provide for each such report to include the test results communicated to the responsible officer under section 62(7)(c) above and the views of the treatment provider as to the treatment and testing of the offender.

(2)　At a review hearing the court, after considering the responsible officer's report, may amend any requirement or provision of the order.

(3)　The court—

(a)　shall not amend the treatment or testing requirement unless the offender expresses his willingness to comply with the requirement as amended;

(b)　shall not amend any provision of the order so as to reduce the treatment and testing period below the minimum specified in section 61(2) above, or to increase it above the maximum so specified; and

(c) except with the consent of the offender, shall not amend any requirement or provision of the order while an appeal against the order is pending.

(4) If the offender fails to express his willingness to comply with the treatment or testing requirement as proposed to be amended by the court, the court may—

(a) revoke the order; and

(b) deal with him, for the offence in respect of which the order was made, in any manner in which it could deal with him if he had just been convicted by the court of the offence.

(5) In dealing with the offender under subsection (4)(b) above, the court—

(a) shall take into account the extent to which the offender has complied with the requirements of the order; and

(b) may impose a custodial sentence notwithstanding anything in section 1(2) of the 1991 Act.

(6) Where the order was made by a magistrates' court in the case of an offender under the age of 18 years in respect of an offence triable only on indictment in the case of an adult, the court's power under subsection (4)(b) above shall be a power to do either or both of the following, namely—

(a) to impose a fine not exceeding £5,000 for the offence in respect of which the order was made;

(b) to deal with the offender for that offence in any way in which it could deal with him if it had just convicted him of an offence punishable with imprisonment for a term not exceeding six months;

and the reference in paragraph (b) above to an offence punishable with imprisonment shall be construed without regard to any prohibition or restriction imposed by or under any enactment on the imprisonment of young offenders.

(7) If at a review hearing the court, after considering the responsible officer's report, is of the opinion that the offender's progress under the order is satisfactory, the court may so amend the order as to provide for each subsequent review to be made by the court without a hearing.

(8) If at a review without a hearing the court, after considering the responsible officer's report, is of the opinion that the offender's progress under the order is no longer satisfactory, the court may require the offender to attend a hearing of the court at a specified time and place.

(9) At that hearing the court, after considering that report, may—

(a) exercise the powers conferred by this section as if the hearing were a review hearing; and

(b) so amend the order as to provide for each subsequent review to be made at a review hearing.

(10) In this section any reference to the court, in relation to a review without a hearing, shall be construed—

(a) in the case of the Crown Court, as a reference to a judge of the court;

(b) in the case of a magistrates' court, as a reference to a justice of the peace acting for the commission area for which the court acts.

64. Supplementary provisions as to orders

(1) Before making a drug treatment and testing order, a court shall explain to the offender in ordinary language—

(a) the effect of the order and of the requirements proposed to be included in it;

(b)   the consequences which may follow (under Schedule 2 to the 1991 Act) if he fails to comply with any of those requirements;

(c)   that the order may be reviewed (under that Schedule) on the application either of the offender or of the responsible officer; and

(d)   that the order will be periodically reviewed at intervals as provided for in the order (by virtue of section 63 above);

and the court shall not make the order unless the offender expresses his willingness to comply with its requirements.

(2)   Where, in the case of a drug treatment and testing order made by a magistrates' court, another magistrates' court is responsible for the order, the court making the order shall forthwith send copies of the order to the other court.

(3)   Where a drug treatment and testing order is made or amended under section 63(2) above, the court responsible for the order shall forthwith or, in a case falling within subsection (2) above, as soon as reasonably practicable give copies of the order, or the order as amended, to a probation officer assigned to the court, and he shall give a copy—

(a)   to the offender;

(b)   to the treatment provider; and

(c)   to the responsible officer.

(4)   Where a drug treatment and testing order has been made on an appeal brought from the Crown Court, or from the criminal division of the Court of Appeal, for the purposes of sections 62 and 63 above it shall be deemed to have been made by the Crown Court.

(5)   Schedule 2 to the 1991 Act (enforcement etc. of community orders) shall have effect subject to the amendments specified in Schedule 4 to this Act, being amendments for applying that Schedule to drug treatment and testing orders.

Young offenders: reprimands and warnings

65.   Reprimands and warnings

(1)   Subsections (2) to (5) below apply where—

(a)   a constable has evidence that a child or young person ('the offender') has committed an offence;

(b)   the constable considers that the evidence is such that, if the offender were prosecuted for the offence, there would be a realistic prospect of his being convicted;

(c)   the offender admits to the constable that he committed the offence;

(d)   the offender has not previously been convicted of an offence; and

(e)   the constable is satisfied that it would not be in the public interest for the offender to be prosecuted.

(2)   Subject to subsection (4) below, the constable may reprimand the offender if the offender has not previously been reprimanded or warned.

(3)   The constable may warn the offender if—

(a)   the offender has not previously been warned; or

(b)   where the offender has previously been warned, the offence was committed more than two years after the date of the previous warning and the constable considers the offence to be not so serious as to require a charge to be brought;

but no person may be warned under paragraph (b) above more than once.

(4)   Where the offender has not been previously reprimanded, the constable shall warn rather than reprimand the offender if he considers the offence to be so serious as to require a warning.

(5)   The constable shall—

(a)   give any reprimand or warning at a police station and, where the offender is under the age of 17, in the presence of an appropriate adult; and

(b)   explain to the offender and, where he is under that age, the appropriate adult in ordinary language—

(i)   in the case of a reprimand, the effect of subsection (5)(a) of section 66 below;

(ii)   in the case of a warning, the effect of subsections (1), (2), (4) and (5)(b) and (c) of that section, and any guidance issued under subsection (3) of that section.

(6)   The Secretary of State shall publish, in such manner as he considers appropriate, guidance as to—

(a)   the circumstances in which it is appropriate to give reprimands or warnings, including criteria for determining—

(i)   for the purposes of subsection (3)(b) above, whether an offence is not so serious as to require a charge to be brought; and

(ii)   for the purposes of subsection (4) above, whether an offence is so serious as to require a warning;

(b)   the category of constable by whom reprimands and warnings may be given; and

(c)   the form which reprimands and warnings are to take and the manner in which they are to be given and recorded.

(7)   In this section 'appropriate adult', in relation to a child or young person, means—

(a)   his parent or guardian or, if he is in the care of a local authority or voluntary organisation, a person representing that authority or organisation;

(b)   a social worker of a local authority social services department;

(c)   if no person falling within paragraph (a) or (b) above is available, any responsible person aged 18 or over who is not a police officer or a person employed by the police.

(8)   No caution shall be given to a child or young person after the commencement of this section.

(9)   Any reference (however expressed) in any enactment passed before or in the same Session as this Act to a person being cautioned shall be construed, in relation to any time after that commencement, as including a reference to a child or young person being reprimanded or warned.

66.   Effect of reprimands and warnings

(1)   Where a constable warns a person under section 65 above, he shall as soon as practicable refer the person to a youth offending team.

(2)   A youth offending team—

(a)   shall assess any person referred to them under subsection (1) above; and

(b)   unless they consider it inappropriate to do so, shall arrange for him to participate in a rehabilitation programme.

(3)   The Secretary of State shall publish, in such manner as he considers appropriate, guidance as to—

(a)   what should be included in a rehabilitation programme arranged for a person under subsection (2) above;

(b)   the manner in which any failure by a person to participate in such a programme is to be recorded; and

    (c)   the persons to whom any such failure is to be notified.

    (4)   Where a person who has been warned under section 65 above is convicted of an offence committed within two years of the warning, the court by or before which he is so convicted—

    (a)   shall not make an order under subsection (1)(b) (conditional discharge) of section 1A of the 1973 Act in respect of the offence unless it is of the opinion that there are exceptional circumstances relating to the offence or the offender which justify its doing so; and

    (b)   where it does so, shall state in open court that it is of that opinion and why it is.

    (5)   The following, namely—

    (a)   any reprimand of a person under section 65 above;

    (b)   any warning of a person under that section; and

    (c)   any report on a failure by a person to participate in a rehabilitation programme arranged for him under subsection (2) above,

may be cited in criminal proceedings in the same circumstances as a conviction of the person may be cited.

    (6)   In this section 'rehabilitation programme' means a programme the purpose of which is to rehabilitate participants and to prevent them from re-offending.

Young offenders: non-custodial orders

67. Reparation orders

    (1)   This section applies where a child or young person is convicted of an offence other than one for which the sentence is fixed by law.

    (2)   Subject to the provisions of this section and section 68 below, the court by or before which the offender is convicted may make an order (a 'reparation order') which requires the offender to make reparation specified in the order:

    (a)   to a person or persons so specified; or

    (b)   to the community at large;

and any person so specified must be a person identified by the court as a victim of the offence or a person otherwise affected by it.

    (3)   The court shall not make a reparation order unless it has been notified by the Secretary of State that arrangements for implementing such orders are available in the area proposed to be named in the order and the notice has not been withdrawn.

    (4)   The court shall not make a reparation order in respect of the offender if it proposes—

    (a)   to pass on him a custodial sentence or a sentence under section 53(1) of the 1933 Act; or

    (b)   to make in respect of him a community service order, a combination order, a supervision order which includes requirements imposed in pursuance of sections 12 to 12C of the 1969 Act or an action plan order.

    (5)   A reparation order shall not require the offender—

    (a)   to work for more than 24 hours in aggregate; or

    (b)   to make reparation to any person without the consent of that person.

    (6)   Subject to subsection (5) above, requirements specified in a reparation order shall be such as in the opinion of the court are commensurate with seriousness of the offence, or the combination of the offence and one or more offences associated with it.

(7)   Requirements so specified shall, as far as practicable, be such as to avoid—
    (a)   any conflict with the offender's religious beliefs or with the requirements of any community order to which he may be subject; and
    (b)   any interference with the times, if any, at which the offender normally works or attends school or any other educational establishment.
(8)   Any reparation required by a reparation order—
    (a)   shall be made under the supervision of the responsible officer; and
    (b)   shall be made within a period of three months from the date of the making of the order.
(9)   A reparation order shall name the petty sessions area in which it appears to the court making the order, or to the court varying any provision included in the order in pursuance of this subsection, that the offender resides or will reside.
(10)   In this section 'responsible officer', in relation to a reparation order, means one of the following who is specified in the order, namely—
    (a)   a probation officer;
    (b)   a social worker of a local authority social services department; and
    (c)   a member of a youth offending team.
(11)   The court shall give reasons if it does not make a reparation order in a case where it has power to do so.

68.   Reparation orders: supplemental

(1)   Before making a reparation order, a court shall obtain and consider a written report by a probation officer, a social worker of a local authority social services department or a member of a youth offending team, indicating—
    (a)   the type of work that is suitable for the offender; and
    (b)   the attitude of the victim or victims to the requirements proposed to be included in the order.
(2)   Before making a reparation order, a court shall explain to the offender in ordinary language—
    (a)   the effect of the order and of the requirements proposed to be included in it;
    (b)   the consequences which may follow (under Schedule 5 to this Act) if he fails to comply with any of those requirements; and
    (c)   that the court has power (under that Schedule) to review the order on the application either of the offender or of the responsible officer.
(3)   Schedule 5 to this Act shall have effect for dealing with failure to comply with the requirements of reparation orders, for varying such orders and for discharging them with or without the substitution of other sentences.

69.   Action plan orders

(1)   This section applies where a child or young person is convicted of an offence other than one for which the sentence is fixed by law.
(2)   Subject to the provisions of this section and section 70 below, the court by or before which the offender is convicted may, if it is of the opinion that it is desirable to do so in the interests of securing his rehabilitation, or of preventing the commission by him of further offences, make an order (an 'action plan order') which—
    (a)   requires the offender, for a period of three months beginning with the date of the order, to comply with an action plan, that is to say, a series of requirements with respect to his actions and whereabouts during that period;

(b) places the offender under the supervision for that period of the responsible officer; and

(c) requires the offender to comply with any directions given by that officer with a view to the implementation of that plan.

(3) The court shall not make an action plan order unless it has been notified by the Secretary of State that arrangements for implementing such orders are available in the area proposed to be named in the order and the notice has not been withdrawn.

(4) The court shall not make an action plan order in respect of the offender if

(a) he is already the subject of such an order; or

(b) the court proposes to pass on him a custodial sentence or a sentence under section 53(1) of the 1933 Act, or to make in respect of him a probation order, a community service order, a combination order, a supervision order or an attendance centre order.

(5) Requirements included in an action plan order, or directions given by a responsible officer, may require the offender to do all or any of the following things, namely—

(a) to participate in activities specified in the requirements or directions at a time or times so specified;

(b) to present himself to a person or persons specified in the requirements or directions at a place or places and at a time or times so specified;

(c) to attend at an attendance centre specified in the requirements or directions for a number of hours so specified;

(d) to stay away from a place or places specified in the requirements or directions;

(e) to comply with any arrangements for his education specified in the requirements or directions;

(f) to make reparation specified in the requirements or directions to a person or persons so specified or to the community at large; and

(g) to attend any hearing fixed by the court under section 70(3) below.

(6) Such requirements and directions shall, as far as practicable, be such as to avoid—

(a) any conflict with the offender's religious beliefs or with the requirements of any other community order to which he may be subject; and

(b) any interference with the times, if any, at which he normally works or attends school or any other educational establishment.

(7) Subsection (5)(c) above does not apply unless the offence committed by the offender is punishable with imprisonment in the case of a person aged 21 or over.

(8) A person shall not be specified in requirements or directions under subsection (5)(f) above unless—

(a) he is identified by the court or, as the case may be, the responsible officer as a victim of the offence or a person otherwise affected by it; and

(b) he consents to the reparation being made.

(9) An action plan order shall name the petty sessions area in which it appears to the court making the order, or to the court varying any provision included in the order in pursuance of this subsection, that the offender resides or will reside.

(10) In this section 'responsible officer', in relation to an action plan order, means one of the following who is specified in the order, namely—

(a) a probation officer;

(b)   a social worker of a local authority social services department; and

(c)   a member of a youth offending team.

(11)   An action plan order shall be a community order for the purposes of Part I of the 1991 Act; and the provisions of that Part, which include provisions with respect to restrictions on imposing, and procedural requirements for, community sentences (sections 6 and 7), shall apply accordingly.

70. Action plan orders: supplemental

(1)   Before making an action plan order, a court shall obtain and consider—

(a)   a written report by a probation officer, a social worker of a local authority social services department or a member of a youth offending team, indicating—

(i)   the requirements proposed by that person to be included in the order;

(ii)   the benefits to the offender that the proposed requirements are designed to achieve; and

(iii)   the attitude of a parent or guardian of the offender to the proposed requirements; and

(b)   where the offender is under the age of 16, information about the offender's family circumstances and the likely effect of the order on those circumstances.

(2)   Before making an action plan order, a court shall explain to the offender in ordinary language—

(a)   the effect of the order and of the requirements proposed to be included in it;

(b)   the consequences which may follow (under Schedule 5 to this Act) if he fails to comply with any of those requirements; and

(c)   that the court has power (under that Schedule) to review the order on the application either of the offender or of the responsible officer.

(3)   Immediately after making an action plan order, a court may—

(a)   fix a further hearing for a date not more than 21 days after the making of the order; and

(b)   direct the responsible officer to make, at that hearing, a report as to the effectiveness of the order and the extent to which it has been implemented.

(4)   At a hearing fixed under subsection (3) above, the court—

(a)   shall consider the responsible officer's report; and

(b)   may, on the application of the responsible officer or the offender, vary the order—

(i)   by cancelling any provision included in it; or

(ii)   by inserting in it (either in addition to or in substitution for any of its provisions) any provision that the court could originally have included in it.

(5)   Schedule 5 to this Act shall have effect for dealing with failure to comply with the requirements of action plan orders, for varying such orders and for discharging them with or without the substitution of other sentences.

71. Supervision orders

(1)   In subsection (3) of section 12A of the 1969 Act (young offenders), after paragraph (a) there shall be inserted the following paragraph—

'(aa)   to make reparation specified in the order to a person or persons so specified or to the community at large;'.

(2)   In subsection (5) of that section, for the words 'subsection (3)(a) or (b)' there shall be substituted the words 'subsection (3)(a), (aa) or (b)'.

(3)   In subsection (7) of that section, after paragraph (a) there shall be inserted the following paragraph—

'(aa)   any requirement to make reparation to any person unless that person—
(i)   is identified by the court as a victim of the offence or a person otherwise affected by it; and
(ii)   consents to the inclusion of the requirement; or'.

(4)   In subsection (6) of section 12AA of the 1969 Act (requirement for young offender to live in local authority accommodation), for paragraphs (b) to (d) there shall be substituted the following paragraphs—

'(b)   that order imposed—
(i)   a requirement under section 12, 12A or 12C of this Act; or
(ii)   a residence requirement;
(c)   he fails to comply with that requirement, or is found guilty of an offence committed while that order was in force; and
(d)   the court is satisfied that—
(i)   the failure to comply with the requirement, or the behaviour which constituted the offence, was due to a significant extent to the circumstances in which he was living; and
(ii)   the imposition of a residence requirement will assist in his rehabilitation;';

and for the words 'the condition in paragraph (d)' there shall be substituted the words 'sub-paragraph (i) of paragraph (d)'.

(5)   In section 13 of the 1969 Act (selection of supervisor), subsection (2) shall cease to have effect.

72.   Breach of requirements in supervision orders

(1)   In subsection (3) of section 15 of the 1969 Act (variation and discharge of supervision orders), for paragraphs (a) and (b) there shall be substituted the following paragraphs—

'(a)   whether or not it also makes an order under subsection (1) above, may order him to pay a fine of an amount not exceeding £1,000, or make in respect of him—
(i)   subject to section 16A(1) of this Act, an order under section 17 of the Criminal Justice Act 1982 (attendance centre orders); or
(ii)   subject to section 16B of this Act, an order under section 12 of the Criminal Justice Act 1991 (curfew orders);
(b)   if the supervision order was made by a relevant court, may discharge the order and deal with him, for the offence in respect of which the order was made, in any manner in which he could have been dealt with for that offence by the court which made the order if the order had not been made; or
(c)   if the order was made by the Crown Court, may commit him in custody or release him on bail until he can be brought or appear before the Crown Court.'

(2)   For subsections (4) to (6) of that section there shall be substituted the following subsections—

'(4)   Where a court deals with a supervised person under subsection (3)(c) above, it shall send to the Crown Court a certificate signed by a justice of the peace giving—
(a)   particulars of the supervised person's failure to comply with the requirement in question; and

(b)   such other particulars of the case as may be desirable;
and a certificate purporting to be so signed shall be admissible as evidence of the
failure before the Crown Court.

(5)   Where—

(a)   by virtue of subsection (3)(c) above the supervised person is brought or
appears before the Crown Court; and

(b)   it is proved to the satisfaction of the court that he has failed to comply
with the requirement in question,
that court may deal with him, for the offence in respect of which the order was
made, in any manner in which it could have dealt with him for that offence if it had
not made the order.

(6)   Where the Crown Court deals with a supervised person under subsection
(5) above, it shall discharge the supervision order if it is still in force.'

(3)   In subsections (7) and (8) of that section, for the words 'or (4)' there shall be
substituted the words 'or (5)'.

Young offenders: detention and training orders

73.   Detention and training orders

(1)   Subject to section 53 of the 1933 Act, section 8 of the Criminal Justice Act
1982 ('the 1982 Act') and subsection (2) below, where—

(a)   a child or young person ('the offender') is convicted of an offence which
is punishable with imprisonment in the case of a person aged 21 or over; and

(b)   the court is of the opinion that either or both of paragraphs (a) or (b) of
subsection (2) of section 1 of the 1991 Act apply or the case falls within subsection
(3) of that section,
the sentence that the court is to pass is a detention and training order.

(2)   A court shall not make a detention and training order—

(a)   in the case of an offender under the age of 15 at the time of the conviction,
unless it is of the opinion that he is a persistent offender;

(b)   in the case of an offender under the age of 12 at that time, unless—

(i)   it is of the opinion that only a custodial sentence would be adequate to
protect the public from further offending by him; and

(ii)   the offence was committed on or after such date as the Secretary of
State may by order appoint.

(3)   A detention and training order is an order that the offender in respect of whom
it is made shall be subject, for the term specified in the order, to a period of detention
and training followed by a period of supervision.

(4)   A detention and training order shall be a custodial sentence for the purposes
of Part I of the 1991 Act; and the provisions of sections 1 to 4 of that Act shall apply
accordingly.

(5)   Subject to subsection (6) below, the term of a detention and training order
shall be 4, 6, 8, 10, 12, 18 or 24 months.

(6)   The term of a detention and training order may not exceed the maximum term
of imprisonment that the Crown Court could (in the case of an offender aged 21 or
over) impose for the offence.

(7)   The following provisions, namely—

(a)   section 1B of the 1982 Act (detention in young offender institutions: special provision for offenders under 18); and
(b)   sections 1 to 4 of the 1994 Act (secure training orders),
which are superseded by this section and sections 74 to 78 below, shall cease to have effect.

74.   Duties and powers of court

(1)   On making a detention and training order in a case where subsection (2) of section 73 above applies, it shall be the duty of the court (in addition to the duty imposed by section 1(4) of the 1991 Act) to state in open court that it is of the opinion mentioned in paragraph (a) or, as the case may be, paragraphs (a) and (b)(i) of that subsection.

(2)   Subject to subsection (3) below, where—
(a)   an offender is convicted of more than one offence for which he is liable to a detention and training order; or
(b)   an offender who is subject to a detention and training order is convicted of one or more further offences for which he is liable to such an order,
the court shall have the same power to pass consecutive detention and training orders as if they were sentences of imprisonment.

(3)   A court shall not make in respect of an offender a detention and training order the effect of which would be that he would be subject to detention and training orders for a term which exceeds 24 months.

(4)   Where the term of the detention and training orders to which an offender would otherwise be subject exceeds 24 months, the excess shall be treated as remitted.

(5)   In determining the term of a detention and training order for an offence, the court shall take account of any period for which the offender has been remanded in custody in connection with the offence, or any other offence the charge for which was founded on the same facts or evidence.

(6)   The reference in subsection (5) above to an offender being remanded in custody is a reference to his being—
(a)   held in police detention;
(b)   remanded in or committed to custody by an order of a court;
(c)   remanded or committed to local authority accommodation under section 23 of the 1969 Act and placed and kept in secure accommodation; or
(d)   remanded, admitted or removed to hospital under section 35, 36, 38 or 48 of the Mental Health Act 1983.

(7)   A person is in police detention for the purposes of subsection (6) above—
(a)   at any time when he is in police detention for the purposes of the 1984 Act; and
(b)   at any time when he is detained under section 14 of the Prevention of Terrorism (Temporary Provisions) Act 1989;
and in that subsection 'secure accommodation' has the same meaning as in section 23 of the 1969 Act.

(8)   For the purpose of any reference in this section or sections 75 to 78 below to the term of a detention and training order, consecutive terms of such orders and terms of such orders which are wholly or partly concurrent shall be treated as a single term if—
(a)   the orders were made on the same occasion; or

(b)   where they were made on different occasions, the offender has not been released (by virtue of subsection (2), (3), (4) or (5) of section 75 below) at any time during the period beginning with the first and ending with the last of those occasions.

75.   The period of detention and training

(1)   An offender shall serve the period of detention and training under a detention and training order in such secure accommodation as may be determined by the Secretary of State or by such other person as may be authorised by him for that purpose.

(2)   Subject to subsections (3) to (5) below, the period of detention and training under a detention and training order shall be one-half of the term of the order.

(3)   The Secretary of State may at any time release the offender if he is satisfied that exceptional circumstances exist which justify the offender's release on compassionate grounds.

(4)   The Secretary of State may release the offender—

(a)   in the case of an order for a term of 8 months or more but less than 18 months, one month before the half-way point of the term of the order; and

(b)   in the case of an order for a term of 18 months or more, one month or two months before that point.

(5)   If the youth court so orders on an application made by the Secretary of State for the purpose, the Secretary of State shall release the offender—

(a)   in the case of an order for a term of 8 months or more but less than 18 months, one month after the half-way point of the term of the order; and

(b)   in the case of an order for a term of 18 months or more, one month or two months after that point.

(6)   An offender detained in pursuance of a detention and training order shall be deemed to be in legal custody.

(7)   In this section and sections 77 and 78 below 'secure accommodation' means—

(a)   a secure training centre;

(b)   a young offender institution;

(c)   accommodation provided by a local authority for the purpose of restricting the liberty of children and young persons;

(d)   accommodation provided for that purpose under subsection (5) of section 82 of the 1989 Act (financial support by the Secretary of State); or

(e)   such other accommodation provided for the purpose of restricting liberty as the Secretary of State may direct.

76.   The period of supervision

(1)   The period of supervision of an offender who is subject to a detention and training order—

(a)   shall begin with the offender's release, whether at the half-way point of the term of the order or otherwise; and

(b)   subject to subsection (2) below, shall end when the term of the order ends.

(2)   The Secretary of State may by order provide that the period of supervision shall end at such point during the term of a detention and training order as may be specified in the order under this subsection.

(3)   During the period of supervision, the offender shall be under the supervision of—

    (a)   a probation officer;

    (b)   a social worker of a local authority social services department; or

    (c)   a member of a youth offending team;

and the category of person to supervise the offender shall be determined from time to time by the Secretary of State.

    (4)   Where the supervision is to be provided by a probation officer, the probation officer shall be an officer appointed for or assigned to the petty sessions area within which the offender resides for the time being.

    (5)   Where the supervision is to be provided by—

    (a)   a social worker of a local authority social services department; or

    (b)   a member of a youth offending team,

the social worker or member shall be a social worker of, or a member of a youth offending team established by, the local authority within whose area the offender resides for the time being.

    (6)   The offender shall be given a notice from the Secretary of State specifying—

    (a)   the category of person for the time being responsible for his supervision; and

    (b)   any requirements with which he must for the time being comply.

    (7)   A notice under subsection (6) above shall be given to the offender—

    (a)   before the commencement of the period of supervision; and

    (b)   before any alteration in the matters specified in subsection (6)(a) or (b) above comes into effect.

77. Breaches of supervision requirements

    (1)   Where a detention and training order is in force in respect of an offender and it appears on information to a justice of the peace acting for a relevant petty sessions area that the offender has failed to comply with requirements under section 76(6)(b) above, the justice—

    (a)   may issue a summons requiring the offender to appear at the place and time specified in the summons before a youth court acting for the area; or

    (b)   if the information is in writing and on oath, may issue a warrant for the offender's arrest requiring him to be brought before such a court.

    (2)   For the purposes of this section a petty sessions area is a relevant petty sessions area in relation to a detention and training order if—

    (a)   the order was made by a youth court acting for it; or

    (b)   the offender resides in it for the time being.

    (3)   If it is proved to the satisfaction of the youth court before which an offender appears or is brought under this section that he has failed to comply with requirements under section 76(6)(b) above, that court may—

    (a)   order the offender to be detained, in such secure accommodation as the Secretary of State may determine, for such period, not exceeding the shorter of three months or the remainder of the term of the detention and training order, as the court may specify; or

    (b)   impose on the offender a fine not exceeding level 3 on the standard scale.

    (4)   An offender detained in pursuance of an order under subsection (3) above shall be deemed to be in legal custody; and a fine imposed under that subsection shall be deemed, for the purposes of any enactment, to be a sum adjudged to be paid by a conviction.

78. Offences during currency of order

(1)   This section applies to a person subject to a detention and training order if—

(a)   after his release and before the date on which the term of the order ends, he commits an offence punishable with imprisonment in the case of a person aged 21 or over; and

(b)   whether before or after that date, he is convicted of that offence ('the new offence').

(2)   Subject to section 7(8) of the 1969 Act, the court by or before which a person to whom this section applies is convicted of the new offence may, whether or not it passes any other sentence on him, order him to be detained in such secure accommodation as the Secretary of State may determine for the whole or any part of the period which—

(a)   begins with the date of the court's order; and

(b)   is equal in length to the period between the date on which the new offence was committed and the date mentioned in subsection (1) above.

(3)   The period for which a person to whom this section applies is ordered under subsection (2) above to be detained in secure accommodation—

(a)   shall, as the court may direct, either be served before and be followed by, or be served concurrently with, any sentence imposed for the new offence; and

(b)   in either case, shall be disregarded in determining the appropriate length of that sentence.

(4)   Where the new offence is found to have been committed over a period of two or more days, or at some time during a period of two or more days, it shall be taken for the purposes of this section to have been committed on the last of those days.

(5)   A person detained in pursuance of an order under subsection (2) above shall be deemed to be in legal custody.

79. Interaction with sentences of detention

(1)   Where a court passes a sentence of detention in a young offender institution in the case of an offender who is subject to a detention and training order, the sentence shall take effect as follows—

(a)   if the offender has been released by virtue of subsection (2), (3), (4) or (5) of section 75 above, at the beginning of the day on which it is passed;

(b)   if not, either as mentioned in paragraph (a) above or, if the court so orders, at the time when the offender would otherwise be released by virtue of that subsection.

(2)   Where a court makes a detention and training order in the case of an offender who is subject to a sentence of detention in a young offender institution, the order shall take effect as follows—

(a)   if the offender has been released under Part II of the 1991 Act, at the beginning of the day on which it is made;

(b)   if not, either as mentioned in paragraph (a) above or, if the court so orders, at the time when the offender would otherwise be released under that Part.

(3)   Subject to subsection (4) below, where at any time an offender is subject concurrently—

(a)   to a detention and training order; and

(b)   to a sentence of detention in a young offender institution,

he shall be treated for the purposes of sections 75 to 78 above, section 1C of the 1982 Act and Part II of the 1991 Act as if he were subject only to the one of them that was imposed on the later occasion.

(4)   Nothing in subsection (3) above shall require the offender to be released in respect of either the order or the sentence unless and until he is required to be released in respect of each of them.

(5)   Where, by virtue of any enactment giving a court power to deal with a person in a manner in which a court on a previous occasion could have dealt with him, a detention and training order for any term is made in the case of a person who has attained the age of 18, the person shall be treated as if he had been sentenced to detention in a young offender institution for the same term.

Sentencing: general

80.   Sentencing guidelines
   (1)   This section applies where the Court—
   (a)   is seised of an appeal against, or a reference under section 36 of the Criminal Justice Act 1988 with respect to, the sentence passed for an offence; or
   (b)   receives a proposal under section 81 below in respect of a particular category of offence;
and in this section 'the relevant category' means any category within which the offence falls or, as the case may be, the category to which the proposal relates.

   (2)   The Court shall consider—
   (a)   whether to frame guidelines as to the sentencing of offenders for offences of the relevant category; or
   (b)   where such guidelines already exist, whether it would be appropriate to review them.

   (3)   Where the Court decides to frame or revise such guidelines, the Court shall have regard to—
   (a)   the need to promote consistency in sentencing;
   (b)   the sentences imposed by courts in England and Wales for offences of the relevant category;
   (c)   the cost of different sentences and their relative effectiveness in preventing re-offending;
   (d)   the need to promote public confidence in the criminal justice system; and
   (e)   the views communicated to the Court, in accordance with section 81(4)(b) below, by the Sentencing Advisory Panel.

   (4)   Guidelines framed or revised under this section shall include criteria for determining the seriousness of offences, including (where appropriate) criteria for determining the weight to be given to any previous convictions of offenders or any failures of theirs to respond to previous sentences.

   (5)   In a case falling within subsection (1)(a) above, guidelines framed or revised under this section shall, if practicable, be included in the Court's judgment in the appeal.

   (6)   Subject to subsection (5) above, guidelines framed or revised under this section shall be included in a judgment of the Court at the next appropriate opportunity (having regard to the relevant category of offence).

   (7)   For the purposes of this section, the Court is seised of an appeal against a sentence if—
   (a)   the Court or a single judge has granted leave to appeal against the sentence under section 9 or 10 of the Criminal Appeal Act 1968; or

(b)   in a case where the judge who passed the sentence granted a certificate of fitness for appeal under section 9 or 10 of that Act, notice of appeal has been given, and (in either case) the appeal has not been abandoned or disposed of.

(8)   For the purposes of this section, the Court is seised of a reference under section 36 of the Criminal Justice Act 1988 if it has given leave under subsection (1) of that section and the reference has not been disposed of.

(9)   In this section and section 81 below—

'the Court' means the criminal division of the Court of Appeal;

'offence' means an indictable offence.

81.   The Sentencing Advisory Panel

(1)   The Lord Chancellor, after consultation with the Secretary of State and the Lord Chief Justice, shall constitute a sentencing panel to be known as the Sentencing Advisory Panel ('the Panel') and appoint one of the members of the Panel to be its chairman.

(2)   Where, in a case falling within subsection (1)(a) of section 80 above, the Court decides to frame or revise guidelines under that section for a particular category of offence, the Court shall notify the Panel.

(3)   The Panel may at any time, and shall if directed to do so by the Secretary of State, propose to the Court that guidelines be framed or revised under section 80 above for a particular category of offence.

(4)   Where the Panel receives a notification under subsection (2) above or makes a proposal under subsection (3) above, the Panel shall—

(a)   obtain and consider the views on the matters in issue of such persons or bodies as may be determined, after consultation with the Secretary of State and the Lord Chief Justice, by the Lord Chancellor;

(b)   formulate its own views on those matters and communicate them to the Court; and

(c)   furnish information to the Court as to the matters mentioned in section 80(3)(b) and (c) above.

(5)   The Lord Chancellor may pay to any member of the Panel such remuneration as he may determine.

82.   Increase in sentences for racial aggravation

(1)   This section applies where a court is considering the seriousness of an offence other than one under sections 29 to 32 above.

(2)   If the offence was racially aggravated, the court—

(a)   shall treat that fact as an aggravating factor (that is to say, a factor that increases the seriousness of the offence); and

(b)   shall state in open court that the offence was so aggravated.

(3)   Section 28 above applies for the purposes of this section as it applies for the purposes of sections 29 to 32 above.

Miscellaneous and supplemental

83.   Power to make confiscation orders on committal for sentence

After subsection (9) of section 71 of the Criminal Justice Act 1988 (confiscation orders) there shall be inserted the following subsection—

'(9A)   Where an offender is committed by a magistrates' court for sentence under section 38 or 38A of the Magistrates' Courts Act 1980 or section 56 of the

Criminal Justice Act 1967, this section and sections 72 to 74C below shall have effect as if the offender had been convicted of the offence in the proceedings before the Crown Court and not in the proceedings before the magistrates' court.'

84.   Football spectators: failure to comply with reporting duty

(1)   In section 16(5) of the Football Spectators Act 1989 (penalties for failure to comply with reporting duty imposed by restriction order)—

(a)   for the words 'one month' there shall be substituted the words 'six months'; and

(b)   for the words 'level 3' there shall be substituted the words 'level 5'.

(2)   In section 24(2) of the 1984 Act (arrestable offences), after paragraph (p) there shall be inserted—

'(q)   an offence under section 16(4) of the Football Spectators Act 1989 (failure to comply with reporting duty imposed by restriction order).'

85.   Interpretation etc. of Chapter I

(1)   In this Chapter—

'action plan order' has the meaning given by section 69(2) above;

'detention and training order' has the meaning given by section 73(3) above;

'drug treatment and testing order' has the meaning given by section 61(2) above;

'make reparation', in relation to an offender, means make reparation for the offence otherwise than by the payment of compensation;

'reparation order' has the meaning given by section 67(2) above;

'responsible officer'—

(a)   in relation to a drug treatment and testing order, has the meaning given by section 62(7) above;

(b)   in relation to a reparation order, has the meaning given by section 67(10) above;

(c)   in relation to an action plan order, has the meaning given by section 69(10) above.

(2)   Where the supervision under a reparation order or action plan order is be provided by a probation officer, the probation officer shall be an officer appointed for or assigned to the petty sessions area named in the order.

(3)   Where the supervision under a reparation order or action plan order is to be provided by—

(a)   a social worker of a local authority social services department; or

(b)   a member of a youth offending team,

the social worker or member shall be a social worker of, or a member of a youth offending team established by, the local authority within whose area it appears to the court that the child or young person resides or will reside.

(4)   In this Chapter, in relation to a drug treatment and testing order—

'the treatment and testing period' has the meaning given by section 61(2) above;

'the treatment provider' and 'the treatment requirement' have the meanings given by subsection (1) of section 62 above;

'the testing requirement' has the meaning given by subsection (4) of that section.

(5)   In this Chapter, unless the contrary intention appears, expressions which are also used in Part I of the 1991 Act have the same meanings as in that Part.

(6)   For the purposes of this Chapter, a sentence falls to be imposed under section 2(2), 3(2) or 4(2) of the 1997 Act if it is required by that provision and the court is not of the opinion there mentioned.

CHAPTER II
SCOTLAND

Sexual or violent offenders

86.   Extended sentences for sex and violent offenders
(1)   After section 210 of the 1995 Act there shall be inserted the following section—

'210A.   Extended sentences for sex and violent offenders
(1)   Where a person is convicted on indictment of a sexual or violent offence, the court may, if it—
(a)   intends, in relation to—
(i)   a sexual offence, to pass a determinate sentence of imprisonment; or
(ii)   a violent offence, to pass such a sentence for a term of four years or more; and
(b)   considers that the period (if any) for which the offender would, apart from this section, be subject to a licence would not be adequate for the purpose of protecting the public from serious harm from the offender,
pass an extended sentence on the offender.
(2)   An extended sentence is a sentence of imprisonment which is the aggregate of—
(a)   the term of imprisonment ("the custodial term") which the court would have passed on the offender otherwise than by virtue of this section; and
(b)   a further period ("the extension period") for which the offender is to be subject to a licence and which is, subject to the provisions of this section, of such length as the court considers necessary for the purpose mentioned in subsection (1)(b) above.
(3)   The extension period shall not exceed, in the case of—
(a)   a sexual offence, ten years; and
(b)   a violent offence, five years.
(4)   A court shall, before passing an extended sentence, consider a report by a relevant officer of a local authority about the offender and his circumstances and, if the court thinks it necessary, hear that officer.
(5)   The term of an extended sentence passed for a statutory offence shall not exceed the maximum term of imprisonment provided for in the statute in respect of that offence.
(6)   Subject to subsection (5) above, a sheriff may pass an extended sentence which is the aggregate of a custodial term not exceeding the maximum term of imprisonment which he may impose and an extension period not exceeding three years.
(7)   The Secretary of State may by order—
(a)   amend paragraph (b) of subsection (3) above by substituting a different period, not exceeding ten years, for the period for the time being specified in that paragraph; and

(b)   make such transitional provision as appears to him to be necessary or expedient in connection with the amendment.

(8)   The power to make an order under subsection (7) above shall be exercisable by statutory instrument; but no such order shall be made unless a draft of the order has been laid before, and approved by a resolution of, each House of Parliament.

(9)   An extended sentence shall not be imposed where the sexual or violent offence was committed before the commencement of section 86 of the Crime and Disorder Act 1998.

(10)   For the purposes of this section—

"licence" and "relevant officer" have the same meaning as in Part I of the Prisoners and Criminal Proceedings (Scotland) Act 1993;

"sexual offence" means—

(i)   rape;

(ii)   clandestine injury to women;

(iii)   abduction of a woman or girl with intent to rape or ravish;

(iv)   assault with intent to rape or ravish;

(v)   indecent assault;

(vi)   lewd, indecent or libidinous behaviour or practices;

(vii)   shameless indecency;

(viii) sodomy;

(ix)   an offence under section 170 of the Customs and Excise Management Act 1979 in relation to goods prohibited to be imported under section 42 of the Customs Consolidation Act 1876, but only where the prohibited goods include indecent photographs of persons;

(x)   an offence under section 52 of the Civic Government (Scotland) Act 1982 (taking and distribution of indecent images of children);

(xi)   an offence under section 52A of that Act (possession of indecent images of children);

(xii)   an offence under section 1 of the Criminal Law (Consolidation) (Scotland) Act 1995 (incest);

(xiii) an offence under section 2 of that Act (intercourse with a stepchild);

(xiv)   an offence under section 3 of that Act (intercourse with child under 16 by person in position of trust);

(xv)   an offence under section 5 of that Act (unlawful intercourse with girl under 16);

(xvi)   an offence under section 6 of that Act (indecent behaviour towards girl between 12 and 16);

(xvii) an offence under section 8 of that Act (abduction of girl under 18 for purposes of unlawful intercourse);

(xviii) an offence under section 10 of that Act (person having parental responsibilities causing or encouraging sexual activity in relation to a girl under 16); and

(xix)   an offence under subsection (5) of section 13 of that Act (homosexual offences);

"imprisonment" includes—

(i)   detention under section 207 of this Act; and

(ii)   detention under section 208 of this Act; and

"violent offence" means any offence (other than an offence which is a sexual offence within the meaning of this section) inferring personal violence.

(11)   Any reference in subsection (10) above to a sexual offence includes—

(a)   a reference to any attempt, conspiracy or incitement to commit that offence; and

(b)   except in the case of an offence in paragraphs (i) to (viii) of the definition of "sexual offence" in that subsection, a reference to aiding and abetting, counselling or procuring the commission of that offence.'

(2)   In section 209 of the 1995 Act (supervised release orders), in subsection (1)—

(a)   after the word 'convicted' there shall be inserted the words 'on indictment';

(b)   after the words 'an offence' there shall be inserted the words ', other than a sexual offence within the meaning of section 210A of this Act,'; and

(c)   the words 'not less than twelve months but' shall cease to have effect.

87.   Further provision as to extended sentences

After section 26 of the Prisoners and Criminal Proceedings (Scotland) Act 1993 ('the 1993 Act') there shall be inserted the following section—

'Extended sentences

26A.   Extended sentences

(1)   This section applies to a prisoner who, on or after the date on which section 87 of the Crime and Disorder Act 1998 comes into force, has been made subject to an extended sentence within the meaning of section 210A of the 1995 Act (extended sentences).

(2)   Subject to the provisions of this section, this Part of this Act, except section 1A, shall apply in relation to extended sentences as if any reference to a sentence or term of imprisonment was a reference to the custodial term of an extended sentence.

(3)   Where a prisoner subject to an extended sentence is released on licence under this Part the licence shall, subject to any revocation under section 17 of this Act, remain in force until the end of the extension period.

(4)   Where, apart from this subsection, a prisoner subject to an extended sentence would be released unconditionally—

(a)   he shall be released on licence; and

(b)   the licence shall, subject to any revocation under section 17 of this Act, remain in force until the end of the extension period.

(5)   The extension period shall be taken to begin as follows—

(a)   for the purposes of subsection (3) above, on the day following the date on which, had there been no extension period, the prisoner would have ceased to be on licence in respect of the custodial term;

(b)   for the purposes of subsection (4) above, on the date on which, apart from that subsection, he would have been released unconditionally.

(6)   Subject to section 1A(c) of this Act and section 210A(3) of the 1995 Act and to any direction by the court which imposes an extended sentence, where a prisoner is subject to two or more extended sentences, the extension period which is taken to begin in accordance with subsection (5) above shall be the aggregate of the extension period of each of those sentences.

(7) For the purposes of sections 12(3) and 17(1) of this Act, and subject to subsection (8) below, the question whether a prisoner is a long-term or short-term prisoner shall be determined by reference to the extended sentence.

(8) Where a short-term prisoner serving an extended sentence in respect of a sexual offence is released on licence under subsection (4)(a) above, the provisions of section 17 of this Act shall apply to him as if he was a long-term prisoner.

(9) In relation to a prisoner subject to an extended sentence, the reference in section 17(5) of this Act to his sentence shall be construed as a reference to the extended sentence.

(10) For the purposes of this section "custodial term", "extension period" and "imprisonment" shall have the same meaning as in section 210A of the 1995 Act.

(11) In section 1A(c) and section 16(1)(a) of this Act, the reference to the date on which a prisoner would have served his sentence in full shall mean, in relation to a prisoner subject to an extended sentence, the date on which the extended sentence, as originally imposed by the court, would expire.'

88. Re-release of prisoners serving extended sentences
After section 3 of the 1993 Act there shall be inserted the following section—

'3A. Re-release of prisoners serving extended sentences
(1) This section applies to a prisoner serving an extended sentence within the meaning of section 210A of the 1995 Act (extended sentences) who has been recalled to prison under section 17(1) of this Act.

(2) Subject to subsection (3) below, a prisoner to whom this section applies may require the Secretary of State to refer his case to the Parole Board—
(a) where his case has previously been referred to the Parole Board under this section or section 17(3) of this Act, not less than one year following the disposal of that referral;
(b) in any other case, at any time.

(3) Where a prisoner to whom this section applies is subject to another sentence which is not treated as a single sentence with the extended sentence, the Secretary of State shall not be required to refer his case to the Parole Board before he has served one half of that other sentence.

(4) Where the case of a prisoner to whom this section applies is referred to the Parole Board under this section or section 17(3) of this Act, the Board shall, if it is satisfied that it is no longer necessary for the protection of the public from serious harm that the prisoner should be confined (but not otherwise), direct that he should be released.

(5) If the Parole Board gives a direction under subsection (4) above, the Secretary of State shall release the prisoner on licence.'

Offenders dependent etc. on drugs

89. Drug treatment and testing orders
After section 234A of the 1995 Act there shall be inserted the following section—

'234B. Drug treatment and testing order
(1) This section applies where a person of 16 years of age or more is convicted of an offence, other than one for which the sentence is fixed by law, committed on or after the date on which section 89 of the Crime and Disorder Act 1998 comes into force.

(2)   Subject to the provisions of this section, the court by or before which the offender is convicted may, if it is of the opinion that it is expedient to do so instead of sentencing him, make an order (a "drug treatment and testing order") which shall—

(a)   have effect for a period specified in the order of not less than six months nor more than three years ("the treatment and testing period"); and

(b)   include the requirements and provisions mentioned in section 234C of this Act.

(3)   A court shall not make a drug treatment and testing order unless it—

(a)   has been notified by the Secretary of State that arrangements for implementing such orders are available in the area of the local authority proposed to be specified in the order under section 234C(6) of this Act and the notice has not been withdrawn;

(b)   has obtained a report by, and if necessary heard evidence from, an officer of the local authority in whose area the offender is resident about the offender and his circumstances; and

(c)   is satisfied that—

(i)   the offender is dependent on, or has a propensity to misuse, drugs;

(ii)   his dependency or propensity is such as requires and is susceptible to treatment; and

(iii)   he is a suitable person to be subject to such an order.

(4)   For the purpose of determining for the purposes of subsection (3)(c) above whether the offender has any drug in his body, the court may by order require him to provide samples of such description as it may specify.

(5)   A drug treatment and testing order or an order under subsection (4) above shall not be made unless the offender expresses his willingness to comply with its requirements.

(6)   The Secretary of State may by order—

(a)   amend paragraph (a) of subsection (2) above by substituting a different period for the minimum or the maximum period for the time being specified in that paragraph; and

(b)   make such transitional provisions as appear to him necessary or expedient in connection with any such amendment.

(7)   The power to make an order under subsection (6) above shall be exercisable by statutory instrument; but no such order shall be made unless a draft of the order has been laid before and approved by resolution of each House of Parliament.

(8)   A drug treatment and testing order shall be as nearly as may be in the form prescribed by Act of Adjournal.'

90.   Requirements and provisions to be included in drug treatment and testing orders

After section 234B of the 1995 Act there shall be inserted the following section—

'234C.   Requirements and provisions of drug treatment and testing orders

(1)   A drug treatment and testing order shall include a requirement ("the treatment requirement") that the offender shall submit, during the whole of the treatment and testing period, to treatment by or under the direction of a specified

person having the necessary qualifications or experience ("the treatment provider") with a view to the reduction or elimination of the offender's dependency on or propensity to misuse drugs.

(2) The required treatment for any particular period shall be—

(a) treatment as a resident in such institution or place as may be specified in the order; or

(b) treatment as a non-resident in or at such institution or place, and at such intervals, as may be so specified;

but the nature of the treatment shall not be specified in the order except as mentioned in paragraph (a) or (b) above.

(3) A court shall not make a drug treatment and testing order unless it is satisfied that arrangements have been made for the treatment intended to be specified in the order (including arrangements for the reception of the offender where he is required to submit to treatment as a resident).

(4) A drug treatment and testing order shall include a requirement ("the testing requirement") that, for the purpose of ascertaining whether he has any drug in his body during the treatment and testing period, the offender shall provide during that period, at such times and in such circumstances as may (subject to the provisions of the order) be determined by the treatment provider, samples of such description as may be so determined.

(5) The testing requirement shall specify for each month the minimum number of occasions on which samples are to be provided.

(6) A drug treatment and testing order shall specify the local authority in whose area the offender will reside when the order is in force and require that authority to appoint or assign an officer (a "supervising officer") for the purposes of subsections (7) and (8) below.

(7) A drug treatment and testing order shall—

(a) provide that, for the treatment and testing period, the offender shall be under the supervision of a supervising officer;

(b) require the offender to keep in touch with the supervising officer in accordance with such instructions as he may from time to time be given by that officer, and to notify him of any change of address; and

(c) provide that the results of the tests carried out on the samples provided by the offender in pursuance of the testing requirement shall be communicated to the supervising officer.

(8) Supervision by the supervising officer shall be carried out to such extent only as may be necessary for the purpose of enabling him—

(a) to report on the offender's progress to the appropriate court;

(b) to report to that court any failure by the offender to comply with the requirements of the order; and

(c) to determine whether the circumstances are such that he should apply to that court for the variation or revocation of the order.'

91. Procedural matters relating to drug treatment and testing orders

After section 234C of the 1995 Act there shall be inserted the following section—

'234D. Procedural matters relating to drug treatment and testing orders

(1) Before making a drug treatment and testing order, a court shall explain to the offender in ordinary language—

(a) the effect of the order and of the requirements proposed to be included in it;

(b) the consequences which may follow under section 234G of this Act if he fails to comply with any of those requirements;

(c) that the court has power under section 234E of this Act to vary or revoke the order on the application of either the offender or the supervising officer; and

(d) that the order will be periodically reviewed at intervals provided for in the order.

(2) Upon making a drug treatment and testing order the court shall—

(a) give, or send by registered post or the recorded delivery service, a copy of the order to the offender;

(b) send a copy of the order to the treatment provider;

(c) send a copy of the order to the chief social work officer of the local authority specified in the order in accordance with section 234C(6) of this Act; and

(d) where it is not the appropriate court, send a copy of the order (together with such documents and information relating to the case as are considered useful) to the clerk of the appropriate court.

(3) Where a copy of a drug treatment and testing order has under subsection (2)(a) been sent by registered post or by the recorded delivery service, an acknowledgment or certificate of delivery of a letter containing a copy order issued by the Post Office shall be sufficient evidence of the delivery of the letter on the day specified in such acknowledgement or certificate.'

92. Amendment and periodic review of drug treatment and testing orders
After section 234D of the 1995 Act there shall be inserted the following sections—

'**234E. Amendment of drug treatment and testing order**

(1) Where a drug treatment and testing order is in force either the offender or the supervising officer may apply to the appropriate court for variation or revocation of the order.

(2) Where an application is made under subsection (1) above by the supervising officer, the court shall issue a citation requiring the offender to appear before the court.

(3) On an application made under subsection (1) above and after hearing both the offender and the supervising officer, the court may by order, if it appears to it in the interests of justice to do so—

(a) vary the order by—

(i) amending or deleting any of its requirements or provisions;

(ii) inserting further requirements or provisions; or

(iii) subject to subsection (4) below, increasing or decreasing the treatment and testing period; or

(b) revoke the order.

(4) The power conferred by subsection (3)(a)(iii) above shall not be exercised so as to increase the treatment and testing period above the maximum for the time being specified in section 234B(2)(a) of this Act, or to decrease it below the minimum so specified.

(5) Where the court, on the application of the supervising officer, proposes to vary (otherwise than by deleting a requirement or provision) a drug treatment and

testing order, sections 234B(5) and 234D(1) of this Act shall apply to the variation of such an order as they apply to the making of such an order.

(6) If an offender fails to appear before the court after having been cited in accordance with subsection (2) above, the court may issue a warrant for his arrest.

234F. Periodic review of drug treatment and testing order

(1) A drug treatment and testing order shall—

(a) provide for the order to be reviewed periodically at intervals of not less than one month;

(b) provide for each review of the order to be made, subject to subsection (5) below, at a hearing held for the purpose by the appropriate court (a "review hearing");

(c) require the offender to attend each review hearing;

(d) provide for the supervising officer to make to the court, before each review, a report in writing on the offender's progress under the order; and

(e) provide for each such report to include the test results communicated to the supervising officer under section 234C(7)(c) of this Act and the views of the treatment provider as to the treatment and testing of the offender.

(2) At a review hearing the court, after considering the supervising officer's report, may amend any requirement or provision of the order.

(3) The court—

(a) shall not amend the treatment or testing requirement unless the offender expresses his willingness to comply with the requirement as amended;

(b) shall not amend any provision of the order so as reduce the treatment and testing period below the minimum specified in section 234B(2)(a) of this Act or to increase it above the maximum so specified; and

(c) except with the consent of the offender, shall not amend any requirement or provision of the order while an appeal against the order is pending.

(4) If the offender fails to express his willingness to comply with the treatment or testing requirement as proposed to be amended by the court, the court may revoke the order.

(5) If at a review hearing the court, after considering the supervising officer's report, is of the opinion that the offender's progress under the order is satisfactory, the court may so amend the order as to provide for each subsequent review to be made without a hearing.

(6) A review without a hearing shall take place in chambers without the parties being present.

(7) If at a review without a hearing the court, after considering the supervising officer's report, is of the opinion that the offender's progress is no longer satisfactory, the court may issue a warrant for the arrest of the offender or may, if it thinks fit, instead of issuing a warrant in the first instance, issue a citation requiring the offender to appear before that court as such time as may be specified in the citation.

(8) Where an offender fails to attend—

(a) a review hearing in accordance with a requirement contained in a drug treatment and testing order; or

(b) a court at the time specified in a citation under subsection (7) above, the court may issue a warrant for his arrest.

(9)   Where an offender attends the court at a time specified by a citation issued under subsection (7) above—

(a)   the court may exercise the powers conferred by this section as if the court were conducting a review hearing; and

(b)   so amend the order as to provide for each subsequent review to be made at a review hearing.'

93.   Consequences of breach of drug treatment and testing order

After section 234F of the 1995 Act there shall be inserted the following sections—

'234G.   Breach of drug treatment testing order

(1)   If at any time when a drug treatment and testing order is in force it appears to the appropriate court that the offender has failed to comply with any requirement of the order, the court may issue a citation requiring the offender to appear before the court at such time as may be specified in the citation or, if it appears to the court to be appropriate, it may issue a warrant for the arrest of the offender.

(2)   If it is proved to the satisfaction of the appropriate court that the offender has failed without reasonable excuse to comply with any requirement of the order, the court may by order—

(a)   without prejudice to the continuation in force of the order, impose a fine not exceeding level 3 on the standard scale;

(b)   vary the order; or

(c)   revoke the order.

(3)   For the purposes of subsection (2) above, the evidence of one witness shall be sufficient evidence.

(4)   A fine imposed under this section in respect of a failure to comply with the requirements of a drug treatment and testing order shall be deemed for the purposes of any enactment to be a sum adjudged to be paid by or in respect of a conviction or a penalty imposed on a person summarily convicted.

234H.   Disposal on revocation of drugs treatment and testing order

(1)   Where the court revokes a drugs treatment and testing order under section 234E(3)(b), 234F(4) or 234G(2)(c) of this Act, it may dispose of the offender in any way which would have been competent at the time when the order was made.

(2)   In disposing of an offender under subsection (1) above, the court shall have regard to the time for which the order has been in operation.

(3)   Where the court revokes a drug treatment and testing order as mentioned in subsection (1) above and the offender is subject to—

(a)   a probation order, by virtue of section 234J of this Act; or

(b)   a restriction of liberty order, by virtue of section 245D of this Act; or

(c)   a restriction of liberty order and a probation order, by virtue of the said section 245D,

the court shall, before disposing of the offender under subsection (1) above—

(i)   where he is subject to a probation order, discharge that order;

(ii)   where he is subject to a restriction of liberty order, revoke that order; and

(iii)   where he is subject to both such orders, discharge the probation order and revoke the restriction of liberty order.'

94. Combination of orders

(1)   After section 234H of the 1995 Act there shall be inserted the following section—

'**234J.   Concurrent drug treatment and testing and probation orders**

(1)   Notwithstanding sections 228(1) and 234B(2) of this Act, where the court considers it expedient that the offender should be subject to a drug treatment and testing order and to a probation order, it may make both such orders in respect of the offender.

(2)   In deciding whether it is expedient for it to exercise the power conferred by subsection (1) above, the court shall have regard to the circumstances, including the nature of the offence and the character of the offender and to the report submitted to it under section 234B(3)(b) of this Act.

(3)   Where the court makes both a drug treatment and testing order and a probation order by virtue of subsection (1) above, the clerk of the court shall send a copy of each of the orders to the following—

(a)   the treatment provider within the meaning of section 234C(1);

(b)   the officer of the local authority who is appointed or assigned to be the supervising officer under section 234C(6) of this Act; and

(c)   if he would not otherwise receive a copy of the order, the officer of the local authority who is to supervise the probationer.

(4)   Where the offender by an act or omission fails to comply with a requirement of an order made by virtue of subsection (1) above—

(a)   if the failure relates to a requirement contained in a probation order and is dealt with under section 232(2)(c) of this Act, the court may, in addition, exercise the power conferred by section 234G(2)(b) of this Act in relation to the drug treatment and testing order; and

(b)   if the failure relates to a requirement contained in a drug treatment and testing order and is dealt with under section 234G(2)(b) of this Act, the court may, in addition, exercise the power conferred by section 232(2)(c) of this Act in relation to the probation order.

(5)   Where an offender by an act or omission fails to comply with both a requirement contained in a drug treatment and testing order and in a probation order to which he is subject by virtue of subsection (1) above, he may, without prejudice to subsection (4) above, be dealt with as respects that act or omission either under section 232(2) of this Act or under section 234G(2) of this Act but he shall not be liable to be otherwise dealt with in respect of that act or omission.'

(2)   Schedule 6 to this Act (Part I of which makes further provision in relation to the combination of drug treatment and testing orders with other orders and Part II of which makes provision in relation to appeals) shall have effect.

95.   Interpretation provision in relation to drug treatment and testing orders

(1)   After section 234J of the 1995 Act there shall be inserted the following section—

'**234K.   Drug treatment and testing orders: interpretation**

In sections 234B to 234J of this Act—

    "the appropriate court" means—

(a)   where the drug treatment and testing order has been made by the High Court, that court;

(b)   in any other case, the court having jurisdiction in the area of the local authority for the time being specified in the order under section 234C(6) of this Act, being a sheriff or district court according to whether the order has been made by a sheriff or district court, but in a case where an order has been made by a district court and there is no district court in that area, the sheriff court; and

"local authority" means a council constituted under section 2 of the Local Government etc. (Scotland) Act 1994 and any reference to the area of such an authority is a reference to the local government area within the meaning of that Act for which it is so constituted.'

(2)   In section 307(1) of the 1995 Act (interpretation), after the definition of 'diet' there shall be inserted the following definition—

' "drug treatment and testing order" has the meaning assigned to it in section 234B(2) of this Act;'.

Racial aggravation

96.   Offences racially aggravated

(1)   The provisions of this section shall apply where it is—

(a)   libelled in an indictment; or

(b)   specified in a complaint,

and, in either case, proved that an offence has been racially aggravated.

(2)   An offence is racially aggravated for the purposes of this section if—

(a)   at the time of committing the offence, or immediately before or after doing so, the offender evinces towards the victim (if any) of the offence malice and ill-will based on the victim's membership (or presumed membership) of a racial group; or

(b)   the offence is motivated (wholly or partly) by malice and ill-will towards members of a racial group based on their membership of that group,

and evidence from a single source shall be sufficient evidence to establish, for the purposes of this subsection, that an offence is racially aggravated.

(3)   In subsection (2)(a) above—

'membership', in relation to a racial group, includes association with members of that group;

'presumed' means presumed by the offender.

(4)   It is immaterial for the purposes of paragraph (a) or (b) of subsection (2) above whether or not the offender's malice and ill-will is also based, to any extent, on—

(a)   the fact or presumption that any person or group of persons belongs to any religious group; or

(b)   any other factor not mentioned in that paragraph.

(5)   Where this section applies, the court shall, on convicting a person, take the aggravation into account in determining the appropriate sentence.

(6)   In this section 'racial group' means a group of persons defined by reference to race, colour, nationality (including citizenship) or ethnic or national origins.

PART V
MISCELLANEOUS AND SUPPLEMENTAL

Remands and committals

97. Remands and committals of children and young persons

(1) In subsection (4) of section 23 of the 1969 Act (remands and committals to local authority accommodation), for the words 'Subject to subsection (5) below,' there shall be substituted the words 'Subject to subsections (5) and (5A) below,'.

(2) In subsection (5) of that section, for the words 'a young person who has attained the age of fifteen' there shall be substituted the words 'a child who has attained the age of twelve, or a young person, who (in either case) is of a prescribed description'.

(3) After that subsection there shall be inserted the following subsection—

'(5A) A court shall not impose a security requirement in respect of a child or young person who is not legally represented in the court unless—

(a) he applied for legal aid and the application was refused on the ground that it did not appear his means were such that he required assistance; or

(b) having been informed of his right to apply for legal aid and had the opportunity to do so, he refused or failed to apply.'

(4) In subsection (12) of that section, after the definition of 'imprisonable offence' there shall be inserted the following definition—

' "prescribed description" means a description prescribed by reference to age or sex or both by an order of the Secretary of State;'.

(5) Section 20 of the 1994 Act (which has not been brought into force and is superseded by this section) is hereby repealed.

98. Remands and committals: alternative provision for 15 or 16 year old boys

(1) Section 23 of the 1969 Act shall have effect with the modifications specified in subsections (2) to (6) below in relation to any male person who—

(a) is of the age of 15 or 16; and

(b) is not of a description prescribed for the purposes of subsection (5) of that section.

(2) In subsection (1), immediately before the words 'the remand' there shall be inserted the words 'then, unless he is remanded to a remand centre or a prison in pursuance of subsection (4)(b) or (c) below,'.

(3) For subsections (4) to (5A) there shall be substituted the following subsections—

'(4) Where a court, after consultation with a probation officer, a social worker of a local authority social services department or a member of a youth offending team, declares a person to be one to whom subsection (5) below applies—

(a) it shall remand him to local authority accommodation and require him to be placed and kept in secure accommodation, if—

(i) it also, after such consultation, declares him to be a person to whom subsection (5A) below applies; and

(ii) it has been notified that secure accommodation is available for him;

(b) it shall remand him to a remand centre, if paragraph (a) above does not apply and it has been notified that such a centre is available for the reception from the court of persons to whom subsection (5) below applies; and

(c)   it shall remand him to a prison, if neither paragraph (a) nor paragraph (b) above applies.

(4A)   A court shall not declare a person who is not legally represented in the court to be a person to whom subsection (5) below applies unless—

(a)   he applied for legal aid and the application was refused on the ground that it did not appear his means were such that he required assistance; or

(b)   having been informed of his right to apply for legal aid and had the opportunity to do so, he refused or failed to apply.

(5)   This subsection applies to a person who—

(a)   is charged with or has been convicted of a violent or sexual offence, or an offence punishable in the case of an adult with imprisonment for a term of fourteen years or more; or

(b)   has a recent history of absconding while remanded to local authority accommodation, and is charged with or has been convicted of an imprisonable offence alleged or found to have been committed while he was so remanded, if (in either case) the court is of opinion that only remanding him to a remand centre or prison, or to local authority accommodation with a requirement that he be placed and kept in secure accommodation, would be adequate to protect the public from serious harm from him.

(5A)   This subsection applies to a person if the court is of opinion that, by reason of his physical or emotional immaturity or a propensity of his to harm himself, it would be undesirable for him to be remanded to a remand centre or a prison.'

(4)   In subsection (6)—

(a)   for the words 'imposes a security requirement in respect of a young person' there shall be substituted the words 'declares a person to be one to whom subsection (5) above applies'; and

(b)   for the words 'subsection (5) above' there shall be substituted the words 'that subsection'.

(5)   In subsection (7), after the words 'a security requirement' there shall be inserted the words '(that is to say, a requirement imposed under subsection (4)(a) above that the person be placed and kept in secure accommodation)'.

(6)   After subsection (9) there shall be inserted the following subsection—

'(9A)   Where a person is remanded to local authority accommodation without the imposition of a security requirement, a relevant court may, on the application of the designated authority, declare him to be a person to whom subsection (5) above applies; and on its doing so, subsection (4) above shall apply.'

(7)   Section 62 of the 1991 Act (which is superseded by this section) shall cease to have effect.

Release and recall of prisoners

99.   Power to release short-term prisoners on licence

Immediately before section 35 of the 1991 Act there shall be inserted the following section—

'34A.   Power to release short-term prisoners on licence

(1)   Subject to subsection (2) below, subsection (3) below applies where a short-term prisoner aged 18 or over is serving a sentence of imprisonment for a term of three months or more.

(2)   Subsection (3) below does not apply where—

(a)   the sentence is an extended sentence within the meaning of section 58 of the Crime and Disorder Act 1998;

(b)   the sentence is for an offence under section 1 of the Prisoners (Return to Custody) Act 1995;

(c)   the sentence was imposed under paragraph 3(1)(d) or 4(1)(d) of Schedule 2 to this Act in a case where the prisoner had failed to comply with a requirement of a curfew order;

(d)   the prisoner is subject to a hospital order, hospital direction or transfer direction under section 37, 45A or 47 of the Mental Health Act 1983;

(e)   the prisoner is liable to removal from the United Kingdom for the purposes of section 46 below;

(f)   the prisoner has been released on licence under this section at any time and has been recalled to prison under section 38A(1)(a) below;

(g)   the prisoner has been released on licence under this section or section 36 below during the currency of the sentence, and has been recalled to prison under section 39(1) or (2) below;

(h)   the prisoner has been returned to prison under section 40 below at any time; or

(j)   the interval between—

(i)   the date on which the prisoner will have served the requisite period for the term of the sentence; and

(ii)   the date on which he will have served one-half of the sentence,
is less than 14 days.

(3)   After the prisoner has served the requisite period for the term of his sentence, the Secretary of State may, subject to section 37A below, release him on licence.

(4)   In this section "the requisite period" means—

(a)   for a term of three months or more but less than four months, a period of 30 days;

(b)   for a term of four months or more but less than eight months, a period equal to one-quarter of the term;

(c)   for a term of eight months or more, a period that is 60 days less than one-half of the term.

(5)   The Secretary of State may by order made by statutory instrument—

(a)   repeal the words "aged 18 or over" in subsection (1) above;

(b)   amend the definition of "the requisite period" in subsection (4) above; and

(c)   make such transitional provision as appears to him necessary or expedient in connection with the repeal or amendment.

(6)   No order shall be made under subsection (5) above unless a draft of the order has been laid before and approved by a resolution of each House of Parliament.'

100.   Curfew condition to be included in licence

(1)   After section 37 of the 1991 Act there shall be inserted the following section—

'37A. Curfew condition to be included in licence under section 34A

(1)   A person shall not be released under section 34A(3) above unless the licence includes a condition ("the curfew condition") which—

(a)   requires the released person to remain, for periods for the time being specified in the condition, at a place for the time being so specified (which may be an approved probation hostel); and

(b)   includes requirements for securing the electronic monitoring of his whereabouts during the periods for the time being so specified.

(2)   The curfew condition may specify different places or different periods for different days, but shall not specify periods which amount to less than 9 hours in any one day (excluding for this purpose the first and last days of the period for which the condition is in force).

(3)   The curfew condition shall remain in force until the date when the released person would (but for his release) have served one-half of his sentence.

(4)   The curfew condition shall include provision for making a person responsible for monitoring the released person's whereabouts during the periods for the time being specified in the condition; and a person who is made so responsible shall be of a description specified in an order made by the Secretary of State.

(5)   The power conferred by subsection (4) above—

(a)   shall be exercisable by statutory instrument; and

(b)   shall include power to make different provision for different cases or classes of case or for different areas.

(6)   Nothing in this section shall be taken to require the Secretary of State to ensure that arrangements are made for the electronic monitoring of released persons' whereabouts in any particular part of England and Wales.

(7)   In this section "approved probation hostel" has the same meaning as in the Probation Service Act 1993.'

(2)   Immediately before section 39 of the 1991 Act there shall be inserted the following section—

'38A. Breach of curfew condition

(1)   If it appears to the Secretary of State, as regards a person released on licence under section 34A(3) above—

(a)   that he has failed to comply with the curfew condition;

(b)   that his whereabouts can no longer be electronically monitored at the place for the time being specified in that condition; or

(c)   that it is necessary to do so in order to protect the public from serious harm from him,

the Secretary of State may, if the curfew condition is still in force, revoke the licence and recall the person to prison.

(2)   A person whose licence under section 34A(3) above is revoked under this section—

(a)   may make representations in writing with respect to the revocation;

(b)   on his return to prison, shall be informed of the reasons for the revocation and of his right to make representations.

(3)   The Secretary of State, after considering any representations made under subsection (2)(b) above or any other matters, may cancel a revocation under this section.

(4) Where the revocation of a person's licence is cancelled under subsection (3) above, the person shall be treated for the purposes of sections 34A(2)(f) and 37(1B) above as if he had not been recalled to prison under this section.

(5) On the revocation under this section of a person's licence under section 34A(3) above, he shall be liable to be detained in pursuance of his sentence and, if at large, shall be deemed to be unlawfully at large.

(6) In this section "the curfew condition" has the same meaning as in section 37A above.'

101. Early release: two or more sentences

(1) For subsection (2) of section 51 of the 1991 Act (interpretation of Part II) there shall be substituted the following subsections—

'(2) For the purposes of any reference in this Part, however expressed, to the term of imprisonment to which a person has been sentenced or which, or part of which, he has served, consecutive terms and terms which are wholly or partly concurrent shall be treated as a single term if—

(a) the sentences were passed on the same occasion; or

(b) where they were passed on different occasions, the person has not been released under this Part at any time during the period beginning with the first and ending with the last of those occasions.

(2A) Where a suspended sentence of imprisonment is ordered to take effect, with or without any variation of the original term, the occasion on which that order is made shall be treated for the purposes of subsection (2) above as the occasion on which the sentence is passed.

(2B) Where a person has been sentenced to two or more terms of imprisonment which are wholly or partly concurrent and do not fall to be treated as a single term—

(a) nothing in this Part shall require the Secretary of State to release him in respect of any of the terms unless and until the Secretary of State is required to release him in respect of each of the others;

(b) nothing in this Part shall require the Secretary of State or the Board to consider his release in respect of any of the terms unless and until the Secretary of State or the Board is required to consider his release, or the Secretary of State is required to release him, in respect of each of the others;

(c) on and after his release under this Part he shall be on licence for so long, and subject to such conditions, as is required by this Part in respect of any of the sentences; and

(d) the date mentioned in section 40(1) above shall be taken to be that on which he would (but for his release) have served each of the sentences in full.

(2C) Where a person has been sentenced to one or more terms of imprisonment and to one or more life sentences (within the meaning of section 34 of the Crime (Sentences) Act 1997), nothing in this Part shall—

(a) require the Secretary of State to release the person in respect of any of the terms unless and until the Secretary of State is required to release him in respect of each of the life sentences; or

(b) require the Secretary of State or the Board to consider the person's release in respect of any of the terms unless and until the Secretary of State or the Board is required to consider his release in respect of each of the life sentences.

(2D)   Subsections (2B) and (2C) above shall have effect as if the term of an extended sentence (within the meaning of section 58 of the Crime and Disorder Act 1998) included the extension period (within the meaning of that section).'

(2)   After subsection (3) of section 34 of the 1997 Act (interpretation of Chapter II) there shall be inserted the following subsection—

'(4)   Where a person has been sentenced to one or more life sentences and to one or more terms of imprisonment, nothing in this Chapter shall require the Secretary of State to release the person in respect of any of the life sentences unless and until the Secretary of State is required to release him in respect of each of the terms.'

102.   Restriction on consecutive sentences for released prisoners

(1)   A court sentencing a person to a term of imprisonment shall not order or direct that the term shall commence on the expiration of any other sentence of imprisonment from which he has been released under Part II of the 1991 Act.

(2)   Expressions used in this section shall be construed as if they were contained in that Part.

103.   Recall to prison of short-term prisoners

(1)   This section has effect for the purpose of securing that, subject to section 100(2) above, the circumstances in which prisoners released on licence under Part II of the 1991 Act may be recalled to prison are the same for short-term prisoners as for long-term prisoners.

(2)   Section 38 of the 1991 Act (breach of licence conditions by short-term prisoners) shall cease to have effect.

(3)   In subsection (1) of section 39 of the 1991 Act (recall of long-term prisoners while on licence), after the words 'in the case of a' there shall be inserted the words 'short-term or'.

104.   Release on licence following recall to prison

(1)   In subsection (3) of section 33 of the 1991 Act (duty to release short-term and long-term prisoners), for the word 'unconditionally' there shall be substituted the words 'on licence'.

(2)   After subsection (1) of section 37 of that Act (duration and conditions of licences) there shall be inserted the following subsection—

'(1A)   Where a prisoner is released on licence under section 33(3) or (3A) above, subsection (1) above shall have effect as if for the reference to three-quarters of his sentence there were substituted a reference to the whole of that sentence.'

105.   Release on licence following return to prison

After section 40 of the 1991 Act there shall be inserted the following section—

'40A.   Release on licence following return to prison

(1)   This section applies (in place of sections 33, 33A, 37(1) and 39 above) where a court passes on a person a sentence of imprisonment which—

(a)   includes, or consists of, an order under section 40 above; and

(b)   is for a term of twelve months or less.

(2)   As soon as the person has served one-half of the sentence, it shall be the duty of the Secretary of State to release him on licence.

(3)   Where the person is so released, the licence shall remain in force for a period of three months.

(4)   If the person fails to comply with such conditions as may for the time being be specified in the licence, he shall be liable on summary conviction—

(a)   to a fine not exceeding level 3 on the standard scale; or

(b)   to a sentence of imprisonment for a term not exceeding the relevant period,

but not liable to be dealt with in any other way.

(5)   In subsection (4) above "the relevant period" means a period which is equal in length to the period between the date on which the failure occurred or began and the date of the expiry of the licence.

(6)   As soon as a person has served one-half of a sentence passed under subsection (4) above, it shall be the duty of the Secretary of State to release him, subject to the licence if it is still subsisting.'

Miscellaneous

106.   Pre-consolidation amendments
The enactments mentioned in Schedule 7 to this Act shall have effect subject to the amendments there specified, being amendments designed to facilitate, or otherwise desirable in connection with, the consolidation of certain enactments relating to the powers of courts to deal with offenders or defaulters.

107.   Amendments to Chapter I of Part II of 1997 Act
(1)   Chapter I of Part II of the 1997 Act (which relates to the effect of determinate custodial sentences) shall be amended as follows.

(2)   Sections 8 and 10 to 27 are hereby repealed.

(3)   After subsection (7) of section 9 (crediting of periods of remand in custody) there shall be inserted the following subsection—

'(7A)   Such rules may make such incidental, supplemental and consequential provisions as may appear to the Secretary of State to be necessary or expedient.'

(4)   After subsection (10) of that section there shall be inserted the following subsections—

'(11)   In this section "sentence of imprisonment" does not include a committal—

(a)   in default of payment of any sum of money other than one adjudged to be paid by a conviction;

(b)   for want of sufficient distress to satisfy any sum of money; or

(c)   for failure to do or abstain from doing anything required to be done or left undone;

and cognate expressions shall be construed accordingly.

(12)   For the purposes of any reference in this section, however expressed, to the term of imprisonment to which a person has been sentenced, consecutive terms and terms which are wholly or partly concurrent shall be treated as a single term if—

(a)   the sentences were passed on the same occasion; or

(b)   where they were passed on different occasions, the person has not been released under Part II of the 1991 Act at any time during the period beginning with the first and ending with the last of those occasions.'

(5)   After that section there shall be inserted the following section—

'9A.   Provision supplementary to section 9
(1)   Section 9 above applies to—
    (a)   a sentence of detention in a young offender institution; and
    (b)   a determinate sentence of detention under section 53 of the Children and Young Persons Act 1933 ("the 1933 Act"),
as it applies to an equivalent sentence of imprisonment.
(2)   Section 9 above applies to—
    (a)   persons remanded or committed to local authority accommodation under section 23 of the Children and Young Persons Act 1969 ("the 1969 Act") and placed and kept in secure accommodation; and
    (b)   persons remanded, admitted or removed to hospital under section 35, 36, 38 or 48 of the Mental Health Act 1983 ("the 1983 Act"),
as it applies to persons remanded in or committed to custody by an order of a court.
(3)   In this section "secure accommodation" has the same meaning as in section 23 of the 1969 Act.'

108.   Repeal of Chapter I of Part III of Crime and Punishment (Scotland) Act 1997
Chapter I of Part III of the Crime and Punishment (Scotland) Act 1997 (early release of prisoners) shall cease to have effect.

109.   Transitional provisions in relation to certain life prisoners
(1)   Section 16 of the Crime and Punishment (Scotland) Act 1997 (designated life prisoners) shall have effect and shall be deemed always to have had effect with the amendments made by subsections (2) and (3) below.
(2)   In subsection (2), at the beginning there shall be inserted the words 'Except in a case to which subsection (3A) or (3B) below applies,'.
(3)   After subsection (3) there shall be inserted the following subsections—
    '(3A)   This subsection applies in a case where a person—
        (a)   was sentenced, prior to 20 October 1997, in respect of a murder committed by him before he attained the age of 18 years; and
        (b)   has been released on licence, other than under section 3 of the 1993 Act, whether before or on that date.
    (3B)   This subsection applies in a case where a person—
        (a)   was sentenced, prior to 20 October 1997, in respect of a murder committed by him before he attained the age of 18 years; and
        (b)   has been released on licence, other than under section 3 of the 1993 Act, after that date without his case having been considered under subsection (2) above.
    (3C)   In a case to which subsection (3A) or (3B) applies, Part I of the 1993 Act shall apply as if the person were a designated life prisoner, within the meaning of section 2 of that Act, whose licence had been granted under subsection (4) of that section on his having served the designated part of his sentence.'
(4)   Where, prior to the commencement of this section, a certificate has been issued under subsection (2) of section 16 of the Crime and Punishment (Scotland) Act 1997 in respect of a case to which subsection (3A) of that section applies, the certificate shall be disregarded.

110. Calculation of period of detention at customs office etc. where person previously detained

In section 24 of the Criminal Law (Consolidation) (Scotland) Act 1995 (detention and questioning by customs officers), in subsection (4)—

(a) for the words from 'he' to 'be' there shall be substituted the words 'and is'; and

(b) after the word 'detention' there shall be inserted the words ', the period of six hours mentioned in subsection (2) above shall be reduced by the length of that earlier detention'.

111. Early release in Scotland: two or more sentences

(1) After section 1 of the 1993 Act there shall be inserted the following section—

'**1A. Application to persons serving more than one sentence**

Where a prisoner has been sentenced to two or more terms of imprisonment which are wholly or partly concurrent and do not fall to be treated as a single term by virtue of section 27(5) of this Act—

(a) nothing in this Part of this Act shall require the Secretary of State to release him in respect of any of the terms unless and until the Secretary of State is required to release him in respect of each of the other terms;

(b) nothing in this Part of this Act shall require the Secretary of State or the Parole Board to consider his release in respect of any of the terms unless and until the Secretary of State or the Parole Board is required to consider his release, or the Secretary of State is required to release him, in respect of each of the other terms; and

(c) where he is released on licence under this Part of this Act, he shall be on a single licence which—

(i) shall (unless revoked) remain in force until the date on which he would (but for his release) have served in full all the sentences in respect of which he has been so released; and

(ii) shall be subject to such conditions as may be specified or required by this Part of this Act in respect of any of the sentences.'

(2) After subsection (7) of section 16 of the 1993 Act (orders for return to prison on commission of further offence) there shall be inserted the following subsection—

'(8) Where a prisoner has been sentenced to two or more terms of imprisonment which are wholly or partly concurrent and do not fall to be treated as a single term by virtue of section 27(5) of this Act, the date mentioned in subsection (1)(a) above shall be taken to be that on which he would (but for his release) have served all of the sentences in full.'

(3) For subsection (5) of section 27 of the 1993 Act (interpretation of Part I) there shall be substituted the following subsection—

'(5) For the purposes of any reference, however expressed, in this Part of this Act to the term of imprisonment or other detention to which a person has been sentenced or which, or any part of which, he has served, consecutive terms and terms which are wholly or partly concurrent shall be treated as a single term if—

(a) the sentences were passed at the same time; or

(b) where the sentences were passed at different times, the person has not been released under this Part of this Act at any time during the period beginning with the passing of the first sentence and ending with the passing of the last.'

(4) In sub-paragraph (1) of paragraph 6B of Schedule 6 to the 1993 Act (aggregation of old and new sentences)—

(a) for the words 'a prisoner' there shall be substituted the words 'an existing prisoner';

(b) the word 'and' after head (a) shall cease to have effect;

(c) in head (b), for the words 'that date' there shall be inserted the words 'the date on which section 111 of the Crime and Disorder Act 1998 comes into force'; and

(d) after head (b) there shall be inserted the following—

'; and

(c) he has not at any time prior to the passing of the sentence or sentences mentioned in head (b) above been released from the sentence or sentences mentioned in head (a) above under the existing provisions.'

(5) After that paragraph there shall be inserted the following paragraph—

'6C.—(1) This paragraph applies where—

(a) an existing prisoner was, at the relevant date, serving a sentence or sentences of imprisonment, on conviction of an offence, passed before that date;

(b) on or after the date on which section 111 of the Crime and Disorder Act 1998 comes into force he is, or has been, sentenced to a further term or terms of imprisonment on conviction of an offence, to be served wholly or partly concurrently with the sentence or sentences mentioned in head (a); and

(c) the sentences do not fall to be treated as a single term by virtue of paragraph 6B(2)(a) above.

(2) In a case to which this paragraph applies the Secretary of State shall not release, or be required to consider the release of, the prisoner unless and until the requirements for release, or for consideration of his release, of the new and the existing provisions are satisfied in relation to each sentence to which they respectively apply.

(3) In a case to which this paragraph applies the Parole Board shall not be required to consider the release of the prisoner unless and until the requirements for release, or for consideration for release, of the new and the existing provisions are satisfied in relation to each sentence to which they respectively apply.

(4) In a case to which this paragraph applies, where the prisoner is released on licence, he shall be on a single licence which—

(a) shall (unless revoked) remain in force until the later of—

(i) the date on which he would have been discharged from prison on remission of part of his sentence or sentences under the existing provisions if, after his release, he had not forfeited remission of any part of that sentence under those provisions; or

(ii) the date on which he would (but for his release) have served in full all the sentences in respect of which he was released on licence and which were imposed after the relevant date; and

(b) shall be deemed to be granted under the new provisions and, subject to sub-paragraph (5) below, those provisions so far as relating to conditions of licences, and recall or return to prison, shall apply as they apply in respect of a prisoner on licence in respect of a sentence passed after the relevant date.

(5) In the application of section 16 to a person whose licence is deemed to be granted under the new provisions by virtue of sub-paragraph (4)(b) above, the reference to the original sentence (within the meaning of that section) shall be

construed as a reference to the further term or terms mentioned in head (b) of sub-paragraph (1) above.'

(6) Subject to subsection (7) below, the amendments made by subsections (1) to (5) above apply where one or more of the sentences concerned was passed after the commencement of this section.

(7) Where the terms of two or more sentences passed before the commencement of this section have been treated, by virtue of section 27(5) of, or paragraph 6B of Schedule 6 to, the 1993 Act, as a single term for the purposes of Part I of that Act, they shall continue to be so treated after that commencement.

(8) In relation to a prisoner released on licence at any time under section 16(7)(b) of the 1993 Act, section 17(1)(a) of that Act shall have effect as if after the word 'Act' there were inserted the words 'or a short term prisoner has been released on licence by virtue of section 16(7)(b) of this Act'.

112. Restriction on consecutive sentences for released prisoners: Scotland
After section 204 of the 1995 Act there shall be inserted the following section—

'204A. **Restriction on consecutive sentences for released prisoners**
A court sentencing a person to imprisonment or other detention shall not order or direct that the term of imprisonment or detention shall commence on the expiration of any other such sentence from which he has been released at any time under the existing or new provisions within the meaning of Schedule 6 to the Prisoners and Criminal Proceedings (Scotland) Act 1993.'

113. Deputy authorising officer under Part III of Police Act 1997
(1) In subsection (1) of section 94 of the Police Act 1997 (authorisations given in absence of authorising officer), for the words '(f) or (g)' there shall be substituted the words '(f), (g) or (h)'.

(2) In subsection (3) of that section, for paragraphs (a) and (b) there shall be substituted the words 'he holds the rank of assistant chief constable in that Service or Squad'.

(3) In subsection (4) of that section, the word 'and' immediately preceding paragraph (c) shall cease to have effect and after that paragraph there shall be inserted the words 'and
(d) in the case of an authorising officer within paragraph (h) of section 93(5), means the customs officer designated by the Commissioners of Customs and Excise to act in his absence for the purposes of this paragraph.'

Supplemental

114. Orders and regulations
(1) Any power of a Minister of the Crown to make an order or regulations under this Act—
(a) is exercisable by statutory instrument; and
(b) includes power to make such transitional provision as appears to him necessary or expedient in connection with any provision made by the order or regulations.

(2) A statutory instrument containing an order under section 5(2) or (3) or 10(6) above, or regulations under paragraph 1 of Schedule 3 to this Act, shall be subject to annulment in pursuance of a resolution of either House of Parliament.

(3)   No order under section 38(5), 41(6), 58(7), 61(7), 73(2)(b)(ii) or 76(2) above shall be made unless a draft of the order has been laid before and approved by a resolution of each House of Parliament.

115. Disclosure of information

(1)   Any person who, apart from this subsection, would not have power to disclose information—

(a)   to a relevant authority; or

(b)   to a person acting on behalf of such an authority,

shall have power to do so in any case where the disclosure is necessary or expedient for the purposes of any provision of this Act.

(2)   In subsection (1) above 'relevant authority' means—

(a)   the chief officer of police for a police area in England and Wales;

(b)   the chief constable of a police force maintained under the Police (Scotland) Act 1967;

(c)   a police authority within the meaning given by section 101(1) of the Police Act 1996;

(d)   a local authority, that is to say—

(i)   in relation to England, a county council, a district council, a London borough council or the Common Council of the City of London;

(ii)   in relation to Wales, a county council or a county borough council;

(iii)   in relation to Scotland, a council constituted under section 2 of the Local Government etc. (Scotland) Act 1994;

(e)   a probation committee in England and Wales;

(f)   a health authority.

116. Transitory provisions

(1)   The Secretary of State may by order provide that, in relation to any time before the commencement of section 73 above, a court shall not make an order under—

(a)   section 1 of the 1994 Act (secure training orders); or

(b)   subsection (3)(a) of section 4 of that Act (breaches of supervision requirements),

unless it has been notified by the Secretary of State that accommodation at a secure training centre, or accommodation provided by a local authority for the purpose of restricting the liberty of children and young persons, is immediately available for the offender, and the notice has not been withdrawn.

(2)   An order under this section may provide that sections 2 and 4 of the 1994 Act shall have effect, in relation to any such time, as if—

(a)   for subsections (2) and (3) of section 2 there were substituted the following subsection—

'(2)   Where accommodation for the offender at a secure training centre is not immediately available—

(a)   the court shall commit the offender to accommodation provided by a local authority for the purpose of restricting the liberty of children and young persons until such time as accommodation for him at such a centre is available; and

(b)   the period of detention in the centre under the order shall be reduced by the period spent by the offender in the accommodation so provided.';

(b)   in subsection (5) of that section, for the words 'subsections (2)(a)(ii) and (4)(b) apply' there were substituted the words 'subsection (4)(b) applies';

(c)   for subsection (8) of that section there were substituted the following subsection—

'(8)   In this section "local authority" has the same meaning as in the Children Act 1989.'; and

(d)   in subsection (4) of section 4, for the words 'paragraphs (a), (b) and (c) of subsection (2) and subsections (5), (7) and (8) of section 2' there were substituted the words 'paragraphs (a) and (b) of subsection (2) and subsections (7) and (8) of section 2'.

(3)   In relation to any time before the commencement of section 73 above, section 4 of the 1994 Act shall have effect as if after subsection (4) there were inserted the following subsection—

'(4A)   A fine imposed under subsection (3)(b) above shall be deemed, for the purposes of any enactment, to be a sum adjudged to be paid by a conviction.'

(4)   In relation to any time before the commencement of section 73 above, section 1B of the 1982 Act (special provision for offenders under 18) shall have effect as if—

(a)   in subsection (4), immediately before the words 'a total term' there were inserted the words 'a term or (in the case of an offender to whom subsection (6) below applies)';

(b)   in subsection (5)—

(i)   immediately before the words 'total term' there were inserted the words 'term or (as the case may be)'; and

(ii)   for the words 'the term' there were substituted the word 'it'; and

(c)   for subsection (6) there were substituted the following subsection—

'(6)   This subsection applies to an offender sentenced to two or more terms of detention in a young offender institution which are consecutive or wholly or partly concurrent if—

(a)   the sentences were passed on the same occasion; or

(b)   where they were passed on different occasions, the offender has not been released under Part 11 of the Criminal Justice Act 1991 at any time during the period beginning with the first and ending with the last of those occasions;

and in subsections (4) and (5) above "the total term", in relation to such an offender, means the aggregate of those terms.'

(5)   In this section 'local authority' has the same meaning as in the 1989 Act.

117. General interpretation

(1)   In this Act—

'the 1933 Act' means the Children and Young Persons Act 1933;

'the 1969 Act' means the Children and Young Persons Act 1969;

'the 1973 Act' means the Powers of Criminal Courts Act 1973;

'the 1980 Act' means the Magistrates' Courts Act 1980;

'the 1982 Act' means the Criminal Justice Act 1982;

'the 1984 Act' means the Police and Criminal Evidence Act 1984;

'the 1985 Act' means the Prosecution of Offences Act 1985;

'the 1989 Act' means the Children Act 1989;

'the 1991 Act' means the Criminal Justice Act 1991;

'the 1994 Act' means the Criminal Justice and Public Order Act 1994;

'the 1997 Act' means the Crime (Sentences) Act 1997;
'caution' has the same meaning as in Part V of the Police Act 1997;
'child' means a person under the age of 14;
'commission area' has the same meaning as in the Justices of the Peace Act 1997;
'custodial sentence' has the same meaning as in Part I of the 1991 Act;
'guardian' has the same meaning as in the 1933 Act;
'prescribed' means prescribed by an order made by the Secretary of State;
'young person' means a person who has attained the age of 14 and is under the age of 18;
'youth offending team' means a team established under section 39 above.

(2)   In this Act—
'the 1993 Act' means the Prisoners and Criminal Proceedings (Scotland) Act 1993; and
'the 1995 Act' means the Criminal Procedure (Scotland) Act 1995.

(3)   For the purposes of this Act, the age of a person shall be deemed to be that which it appears to the court to be after considering any available evidence.

118.   Provision for Northern Ireland
An Order in Council under paragraph 1(1)(b) of Schedule 1 to the Northern Ireland Act 1974 (legislation for Northern Ireland in the interim period) which contains a statement that it is made only for purposes corresponding to those of sections 2 to 4, 34, 47(5), 57, 61 to 64 and 85 above—

(a)   shall not be subject to paragraph 1(4) and (5) of that Schedule (affirmative resolution of both Houses of Parliament); but

(b)   shall be subject to annulment in pursuance of a resolution of either House of Parliament.

119.   Minor and consequential amendments
The enactments mentioned in Schedule 8 to this Act shall have effect subject to the amendments there specified, being minor amendments and amendments consequential on the provisions of this Act.

120.   Transitional provisions, savings and repeals
(1)   The transitional provisions and savings contained in Schedule 9 to this Act shall have effect; but nothing in this subsection shall be taken as prejudicing the operation of sections 16 and 17 of the Interpretation Act 1978 (which relate to the effect of repeals).

(2)   The enactments specified in Schedule 10 to this Act, which include some that are spent, are hereby repealed to the extent specified in the third column of that Schedule.

121.   Short title, commencement and extent
(1)   This Act may be cited as the Crime and Disorder Act 1998.

(2)   This Act, except this section, sections 109 and 111(8) above and paragraphs 55, 99 and 117 of Schedule 8 to this Act, shall come into force on such day as the Secretary of State may by order appoint; and different days may be appointed for different purposes or different areas.

(3)   Without prejudice to the provisions of Schedule 9 to this Act, an order under subsection (2) above may make such transitional provisions and savings as appear to the Secretary of State necessary or expedient in connection with any provision brought into force by the order.

(4)   Subject to subsections (5) to (12) below, this Act extends to England and Wales only.

(5)   The following provisions extend to Scotland only, namely—
   (a)   Chapter II of Part I;
   (b)   section 33;
   (c)   Chapter II of Part IV;
   (d)   sections 108 to 112 and 117(2); and
   (e)   paragraphs 55, 70, 71, 98 to 108, 115 to 124 and 140 to 143 of Schedule 8 and section 119 above so far as relating to those paragraphs.

(6)   The following provisions also extend to Scotland, namely—
   (a)   Chapter III of Part I;
   (b)   section 36(3) to (5);
   (c)   section 65(9);
   (d)   section 115;
   (e)   paragraph 3 of Schedule 3 to this Act and section 52(6) above so far as relating to that paragraph;
   (f)   paragraph 15 of Schedule 7 to this Act and section 106 above so far as relating to that paragraph;
   (g)   paragraphs 1, 7(1) and (3), 14(1) and (2), 35, 36, 45, 135, 136 and 138 of Schedule 8 to this Act and section 119 above so far as relating to those paragraphs; and
   (h)   this section.

(7)   Sections 36(1), (2)(a), (b) and (d) and (6)(b) and section 118 above extend to Northern Ireland only.

(8)   Section 36(3)(b), (4) and (5) above, paragraphs 7(1) and (3), 45, 135 and 138 of Schedule 8 to this Act, section 119 above so far as relating to those paragraphs and this section also extend to Northern Ireland.

(9)   Section 36(5) above, paragraphs 7(1) and (3), 45 and 134 of Schedule 8 to this Act, section 119 above so far as relating to those paragraphs and this section also extend to the Isle of Man.

(10)   Section 36(5) above, paragraphs 7(1) and (3), 45 and 135 of Schedule 8 to this Act, section 119 above so far as relating to those paragraphs and this section also extend to the Channel Islands.

(11)   The repeals in Schedule 10 to this Act, and section 120(2) above so far as relating to those repeals, have the same extent as the enactments on which the repeals operate.

(12)   Section 9(4) of the Repatriation of Prisoners Act 1984 (power to extend Act to Channel Islands and Isle of Man) applies to the amendments of that Act made by paragraphs 56 to 60 of Schedule 8 to this Act; and in Schedule 1 to the 1997 Act—
   (a)   paragraph 14 (restricted transfers between the United Kingdom and the Channel Islands) as applied in relation to the Isle of Man; and
   (b)   paragraph 19 (application of Schedule in relation to the Isle of Man), apply to the amendments of that Schedule made by paragraph 135 of Schedule 8 to this Act.

SCHEDULES

Section 24(4)   SCHEDULE 1
SCHEDULE 2A TO THE CIVIC GOVERNMENT (SCOTLAND) ACT 1982

Section 54(2C)   'SCHEDULE 2A
RETENTION AND DISPOSAL OF PROPERTY SEIZED UNDER
SECTION 54(2A) OF THIS ACT

Application
1. This schedule applies to property seized under section 54(2A) of this Act.

Retention
2.—(1) Subject to sub-paragraph (2) below, property to which this Schedule applies may be retained for a period of twenty-eight days beginning with the day on which it was seized.

(2) Where proceedings for an offence are instituted within the period specified in sub-paragraph (1) above against any person, the property may be retained for a period beginning on the day on which it was seized and ending on the day when—

(a) the prosecutor certifies that the property is not, or is no longer, required as a production in criminal proceedings or for any purpose relating to such proceedings;

(b) the accused in such proceedings—

(i) is sentenced or otherwise dealt with for the offence; or

(ii) is acquitted of the offence; or

(c) the proceedings are expressly abandoned by the prosecutor or are deserted *simpliciter.*

Arrangements for custody of property

3.—(1) Subject to the proviso to section 17(3)(b) of the Police (Scotland) Act 1967 (duty to comply with instructions received from prosecutor), the chief constable shall, in accordance with the provisions of this Schedule, make such arrangements as he considers appropriate for the care, custody, return or disposal of property to which this Schedule applies.

(2) Any reference in this Schedule to property being in the possession of, delivered by or disposed of by, the chief constable includes a reference to its being in the possession of, delivered by or disposed of by, another person under arrangements made under sub-paragraph (1) above.

Disposal

4. Where the period of retention permitted by paragraph 2 above expires and the chief constable has reason to believe that the person from whom the property was seized is not the owner or the person having right to possession of it, he shall take reasonable steps to ascertain the identity of the owner or of the person with that right and to notify him of the procedures determined under paragraph 5(1) below.

5.—(1) Subject to sub-paragraphs (5) and (6) below, the owner or any person having right to possession of any property to which this Schedule applies and which, at the expiry of the period of retention permitted by paragraph 2 above, is in the possession of the chief constable may at any time prior to its disposal under paragraph 6 below claim that property in accordance with such procedure as the chief constable may determine.

(2) Subject to sub-paragraphs (3), (5) and (6) below, where the chief constable considers that the person making a claim in accordance with the procedure determined under sub-paragraph (1) above is the owner of the property or has a right to possession of it, he shall deliver the property to the claimant.

(3) Subject to sub-paragraph (4) below, the chief constable may impose such conditions connected with the delivery to the claimant of property under sub-paragraph (2) above as he thinks fit and, without prejudice to that generality, such conditions may relate to the payment of such reasonable charges (including any reasonable expenses incurred in relation to the property by or on behalf of him) as he may determine.

(4) No condition relating to the payment of any charge shall be imposed by the chief constable on the owner or person having right of possession of the property where he is satisfied that that person did not know, and had no reason to suspect, that the property to which this Schedule applies was likely to be used in a manner which gave rise to its seizure.

(5) This paragraph does not apply where the period of retention expires in such manner as is mentioned in paragraph 2(2)(b)(i) above and the court by which he was convicted has made a suspended forfeiture order or a restraint order in respect of the property to which this Schedule applies.

(6) This paragraph shall cease to apply where at any time—
    (a) the property to which this Schedule applies—
        (i) is seized under any other power available to a constable; or
        (ii) passes into the possession of the prosecutor; or
    (b) proceedings for an offence are instituted, where the property to which this Schedule applies is required as a production.

6.—(1) Where this sub-paragraph applies, the chief constable may—
    (a) sell property to which this Schedule applies; or
    (b) if in his opinion it would be impracticable to sell such property, dispose of it.

(2) Sub-paragraph (1) above applies—
    (a) at any time after the expiry of the relevant period where, within that period—
        (i) no claim has been made under paragraph 5 above; or
        (ii) any such a claim which has been made has been rejected by the chief constable; and
    (b) where a claim has been made under paragraph 5 above and not determined within the relevant period, at any time after the rejection of that claim by the chief constable.

(3) In sub-paragraph (2) above, the "relevant period" means a period of six months beginning with the day on which the period of retention permitted by paragraph 2 above expired.

(4)   Sections 71, 72 and 77(1) of this Act shall apply to a disposal under this paragraph as they apply to a disposal under section 68 of this Act.

Appeals

7.—(1)   A claimant under sub-paragraph (2) of paragraph 5 above may appeal to the sheriff against any decision of the chief constable made under that paragraph as respects the claim.

(2)   The previous owner of any property disposed of for value under paragraph 6 above may appeal to the sheriff against any decision of the chief constable made under section 72 of this Act as applied by sub-paragraph (4) of that paragraph.

(3)   Subsections (3) to (5) of section 76 of this Act shall apply to an appeal under this paragraph as they apply to an appeal under that section.

Interpretation

8.   In this Schedule—
"chief constable" means the chief constable for the police area in which the property to which this Schedule applies was seized, and includes a constable acting under the direction of the chief constable for the purposes of this Schedule;
"restraint order" shall be construed in accordance with section 28(1) of the Proceeds of Crime (Scotland) Act 1995;
"suspended forfeiture order" shall be construed in accordance with section 21(2) of that Act.'

Section 41 (11)   SCHEDULE 2
THE YOUTH JUSTICE BOARD: FURTHER PROVISIONS

Membership

1.   The Secretary of State shall appoint one of the members of the Board to be their chairman.

2.—(1)   Subject to the following provisions of this paragraph, a person shall hold and vacate office as a member of the Board, or as chairman of the Board, in accordance with the terms of his appointment.

(2)   An appointment as a member of the Board may be full-time or part-time.

(3)   The appointment of a person as a member of the Board, or as chairman of the Board, shall be for a fixed period of not longer than five years.

(4)   Subject to sub-paragraph (5) below, a person whose term of appointment as a member of the Board, or as chairman of the Board, expires shall be eligible for re-appointment.

(5)   No person may hold office as a member of the Board for a continuous period which is longer than ten years.

(6)   A person may at any time resign his office as a member of the Board, or as chairman of the Board, by notice in writing addressed to the Secretary of State.

(7)   The terms of appointment of a member of the Board, or the chairman of the Board, may provide for his removal from office (without cause being assigned) on notice from the Secretary of State of such length as may be specified in those terms, subject (if those terms so provide) to compensation from the Secretary of State; and in any such case the Secretary of State may remove that member from office in accordance with those terms.

(8) Where—

(a) the terms of appointment of a member of the Board, or the chairman of the Board, provide for compensation on his removal from office in pursuance of sub-paragraph (7) above; and

(b) the member or chairman is removed from office in pursuance of that sub-paragraph,

the Board shall pay to him compensation of such amount, and on such terms, as the Secretary of State may with the approval of the Treasury determine.

(9) The Secretary of State may also at any time remove a person from office as a member of the Board if satisfied—

(a) that he has without reasonable excuse failed to discharge his functions as a member for a continuous period of three months beginning not earlier than six months before that time;

(b) that he has been convicted of a criminal offence;

(c) that a bankruptcy order has been made against him, or his estate has been sequestrated, or he has made a composition or arrangement with, or granted a trust deed for, his creditors; or

(d) that he is unable or unfit to discharge his functions as a member.

(10) The Secretary of State shall remove a member of the Board, or the chairman of the Board, from office in pursuance of this paragraph by declaring his office as a member of the Board to be vacant and notifying that fact in such manner as the Secretary of State thinks fit; and the office shall then become vacant.

(11) If the chairman of the Board ceases to be a member of the Board he shall also cease to be chairman.

Members and employees

3.—(1) The Board shall—

(a) pay to members of the Board such remuneration;

(b) pay to or in respect of members of the Board any such allowances, fees, expenses and gratuities; and

(c) pay towards the provision of pensions to or in respect of members of the Board any such sums,

as the Board are required to pay by or in accordance with directions given by the Secretary of State.

(2) Where a member of the Board was, immediately before becoming a member, a participant in a scheme under section 1 of the Superannuation Act 1972, the Minister for the Civil Service may determine that his term of office as a member shall be treated for the purposes of the scheme as if it were service in the employment or office by reference to which he was a participant in the scheme; and his rights under the scheme shall not be affected by sub-paragraph (1)(c) above.

(3) Where—

(a) a person ceases to hold office as a member of the Board otherwise than on the expiry of his term of appointment; and

(b) it appears to the Secretary of State that there are special circumstances which make it right for him to receive compensation,

the Secretary of State may direct the Board to make to the person a payment of such amount as the Secretary of State may determine.

4.—(1) The Board may appoint a chief executive and such other employees as the Board think fit, subject to the consent of the Secretary of State as to their number and terms and conditions of service.

(2) The Board shall—

(a) pay to employees of the Board such remuneration; and

(b) pay to or in respect of employees of the Board any such allowances, fees, expenses and gratuities,

as the Board may, with the consent of the Secretary of State, determine.

(3) Employment by the Board shall be included among the kinds of employment to which a scheme under section 1 of the Superannuation Act 1972 may apply.

5. The Board shall pay to the Minister for the Civil Service, at such times as he may direct, such sums as he may determine in respect of any increase attributable to paragraph 3(2) or 4(3) above in the sums payable out of money provided by Parliament under the Superannuation Act 1972.

House of Commons disqualification

6. In Part II of Schedule 1 to the House of Commons Disqualification Act 1975 (bodies of which all members are disqualified), there shall be inserted at the appropriate place the following entry—

'The Youth Justice Board for England and Wales'.

Procedure

7.—(1) The arrangements for the procedure of the Board (including the quorum for meetings) shall be such as the Board may determine.

(2) The validity of any proceedings of the Board (or of any committee of the Board) shall not be affected by—

(a) any vacancy among the members of the Board or in the office of chairman of the Board; or

(b) any defect in the appointment of any person as a member of the Board or as chairman of the Board.

Annual reports and accounts

8.—(1) As soon as possible after the end of each financial year of the Board, the Board shall send to the Secretary of State a report on the discharge of their functions during that year.

(2) The Secretary of State shall lay before each House of Parliament, and cause to be published, a copy of every report sent to him under this paragraph.

9.—(1) The Board shall—

(a) keep proper accounts and proper records in relation to the accounts; and

(b) prepare a statement of accounts in respect of each financial year of the Board.

(2) The statement of accounts shall contain such information and shall be in such form as the Secretary of State may, with the consent of the Treasury, direct.

(3) The Board shall send a copy of the statement of accounts to the Secretary of State and to the Comptroller and Auditor General within such period after the end of the financial year to which the statement relates as the Secretary of State may direct.

(4) The Comptroller and Auditor General shall—

(a) examine, certify and report on the statement of accounts; and

(b) lay a copy of the statement of accounts and of his report before each House of Parliament.

10. For the purposes of this Schedule the Board's financial year shall be the period of twelve months ending with 31st March; but the first financial year of the Board shall be the period beginning with the date of establishment of the Board and ending with the first 31st March which falls at least six months after that date.

Expenses

11. The Secretary of State shall out of money provided by Parliament pay to the Board such sums towards their expenses as he may determine.

Section 52(6)   SCHEDULE 3
PROCEDURE WHERE PERSONS ARE SENT FOR TRIAL UNDER
SECTION 51

Regulations

1. The Attorney General shall by regulations provide that, where a person is sent for trial under section 51 of this Act on any charge or charges, copies of the documents containing the evidence on which the charge or charges are based shall, on or before the relevant date—

(a) be served on that person; and

(b) be given to the Crown Court sitting at the place specified in the notice under subsection (7) of that section.

(2) In sub-paragraph (1) above 'the relevant date' means the date prescribed by the regulations.

Applications for dismissal

2.—(1) A person who is sent for trial under section 51 of this Act on any charge or charges may, at any time—

(a) after he is served with copies of the documents containing the evidence on which the charge or charges are based; and

(b) before he is arraigned (and whether or not an indictment has been preferred against him),

apply orally or in writing to the Crown Court sitting at the place specified in the notice under subsection (7) of that section for the charge, or any of the charges, in the case to be dismissed.

(2) The judge shall dismiss a charge (and accordingly quash any count relating to it in any indictment preferred against the applicant) which is the subject of any such application if it appears to him that the evidence against the applicant would not be sufficient for a jury properly to convict him.

(3) No oral application may be made under sub-paragraph (1) above unless the applicant has given to the Crown Court sitting at the place in question written notice of his intention to make the application.

(4) Oral evidence may be given on such an application only with the leave of the judge or by his order; and the judge shall give leave or make an order only if it appears to him, having regard to any matters stated in the application for leave, that the interests of justice require him to do so.

(5)   If the judge gives leave permitting, or makes an order requiring, a person to give oral evidence, but that person does not do so, the judge may disregard any document indicating the evidence that he might have given.

(6)   If the charge, or any of the charges, against the applicant is dismissed—

(a)   no further proceedings may be brought on the dismissed charge or charges except by means of the preferment of a voluntary bill of indictment; and

(b)   unless the applicant is in custody otherwise than on the dismissed charge or charges, he shall be discharged.

(7)   Crown Court Rules may make provision for the purposes of this paragraph and, without prejudice to the generality of this sub-paragraph, may make provision—

(a)   as to the time or stage in the proceedings at which anything required to be done is to be done (unless the court grants leave to do it at some other time or stage);

(b)   as to the contents and form of notices or other documents;

(c)   as to the manner in which evidence is to be submitted; and

(d)   as to persons to be served with notices or other material.

Reporting restrictions

3.—(1)   Except as provided by this paragraph, it shall not be lawful—

(a)   to publish in Great Britain a written report of an application under paragraph 2(1) above; or

(b)   to include in a relevant programme for reception in Great Britain a report of such an application,

if (in either case) the report contains any matter other than that permitted by this paragraph.

(2)   An order that sub-paragraph (1) above shall not apply to reports of an application under paragraph 2(1) above may be made by the judge dealing with the application.

(3)   Where in the case of two or more accused one of them objects to the making of an order under sub-paragraph (2) above, the judge shall make the order if, and only if, he is satisfied, after hearing the representations of the accused, that it is in the interests of justice to do so.

(4)   An order under sub-paragraph (2) above shall not apply to reports of proceedings under sub-paragraph (3) above, but any decision of the court to make or not to make such an order may be contained in reports published or included in a relevant programme before the time authorised by sub-paragraph (5) below.

(5)   It shall not be unlawful under this paragraph to publish or include in a relevant programme a report of an application under paragraph 2(1) above containing any matter other than that permitted by sub-paragraph (8) below where the application is successful.

(6)   Where—

(a)   two or more persons were jointly charged; and

(b)   applications under paragraph 2(1) above are made by more than one of them,

sub-paragraph (5) above shall have effect as if for the words 'the application is' there were substituted the words 'all the applications are'.

(7)   It shall not be unlawful under this paragraph to publish or include in a relevant programme a report of an unsuccessful application at the conclusion of the trial of the person charged, or of the last of the persons charged to be tried.

(8)   The following matters may be contained in a report published or included in a relevant programme without an order under sub-paragraph (2) above before the time authorised by sub-paragraphs (5) and (6) above, that is to say—

(a)   the identity of the court and the name of the judge;

(b)   the names, ages, home addresses and occupations of the accused and witnesses;

(c)   the offence or offences, or a summary of them, with which the accused is or are charged;

(d)   the names of counsel and solicitors engaged in the proceedings;

(e)   where the proceedings are adjourned, the date and place to which they are adjourned;

(f)   the arrangements as to bail;

(g)   whether legal aid was granted to the accused or any of the accused.

(9)   The addresses that may be published or included in a relevant programme under sub-paragraph (8) above are addresses—

(a)   at any relevant time; and

(b)   at the time of their publication or inclusion in a relevant programme.

(10)   If a report is published or included in a relevant programme in contravention of this paragraph, the following persons, that is to say—

(a)   in the case of a publication of a written report as part of a newspaper or periodical, any proprietor, editor or publisher of the newspaper or periodical;

(b)   in the case of a publication of a written report otherwise than as part of a newspaper or periodical, the person who publishes it;

(c)   in the case of the inclusion of a report in a relevant programme, any body corporate which is engaged in providing the service in which the programme is included and any person having functions in relation to the programme corresponding to those of the editor of a newspaper;

shall be liable on summary conviction to a fine not exceeding level 5 on the standard scale.

(11)   Proceedings for an offence under this paragraph shall not, in England and Wales, be instituted otherwise than by or with the consent of the Attorney General.

(12)   Sub-paragraph (1) above shall be in addition to, and not in derogation from, the provisions of any other enactment with respect to the publication of reports of court proceedings.

(13)   In this paragraph—

'publish', in relation to a report, means publish the report, either by itself or as part of a newspaper or periodical, for distribution to the public;

'relevant programme' means a programme included in a programme service (within the meaning of the Broadcasting Act 1990);

'relevant time' means a time when events giving rise to the charges to which the proceedings relate occurred.

Power of justice to take depositions etc.

4.—(1)   Sub-paragraph (2) below applies where a justice of the peace for any commission area is satisfied that—

(a)   any person in England and Wales ('the witness') is likely to be able to make on behalf of the prosecutor a written statement containing material evidence, or produce on behalf of the prosecutor a document or other exhibit likely to be material evidence, for the purposes of proceedings for an offence for which a person has been sent for trial under section 51 of this Act by a magistrates' court for that area; and

(b)   the witness will not voluntarily make the statement or produce the document or other exhibit.

(2)   In such a case the justice shall issue a summons directed to the witness requiring him to attend before a justice at the time and place appointed in the summons, and to have his evidence taken as a deposition or to produce the document or other exhibit.

(3)   If a justice of the peace is satisfied by evidence on oath of the matters mentioned in sub-paragraph (1) above, and also that it is probable that a summons under sub-paragraph (2) above would not procure the result required by it, the justice may instead of issuing a summons issue a warrant to arrest the witness and to bring him before a justice at the time and place specified in the warrant.

(4)   A summons may also be issued under sub-paragraph (2) above if the justice is satisfied that the witness is outside the British Islands, but no warrant may be issued under sub-paragraph (3) above unless the justice is satisfied by evidence on oath that the witness is in England and Wales.

(5)   If—

(a)   the witness fails to attend before a justice in answer to a summons under this paragraph;

(b)   the justice is satisfied by evidence on oath that the witness is likely to be able to make a statement or produce a document or other exhibit as mentioned in sub-paragraph (1)(a) above;

(c)   it is proved on oath, or in such other manner as may be prescribed, that he has been duly served with the summons and that a reasonable sum has been paid or tendered to him for costs and expenses; and

(d)   it appears to the justice that there is no just excuse for the failure,
the justice may issue a warrant to arrest the witness and to bring him before a justice at the time and place specified in the warrant.

(6)   Where—

(a)   a summons is issued under sub-paragraph (2) above or a warrant is issued under sub-paragraph (3) or (5) above; and

(b)   the summons or warrant is issued with a view to securing that the witness has his evidence taken as a deposition,
the time appointed in the summons or specified in the warrant shall be such as to enable the evidence to be taken as a deposition before the relevant date.

(7)   If any person attending or brought before a justice in pursuance of this paragraph refuses without just excuse to have his evidence taken as a deposition, or to produce the document or other exhibit, the justice may do one or both of the following—

(a)   commit him to custody until the expiration of such period not exceeding one month as may be specified in the summons or warrant or until he sooner has his evidence taken as a deposition or produces the document or other exhibit;

(b)   impose on him a fine not exceeding £2,500.

(8)   A fine imposed under sub-paragraph (7) above shall be deemed, for the purposes of any enactment, to be a sum adjudged to be paid by a conviction.

(9) If in pursuance of this paragraph a person has his evidence taken as a deposition, the clerk of the justice concerned shall as soon as is reasonably practicable send a copy of the deposition to the prosecutor and the Crown Court.

(10) If in pursuance of this paragraph a person produces an exhibit which is a document, the clerk of the justice concerned shall as soon as is reasonably practicable send a copy of the document to the prosecutor and the Crown Court.

(11) If in pursuance of this paragraph a person produces an exhibit which is not a document, the clerk of the justice concerned shall as soon as is reasonably practicable inform the prosecutor and the Crown Court of that fact and of the nature of the exhibit.

(12) In this paragraph—
'prescribed' means prescribed by rules made under section 144 of the 1980 Act;
'the relevant date' has the meaning given by paragraph 1(2) above.

Use of depositions as evidence

5.—(1) Subject to sub-paragraph (3) below, sub-paragraph (2) below applies where in pursuance of paragraph 4 above a person has his evidence taken as a deposition.

(2) Where this sub-paragraph applies the deposition may without further proof be read as evidence on the trial of the accused, whether for an offence for which he was sent for trial under section 51 of this Act or for any other offence arising out of the same transaction or set of circumstances.

(3) Sub-paragraph (2) above does not apply if—
    (a) it is proved that the deposition was not signed by the justice by whom it purports to have been signed;
    (b) the court of trial at its discretion orders that sub-paragraph (2) above shall not apply; or
    (c) a party to the proceedings objects to sub-paragraph (2) above applying.

(4) If a party to the proceedings objects to sub-paragraph (2) applying the court of trial may order that the objection shall have no effect if the court considers it to be in the interests of justice so to order.

Power of Crown Court to deal with summary offence

6.—(1) This paragraph applies where a magistrates' court has sent a person for trial under section 51 of this Act for offences which include a summary offence.

(2) If the person is convicted on the indictment, the Crown Court shall consider whether the summary offence is related to the offence that is triable only on indictment or, as the case may be, any of the offences that are so triable.

(3) If it considers that the summary offence is so related, the court shall state to the person the substance of the offence and ask him whether he pleads guilty or not guilty.

(4) If the person pleads guilty, the Crown Court shall convict him, but may deal with him in respect of the summary offence only in a manner in which a magistrates' court could have dealt with him.

(5) If he does not plead guilty, the powers of the Crown Court shall cease in respect of the summary offence except as provided by sub-paragraph (6) below.

(6) If the prosecution inform the court that they would not desire to submit evidence on the charge relating to the summary offence, the court shall dismiss it.

(7)   The Crown Court shall inform the clerk of the magistrates' court of the outcome of any proceedings under this paragraph.

(8)   If the summary offence is one to which section 40 of the Criminal Justice Act 1988 applies, the Crown Court may exercise in relation to the offence the power conferred by that section; but where the person is tried on indictment for such an offence, the functions of the Crown Court under this paragraph in relation to the offence shall cease.

(9)   Where the Court of Appeal allows an appeal against conviction of an indictable-only offence which is related to a summary offence of which the appellant was convicted under this paragraph—

(a)   it shall set aside his conviction of the summary offence and give the clerk of the magistrates' court notice that it has done so; and

(b)   it may direct that no further proceedings in relation to the offence are to be undertaken;

and the proceedings before the Crown Court in relation to the offence shall thereafter be disregarded for all purposes.

(10)   A notice under sub-paragraph (9) above shall include particulars of any direction given under paragraph (b) of that sub-paragraph in relation to the offence.

(11)   The references to the clerk of the magistrates' court in this paragraph shall be construed in accordance with section 141 of the 1980 Act.

(12)   An offence is related to another offence for the purposes of this paragraph if it arises out of circumstances which are the same as or connected with those giving rise to the other offence.

Procedure where no indictable-only offence remains

7.—(1)   Subject to paragraph 13 below, this paragraph applies where—

(a)   a person has been sent for trial under section 51 of this Act but has not been arraigned; and

(b)   the person is charged on an indictment which (following amendment of the indictment, or as a result of an application under paragraph 2 above, or for any other reason) includes no offence that is triable only on indictment.

(2)   Everything that the Crown Court is required to do under the following provisions of this paragraph must be done with the accused present in court.

(3)   The court shall cause to be read to the accused each count of the indictment that charges an offence triable either way.

(4)   The court shall then explain to the accused in ordinary language that, in relation to each of those offences, he may indicate whether (if it were to proceed to trial) he would plead guilty or not guilty, and that if he indicates that he would plead guilty the court must proceed as mentioned in sub-paragraph (6) below.

(5)   The court shall then ask the accused whether (if the offence in question were to proceed to trial) he would plead guilty or not guilty.

(6)   If the accused indicates that he would plead guilty the court shall proceed as if he had been arraigned on the count in question and had pleaded guilty.

(7)   If the accused indicates that he would plead not guilty, or fails to indicate how he would plead, the court shall consider whether the offence is more suitable for summary trial or for trial on indictment.

(8)   Subject to sub-paragraph (6) above, the following shall not for any purpose be taken to constitute the taking of a plea—

(a) asking the accused under this paragraph whether (if the offence were to proceed to trial) he would plead guilty or not guilty;

(b) an indication by the accused under this paragraph of how he would plead.

8.—(1) Subject to paragraph 13 below, this paragraph applies in a case where—

(a) a person has been sent for trial under section 51 of this Act but has not been arraigned;

(b) he is charged on an indictment which (following amendment of the indictment, or as a result of an application under paragraph 2 above, or for any other reason) includes no offence that is triable only on indictment;

(c) he is represented by a legal representative;

(d) the Crown Court considers that by reason of his disorderly conduct before the court it is not practicable for proceedings under paragraph 7 above to be conducted in his presence; and

(e) the court considers that it should proceed in his absence.

(2) In such a case—

(a) the court shall cause to be read to the representative each count of the indictment that charges an offence triable either way;

(b) the court shall ask the representative whether (if the offence in question were to proceed to trial) the accused would plead guilty or not guilty;

(c) if the representative indicates that the accused would plead guilty the court shall proceed as if the accused had been arraigned on the count in question and had pleaded guilty;

(d) if the representative indicates that the accused would plead not guilty, or fails to indicate how the accused would plead, the court shall consider whether the offence is more suitable for summary trial or for trial on indictment.

(3) Subject to sub-paragraph (2)(c) above, the following shall not for any purpose be taken to constitute the taking of a plea—

(a) asking the representative under this section whether (if the offence were to proceed to trial) the accused would plead guilty or not guilty;

(b) an indication by the representative under this paragraph of how the accused would plead.

9.—(1) This paragraph applies where the Crown Court is required by paragraph 7(7) or 8(2)(d) above to consider the question whether an offence is more suitable for summary trial or for trial on indictment.

(2) Before considering the question, the court shall afford first the prosecutor and then the accused an opportunity to make representations as to which mode of trial would be more suitable.

(3) In considering the question, the court shall have regard to—

(a) any representations made by the prosecutor or the accused;

(b) the nature of the case;

(c) whether the circumstances make the offence one of a serious character;

(d) whether the punishment which a magistrates' court would have power to impose for it would be adequate; and

(e) any other circumstances which appear to the court to make it more suitable for the offence to be dealt tried in one way rather than the other.

10.—(1) This paragraph applies (unless excluded by paragraph 15 below) where the Crown Court considers that an offence is more suitable for summary trial.

(2) The court shall explain to the accused in ordinary language—

(a)   that it appears to the court more suitable for him to be tried summarily for the offence, and that he can either consent to be so tried or, of he wishes, be tried by a jury; and

(b)   that if he is tried summarily and is convicted by the magistrates' court, he may be committed for sentence to the Crown Court under section 38 of the 1980 Act if the convicting court is of such opinion as is mentioned in subsection (2) of that section.

(3)   After explaining to the accused as provided by sub-paragraph (2) above the court shall ask him whether he wishes to be tried summarily or by a jury, and

(a)   if he indicates that he wishes to be tried summarily, shall remit him for trial to a magistrates' court acting for the place where he was sent to the Crown Court for trial;

(b)   if he does not give such an indication, shall retain its functions in relation to the offence and proceed accordingly.

11.   If the Crown Court considers that an offence is more suitable for trial on indictment, the court—

(a)   shall tell the accused that it has decided that it is more suitable for him to be tried for the offence by a jury; and

(b)   shall retain its functions in relation to the offence and proceed accordingly.

12.—(1)   Where the prosecution is being carried on by the Attorney General, the Solicitor General or the Director of Public Prosecutions and he applies for an offence which may be tried on indictment to be so tried—

(a)   sub-paragraphs (4) to (8) of paragraph 7, sub-paragraphs (2)(b) to (d) and (3) of paragraph 8 and paragraphs 9 to 11 above shall not apply; and

(b)   the Crown Court shall retain its functions in relation to the offence and proceed accordingly.

(2)   The power of the Director of Public Prosecutions under this paragraph to apply for an offence to be tried on indictment shall not be exercised except with the consent of the Attorney General.

13.—(1)   This paragraph applies, in place of paragraphs 7 to 12 above, in the case of a child or young person who—

(a)   has been sent for trial under section 51 of this Act but has not been arraigned; and

(b)   is charged on an indictment which (following amendment of the indictment, or as a result of an application under paragraph 2 above, or for any other reason) includes no offence that is triable only on indictment.

(2)   The Crown Court shall remit the child or young person for trial to a magistrates' court acting for the place where he was sent to the Crown Court for trial unless—

(a)   he is charged with such an offence as is mentioned in subsection (2) of section 53 of the 1933 Act (punishment of certain grave crimes) and the Crown Court considers that if he is found guilty of the offence it ought to be possible to sentence him in pursuance of subsection (3) of that section; or

(b)   he is charged jointly with an adult with an offence triable either way and the Crown Court considers it necessary in the interests of justice that they both be tried for the offence in the Crown Court.

(3)   In sub-paragraph (2) above 'adult' has the same meaning as in section 51 of this Act.

*Procedure for determining whether offences of criminal damage etc. are
summary offences*

14.—(1) This paragraph applies where the Crown Court has to determine, for the purposes of this Schedule, whether an offence which is listed in the first column of Schedule 2 to the 1980 Act (offences for which the value involved is relevant to the mode of trial) is a summary offence.

(2) The court shall have regard to any representations made by the prosecutor or the accused.

(3) If it appears clear to the court that the value involved does not exceed the relevant sum, it shall treat the offence as a summary offence.

(4) If it appears clear to the court that the value involved exceeds the relevant sum, it shall treat the offence as an indictable offence.

(5) If it appears to the court for any reason not clear whether the value involved does or does not exceed the relevant sum, the court shall ask the accused whether he wishes the offence to be treated as a summary offence.

(6) Where sub-paragraph (5) above applies—

(a) if the accused indicates that he wishes the offence to be treated as a summary offence, the court shall so treat it;

(b) if the accused does not give such an indication, the court shall treat the offence as an indictable offence.

(7) In this paragraph 'the value involved' and 'the relevant sum' have the same meanings as in section 22 of the 1980 Act (certain offences triable either way to be tried summarily if value involved is small).

*Power of Crown Court, with consent of legally-represented accused, to proceed
in his absence*

15.—(1) The Crown Court may proceed in the absence of the accused in accordance with such of the provisions of paragraphs 9 to 14 above as are applicable in the circumstances if—

(a) the accused is represented by a legal representative who signifies to the court the accused's consent to the proceedings in question being conducted in his absence; and

(b) the court is satisfied that there is good reason for proceeding in the absence of the accused.

(2) Sub-paragraph (1) above is subject to the following provisions of this paragraph which apply where the court exercises the power conferred by that sub-paragraph.

(3) If, where the court has considered as required by paragraph 7(7) or 8(2)(d) above, it appears to the court that an offence is more suitable for summary trial, paragraph 10 above shall not apply and—

(a) if the legal representative indicates that the accused wishes to be tried summarily, the court shall remit the accused for trial to a magistrates' court acting for the place where he was sent to the Crown Court for trial;

(b) if the legal representative does not give such an indication, the court shall retain its functions and proceed accordingly.

(4) If, where the court has considered as required by paragraph 7(7) or 8(2)(d) above, it appears to the court that an offence is more suitable for trial on indictment, paragraph 11 above shall apply with the omission of paragraph (a).

(5) Where paragraph 14 above applies and it appears to the court for any reason not clear whether the value involved does or does not exceed the relevant sum, sub-paragraphs (5) and (6) of that paragraph shall not apply and—

(a) the court shall ask the legal representative whether the accused wishes the offence to be treated as a summary offence;

(b) if the legal representative indicates that the accused wishes the offence to be treated as a summary offence, the court shall so treat it;

(c) if the legal representative does not give such an indication, the court shall treat the offence as an indictable offence.

Section 64(5) SCHEDULE 4
ENFORCEMENT ETC. OF DRUG TREATMENT AND TESTING ORDERS

Preliminary

1. Schedule 2 to the 1991 Act (enforcement etc. of community orders) shall be amended as follows.

Meaning of 'relevant order' etc.

2.—(1) In sub-paragraph (1) of paragraph 1 (preliminary)—

(a) after the words 'a probation order,' there shall be inserted the words 'a drug treatment and testing order,'; and

(b) in paragraph (a), for the words 'probation or community service order' there shall be substituted the words 'probation, community service or drug treatment and testing order'.

(2) After sub-paragraph (3) of that paragraph there shall be inserted the following sub-paragraph—

'(4) In this Schedule, references to the court responsible for a drug treatment and testing order shall be construed in accordance with section 62(9) of the Crime and Disorder Act 1998.'

Breach of requirements of order

3. In sub-paragraph (2) of paragraph 2 (issue of summons or warrant), for the words 'before a magistrates' court acting for the petty sessions area concerned' there shall be substituted the following paragraphs—

'(a) except where the relevant order is a drug treatment and testing order, before a magistrates' court acting for the petty sessions area concerned;

(b) in the excepted case, before the court responsible for the order.'

4. In sub-paragraph (1) of paragraph 4 (powers of Crown Court), after the word 'Where' there shall be inserted the words 'under paragraph 2 or'.

5. In sub-paragraph (2) of paragraph 5 (exclusions), for the words 'is required by a probation order to submit to treatment for his mental condition, or his dependency on drugs or alcohol,' there shall be substituted the following paragraphs—

'(a) is required by a probation order to submit to treatment for his mental condition, or his dependency on or propensity to misuse drugs or alcohol; or

(b) is required by a drug treatment and testing order to submit to treatment for his dependency on or propensity to misuse drugs,'.

Revocation of order

6.—(1) In sub-paragraph (1) of paragraph 7 (revocation of order by magistrates' court), after the words 'the petty sessions area concerned' there shall be inserted the words 'or, where the relevant order is a drug treatment and testing order for which a magistrates' court is responsible, to that court'.

(2) In sub-paragraph (3) of that paragraph—

(a) after the words 'a probation order' there shall be inserted the words 'or drug treatment and testing order'; and

(b) after the word 'supervision' there shall be inserted the words 'or, as the case may be, treatment'.

7.—(1) After sub-paragraph (1) of paragraph 8 (revocation of order by Crown Court) there shall be inserted the following sub-paragraph—

'(1A) This paragraph also applies where—

(a) a drug treatment and testing order made by the Crown Court is in force in respect of an offender; and

(b) the offender or the responsible officer applies to the Crown Court for the order to be revoked or for the offender to be dealt with in some other manner for the offence in respect of which the order was made.'

(2) In sub-paragraph (3) of that paragraph—

(a) after the words 'a probation order' there shall be inserted the words 'or drug treatment and testing order'; and

(b) after the word 'supervision' there shall be inserted the words 'or, as the case may be, treatment'.

8. In sub-paragraph (1) of paragraph 9 (revocation of order following custodial sentence), for paragraph (a) there shall be substituted the following paragraph—

'(a) an offender in respect of whom a relevant order is in force is convicted of an offence—

(i) by a magistrates' court other than a magistrates' court acting for the petty sessions area concerned; or

(ii) where the relevant order is a drug treatment and testing order, by a magistrates' court which is not responsible for the order; and'.

Amendment of order

9. In sub-paragraph (1) of paragraph 12 (amendment by reason of change of residence), after the words 'a relevant order' there shall be inserted the words '(other than a drug treatment and testing order)'.

10. After paragraph 14 there shall be inserted the following paragraph—

'Amendment of drug treatment and testing order

14A.—(1) Without prejudice to the provisions of section 63(2), (7) and (9) of the Crime and Disorder Act 1998, the court responsible for a drug treatment and testing order may by order—

(a) vary or cancel any of the requirements or provisions of the order on an application by the responsible officer under sub-paragraph (2) or (3)(a) or (b) below; or

(b)   amend the order on an application by that officer under sub-paragraph (3)(c) below.

(2)   Where the treatment provider is of the opinion that the treatment or testing requirement of the order should be varied or cancelled—

(a)   he shall make a report in writing to that effect to the responsible officer; and

(b)   that officer shall apply to the court for the variation or cancellation of the requirement.

(3)   Where the responsible officer is of the opinion—

(a)   that the treatment or testing requirement of the order should be so varied as to specify a different treatment provider;

(b)   that any other requirement of the order, or a provision of the order, should be varied or cancelled; or

(c)   that the order should be so amended as to provide for each subsequent review under section 63 of the Crime and Disorder Act 1998 to be made without a hearing instead of at a review hearing, or vice versa,

he shall apply to the court for the variation or cancellation of the requirement or provision or the amendment of the order.

(4)   The court—

(a)   shall not amend the treatment or testing requirement unless the offender expresses his willingness to comply with the requirement as amended; and

(b)   shall not amend any provision of the order so as to reduce the treatment and testing period below the minimum specified in section 61(2) of the Crime and Disorder Act 1998 or to increase it above the maximum so specified.

(5)   If the offender fails to express his willingness to comply with the treatment or testing requirement as proposed to be amended by the court, the court may—

(a)   revoke the order; and

(b)   deal with him, for the offence in respect of which the order was made, in any manner in which it could deal with him if he had just been convicted by the court of the offence.

(6)   In dealing with the offender under sub-paragraph (5)(b) above, the court—

(a)   shall take into account the extent to which the offender has complied with the requirements of the order; and

(b)   may impose a custodial sentence notwithstanding anything in section 1(2) of this Act.

(7)   Paragraph 6A above shall apply for the purposes of this paragraph as it applies for the purposes of paragraph 3 above, but as if for the words 'paragraph 3(1)(d) above' there were substituted the words 'paragraph 14A(5)(b) below'.

(8)   In this paragraph—

'review hearing' has the same meaning as in section 63 of the Crime and Disorder Act 1998;

'the treatment requirement' and 'the testing requirement' have the same meanings as in Chapter I of Part IV of that Act.'

11.   In paragraph 16 (order not to be amended pending appeal), after the words 'paragraph 13 or 15 above' there shall be inserted the words 'or, except with the consent of the offender, under paragraph 14A above'.

12.—(1)   In sub-paragraph (1) of paragraph 18 (notification of amended order), after the words 'a relevant order' there shall be inserted the words '(other than a drug treatment and testing order)'.

(2)   After that sub-paragraph there shall be inserted the following sub-paragraph—

'(1A)   On the making under this Part of this Schedule of an order amending a drug treatment and testing order, the clerk to the court shall forthwith give copies of the amending order to the responsible officer.'

(3)   In sub-paragraph (2) of that paragraph, after the words 'sub-paragraph (1)' there shall be inserted the words 'or (1A)'.

Sections 68(3) and 70(5)   SCHEDULE 5
ENFORCEMENT ETC. OF REPARATION AND ACTION PLAN ORDERS

Preliminary

1.   In this Schedule—
'the appropriate court', in relation to a reparation order or action plan order, means the youth court acting for the petty sessions area for the time being named in the order in pursuance of section 67(9) or, as the case may be, section 69(9) of this Act;
'local authority accommodation' means accommodation provided by or on behalf of a local authority (within the meaning of the 1989 Act).

General power to discharge or vary order

2.—(1)   If while a reparation order or action plan order is in force in respect of an offender it appears to the appropriate court, on the application of the responsible officer or the offender, that it is appropriate to make an order under this sub-paragraph, the court may make an order discharging the reparation order or action plan order or varying it—

(a)   by cancelling any provision included in it; or

(b)   by inserting in it (either in addition to or in substitution for any of its provisions) any provision that could have been included in the order if the court had then had power to make it and were exercising the power.

(2)   Where an application under this paragraph for the discharge of a reparation order or action plan order is dismissed, no further application for its discharge shall be made under this paragraph by any person except with the consent of the appropriate court.

Failure to comply with order

3.—(1)   This paragraph applies where a reparation order or action plan order is in force and it is proved to the satisfaction of the appropriate court, on the application of the responsible officer, that the offender has failed to comply with any requirement included in the order.

(2)   The court—

(a)   whether or not it also makes an order under paragraph 2 above, may order the offender to pay a fine of an amount not exceeding £1,000, or make an attendance centre order or curfew order in respect of him; or

(b)   if the reparation order or action plan order was made by a youth court, may discharge the order and deal with him, for the offence in respect of which the order was made, in any manner in which he could have been dealt with for that offence by the court which made the order if the order had not been made; or

(c) if the reparation order or action plan order was made by the Crown Court, may commit him in custody or release him on bail until he can be brought or appear before the Crown Court.

(3) For the purposes of sub-paragraph (2)(b) and (c) above, a reparation order or action plan order made on appeal from a decision of a magistrates' court or the Crown Court shall be treated as if it had been made by a magistrates' court or the Crown Court, as the case may be.

(4) Where a court deals with an offender under sub-paragraph (2)(c) above, it shall send to the Crown Court a certificate signed by a justice of the peace giving—

(a) particulars of the offender's failure to comply with the requirement in question; and

(b) such other particulars of the case as may be desirable;

and a certificate purporting to be so signed shall be admissible as evidence of the failure before the Crown Court.

(5) Where—

(a) by virtue of sub-paragraph (2)(c) above the offender is brought or appears before the Crown Court; and

(b) it is proved to the satisfaction of the court that he has failed to comply with the requirement in question,

that court may deal with him, for the offence in respect of which the order was made, in any manner in which it could have dealt with him for that offence if it had not made the order.

(6) Where the Crown Court deals with an offender under sub-paragraph (5) above, it shall revoke the reparation order or action plan order if it is still in force.

(7) A fine imposed under this paragraph shall be deemed, for the purposes of any enactment, to be a sum adjudged to be paid by a conviction.

(8) In dealing with an offender under this paragraph, a court shall take into account the extent to which he has complied with the requirements of the reparation order or action plan order.

Presence of offender in court, remands etc.

4.—(1) Where the responsible officer makes an application under paragraph 2 or 3 above to the appropriate court, he may bring the offender before the court and, subject to sub-paragraph (9) below, the court shall not make an order under that paragraph unless the offender is present before it.

(2) Without prejudice to any power to issue a summons or warrant apart from this sub-paragraph, the court to which an application under paragraph 2 or 3 above is made may issue a summons or warrant for the purpose of securing the attendance of the offender before it.

(3) Subsections (3) and (4) of section 55 of the 1980 Act (which among other things restrict the circumstances in which a warrant may be issued) shall apply with the necessary modifications to a warrant under sub-paragraph (2) above as they apply to a warrant under that section and as if in subsection (3) after the word 'summons' there were inserted the words 'cannot be served or'.

(4) Where the offender is arrested in pursuance of a warrant under sub-paragraph (2) above and cannot be brought immediately before the appropriate court, the person in whose custody he is—

(a)   may make arrangements for his detention in a place of safety for a period of not more than 72 hours from the time of the arrest (and it shall be lawful for him to be detained in pursuance of the arrangements); and

(b)   shall within that period bring him before a youth court.

(5)   Where an offender is, under sub-paragraph (4) above, brought before a youth court other than the appropriate court, that court may—

(a)   direct that he be released forthwith; or

(b)   subject to sub-paragraph (6) below, remand him to local authority accommodation.

(6)   Where the offender is aged 18 or over at the time when he is brought before the court, he shall not be remanded to local authority accommodation but may instead be remanded—

(a)   to a remand centre, if the court has been notified that such a centre is available for the reception of persons under this sub-paragraph; or

(b)   to a prison, if it has not been so notified.

(7)   Where an application is made to a court under paragraph 2(1) above, the court may remand (or further remand) the offender to local authority accommodation if—

(a)   a warrant has been issued under sub-paragraph (2) of this paragraph for the purpose of securing the attendance of the offender before the court; or

(b)   the court considers that remanding (or further remanding) him will enable information to be obtained which is likely to assist the court in deciding whether and, if so, how to exercise its powers under paragraph 2(1) above.

(8) A court remanding an offender to local authority accommodation under this paragraph shall designate, as the authority who are to receive him, the local authority for the area in which the offender resides or, where it appears to the court that he does not reside in the area of a local authority, the local authority—

(a)   specified by the court; and

(b)   in whose area the offence or an offence associated with it was committed.

(9)   A court may make an order under paragraph 2 above in the absence of the offender if the effect of the order is one or more of the following, that is to say—

(a)   discharging the reparation order or action plan order;

(b)   cancelling a requirement included in the reparation order or action plan order;

(c)   altering in the reparation order or action plan order the name of any area;

(d)   changing the responsible officer.

Supplemental

5.—(1)   The provisions of section 17 of the 1982 Act (attendance centre orders) shall apply for the purposes of paragraph 3(2)(a) above but as if—

(a)   in subsection (1), for the words from 'has power' to 'probation order' there were substituted the words 'considers it appropriate to make an attendance centre order in respect of any person in pursuance of paragraph 3(2) of Schedule 5 to the Crime and Disorder Act 1998'; and

(b)   subsection (13) were omitted.

(2)   Sections 18 and 19 of the 1982 Act (discharge and variation of attendance centre order and breach of attendance centre orders or attendance centre rules) shall also apply for the purposes of that paragraph but as if there were omitted—

(a)   from subsection (4A) of section 18 and subsections (3) and (5) of section 19, the words ', for the offence in respect of which the order was made,' and 'for that offence'; and

(b)   from subsection (4B) of section 18 and subsection (6) of section 19, the words 'for an offence'.

(3)   The provisions of section 12 of the 1991 Act (curfew orders) shall apply for the purposes of paragraph 3(2)(a) above but as if—

(a)   in subsection (1), for the words from the beginning to 'before which he is convicted' there were substituted the words 'Where a court considers it appropriate to make a curfew order in respect of any person in pursuance of paragraph 3(2)(a) of Schedule 5 to the Crime and Disorder Act 1998, the court'; and

(b)   in subsection (8), for the words 'on conviction' there were substituted the words 'on the date on which his failure to comply with a requirement included in the reparation order or action plan order was proved to the court'.

(4)   Schedule 2 to the 1991 Act (enforcement etc. of community orders), so far as relating to curfew orders, shall also apply for the purposes of that paragraph but as if—

(a)   the power conferred on the magistrates' court by each of paragraphs 3(1)(d) and 7(2)(a)(ii) to deal with the offender for the offence in respect of which the order was made were a power to deal with the offender, for his failure to comply with a requirement included in the reparation order or action plan order, in any manner in which the appropriate court could deal with him for that failure to comply if it had just been proved to the satisfaction of that court;

(b)   the power conferred on the Crown Court by paragraph 4(1)(d) to deal with the offender for the offence in respect of which the order was made were a power to deal with the offender, for his failure to comply with such a requirement, in any manner in which that court could deal with him for that failure to comply if it had just been proved to its satisfaction;

(c)   the reference in paragraph 7(1)(b) to the offence in respect of which the order was made were a reference to the failure to comply in respect of which the curfew order was made; and

(d)   the power conferred on the Crown Court by paragraph 8(2)(b) to deal with the offender for the offence in respect of which the order was made were a power to deal with the offender, for his failure to comply with a requirement included in the reparation order or action plan order, in any manner in which the appropriate court (if that order was made by a magistrates' court) or the Crown Court (if that order was made by the Crown Court) could deal with him for that failure to comply if it had just been proved to the satisfaction of that court.

(5)   For the purposes of the provisions mentioned in sub-paragraph (4)(a) and (d) above, as applied by that sub-paragraph, if the reparation order or action plan order is no longer in force the appropriate court's powers shall be determined on the assumption that it is still in force.

(6)   If while an application to the appropriate court in pursuance of paragraph 2 or 3 above is pending the offender attains the age of 18 years, the court shall, subject to paragraph 4(6) above, deal with the application as if he had not attained that age.

(7)   The offender may appeal to the Crown Court against—

(a)   any order made under paragraphs 2 or 3 above, except an order made or which could have been made in his absence (by virtue of paragraph 4(9) above);

(b) the dismissal of an application under paragraph 2 above to discharge a reparation order or action plan order.

Section 94(2) SCHEDULE 6

DRUG TREATMENT AND TESTING ORDERS:
AMENDMENT OF THE 1995 ACT

PART I
AMENDMENTS RELATING TO COMBINATION OF ORDERS

1. In section 228(1) (probation orders), for the words 'section 245U' there shall be substituted the words 'sections 234J and 245D'.

2.—(1) Section 232 (failure to comply with requirements of probation orders) shall be amended as follows.

(2) In subsection (3A)—

(a) for the words 'a restriction of liberty order' there shall be substituted—

'(a) a restriction of liberty order; or

(b) a restriction of liberty order and a drug treatment and testing order'; and

(b) at the end there shall be added the words 'or, as the case may be, the restriction of liberty order and the drug treatment and testing order.'

(3) After that subsection there shall be inserted the following subsection—

'(3B) Where the court intends to sentence an offender under subsection (2)(b) above and the offender is by virtue of section 234J of this Act subject to a drug treatment and testing order, it shall, before sentencing the offender under that paragraph, revoke the drug treatment and testing order.'

3. For section 245D there shall be substituted the following section—

'**245D. Combination of restriction of liberty order with other orders**

(1) Subsection (3) applies where the court—

(a) intends to make a restriction of liberty order under section 245A(1) of this Act; and

(b) considers it expedient that the offender should also be subject to a probation order made under section 228(1) of this Act or to a drug treatment and testing order made under section 234B(2) of this Act or to both such orders.

(2) In deciding whether it is expedient to make a probation order or a drug treatment and testing order by virtue of paragraph (b) of subsection (1) above, the court shall—

(a) have regard to the circumstances, including the nature of the offence and the character of the offender; and

(b) obtain a report as to the circumstances and character of the offender.

(3) Where this subsection applies, the court, notwithstanding sections 228(1), 234B(2) and 245A(1) of this Act, may make a restriction of liberty order and either or both of a probation order and a drug treatment and testing order.

(4) Where the court makes a restriction of liberty order and a probation order by virtue of subsection (3) above, the clerk of the court shall send a copy of each order to—

(a) any person responsible for monitoring the offender's compliance with the restriction of liberty order; and

(b) the officer of the local authority who is to supervise the probationer.

(5) Where the court makes a restriction of liberty order and a drug treatment and testing order by virtue of subsection (3) above, the clerk of the court shall send a copy of each order to—

(a) any person responsible for monitoring the offender's compliance with the restriction of liberty order;

(b) the treatment provider, within the meaning of section 234C(1) of this Act; and

(c) the officer of the local authority who is appointed or assigned to be the supervising officer under section 234C(6) of this Act.

(6) Where the court makes a restriction of liberty order, a probation order and a drug treatment and testing order the clerk of the court shall send copies of each of the orders to the persons mentioned—

(a) in subsection (4) above;

(b) in paragraph (b) of subsection (5) above; and

(c) in paragraph (c) of that subsection, if that person would not otherwise receive such copies.

(7) Where the offender by an act or omission fails to comply with a requirement of an order made by virtue of subsection (3) above—

(a) if the failure relates to a requirement contained in a probation order and is dealt with under section 232(2)(c) of this Act, the court may, in addition, exercise the powers conferred by section 234G(2)(b) of this Act in relation to a drug treatment and testing order to which the offender is subject by virtue of subsection (3) above and by section 245F(2) of this Act in relation to the restriction of liberty order;

(b) if the failure relates to a requirement contained in a drug treatment and testing order and is dealt with under section 234G(2)(b) of this Act, the court may, in addition, exercise the powers conferred by section 232(2)(c) of this Act in relation to a probation order to which the offender is subject by virtue of subsection (3) above and by section 245F(2)(b) of this Act in relation to the restriction of liberty order; and

(c) if the failure relates to a requirement contained in a restriction of liberty order and is dealt with under section 245F(2)(b) of this Act, the court may, in addition, exercise the powers conferred by section 232(2)(c) of this Act in relation to a probation order and by section 234G(2)(b) of this Act in relation to a drug treatment and testing order to which, in either case, the offender is subject by virtue of subsection (3) above.

(8) In any case to which this subsection applies, the offender may, without prejudice to subsection (7) above, be dealt with as respects that case under section 232(2) or, as the case may be, section 234G or section 245F(2) of this Act but he shall not be liable to be otherwise dealt with as respects that case.

(9) Subsection (8) applies in a case where—

(a) the offender by an act or omission fails to comply with both a requirement contained in a restriction of liberty order and in a probation order to which he is subject by virtue of subsection (3) above;

(b) the offender by an act or omission fails to comply with both a requirement contained in a restriction of liberty order and in a drug treatment and testing order to which he is subject by virtue of subsection (3) above;

(c)   the offender by an act or omission fails to comply with a requirement contained in each of a restriction of liberty order, a probation order and a drug treatment and testing order to which he is subject by virtue of subsection (3) above.'

4.—(1)   Section 245G (disposal on revocation of restriction of liberty order) shall be amended as follows.

(2)   In subsection (2), for the words from 'by' to the end there shall be substituted the words 'by virtue of section 245ID(3) of this Act, subject to a probation order or a drug treatment and testing order or to both such orders, it shall, before disposing the offender under subsection (1) above—

(a)   where he is subject to a probation order, discharge that order;

(b)   where he is subject to a drug treatment and testing order, revoke that order; and

(c)   where he is subject to both such orders, discharge the probation order and revoke the drug treatment and testing order.'

(3)   After subsection (2) there shall be added—

'(3)   Where the court orders a probation order discharged or a drug treatment and testing order revoked the clerk of the court shall forthwith give copies of that order to the persons mentioned in subsection (4) or, as the case may be, (5) of section 245D of this Act.

(4)   Where the court orders a probation order discharged and a drug treatment and testing order revoked, the clerk of the court shall forthwith give copies of that order to the persons mentioned in section 245D(6) of this Act.'

PART II
AMENDMENTS RELATING TO APPEALS

5.   In section 106 (solemn appeals), in paragraph (d), after the words 'probation order' there shall be inserted the words ', drug treatment and testing order'.

6.—(1)   Section 108 (right of appeal of prosecutor) shall be amended as follows.

(2)   In subsection (1), after paragraph (d) there shall be inserted the following paragraph—

'(dd)   a drug treatment and testing order;'.

(3)   In subsection (2)(b)(iii), for the word 'or', where it first occurs, there shall be substituted the word 'to'.

7.—(1)   Section 175 (appeals in summary cases) shall be amended as follows.

(2)   In subsection (2)(c), after the words 'probation order' there shall be inserted the words ', drug treatment and testing order'.

(3)   In subsection (4), after paragraph (d) there shall be inserted the following paragraph—

'(dd)   a drug treatment and testing order;'.

(4)   In subsection (4A)(b)(iii), for the word 'or', where it first occurs, there shall be substituted the word 'to'.

Section 106   SCHEDULE 7

PRE-CONSOLIDATION AMENDMENTS:
POWERS OF CRIMINAL COURTS

Children and Young Persons Act 1933 (c. 12)

1.—(1)   In subsection (1A) of section 55 of the 1933 Act (power to order parent or guardian to pay fine etc.), in paragraph (a), for the words 'section 15(2A)' there shall be substituted the words 'section 15(3)(a)'.

(2)   For paragraph (b) of that subsection there shall be substituted the following paragraphs—

'(b)   a court would impose a fine on a child or young person under section 19(3) of the Criminal Justice Act 1982 (breach of attendance centre order or attendance centre rules); or

(bb)   a court would impose a fine on a child or young person under paragraph 3(1)(a) or 4(1)(a) of Schedule 2 to the Criminal Justice Act 1991 (breach of requirement of a relevant order (within the meaning given by that Schedule) or of a combination order);'.

(3)   After subsection (5) of that section there shall be added the following subsection

'(6)   In relation to any other child or young person, references in this section to his parent shall be construed in accordance with section 1 of the Family Law Reform Act 1987.'

Criminal Justice Act 1967 (c. 80)

2.—(1)   In subsection (1)(b)(i) of section 56 of the Criminal Justice Act 1967 (committal for sentence for offences tried summarily), for the words from 'section 93' to '34 to 36' there shall be substituted the words 'section 34, 35 or 36'.

(2)   In subsection (2) of that section, for the words from 'section 8(6)' to the end there shall be substituted the words 'section 1B(5) of the Powers of Criminal Courts Act 1973 (conditionally discharged person convicted of further offence) and section 24(2) of that Act (offender convicted during operational period of suspended sentence).'

(3)   Subsection (3) of that section shall cease to have effect.

(4)   For subsection (5) of that section there shall be substituted the following subsections—

'(5)   Where under subsection (1) above a magistrates' court commits a person to be dealt with by the Crown Court in respect of an offence, the Crown Court may after inquiring into the circumstances of the case deal with him in any way in which the magistrates' court could deal with him if it had just convicted him of the offence.

(5A)   Subsection (5) above does not apply where under subsection (1) above a magistrates' court commits a person to be dealt with by the Crown Court in respect of a suspended sentence, but in such a case the powers under section 23 of the Powers of Criminal Courts Act 1973 (power of court to deal with suspended sentence) shall be exercisable by the Crown Court.

(5B)   Without prejudice to subsections (5) and (5A) above, where under subsection (1) above or any enactment to which this section applies a magistrates' court commits a person to be dealt with by the Crown Court, any duty or power which, apart from this subsection, would fall to be discharged or exercised by the magistrates' court shall not be discharged or exercised by that court but shall instead be discharged or may instead be exercised by the Crown Court.

(5C)   Where under subsection (1) above a magistrates' court commits a person to be dealt with by the Crown Court in respect of an offence triable only on indictment in the case of an adult (being an offence which was tried summarily because of the offender's being under 18 years of age), the Crown Court's powers under subsection (5) above in respect of the offender after he attains the age of 18 years shall be powers to do either or both of the following—

    (a)   to impose a fine not exceeding £5,000;

    (b)   to deal with the offender in respect of the offence in any way in which the magistrates' court could deal with him if it had just convicted him of an offence punishable with imprisonment for a term not exceeding six months.

    (5D) For the purposes of this section the age of an offender shall be deemed to be that which it appears to the court to be after considering any available evidence.'

  (5)   Subsection (13) of that section shall cease to have effect.

Children and Young Persons Act 1969 (c. 54)

3.   After subsection (8) of section 7 of the 1969 Act (alterations in treatment of young offenders etc.) there shall be added the following subsection—

    '(9)   The reference in subsection (8) above to a person's parent shall be construed in accordance with section 1 of the Family Law Reform Act 1987 (and not in accordance with section 70(1A) of this Act).'

4.   In section 12 of the 1969 Act (power to include requirements in supervision orders), after subsection (3) there shall be added the following subsection—

    '(4)   Directions given by the supervisor by virtue of subsection (2)(b) or (c) above shall, as far as practicable, be such as to avoid—

    (a)   any conflict with the offender's religious beliefs or with the requirements of any other community order (within the meaning of Part I of the Criminal Justice Act 1991) to which he may be subject; and

    (b)   any interference with the times, if any, at which he normally works or attends school or any other educational establishment.'

5.—(1)   In subsection (1) of section 12B of the 1969 Act (power to include in supervision order requirements as to mental treatment)—

    (a)   for the words 'medical practitioner', in the first place where they occur, there shall be substituted the words 'registered medical practitioner';

    (b)   for the words 'his detention in pursuance of a hospital order under Part III' there shall be substituted the words 'the making of a hospital order or guardianship order within the meaning';

    (c)   in paragraph (a), for the words 'fully registered medical practitioner' there shall be substituted the words 'registered medical practitioner';

    (d)   after that paragraph there shall be inserted the following paragraph—

    '(aa) treatment by or under the direction of a chartered psychologist specified in the order;';

    (e)   in paragraph (b), for the words 'a place' there shall be substituted the words 'an institution or place'; and

    (f)   in paragraph (c), for the words 'the said Act of 1983' there shall be substituted the words 'the Mental Health Act 1983'.

  (2)   After that subsection there shall be inserted the following subsection—

    '(1A)   In subsection (1) of this section "registered medical practitioner" means a fully registered person within the meaning of the Medical Act 1983 and "chartered psychologist" means a person for the time being listed in the British Psychological Society's Register of Chartered Psychologists.'

(3)   After subsection (2) of that section there shall be added the following subsection—

'(3)   Subsections (2) and (3) of section 54 of the Mental Health Act 1983 shall have effect with respect to proof for the purposes of subsection (1) above of a supervised person's mental condition as they have effect with respect to proof of an offender's mental condition for the purposes of section 37(2)(a) of that Act.'

6.   In section 16(11) of the 1969 Act (provisions supplementary to section 15), the words 'seventeen or' shall cease to have effect.

7.—(1)   In subsection (1)(a) of section 16A of the 1969 Act (application of sections 17 to 19 of Criminal Justice Act 1982), for the words 'section 15(2A) or (4)' there shall be substituted the words 'section 15(3)(a)'.

(2)   In subsection (2)(b) of that section—

(a)   in sub-paragraph (i), after the word 'from' there shall be inserted the words 'subsection (4A) of section 18 and'; and

(b)   in sub-paragraph (ii), for the words 'subsection (6)' there shall be substituted the words 'subsection (4B) of section 18 and subsection (6) of section 19'.

8.   In section 34(1)(c) of the 1969 Act (power of Secretary of State to amend references to young person), the words '7(7), 7(8),' shall cease to have effect.

9.   Section 69(5) of the 1969 Act (power to include in commencement order certain consequential provisions) shall cease to have effect.

10.   In section 70 of the 1969 Act (interpretation), for subsections (1A) and (1B) there shall be substituted the following subsections—

'(1A)   In the case of a child or young person—

(a)   whose father and mother were not married to each other at the time of his birth, and

(b)   with respect to whom a residence order is in force in favour of the father,

any reference in this Act to the parent of the child or young person includes (unless the contrary intention appears) a reference to the father.

(1B)   In subsection (1A) of this section, the reference to a child or young person whose father and mother were not married to each other at the time of his birth shall be construed in accordance with section 1 of the Family Law Reform Act 1987 and "residence order" has the meaning given by section 8(1) of the Children Act 1989.'

11.   In Schedule 6 to the 1969 Act (repeals), the entries relating to sections 55, 56(1) and 59(1) of the 1933 Act (which entries have never come into force or are spent) are hereby repealed.

Criminal Justice Act 1972 (c. 71)

12.   Section 49 of the Criminal Justice Act 1972 (community service order in lieu of warrant of commitment for failure to pay fine etc.) shall cease to have effect.

Powers of Criminal Courts Act 1973 (c. 62)

13.—(1)   In subsection (6) of section 1 of the 1973 Act (deferment of sentence), for the words '13(1), (2) and (5)' there shall be substituted the words '13(1) to (3) and (5)'.

(2)   In subsection (8) of that section, for paragraph (a) there shall be substituted the following paragraph—

'(a)   is power to deal with him, in respect of the offence for which passing of sentence has been deferred, in any way in which the court which deferred passing sentence could have dealt with him; and'.

14.—(1)   In subsection (9) of section 1B of the 1973 Act (commission of further offence by person conditionally discharged), for the words from 'those which' to the end there shall be substituted the words 'powers to do either or both of the following—

(a)   to impose a fine not exceeding £5,000 for the offence in respect of which the order was made;

(b)   to deal with the offender for that offence in any way in which a magistrates' court could deal with him if it had just convicted him of an offence punishable with imprisonment for a term not exceeding six months.'

(2)   Subsection (10) of that section (which is superseded by provision inserted by this Schedule in section 57 of the 1973 Act) shall cease to have effect.

15.   In section 1C(1) of the 1973 Act (effect of absolute or conditional discharge)—

(a)   in paragraph (a), for the words 'the following provisions' there shall be substituted the words 'section 1B'; and

(b)   paragraph (b) and the word 'and' immediately preceding it shall cease to have effect.

16.   In section 2(1) of the 1973 Act (probation orders), the words from 'For the purposes' to 'available evidence' (which are superseded by provision inserted by this Schedule in section 57 of the 1973 Act) shall cease to have effect.

17.   Section 11 of the 1973 Act (which is superseded by the paragraph 8A inserted by this Schedule in Schedule 2 to the 1991 Act) shall cease to have effect.

18.—(1)   For subsection (2) of section 12 of the 1973 Act (supplementary provision as to probation and discharge) there shall be substituted the following subsection—

'(2) Where an order for conditional discharge has been made on appeal, for the purposes of this Act it shall be deemed—

(a)   if it was made on an appeal brought from a magistrates' court, to have been made by that magistrates' court;

(b)   if it was made on an appeal brought from the Crown Court or from the criminal division of the Court of Appeal, to have been made by the Crown Court.'

(2)   In subsection (3) of that section, for the words from 'any question whether a probationer' to 'period of conditional discharge,' there shall be substituted the words 'any question whether any person in whose case an order for conditional discharge has been made has been convicted of an offence committed during the period of conditional discharge'.

(3)   For subsection (4) of that section there shall be substituted the following subsection—

'(4)   Nothing in section 1A of this Act shall be construed as preventing a court, on discharging an offender absolutely or conditionally in respect of any offence, from making an order for costs against the offender or imposing any disqualification on him or from making in respect of the offence an order under section 35 or 43 of this Act or section 28 of the Theft Act 1968.'

19.—(1)   In subsection (1) of section 14 of the 1973 Act (community service orders in respect of convicted persons), after the word 'imprisonment', in the first place where it occurs, there shall be inserted the words '(not being an offence the sentence for which is fixed by law or falls to be imposed under section 2(2), 3(2) or 4(2) of the Crime (Sentences) Act 1997)'.

(2) In that subsection, after the words 'young offenders' there shall be inserted the words '; and for the purposes of this subsection a sentence falls to be imposed under section 2(2), 3(2) or 4(2) of the Crime (Sentences) Act 1997 if it is required by that provision and the court is not of the opinion there mentioned'.

(3) In subsection (7) of that section, for the words 'paragraph (b)(i) or (ii)' there shall be substituted the words 'paragraph (b)'.

(4) Subsection (8) of that section shall cease to have effect.

20. For subsection (3) of section 15 of the 1973 Act (obligations of person subject to community service order) there shall be substituted the following subsection—

'(3) The instructions given by the relevant officer under this section shall, as far as practicable, be such as to avoid—

(a) any conflict with the offender's religious beliefs or with the requirements of any other community order (within the meaning of Part I of the Criminal Justice Act 1991) to which he may be subject; and

(b) any interference with the times, if any, at which he normally works or attends school or any other educational establishment.'

21. In section 21(3)(b) of the 1973 Act (meaning of 'sentence of imprisonment' for purposes of restriction on imposing sentences of imprisonment on persons not legally represented), after the words 'contempt of court' there shall be inserted the words 'or any kindred offence'.

22. In subsection (3) of section 22 of the 1973 Act (suspended sentences of imprisonment)—

(a) for the words 'make a probation order in his case in respect of another offence' there shall be substituted the words 'impose a community sentence in his case in respect of that offence or any other offence'; and

(b) at the end there shall be inserted the words '; and in this subsection community sentence' has the same meaning as in Part I of the Criminal Justice Act 1991.'

23.—(1) In section 31 of the 1973 Act (powers etc. of Crown Court in relation to fines and forfeited recognizances), the following provisions shall cease to have effect—

(a) in subsection (3A), the words 'Subject to subsections (3B)(3C) and (3C) below,';

(b) subsections (3B) and (3C); and

(c) in subsection (4), the words '4 or'.

(2) In subsection (6) of that section—

(a) the words 'about committal by a magistrates' court to the Crown Court' shall cease to have effect; and

(b) after the words 'dealt with him' there shall be inserted the words 'or could deal with him'.

(3) In subsection (8) of that section, for the words '(2) to (3C)' there shall be substituted the words '(2) to (3A)'.

24.—(1) In subsection (2) of section 32 of the 1973 Act (enforcement etc. of fines imposed and recognizances forfeited by Crown Court), for the words 'section 85(1)' there shall be substituted the words 'section 85(2)'.

(2) In subsection (3) of that section, after the words 'to the Crown Court' there shall be inserted the words '(except the reference in subsection (1)(b) above)'.

(3) For subsection (4) of that section there shall be substituted the following subsection—

'(4) A magistrates' court shall not, under section 85(1) or 120 of the Magistrates' Courts Act 1980 as applied by subsection (1) above, remit the whole or any part of a fine imposed by, or sum due under a recognizance forfeited by—

(a) the Crown Court,

(b) the criminal division of the Court of Appeal, or

(c) the House of Lords on appeal from that division,

without the consent of the Crown Court.'

(4) Subsection (5) of that section shall cease to have effect.

25. In section 46 of the 1973 Act (reports of probation officers), after subsection (2) there shall be added the following subsection—

'(3) For the purposes of this section—

(a) references to an offender's parent shall be construed in accordance with section 1 of the Family Law Reform Act 1987; and

(b) "guardian" has the same meaning as in the Children and Young Persons Act 1933.'

26.—(1) For subsection (5) of section 57 of the 1973 Act (interpretation) there shall be substituted the following subsection—

'(5) Where a compensation order or supervision order has been made on appeal, for the purposes of this Act (except section 26(5)) it shall be deemed—

(a) if it was made on an appeal brought from a magistrates' court, to have been made by that magistrates' court;

(b) if it was made on an appeal brought from the Crown Court or from the criminal division of the Court of Appeal, to have been made by the Crown Court.'

(2) After subsection (6) of that section there shall be added the following subsection—

'(7) For the purposes of any provision of this Act which requires the determination of the age of a person by the court, his age shall be deemed to be that which it appears to the court to be after considering any available evidence.'

27.—(1) In paragraph 2 of Schedule 1A to the 1973 Act (additional requirements in probation orders), for sub-paragraph (7) there shall be substituted the following sub-paragraph—

'(7) Instructions given by a probation officer under sub-paragraph (4) or (6) above shall, as far as practicable, be such as to avoid—

(a) any conflict with the offender's religious beliefs or with the requirements of any other community order (within the meaning of Part I of the Criminal Justice Act 1991) to which he may be subject; and

(b) any interference with the times, if any, at which he normally works or attends school or any other educational establishment.'

(2) In paragraph 3 of that Schedule, for sub-paragraph (4) there shall be substituted the following sub-paragraph—

'(4) Instructions given by a probation officer under sub-paragraph (3) above shall, as far as practicable, be such as to avoid—

(a)   any conflict with the offender's religious beliefs or with the requirements of any other community order (within the meaning of Part I of the Criminal Justice Act 1991) to which he may be subject; and

(b)   any interference with the times, if any, at which he normally works or attends school or any other educational establishment.'

(3)   In paragraph 5 of that Schedule, for the words 'duly qualified medical practitioner', wherever they occur, there shall be substituted the words 'registered medical practitioner'.

(4)   In that paragraph (both as amended by subsection (3) of section 38 of the 1997 Act and so far as that paragraph has effect without that amendment), in sub-paragraph (4), after the words 'have been' there shall be inserted the words 'or can be'.

(5)   In sub-paragraph (10) of that paragraph, before the definition of 'chartered psychologist' there shall be inserted the following definition—

'"registered medical practitioner" means a fully registered person within the meaning of the Medical Act 1983;'.

(6)   In paragraph 6 of that Schedule (both as amended by subsection (4) of section 38 of the 1997 Act and so far as that paragraph has effect without that amendment), in sub-paragraph (4), after the words 'have been' there shall be inserted the words 'or can be'.

(7) Sub-paragraph (7) of that paragraph shall cease to have effect.

Magistrates' Courts Act 1980 (c. 43)

28.   In section 30(2)(a) of the 1980 Act (remand for medical examination), for the words 'duly qualified medical practitioner' there shall be substituted the words 'registered medical practitioner'.

29.—(1)   In subsection (2) of section 38 of the 1980 Act (committal for sentence on summary trial of offence triable either way), the words ', in accordance with section 56 of the Criminal Justice Act 1967,' shall cease to have effect.

(2)   After that subsection there shall be inserted the following subsection—

'(2A)   Where the court commits a person under subsection (2) above, section 56 of the Criminal Justice Act 1967 (which enables a magistrates' court, where it commits a person under this section in respect of an offence, also to commit him to the Crown Court to be dealt with in respect of certain other offences) shall apply accordingly.'

30.—(1)   In subsection (2) of section 38A of the 1980 Act (committal for sentence on indication of guilty plea to offence triable either way), the words ', in accordance with section 56 of the Criminal Justice Act 1967,' shall cease to have effect.

(2)   In subsection (5) of that section, for the words 'the court might have dealt with him' there shall be substituted the words 'the magistrates' court could deal with him if it had just convicted him of the offence'.

(3)   After that subsection there shall be inserted the following subsection—

'(5A)   Where the court commits a person under subsection (2) above, section 56 of the Criminal Justice Act 1967 (which enables a magistrates' court, where it commits a person under this section in respect of an offence, also to commit him to the Crown Court to be dealt with in respect of certain other offences) shall apply accordingly.'

31.   In section 39(6)(b) of the 1980 Act (cases where magistrates' court may remit offender to another such court for sentence), for the words 'section 34 or 36' there shall be substituted the words 'section 34, 35 or 36'.

32.   In section 85(1)(a) of the 1980 Act (power to remit fine), for the words 'section 74' there shall be substituted the words 'section 77'.

Criminal Justice Act 1982 (c. 48)

33.   In section 3(1) of the 1982 Act (restriction on imposing custodial sentences on persons under 21 not legally represented)—

(a)   in paragraph (a), the words 'under section 1A above' shall cease to have effect;

(b)   in paragraph (c), for the words 'section 8(2)' there shall be substituted the words 'section 8(1) or (2)'; and

(c)   in paragraph (d), for the words 'section 53(2)' there shall be substituted the words 'section 53(1) or (3)'.

34.—(1)   In subsection (3) of section 13 of the 1982 Act (conversion of sentence of detention in a young offender institution to sentence of imprisonment), for the words 'section 15 below' there shall be substituted the words 'section 65 of the Criminal Justice Act 1991 (supervision of young offenders after release)'.

(2)   In subsection (6) of that section, for the words 'section 8(2)' there shall be substituted the words 'section 8(1) or (2)'.

35.   In subsection (2) of section 16 of the 1982 Act (meaning of 'attendance centre'), for the words from ' of orders made' to the end there shall be substituted the words 'of orders made under section 17 below.'

36.—(1)   In subsection (1) of section 17 of the 1982 Act (attendance centre orders), for the words 'Subject to subsections (3) and (4) below,' there shall be substituted the words 'Where a person under 21 years of age is convicted by or before a court of an offence punishable with imprisonment (not being an offence the sentence for which is fixed by law or falls to be imposed under section 2(2), 3(2) or 4(2) of the Crime (Sentences) Act 1997), or'.

(2)   In that subsection, for paragraph (a) there shall be substituted the following paragraph—

'(a)   would have power, but for section 1 above, to commit a person under 21 years of age to prison in default of payment of any sum of money or for failing to do or abstain from doing anything required to be done or left undone, or'.

(3)   In that subsection, in paragraph (b), for the words 'any such person' there shall be substituted the words 'a person under 21 years of age' and after that paragraph there shall be inserted the following paragraph—

'(bb) has power to deal with a person under 16 years of age under that Part of that Schedule for failure to comply with any of the requirements of a curfew order, or'.

(4)   After that subsection there shall be inserted the following subsection—

'(1A)   For the purposes of subsection (1) above—

(a)   the reference to an offence punishable with imprisonment shall be construed without regard to any prohibition or restriction imposed by or under any enactment on the imprisonment of young offenders; and

(b)   a sentence falls to be imposed under section 2(2), 3(2) or 4(2) of the Crime (Sentences) Act 1997 if it is required by that provision and the court is not of the opinion there mentioned.'

(5)   For subsection (8) of that section there shall be substituted the following subsection—

'(8)   The times at which an offender is required to attend at an attendance centre shall, as far as practicable, be such as to avoid—

(a)   any conflict with the offender's religious beliefs or with the requirements of any other community order (within the meaning of Part I of the Criminal Justice Act 1991) to which he may be subject; and

(b)   any interference with the times, if any, at which he normally works or attends school or any other educational establishment.'

37.—(1)   In section 18 of the 1982 Act (discharge and variation of attendance centre orders), for subsection (4A) there shall be substituted the following subsections—

'(4A)   Any power conferred by this section—

(a)   on a magistrates' court to discharge an attendance centre order made by such a court, or

(b)   on the Crown Court to discharge an attendance centre order made by the Crown Court,

includes power to deal with the offender, for the offence in respect of which the order was made, in any manner in which he could have been dealt with for that offence by the court which made the order if the order had not been made.

(4B)   A person sentenced by a magistrates' court under subsection (4A) above for an offence may appeal to the Crown Court against the sentence.'

(2)   Subsection (7) of that section shall cease to have effect.

(3)   In that section, after subsection (9) there shall be added the following subsections—

'(10)   Where an offender has been ordered to attend at an attendance centre in default of the payment of a sum of money or for such a failure or abstention as is mentioned in section 17(1)(a) above, subsection (4A) above shall have effect in relation to the order as if the words ", for the offence in respect of which the order was made," and "for that offence" were omitted.

(11)   Where an attendance centre order has been made on appeal, for the purposes of this section it shall be deemed—

(a)   if it was made on an appeal brought from a magistrates' court, to have been made by that magistrates' court;

(b)   if it was made on an appeal brought from the Crown Court or from the criminal division of the Court of Appeal, to have been made by the Crown Court;

and subsection (4A) above shall have effect in relation to an attendance centre order made on appeal as if the words "if the order had not been made" were omitted.'

38.—(1)   In subsection (1) of section 19 of the 1982 Act (breaches of attendance centre orders or attendance centre rules), for the words 'has been made' there shall be substituted the words 'is in force'.

(2)   In subsection (5) of that section, after the word 'failed' there shall be inserted the words 'without reasonable excuse'.

(3)   After subsection (7) of that section there shall be added the following subsections—

'(8) Where an offender has been ordered to attend at an attendance centre in default of the payment of a sum of money or for such a failure or abstention as is mentioned in section 17(1)(a) above, subsections (3) and (5) above shall have effect in relation to the order as if the words ", for the offence in respect of which the order was made," and "for that offence" were omitted.

(9) Where an attendance centre order has been made on appeal, for the purposes of this section it shall be deemed—

(a) if it was made on an appeal brought from a magistrates' court, to have been made by that magistrates' court;

(b) if it was made on an appeal brought from the Crown Court or from the criminal division of the Court of Appeal, to have been made by the Crown Court;

and, in relation to an attendance centre order made on appeal, subsection (3)(a) above shall have effect as if the words "if the order had not been made" were omitted and subsection (5) above shall have effect as if the words "if it had not made the order" were omitted.'

Criminal Justice Act 1988 (c. 33)

39. Paragraph 40 of Schedule 15 to the Criminal Justice Act 1988 (minor and consequential amendments) shall cease to have effect.

Criminal Justice Act 1991 (c. 53)

40. In section 11 of the 1991 Act (orders combining probation and community service), after subsection (1) there shall be inserted the following subsection—

'(1A) The reference in subsection (1) above to an offence punishable with imprisonment shall be construed without regard to any prohibition or restriction imposed by or under any enactment on the imprisonment of young offenders.'

41.—(1) In subsection (5)(c) of section 12 of the 1991 Act (curfew orders), for the words 'supervising office?' there shall be substituted the words 'responsible officer'.

(2) After subsection (6A) of that section there shall be inserted the following subsection—

'(6B) The court by which a curfew order is made shall give a copy of the order to the offender and to the person responsible for monitoring the offender's whereabouts during the curfew periods specified in the order.'

(3) After subsection (7) of that section there shall be added the following subsection—

'(8) References in this section to the offender's being under the age of sixteen years are references to his being under that age on conviction.'

42. In section 31(1) of the 1991 Act (interpretation of Part I), in paragraph (b) of the definition of 'custodial sentence', for the words 'section 53' there shall be substituted the words 'section 53(3)'.

43.—(1) In subsection (3) of section 40 of the 1991 Act (convictions during currency of original sentences), for the words from 'for sentence' to the end there shall be substituted the words 'to be dealt with under subsection (3A) below'.

(2) After that subsection there shall be inserted the following subsections—

'(3A) Where a person is committed to the Crown Court under subsection (3) above, the Crown Court may order him to be returned to prison for the whole or any part of the period which—

(a) begins with the date of the order; and

(b) is equal in length to the period between the date on which the new offence was committed and the date mentioned in subsection (1) above.

(3B) Subsection (3)(b) above shall not be taken to confer on the magistrates' court a power to commit the person to the Crown Court for sentence for the new offence, but this is without prejudice to any such power conferred on the magistrates' court by any other enactment.'

(3) In subsection (4) of that section, for the words 'subsection (2)' there shall be substituted the words 'subsection (2) or (3A)'.

44. In each of subsections (3)(b) and (4)(a) of section 57 of the 1991 Act (responsibility of parent or guardian for financial penalties), for the words 'section 35(4)(a)' there shall be substituted the words 'section 35(4)'.

45. In section 58 of the 1991 Act (binding over of parent or guardian), after subsection (8) there shall be added the following subsection—

'(9) For the purposes of this section—

(a) "guardian" has the same meaning as in the 1933 Act; and

(b) taking "care" of a person includes giving him protection and guidance and "control" includes discipline.'

46.—(1) In paragraph 1 of Schedule 2 to the 1991 Act (enforcement etc. of community orders), after sub-paragraph (4) there shall be added the following sub-paragraph—

'(5) Where a probation order, community service order, combination order or curfew order has been made on appeal, for the purposes of this Schedule it shall be deemed—

(a) if it was made on an appeal brought from a magistrates' court, to have been made by a magistrates' court;

(b) if it was made on an appeal brought from the Crown Court or from the criminal division of the Court of Appeal, to have been made by the Crown Court.'

20.—(1) In subsection (8) of section 16 of the 1969 Act (provisions supplementary to section 15), after the words 'under the preceding section' there shall be inserted the words 'by a relevant court (within the meaning of that section)'.

(2) Subsection (10) of that section shall cease to have effect.

21. After section 16A of the 1969 Act there shall be inserted the following section—

'**16B. Application of section 12 of Criminal Justice Act 1991 etc.**

(1) The provisions of section 12 of the Criminal Justice Act 1991 (curfew orders) shall apply for the purposes of section 15(3)(a) of this Act but as if—

(a) in subsection (1), for the words from the beginning to "before which he is convicted" there were substituted the words "Where a court considers it appropriate to make a curfew order in respect of any person in pursuance of section 15(3)(a) of the Children and Young Persons Act 1969, the court"; and

(b)   in subsection (8), for the words "on conviction" there were substituted the words "on the date on which his failure to comply with a requirement included in the supervision order was proved to the court".

(2)   Schedule 2 to the Criminal Justice Act 1991 (enforcement etc. of community orders), so far as relating to curfew orders, shall also apply for the purposes of that section but as if—

(a)   the power conferred on the magistrates' court by each of paragraphs 3(1)(d) and 7(2)(a)(ii) to deal with the offender for the offence in respect of which the order was made were a power to deal with the offender, for his failure to comply with a requirement included in the supervision order, in any manner in which the relevant court could deal with him for that failure to comply if it had just been proved to the satisfaction of that court;

(b)   the power conferred on the Crown Court by paragraph 4(1)(d) to deal with the offender for the offence in respect of which the order was made were a power to deal with the offender, for his failure to comply with such a requirement, in any manner in which that court could deal with him for that failure to comply if it had just been proved to its satisfaction;

(c)   the reference in paragraph 7(1)(b) to the offence in respect of which the order was made were a reference to the failure to comply in respect of which the curfew order was made; and

(d)   the power conferred on the Crown Court by paragraph 8(2)(b) to deal with the offender for the offence in respect of which the order was made were a power to deal with the offender, for his failure to comply with a requirement included in the supervision order, in any manner in which the relevant court (if that order was made by a magistrates' court) or the Crown Court (if that order was made by the Crown Court) could deal with him for that failure to comply if it had just been proved to the satisfaction of that court.

(3)   For the purposes of the provisions mentioned in subsection (2)(a) and (d) above, as applied by that subsection, if the supervision order is no longer in force the relevant court's powers shall be determined on the assumption that it is still in force.

(4)   In this section 'relevant court' has the same meaning as in section 15 above.'

22.   In subsection (14) of section 23 of the 1969 Act (remands and committals to local authority accommodation), paragraph (a) shall cease to have effect.

23.   In subsection (1) of section 70 of the 1969 Act (interpretation), after the definition of 'young person' there shall be inserted the following definition—

'youth offending team' means a team established under section 39 of the Crime and Disorder Act 1998.'

Superannuation Act 1972 (c. 11)

24.   In Schedule 1 to the Superannuation Act 1972 (kinds of employment to which a scheme under section 1 of that Act may apply), at the end of the list of 'Other Bodies' there shall be inserted the following entry—

'Youth Justice Board for England and Wales.'

Powers of Criminal Courts Act 1973 (c. 62)

25. After subsection (1) of section IA of the 1973 Act (absolute and conditional discharge) there shall be inserted the following subsection—

'(1A) Subsection (1)(b) above has effect subject to section 66(4) of the Crime and Disorder Act 1998 (effect of reprimands and warnings).'

26.—(1) In subsection (1) of section 2 of the 1973 Act (probation orders), the words 'by a probation officer' shall cease to have effect and for the words 'the supervision of a probation officer' there shall be substituted the word 'supervision'.

(2) In subsection (2) of that section, for the words 'a probation officer appointed for or assigned to that area' there shall be substituted the following paragraphs—

'(a) a probation officer appointed for or assigned to that area; or

(b) where the offender is under the age of 18 years when the order is made, a member of a youth offending team established by a local authority specified in the order.'

(3) After that subsection there shall be inserted the following subsection—

'(2A) The local authority specified as mentioned in subsection (2)(b) above shall be the local authority within whose area it appears to the court that the offender resides or will reside.'

(4) In subsection (4) of that section, for the words 'the probation officer' there shall be substituted the words 'the person'.

(5) After that subsection there shall be inserted the following subsection—

'(4A) In the case of an offender under the age of 18 years, the reference in subsection (4) above to a probation officer includes a reference to a member of a youth offending team.'

(6) In subsection (6) of that section—

(a) for the words 'the probation officer' there shall be substituted the words 'the person'; and

(b) for the words 'that officer' there shall be substituted the words 'that person'.

27.—(1) In subsection (4) of section 14 of the 1973 Act (community service orders), for the words from 'a probation officer' to the end there shall be substituted the following paragraphs—

'(a) a probation officer appointed for or assigned to the area for the time being specified in the order (whether under this subsection or by virtue of Part IV of Schedule 2 to the Criminal Justice Act 1991);

(b) a person appointed for the purposes of those provisions by the probation committee for that area; or

(c) in the case of an offender under the age of 18 years when the order is made, a member of a youth offending team established by a local authority for the time being specified in the order (whether under this subsection or by virtue of that Part).'

(2) After that subsection there shall be inserted the following subsection—

'(4A) The local authority specified as mentioned in subsection (4)(c) above shall be the local authority within whose area it appears to the court that the offender resides or will reside.'

(3) After subsection (8) of that section there shall be inserted the following subsection—

'(9)   In the case of an offender under the age of 18 years, references in subsections (2), (5)(c) or (6) above to a probation officer include references to a member of a youth offending team.'

28.   In subsection (2) of section 21 of the 1973 Act (restriction on imposing sentences of imprisonment etc. on persons not legally represented)—

(a)   after the words 'sentence or trial,' there shall be inserted the words 'or sent to that Court for trial under section 51 of the Crime and Disorder Act 1998,'; and

(b)   for the words 'which committed him' there shall be substituted the words 'which committed or sent him'.

29.   In subsection (1)(b) of section 32 of the 1973 Act (enforcement etc. of fines imposed and recognizances forfeited by Crown Court), after the words 'or dealt with' there shall be inserted the words ', or by which he was sent to that Court for trial under section 51 of the Crime and Disorder Act 1998'.

30.   After subsection (2) of section 23 of the 1973 Act (power of court on conviction of further offence to deal with suspended sentence) there shall be inserted the following subsection—

'(2A)   The power to make an order under subsection (2) above has effect subject to section 102 of the Crime and Disorder Act 1998.'

31.   In section 42 of the 1973 Act (power of Crown Court on committal for sentence), subsection (2) shall cease to have effect.

32.   In subsection (1) of section 46 of the 1973 Act (reports of probation officers), after the words 'probation officer' there shall be inserted the words 'or a member of a youth offending team'.

33.   In subsection (1) of section 57 of the 1973 Act (interpretation), after the definition of 'suspended sentence' there shall be inserted the following definition—

'youth offending team' means a team established under section 39 of the Crime and Disorder Act 1998.'

34.—(1)   At the beginning of sub-paragraph (1) of paragraph 6 (requirements as to drug or alcohol dependency) of Schedule 1A to the 1973 Act there shall be inserted the words 'Subject to sub-paragraph (1A) below,'.

(2)   After that sub-paragraph there shall be inserted the following sub-paragraph—

'(1A)   If the court has been notified by the Secretary of State that arrangements for implementing orders under section 61 of the Crime and Disorder Act 1998 (drug treatment and testing orders) are available in the area proposed to be specified in the probation order, and the notice has not been withdrawn, this paragraph shall have effect as if the words "drugs or", in each place where they occur, were omitted.'

(3)   After that paragraph there shall be inserted the following paragraph—

'Interpretation

7.   In the case of an offender under the age of 18 years, references in this Schedule to a probation officer include references to a member of a youth offending team.'

Rehabilitation of Offenders Act 1974 (c. 53)

35.   After subsection (6) of section 5 of the Rehabilitation of Offenders Act 1974 (rehabilitation periods for particular sentences) there shall be inserted the following subsection—

'(6A)   Where in respect of a conviction a detention and training order was made under section 73 of the Crime and Disorder Act 1998, the rehabilitation period applicable to the sentence shall be—

(a)   in the case of a person aged fifteen years or over at the date of his conviction, five years if the order was, and three and a half years if the order was not, for a term exceeding six months;

(b)   in the case of a person aged under fifteen years at the date of his conviction, a period beginning with that date and ending one year after the date on which the order ceases to have effect.'

36.   In subsection (2) of section 7 of that Act (limitations on rehabilitation under Act etc.), after paragraph (b) there shall be inserted the following paragraph—

'(bb)   in any proceedings on an application for a sex offender order under section 2 or, as the case may be, 20 of the Crime and Disorder Act 1998 or in any appeal against the making of such an order;'.

Bail Act 1976 (c. 63)

37.   After subsection (8A) of section 3 of the Bail Act 1976 (general provisions) there shall be inserted the following subsection—

'(8B)   Subsection (8) above applies where a court has sent a person on bail to the Crown Court for trial under section 51 of the Crime and Disorder Act 1998 as it applies where a court has committed a person on bail to the Crown Court for trial.'

38.   In paragraph 8(1) of Schedule 1 to that Act (persons entitled to bail: supplementary provisions), after the words 'subsection (6)(d)' there shall be inserted the words 'or (e)'.

Magistrates' Courts Act 1980 (c. 43)

39.   In subsection (3) of section 11 of the 1980 Act (certain sentences and orders not to be made in absence of accused), for the words 'secure training order' there shall be substituted the words 'detention and training order'.

40.—(1)   In subsection (1)(a) of section 24 of the 1980 Act (summary trial of information against child or young person for indictable offence), for the words 'that subsection' there shall be substituted the words 'subsection (3) of that section'.

(2)   In subsection (2) of that section, for the words from 'that other offence' to the end there shall be substituted the words 'the charges for both offences could be joined in the same indictment'.

41.   Section 37 of the 1980 Act (committal to Crown Court with a view to greater term of detention in a young offender institution) shall cease to have effect.

42.   In subsection (1) of section 65 of the 1980 Act (meaning of 'family proceedings'), after paragraph (p) there shall be inserted the following paragraph—

'(q)   sections 11 and 12 of the Crime and Disorder Act 1998;'.

43.   In subsection (2) of section 108 of the 1980 Act (right of appeal to the Crown Court), the words 'a probation order or' shall cease to have effect.

44.   In subsection (4)(c) of section 125 of the 1980 Act (warrants)—

(a)   the word 'and' at the end of sub-paragraph (ii) shall cease to have effect;

(b)   in sub-paragraph (iii), for the words 'or 97 above' there shall be substituted the words ', 97 or 97A above; and'; and

(c) after that sub-paragraph there shall be inserted the following sub-paragraph—

'(iv) paragraph 4 of Schedule 3 to the Crime and Disorder Act 1998.'
45. In section 126 of the 1980 Act (execution of certain warrants outside England and Wales)—
    (a) the word 'and' at the end of paragraph (c) shall cease to have effect;
    (b) after that paragraph there shall be inserted the following paragraph—
'(cc) warrants of arrest issued under section 97A above;'; and
    (c) after paragraph (d) there shall be inserted the words '; and
    (e) warrants of arrest issued under paragraph 4 of Schedule 3 to the Crime and Disorder Act 1998.'
46. At the beginning of subsection (1) of section 133 of the 1980 Act (consecutive terms of imprisonment) there shall be inserted the words 'Subject to section 102 of the Crime and Disorder Act 1998,'.

Supreme Court Act 1981 (c. 54)
47. After subsection (1) of section 47 of the Supreme Court Act 1981 (sentences and other orders of Crown Court when dealing with offenders) there shall be inserted the following subsection—

'(1A) The power to give a direction under subsection (1) above has effect subject to section 102 of the Crime and Disorder Act 1998.'
48. In subsection (1)(a) of section 81 of the Supreme Court Act 1981 (bail), after the words 'Criminal Justice Act 1987' there shall be inserted the words 'or who has been sent in custody to the Crown Court for trial under section 51 of the Crime and Disorder Act 1998'.

Criminal Justice Act 1982 (c. 48)
49. In subsection (2) of section 1 of the 1982 Act (general restriction on custodial sentences), for the words from 'remanded in custody' to the end there shall be substituted the following paragraphs—
'(a) remanded in custody;
(b) committed in custody for trial or sentence; or
(c) sent in custody for trial under section 51 of the Crime and Disorder Act 1998.'
50.—(1) In subsection (1) of section 1A of the 1982 Act (detention in a young offender institution), for the words 'not less than 15 years of age' there shall be substituted the words 'not less than 18 years of age'.
(2) In subsection (3) of that section, for the words 'the minimum period applicable to the offender under subsection (4A) below' there shall be substituted the words '21 days'.
(3) In subsection (4) of that section, for the words 'the minimum period applicable' there shall be substituted the words '21 days'.
(4) Subsection (4A) of that section shall cease to have effect.
(5) At the beginning of subsection (6) of that section there shall be inserted the words 'Subject to section 102 of the Crime and Disorder Act 1998,'
51. In subsection (2) of section 1C of the 1982 Act (accommodation of offenders sentenced to detention in a young offender institution), the words 'but if he is under 18 at the time of the direction, only for a temporary purpose' shall cease to have effect.

52.—(1)   In subsection (1) of section 3 of the 1982 Act (restriction on certain sentences where offender not legally represented), for paragraph (e) there shall be substituted the following paragraph—
'(e)   make a detention and training order,'.
(2)   In subsection (2) of that section—
(a)   after the words 'sentence or trial,' there shall be inserted the words 'or sent to that Court for trial under section 51 of the Crime and Disorder Act 1998,'; and
(b)   for the words 'which committed him' there shall be substituted the words 'which committed or sent him'.

53.—(1)   In subsection (3)(a) of section 19 of the 1982 Act (breaches of attendance centre orders or attendance centre rules), the words 'revoke it and' shall cease to have effect.
(2)   In subsection (5) of that section, the words 'revoke the attendance centre order and' shall cease to have effect.
(3)   In subsection (5A) of that section, for paragraph (b) there shall be substituted the following paragraph—
'(b)   in the case of an offender who has wilfully and persistently failed to comply with those requirements, may impose a custodial sentence notwithstanding anything in section 1(2) of the Criminal Justice Act 1991.'
(4)   After that subsection there shall be inserted the following subsection—
'(5B)   Where a court deals with an offender under subsection (3)(a) or (5) above, it shall revoke the attendance centre order if it is still in force.'

Mental Health Act 1983 (c. 20)

54.   In subsection (8) of section 37 of the Mental Health Act 1983 (powers of courts to order hospital admission or guardianship), for the words from 'pass sentence of imprisonment' to 'in respect of the offender' there shall be inserted the following paragraphs—
'(a)   pass a sentence of imprisonment, impose a fine or make a community order (within the meaning of Part I of the Criminal Justice Act 1991) in respect of the offence; or
(b)   make an order under section 58 of that Act (binding over of parent or guardian) in respect of the offender,'.

Mental Health (Scotland) Act 1984 (c. 36)

55.—(1)   In subsection (8A) of section 74 of the Mental Health (Scotland) Act 1984 (effect of certain directions), for the words 'the Crime and Punishment (Scotland) Act 1997' there shall be substituted the words 'Part I of the Prisoners and Criminal Proceedings (Scotland) Act 1993'.
(2)   The amendment made by sub-paragraph (1) above shall be deemed to have had effect from 1 January 1998.

Repatriation of Prisoners Act 1984 (c. 47)

56.   In subsection (4)(b) of section 2 (transfer of prisoners out of United Kingdom) of the Repatriation of Prisoners Act 1984, for sub-paragraph (i) there shall be substituted the following sub-paragraph—

'(i) released on licence under section 33(1)(b), (2) or (3), 33A(2), 34A(3) or 35(1) of the Criminal Justice Act 1991 or section 28(5) or 29(1) of the Crime (Sentences) Act 1997;'.

57. In subsection (9) of section 3 of that Act (transfer of prisoners into United Kingdom)—

(a) for the words 'section 48 of the Criminal Justice Act 1991 (discretionary life prisoners transferred to England and Wales)' there shall be substituted the words 'section 33 of the Crime (Sentences) Act 1997 (life prisoner transferred to England and Wales)'; and

(b) for the words 'section 34 of that Act (duty of Secretary of State to release discretionary life prisoners)' there shall be substituted the words 'section 28 of that Act (duty to release certain life prisoners)'.

58.—(1) Paragraph 2 of the Schedule to that Act as it has effect, and is deemed always to have had effect, by virtue of paragraph 2 of Schedule 2 to the 1997 Act shall be amended as follows.

(2) In sub-paragraph (4), for the definition of 'the enactments relating to release on licence' there shall be substituted the following definition—

' "the enactments relating to release on licence" means sections 33(1)(b), (2) and (3), 33A(2), 34A(3), 35(1) and 37(1) and (2) of the Criminal Justice Act 1991 and section 28(5) and (7) of the Crime (Sentences) Act 1997;'.

59.—(1) Paragraph 2 of the Schedule to that Act (operation of certain enactments in relation to the prisoner) as it has effect by virtue of paragraph 3 of Schedule 2 to the 1997 Act—

(a) shall have effect in relation to all prisoners repatriated to England and Wales after the commencement of Schedule 2; and

(b) as it so has effect, shall be amended as follows.

(2) In sub-paragraph (2), for the words '34(3) and (5) and 35(1) of the Criminal Justice Act 1991' there shall be substituted the words '35(1) of the Criminal Justice Act 1991 and section 28(5) and (7) of the Crime (Sentences) Act 1997'.

(3) In sub-paragraph (4), for the definition of 'the enactments relating to release on licence' there shall be substituted the following definition—

' "the enactments relating to release on licence" means sections 33(1)(b), (2) and (3), 33A(2), 34A(3), 35(1) and 37(1) and (2) of the Criminal Justice Act 1991 and section 28(5) and (7) of the Crime (Sentences) Act 1997;'.

60. For paragraph 3 of the Schedule to that Act there shall be substituted the following paragraph—

'Life imprisonment

3. Where the relevant provisions include provision equivalent to a sentence in relation to which subsection (1) of section 29 of the Crime (Sentences) Act 1997 (power to release certain life prisoners etc.) applies, that subsection shall have effect as if the reference to consultation with the trial judge if available were omitted.'

Police and Criminal Evidence Act 1984 (c. 60)

61. After subsection (4) of section 27 of the 1984 Act (fingerprinting of certain offenders and recording of offences) there shall be inserted the following subsection—

'(4A)   In subsection (4) above "conviction" includes—

(a)   a caution within the meaning of Part V of the Police Act 1997; and

(b)   a reprimand or warning given under section 65 of the Crime and Disorder Act 1998.'

62.   After section 47 of the 1984 Act there shall be inserted the following section—

'**47A.   Early administrative hearings conducted by justices' clerks**

Where a person has been charged with an offence at a police station, any requirement imposed under this Part for the person to appear or be brought before a magistrates' court shall be taken to be satisfied if the person appears or is brought before the clerk to the justices for a petty sessions area in order for the clerk to conduct a hearing under section 50 of the Crime and Disorder Act 1998 (early administrative hearings).'

Prosecution of Offences Act 1985 (c. 23)

63.   In subsection (2) of section 23 of the 1985 Act (discontinuance of proceedings), after paragraph (b) there shall be inserted the following paragraph—

(c)   in the case of any offence, any stage of the proceedings after the accused has been sent for trial under section 51 of the Crime and Disorder Act 1998 (no committal proceedings for indictable-only and related offences).'

64.   After that section there shall be inserted the following section—

'**23A.   Discontinuance of proceedings after accused has been sent for trial**

(1)   This section applies where—

(a)   the Director of Public Prosecutions, or a public authority (within the meaning of section 17 of this Act), has the conduct of proceedings for an offence; and

(b)   the accused has been sent for trial under section 51 of the Crime and Disorder Act 1998 for the offence.

(2)   Where, at any time before the indictment is preferred, the Director or authority gives notice under this section to the Crown Court sitting at the place specified in the notice under section 51(7) of the Crime and Disorder Act 1998 that he or it does not want the proceedings to continue, they shall be discontinued with effect from the giving of that notice.

(3)   The Director or authority shall, in any notice given under subsection (2) above, give reasons for not wanting the proceedings to continue.

(4)   On giving any notice under subsection (2) above the Director or authority shall inform the accused of the notice; but the Director or authority shall not be obliged to give the accused any indication of his reasons for not wanting the proceedings to continue.

(5)   The discontinuance of any proceedings by virtue of this section shall not prevent the institution of fresh proceedings in respect of the same offence.'

Criminal Justice Act 1987 (c. 38)

65.   After subsection (3) of section 4 of the Criminal Justice Act 1987 (notices of transfer in serious fraud cases) there shall be inserted the following subsection—

'(4) This section and sections 5 and 6 below shall not apply in any case in which section 51 of the Crime and Disorder Act 1998 (no committal proceedings for indictable-only offences) applies.'

Criminal Justice Act 1988 (c. 33)

66. In subsection (1) of section 40 of the Criminal Justice Act 1988 (power to join in indictment count for common assault etc.), at the end there shall be inserted the words 'or are disclosed by material which, in pursuance of regulations made under paragraph 1 of Schedule 3 to the Crime and Disorder Act 1998 (procedure where person sent for trial under section 51), has been served on the person charged'.

Legal Aid Act 1988 (c. 34)

67.—(1) In subsection (4) of section 20 of the Legal Aid Act 1988 (competent authorities to grant representation under Part V), after paragraph (a) there shall be inserted the following paragraph—

'(aa) which sends a person for trial under section 51 of the Crime and Disorder Act 1998 (no committal proceedings for indictable-only offences),'.

(2) After subsection (5) of that section there shall be inserted the following subsection—

'(5A) A magistrates' court which has a duty or a power to send a person for trial under section 51 of the Crime and Disorder Act 1998 is also competent, before discharging that duty or (as the case may be) deciding whether to exercise that power, as respects any proceedings before the Crown Court on the person's trial.'

(3) In subsection (3)(a) of section 21 of that Act (availability of representation under Part V), after the word 'committed' there shall be inserted the words 'or sent'.

(4) In subsection (4) of that section, after the word 'commits' there shall be inserted the words 'or sends'.

Children Act 1989 (c. 41)

68. In subsection (4) of section 8 of the 1989 Act (which defines 'family proceedings'), after paragraph (h) there shall be inserted the following paragraph—

'(i) sections 11 and 12 of the Crime and Disorder Act 1998.'

69. In subsection (3) of section 47 of the 1989 Act (local authority's duty to investigate), after the words 'this Act' there shall be inserted the words 'or section 11 of the Crime and Disorder Act 1998 (child safety orders)'.

Prisons (Scotland) Act 1989 (c. 45)

70.—(1) Section 16 of the Prisons (Scotland) Act 1989 (discharge of prisoners) which, notwithstanding its repeal by the Prisoners and Criminal Proceedings (Scotland) Act 1993, is an 'existing provision' for the purposes of Schedule 6 to that Act of 1993, shall for those purposes be amended as follows.

(2) In subsection (1), for the words 'or Sunday' there shall be substituted the words 'Sunday or public holiday'.

(3) At the end there shall be inserted the following subsection—

'(3) For the purposes of this section 'public holiday' means any day on which, in the opinion of the Secretary of State, public offices or other facilities likely to be of use to the prisoner in the area in which he is likely to be following his discharge from prison will be closed.'

71. In section 39 of that Act (rules for the management of prisons)—

(a) in subsection (7)—

(i)   at the beginning there shall be inserted the words 'Subject to subsection (7A) below,';

(ii)   for the words 'a short-term or long-term prisoner within the meaning of' there shall be substituted the words 'any person who is, or is treated as, a long-term or short-term prisoner for the purposes of any provision of'; and

(iii)   the words from 'and the foregoing' to the end shall cease to have effect; and

(b)   after that subsection there shall be inserted the following subsections—

'(7A)   Additional days shall not be awarded under rules made under subsection (7) above in respect of a sentence where the prisoner has at any time been released on licence, in relation to that sentence, under Part I of the Prisoners and Criminal Proceedings (Scotland) Act 1993; and any reference to a sentence in such rules shall be construed in accordance with section 27(5) of that Act.

(7B)   In the application of subsection (7) above to a prisoner subject to an extended sentence within the meaning of section 210A of the 1995 Act, the reference to his sentence shall be construed as a reference to the custodial term of that extended sentence.'

Criminal Justice Act 1991 (c. 53)

72.   For subsection (3) of section 1 of the 1991 Act (restrictions on imposing custodial sentences) there shall be substituted the following subsection—

'(3)   Nothing in subsection (2) above shall prevent the court from passing a custodial sentence on the offender if he fails to express his willingness to comply with—

(a)   a requirement which is proposed by the court to be included in a probation order or supervision order and which requires an expression of such willingness; or

(b)   a requirement which is proposed by the court to be included in a drug treatment and testing order or an order under section 61(6) of the Crime and Disorder Act 1998.'

73.   In subsection (5)(a) of section 3 of the 1991 Act (procedural requirements for custodial sentences), for the words 'a probation officer or by a social worker of a local authority social services department' there shall be substituted the following sub-paragraphs—

'(i)   a probation officer;

(ii)   a social worker of a local authority social services department; or

(iii)   where the offender is under the age of 18 years, a member of a youth offending team;'.

74.   In subsection (4) of section 6 of the 1991 Act (restrictions on imposing community sentences)—

(a)   after paragraph (a) there shall be inserted the following paragraph—

'(aa)   a drug treatment and testing order;';

(b)   the word 'and' immediately following paragraph (e) shall cease to have effect; and

(c)   after paragraph (f) there shall be inserted the following paragraph—

'(g)   an action plan order.'

75. In subsection (3) of section 7 of the 1991 Act (procedural requirements for community sentences), after paragraph (a) there shall be inserted the following paragraph—

　　　'(aa)　a drug treatment and testing order;'.

76. In subsection (1) of section 11 of the 1991 Act (combination orders), for the words 'the supervision of a probation officer' there shall be substituted the word 'supervision'.

77. In subsection (3) of section 15 of the 1991 Act (regulation of community orders)—

　　(a)　in paragraph (a), after the words 'probation officer' there shall be inserted the words 'or member of a youth offending team'; and

　　(b)　after that paragraph there shall be inserted the following paragraph—

　　　'(aa)　in relation to an offender who is subject to a drug treatment and testing order, the probation officer responsible for his supervision;'.

78. In subsection (1) of section 31 of the 1991 Act (interpretation of Part I)—

　　(a)　immediately before the definition of 'attendance centre order' there shall be inserted the following definition—

　　　' "action plan order" means an order under section 69 of the Crime and Disorder Act 1998;';

　　(b)　in the definition of 'custodial sentence', in paragraph (b), after the word 'age,' there shall be inserted the words 'a detention and training order,' and the words 'or a secure training order under section 1 of the Criminal Justice and Public Order Act 1994' shall cease to have effect; and

　　(c)　after that definition there shall be inserted the following definitions—

　　　' "detention and training order" has the meaning given by section 73(3) of the Crime and Disorder Act 1998;

　　　"drug treatment and testing order" means an order under section 61 of that Act;'.

79.—(1)　In subsection (1)(b) of section 32 of the 1991 Act (Parole Board), for the words 'the functions conferred by Part II of the Crime (Sentences) Act 1997 ("Part II")' there shall be substituted the words 'the functions conferred by this Part in respect of long-term and short-term prisoners and by Chapter II of Part II of the Crime (Sentences) Act 1997 ("Chapter II") in respect of life prisoners within the meaning of that Chapter'.

　　(2)　In subsections (3), (4) and (6) of that section, for the words 'Part II' there shall be substituted the words 'this Part or Chapter II'.

80.—(1)　In subsection (3) of section 33 of the 1991 Act (duty to release short-term and long-term prisoners)—

　　(a)　in paragraph (a), for the words 'subsection (1)(b) or (2) above or section 35 or 36(1) below' there shall be substituted the words 'this Part'; and

　　(b)　in paragraph (b), for the words '38(2) or 39(1)' there shall be substituted the words '39(1) or (2)'.

　　(2)　After that subsection there shall be inserted the following subsection—

　　　'(3A)　In the case of a prisoner to whom section 44A below applies, it shall be the duty of the Secretary of State to release him on licence at the end of the extension period (within the meaning of section 58 of the Crime and Disorder Act 1998).'

　　(3)　Sub section (4) of that section shall cease to have effect.

81. After that section there shall be inserted the following section—
  '33A. Duty to release prisoners: special cases
  (1) As soon as a prisoner—
    (a) whose sentence is for a term of less than twelve months; and
    (b) who has been released on licence under section 34A(3)
or 36(1) below and recalled to prison under section 38A(1) or 39(1) or (2) below, would (but for his release) have served one-half of his sentence, it shall be the duty of the Secretary of State to release him unconditionally.
  (2) As soon as a prisoner—
    (a) whose sentence is for a term of twelve months or more; and
    (b) who has been released on licence under section 34A(3) below and recalled to prison under section 38A(1) below,
would (but for his release) have served one-half of his sentence, it shall be the duty of the Secretary of State to release him on licence.
  (3) In the case of a prisoner who—
    (a) has been released on licence under this Part and recalled to prison under section 39(1) or (2) below; and
    (b) has been subsequently released on licence under section 33(3) or (3A) above and recalled to prison under section 39(1) or (2) below,
section 33(3) above shall have effect as if for the words "threequarters" there were substituted the words "the whole" and the words "on licence" were omitted.'

82. In subsection (1) of section 36 of the 1991 Act (power to release prisoners on compassionate grounds), for the word 'prisoner' there shall be substituted the words 'short-term or long-term prisoner'.

83.—(1) In subsection (1) of section 37 of the 1991 Act (duration and conditions of licences)—
  (a) for the words 'subsection (2)' there shall be substituted the words 'subsections (1A), (1B) and (2)'; and
  (b) the words 'any suspension under section 38(2) below or, as the case may be,' shall cease to have effect.
  (2) After subsection (1A) of that section there shall be inserted the following subsection—
    '(1B) Where a prisoner whose sentence is for a term of twelve months or more is released on licence under section 33A(2) or 34A(3) above, subsection (1) above shall have effect as if for the reference to threequarters of his sentence there were substituted a reference to the difference between—
    (a) that proportion of his sentence; and
    (b) the duration of the curfew condition to which he is or was subject.'
  (3) In subsection (2) of that section, for the words 'section 36(1) above' there shall be substituted the words 'section 34A(3) or 36(1) above'.
  (4) In subsection (4) of that section—
    (a) after the words 'a licence' there shall be inserted the words 'under this Part'; and
    (b) the words '(which shall include on his release conditions as to his supervision by a probation officer)' shall cease to have effect.
  (5) After that subsection there shall be inserted the following subsection—
    '(4A) The conditions so specified may in the case of a person released on licence under section 34A above whose sentence is for a term of less than twelve

months, and shall in any other case, include on the person's release conditions as to his supervision by—

    (a)   a probation officer appointed for or assigned to the petty sessions area within which the person resides for the time being; or

    (b)   where the person is under the age of 18 years, a member of a youth offending team established by the local authority within whose area the person resides for the time being.'

(6)   For subsection (5) of that section there shall be substituted the following subsection—

    '(5)   The Secretary of State shall not include on release, or subsequently insert, a condition in the licence of a long-term prisoner, or vary or cancel any such condition, except after consultation with the Board.'

84.   After subsection (5) of section 39 of the 1991 Act (recall of prisoners while on licence) there shall be inserted the following subsection—

    '(5A)   In the case of a prisoner to whom section 44A below applies, subsections (4)(b) and (5) of that section apply in place of subsection (5) above.'

85.   After subsection (4) of section 40 of the 1991 Act (convictions during currency of original sentences) there shall be inserted the following subsections—

    '(5)   Where the new offence is found to have been committed over a period of two or more days, or at some time during a period of two or more days, it shall be taken for the purposes of this section to have been committed on the last of those days.

    (6)   For the purposes of any enactment conferring rights of appeal in criminal cases, any such order as is mentioned in subsection (2) or (3A) above made with regard to any person shall be treated as a sentence passed on him for the offence for which the sentence referred to in subsection (1) above was passed.'

86.—(1)   For subsections (1) and (2) of section 41 of the 1991 Act (remand time to count towards time served) there shall be substituted the following subsections—

    '(1)   Where a person is sentenced to imprisonment for a term in respect of an offence, this section applies to him if the court directs under section 9 of the Crime (Sentences) Act 1997 that the number of days for which he was remanded in custody in connection with—

    (a)   the offence; or

    (b)   any other offence the charge for which was founded on the same facts or evidence,

shall count as time served by him as part of the sentence.

    (2)   For the purpose of determining for the purposes of this Part whether a person to whom this section applies—

    (a)   has served, or would (but for his release) have served, a particular proportion of his sentence; or

    (b)   has served a particular period,

the number of days specified in the direction shall, subject to subsections (3) and (4) below, be treated as having been served by him as part of that sentence or period.'

(2)   After subsection (3) of that section there shall be inserted the following subsection—

'(4)   Where the period for which a licence granted under section 33A(2), 34A(3) or 36(1) above to a short-term prisoner remains in force cannot exceed one-quarter of his sentence, nothing in subsection (2) above shall have the effect of reducing that period.'

87.—(1)   In subsection (3) of section 43 of the 1991 Act (young offenders), for the words 'subsections (1)' there shall be substituted the words 'subsection (1)'.

(2)   In subsection (5) of that section, for the words 'section 37(4)' there shall be substituted the words 'section 37(4A)'.

88.—(1)   In subsection (1) of section 45 of the 1991 Act (fine defaulters and contemnors), for the words 'except sections 35 and 40' there shall be substituted the words 'except sections 33A, 34A, 35 and 40'.

(2)   In subsection (3) of that section—

(a)   for the words 'subsections (1) to (4)' there shall be substituted the words 'subsections (1) to (3)'; and

(b)   for the words 'section 38(2) or 39(1)' there shall be substituted the words 'section 39(1) or (2)'.

(3)   In subsection (4) of that section—

(a)   the words 'any suspension under section 38(2) below; or' shall cease to have effect; and

(b)   for the words 'section 39(1)' there shall be substituted the words 'section 39(1) or (2)'.

89.   In subsection (2) of section 46 of the 1991 Act (persons liable to removal from the United Kingdom), for the words from 'section 37(4)' to the end there shall be substituted the words 'section 37 above shall have effect as if subsection (4A) were omitted'.

90.   For subsection (2) of section 47 of the 1991 Act (persons extradited to the United Kingdom) there shall be substituted the following subsection—

'(2)   In the case of an extradited prisoner, section 9 of the Crime (Sentences) Act 1997 (crediting of periods of remand in custody) shall have effect as if the days for which he was kept in custody while awaiting extradition were days for which he was remanded in custody in connection with the offence, or any other offence the charge for which was founded on the same facts or evidence.'

91.   In section 50 of the 1991 Act (transfer by order of certain functions to Board), for subsection (3) (including that subsection as applied by any order under subsection (1) of that section) there shall be substituted the following subsection—

'(3)   In section 37 above, in subsection (5) for the words 'after consultation with the Board' there shall be substituted the words 'in accordance with recommendations of the Board', and subsection (6) shall be omitted.'

92.   In subsection (4) of section 51 of the 1991 Act (interpretation of Part II)—

(a)   for the words 'Subsections (2) and (3)' there shall be substituted the words 'Subsection (3)'; and

(b)   for the words 'as they apply' there shall be substituted the words 'as it applies'.

93.   After subsection (7) of section 53 of the 1991 Act (notices of transfer in certain cases involving children) there shall be inserted the following subsection—

'(8)   This section shall not apply in any case in which section 51 of the Crime and Disorder Act 1998 (no committal proceedings for indictable-only offences) applies.'

94.—(1) In subsection (1) of section 65 of the 1991 Act (supervision of young offenders after release), for the words from 'a probation officer' to the end there shall be substituted the following paragraphs—

'(a) a probation officer;

(b) a social worker of a local authority social services department; or

(c) in the case of a person under the age of 18 years on his release, a member of a youth offending team.'

(2) After that subsection there shall be inserted the following subsections—

'(1A) Where the supervision is to be provided by a probation officer, the probation officer shall be an officer appointed for or assigned to the petty sessions area within which the offender resides for the time being.

(1B) Where the supervision is to be provided by—

(a) a social worker of a local authority social services department; or

(b) a member of a youth offending team,

the social worker or member shall be a social worker of, or a member of a youth offending team established by, the local authority within whose area the offender resides for the time being.'

95. In subsection (1) of section 99 of the 1991 Act (general interpretation), after the definition of 'young person' there shall be inserted the following definition—

'"youth offending team" means a team established under section 39 of the Crime and Disorder Act 1998.'

96.—(1) After sub-paragraph (5) of paragraph 1 of Schedule 2 to the 1991 Act (enforcement etc. of community orders) there shall be inserted the following sub-paragraph—

'(6) Where a drug treatment and testing order has been made on an appeal brought from the Crown Court, or from the criminal division of the Court of Appeal, for the purposes of this Schedule it shall be deemed to have been made by the Crown Court.'

(2) In sub-paragraph (1)(d) of paragraph 3 of that Schedule, the words 'revoke the order and' shall cease to have effect.

(3) After sub-paragraph (2) of that paragraph there shall be inserted the following sub-paragraph—

'(2A) Where a magistrates' court deals with an offender under sub-paragraph (1)(d) above, it shall revoke the relevant order if it is still in force.'

(4) In sub-paragraph (1)(d) of paragraph 4 of that Schedule, the words 'revoke the order and' shall cease to have effect.

(5) After sub-paragraph (2) of that paragraph there shall be inserted the following sub-paragraph—

'(2A) Where the Crown Court deals with an offender under sub-paragraph (1)(d) above, it shall revoke the relevant order if it is still in force.'

(6) After paragraph 12(4) of that Schedule there shall be inserted the following sub-paragraphs—

'(5) Where—

(a) the court amends a probation order or community service order under this paragraph;

(b) a local authority is specified in the order in accordance with section 2(2)(b) or 14(4)(c) of the 1973 Act; and

(c)   the change, or proposed change, of residence also is or would be a change of residence from the area of that authority to the area of another such authority,

the court shall further amend the order by substituting the other authority for the authority specified in the order.

(6)   In sub-paragraph (5) above "local authority" has the meaning given by section 42 of the Crime and Disorder Act 1998, and references to the area of a local authority shall be construed in accordance with that section.'

(7)   In paragraph 17(1) of that Schedule, the words from 'and the court shall not' to the end shall cease to have effect.

97.   In paragraph 1(2) of Schedule 5 to the 1991 Act (Parole Board: supplementary provisions), for the words 'its functions under Part II of this Act' there shall be substituted the following paragraphs—

'(a)   its functions under this Part in respect of long-term and short-term prisoners; and

(b)   its functions under Chapter II of Part II of the Crime (Sentences) Act 1997 in respect of life prisoners within the meaning of that Chapter'.

Prisoners and Criminal Proceedings (Scotland) Act 1993 (c. 9)

98.—(1)   In subsection (1) of section 1 of the 1993 Act (release of short-term, long-term and life prisoners), at the beginning there shall be inserted the words 'Subject to section 26A(4) of this Act,'.

(2)   In subsection (2) of that section, at the end there shall be added the words 'unless he has before that time been so released, in relation to that sentence, under any provision of this Act'.

(3)   After subsection (3) of that section there shall be inserted the following subsection—

'(3A)   Subsections (1) to (3) above are subject to section 1A of this Act.'

99.—(1)   After subsection (1) of section 4 of the 1993 Act (persons detained under the Mental Health (Scotland) Act 1984) there shall be inserted the following subsection—

'(1A)   This Part of this Act shall apply to a person conveyed to and detained in a hospital pursuant to a hospital direction under section 59A of the 1995 Act as if, while so detained, he was serving the sentence of imprisonment imposed on him at the time at which that direction was made.'

(2)   The amendment made by sub-paragraph (1) above shall be deemed to have had effect from 1 January 1998.

100.   In section 5 of the 1993 Act (fine defaulters and persons in contempt of court)—

(a)   in subsection (1), for the words 'and (3)' there shall be substituted the words 'to (4)'; and

(b)   after subsection (3) there shall be inserted the following subsection—

'(4)   Where a person has had imposed on him two or more terms of imprisonment or detention mentioned in subsection (1)(a) or (b) above, sections 1A and 27(5) of this Act shall apply to those terms as if they were terms of imprisonment.'

101.   In section 7 of the 1993 Act (children detained in solemn proceedings)—
   (a)   in subsection (1)(b), at the end there shall be added the words 'unless he has before that time been so released, in relation to that sentence, under any provision of this Act';
   (b)   after that subsection there shall be inserted the following subsections—
      '(2A)   This subsection applies where a child detained under section 208 of the 1995 Act is sentenced, while so detained, to a determinate term of detention in a young offenders institution or imprisonment and, by virtue of section 27(5) of this Act, such terms of detention or imprisonment are treated as single term.
      (2B)   In a case where subsection (2A) applies and the single term mentioned in that subsection is less than four years, the provisions of this section shall apply.
      (2C)   In a case where subsection (2A) applies and the single term mentioned in that subsection is of four or more years—
         (a)   section 6 of this Act shall apply to him as if the single term were an equivalent sentence of detention in a young offenders institution, if that term is served in such an institution; and
         (b)   the provisions of this Act shall apply to him as if the single term were an equivalent sentence of imprisonment, if that term is served in a remand centre or a prison.';
   (c)   after subsection (4) there shall be inserted the following subsection—
      '(4A)   Where an order under subsection (3) above is made, the making of the order shall, if there is in force a licence relating to the person in respect of whom the order is made, have the effect of revoking that licence.'; and
   (d)   in subsection (5), after the word "construed" there shall be inserted the words 'and sections 1A and 27 shall apply'.
102.   In section 11 of the 1993 Act (duration of licences), subsections (3)(b) and (4) shall cease to have effect.
103.   In section 14 of the 1993 Act (supervised release of short-term prisoners), subsections (2) and (3) shall cease to have effect.
104.—(1)   In subsection (1) of section 16 of the 1993 Act (orders for return to prison after commission of further offence), after the word 'released' there shall be inserted the words 'at any time'.
   (2)   In paragraph (a) of subsection (7) of that section, after the word 'shall' there shall be inserted the words ', if the licence is in force when the order is made,'.
   (3)   Paragraph (b) of that subsection shall cease to have effect.
105.   In section 17 of the 1993 Act (revocation of licence), after subsection (4) there shall be inserted the following subsection—
      '(4A)   Where the case of a prisoner to whom section 3A of this Act applies is referred to the Parole Board under subsection (3) above, subsection (4) of that section shall apply to that prisoner in place of subsection (4) above.'
106.   In section 20 of the 1993 Act (Parole Board for Scotland), at the end of subsection (4) there shall be inserted the words—
      'and rules under this section may make different provision for different classes of prisoner.'
107.   After subsection (7) of section 27 of the 1993 Act (interpretation) there shall be inserted the following subsection—
      '(8)   For the purposes of this section 'public holiday' means any day on which, in the opinion of the Secretary of State, public offices or other facilities

likely to be of use to the prisoner in the area in which he is likely to be following his discharge from prison will be closed.'

108. In Schedule 6 to the 1993 Act (transitional provisions), after paragraph 6C there shall be inserted the following paragraph—

'6D. Where a prisoner released on licence is treated by virtue of the provisions of this or any other enactment as a prisoner whose licence was granted under section 2(4) of this Act, the validity of his licence shall not be affected by the absence in the licence of such a condition as is specified in section 12(2) of this Act.'

Probation Service Act 1993 (c. 47)

109. In subsection (1)(dd) of section 4 of the Probation Service Act 1993 (functions of probation committee), for the words 'a secure training order (within the meaning of section 1 of the Criminal Justice and Public Order Act 1994)' there shall be substituted the words 'a detention and training order (within the meaning of section 73 of the Crime and Disorder Act 1998)'.

110.—(1) In subsection (1) of section 17 of that Act (probation committee expenditure), for the words '(5) and (5A)' there shall be substituted the words 'and (5)'.

(2) Subsection (5A) of that section shall cease to have effect.

Criminal Justice and Public Order Act 1994 (c. 33)

111. In subsection (3) of section 12 of the 1994 Act (escort arrangements and officers), after the words 'secure training orders' there shall be inserted the words 'or detention and training orders'.

112. In paragraph 4 of Schedule 1 to the 1994 Act (escort arrangements: England and Wales), in the definition of 'the offender', after the words 'section 1 of this Act' there shall be inserted the words 'or detention and training under section 73 of the Crime and Disorder Act 1998'.

113.—(1) In sub-paragraph (1) of paragraph 3 of Schedule 2 to the 1994 Act (certification of custody officers: England and Wales)—

(a) in paragraph (b), for the words 'person in charge' there shall be substituted the word 'monitor'; and

(b) in paragraph (e), for the words 'person in charge' there shall be substituted the word 'governor'.

(2) In sub-paragraph (2) of that paragraph, for the words 'or person in charge' there shall be substituted the words ', monitor or governor'.

Drug Trafficking Act 1994 (c. 37)

114. In subsection (7) of section 2 of the Drug Trafficking Act 1994 (confiscation orders), paragraph (a) shall cease to have effect.

Proceeds of Crime (Scotland) Act 1995 (c. 43)

115. At the end of section 18 of the Proceeds of Crime (Scotland) Act 1995 (order to make material available) there shall be added the following subsection—

'(12) In this section "constable" includes a person commissioned by the Commissioners of Customs and Excise.'

116. In subsection (6) of section 19 of that Act (authority for search)—
(a) for the words 'subsection (10)' there shall be substituted the words 'subsections (10) and (12)'; and
(b) for the words 'it applies' there shall be substituted the words 'they apply'.

Criminal Procedure (Scotland) Act 1995 (c. 46)

117.—(1) For section 18(3) of the 1995 Act (prints and samples) there shall be substituted the following subsection—
'(3) Subject to subsection (4) below, all record of any relevant physical data taken from or provided by a person under subsection (2) above, all samples taken under subsection (6) below and all information derived from such samples shall be destroyed as soon as possible following a decision not to institute criminal proceedings against the person or on the conclusion of such proceedings otherwise than with a conviction or an order under section 246(3) of this Act.'

(2) The amendment made by sub-paragraph (1) above shall be deemed to have had effect from 1 August 1997.

118. In subsection (3) of section 49 of the 1995 Act (references to children's hearings), in paragraph (b), after the words 'the sheriff' there shall be inserted the words 'or district'.

119. In section 106(1)(bb) of the 1995 Act (appeals against automatic sentences), which is prospectively inserted by section 18(1) of the Crime and Punishment (Scotland) Act 1997, for the words '205B(3) or 209(1A)' there shall be substituted the words 'or 205B(3)'.

120. In section 108A of the 1995 Act (prosecutor's right of appeal against refusal to impose automatic sentence), which is prospectively inserted by section 18(2) of the Crime and Punishment (Scotland) Act 1997, for the words '205B(3) or 209(1A)' there shall be substituted the words 'or 205B(3)'.

121. In section 118(4A) of the 1995 Act (disposal of appeals), which is prospectively inserted by section 18(5) of the Crime and Punishment (Scotland) Act 1997, in paragraph (c), sub-paragraph (iii) shall cease to have effect.

122. In section 167 of the 1995 Act (findings and sentences in summary proceedings), in subsection (7), at the beginning there shall be inserted the words 'Subject to section 204A of this Act,'.

123. In subsection (5C) of section 175 of the 1995 Act (right of appeal in summary proceedings), the words 'paragraph (a) of' shall be omitted.

124. In subsection (1) of section 307 of the 1995 Act (interpretation), in the definition of 'officer of law'—
(a) after paragraph (b) there shall be inserted the following paragraph—
'(ba) any person commissioned by the Commissioners of Customs and Excise;'; and
(b) in paragraph (e), for the words 'class or persons' there shall be substituted the words 'class of persons'.

Criminal Procedure and Investigations Act 1996 (c. 25)

125. In subsection (2) of section 1 of the Criminal Procedure and Investigations Act 1996 (application of Part I of that Act)—
(a) after paragraph (c) there shall be inserted the following paragraph—

'(cc)   a person is charged with an offence for which he is sent for trial under section 51 (no committal proceedings for indictable-only offences) of the Crime and Disorder Act 1998,'; and

(b)   at the end there shall be inserted the words 'or

(f)   a bill of indictment charging a person with an indictable offence is preferred under section 22B(3)(a) of the Prosecution of Offences Act 1985.'

126.   In section 5 of that Act (compulsory disclosure by accused), after subsection (3) there shall be inserted the following subsection—

'(3A)   Where this Part applies by virtue of section 1(2)(cc), this section does not apply unless—

(a)   copies of the documents containing the evidence have been served on the accused under regulations made under paragraph 1 of Schedule 3 to the Crime and Disorder Act 1998; and

(b)   a copy of the notice under subsection (7) of section 51 of that Act has been served on him under that subsection.'

127.   In subsection (1) of section 13 of that Act (time limits: transitional)—

(a)   after the words 'section 1(2)(b) or (c),' there shall be inserted the words—

'(cc)   the accused is sent for trial under section 51 of the Crime and Disorder Act 1998 (where this Part applies by virtue of section 1(2)(cc)),'; and

(b)   after the words 'section 1(2)(e)' there shall be inserted the words 'or (f)'.

128.   In subsection (1)(a) of section 28 of that Act (introduction to Part III), after the words 'committed for trial' there shall be inserted the words ', or sent for trial under section 51 of the Crime and Disorder Act 1998,'.

129.   In subsection (1) of section 39 of that Act (meaning of pre-trial hearing), after the words 'committed for trial for the offence concerned' there shall be inserted the words ', after the accused has been sent for trial for the offence under section 51 of the Crime and Disorder Act 1998,'.

Crime (Sentences) Act 1997 (c. 43)

130.—(1)   In subsection (3) of section 28 of the 1997 Act (duty to release certain life prisoners), after paragraph (b) there shall be inserted the words 'and

(c)   the provisions of this section as compared with those of sections 33(2) and 35(1) of the Criminal Justice Act 1991 ("the 1991 Act")'.

(2)   In subsection (7) of that section, in paragraph (c), for the words from 'the time when' to the end there shall be substituted the words 'he has served one-half of that sentence'.

131.—(1)   In subsection (2) of section 31 of the 1997 Act (duration and conditions of licences), the words '(which shall include on his release conditions as to his supervision by a probation officer)' shall cease to have effect.

(2)   After that subsection there shall be inserted the following subsection—

'(2A)   The conditions so specified shall include on the prisoner's release conditions as to his supervision by—

(a)   a probation officer appointed for or assigned to the petty sessions area within which the prisoner resides for the time being;

(b)   where the prisoner is under the age of 22, a social worker of the social services department of the local authority within whose area the prisoner resides for the time being; or

(c)   where the prisoner is under the age of 18, a member of a youth offending team established by that local authority under section 39 of the Crime and Disorder Act 1998.'

(3)   In subsection (6) of that section, for the words 'section 24(2) above' there shall be substituted the words 'section 46(3) of the 1991 Act', and for the words 'the words in parentheses' there shall be substituted the words 'subsection (2A) above'.

132.—(1)   In subsection (1) of section 35 of the 1997 Act (fine defaulters: general), for the words 'the 1980 Act' there shall be substituted the words 'the Magistrates' Courts Act 1980 ("the 1980 Act")'.

(2)   In subsection (5)(e) of that section, for the words 'paragraph 3(2)(a)' there shall be substituted the words 'sub-paragraphs (2)(a) and (2A) of paragraph 3'.

(3)   In subsection (8) of that section—

(a)   in paragraph (a), the words 'to revoke the order and deal with an offender for the offence in respect of which the order was made' shall cease to have effect; and

(b)   in paragraph (b), for the words 'paragraph 3(2)(a)' there shall be substituted the words 'sub-paragraphs (2)(a) and (2A) of paragraph 3'.

133.   In section 54 of the 1997 Act (general interpretation), subsection (2) shall cease to have effect.

134.   Subsection (5)(b) of section 57 of the 1997 Act (short title, commencement and extent) shall have effect as if the reference to the Channel Islands included a reference to the Isle of Man.

135.—(1)   Schedule 1 to the 1997 Act (transfer of prisoners within the British Islands) shall be amended as follows.

(2)   In sub-paragraph (3) of paragraph 6—

(a)   after paragraph (a) there shall be inserted the following paragraph—

'(aa)   in relation to a person who is supervised in pursuance of a detention and training order, being ordered to be detained for any failure to comply with requirements under section 76(6)(b) of the Crime and Disorder Act 1998;'; and

(b)   in paragraph (b), for the words 'recalled to prison under the licence' there shall be substituted the words 'recalled or returned to prison'.

(3)   In paragraph 8—

(a)   in sub-paragraph (2), for the words from 'sections 10 to '27 of this Act' there shall be substituted the words 'sections 33 to 39, 41 to 46 and 65 of the 1991 Act, paragraphs 8, 10 to 13 and 19 of Schedule 12 to that Act and sections 75 to 77 of the Crime and Disorder Act 1998';

(b)   in sub-paragraph (4), for the words from 'sections 16' to '27 of this Act' there shall be substituted the words 'sections 37 to 39, 43 to 46 and 65 of the 1991 Act, paragraphs 8, 10 to 13 and 19 of Schedule 12 to that Act and sections 76 and 77 of the Crime and Disorder Act 1998';

(c)   in sub-paragraph (5), after the words 'Any provision of' there shall be inserted the words 'Part II of the 1991 Act or'; and

(d)   after sub-paragraph (5) there shall be inserted the following sub-paragraphs—

'(6)   Section 41 of the 1991 Act, as applied by sub-paragraph (2) or (4) above, shall have effect as if section 67 of the Criminal Justice Act 1967 (computation of sentences of imprisonment passed in England and Wales) or, as the case may require, section 9 of this Act extended to Scotland.

(7) Section 65(7)(b) of the 1991 Act, as applied by sub-paragraph (2) or (4) above, shall have effect as if the reference to a young offender institution were a reference to a young offenders institution.'

(4) In paragraph 9—

(a) in sub-paragraph (1), paragraph (a) and, in paragraph (b), the words 'to that and' shall cease to have effect;

(b) in sub-paragraph (2), for the words from 'sections 10' to '27 of this Act' there shall be substituted the words 'sections 33 to 46 and 65 of the 1991 Act, paragraphs 8, 10 to 13 and 19 of Schedule 12 to that Act and sections 75 to 77 of the Crime and Disorder Act 1998';

(c) in sub-paragraph (4), for the words from 'section 16' to '27 of this Act' there shall be substituted the words 'sections 37 to 40A, 43 to 46 and 65 of the 1991 Act, paragraphs 8, 10 to 13 and 19 of Schedule 12 to that Act and sections 76 and 77 of the Crime and Disorder Act 1998';

(d) sub-paragraph (5) shall cease to have effect;

(e) in sub-paragraph (6), after the words 'Any provision of' there shall be inserted the words 'Part II of the 1991 Act or'; and

(f) after sub-paragraph (6) there shall be inserted the following sub-paragraphs—

'(7) Section 41 of the 1991 Act, as applied by sub-paragraph (2) or (4) above, shall have effect as if section 67 of the Criminal Justice Act 1967 or, as the case may require, section 9 of this Act extended to Northern Ireland.

(8) Section 65(7)(b) of the 1991 Act, as applied by sub-paragraph (1), (2) or (4) above, shall have effect as if the reference to a young offender institution were a reference to a young offenders centre.'

(5) In paragraph 10—

(a) in sub-paragraph (2)(a)—

(i) for the words from 'sections' to '1997 Act' there shall be substituted the words 'sections 1, 1A, 3, 3A, 5, 6(1)(a), 7, 9, 11 to 13, 15 to 21, 26A and 27 of, and Schedules 2 and 6 to, the Prisoners and Criminal Proceedings (Scotland) Act 1993 ("the 1993 Act")'; and

(ii) after the word '3,' there shall be inserted words '6(1)(b)(i) and (iii)';

(b) in sub-paragraph (2)(b), for the words 'sub-paragraphs (3) and (4)' there shall be substituted the words 'sub-paragraph (3)';

(c) sub-paragraph (4) shall cease to have effect;

(d) in sub-paragraph (5)(a), for the words from 'sections 15,' to '37 of the 1997 Act' there shall be substituted the words 'sections 1A, 2(4), 3A, 11 to 13, 15 to 21, 26A and 27 of, and Schedules 2 and 6 to, the 1993 Act';

(e) for sub-paragraph (6)(b) there shall be substituted the following sub-paragraph—

'(b) in the said sub-paragraph (2) the reference to section 6(1)(b)(i) of the 1993 Act is a reference to that provision so far as it relates to a person sentenced under section 205(3) of the Criminal Procedure (Scotland) Act 1995.'; and

(f) for sub-paragraph (7) there shall be substituted the following sub-paragraph—

'(7) Any provision of Part I of the 1993 Act which is applied by sub-paragraph (2) or (5) above shall have effect (as so applied) as if any reference to a chief social work officer were a reference to a chief social worker of a local authority social services department.'

(6) In paragraph 11—
    (a) in sub-paragraph (2)(a)—
        (i) for the words from 'sections' to '1997 Act')' there shall be substituted the words 'sections 1, 1A, 3, 3A, 5, 6(1)(a), 7, 9, 11 to 13, 15 to 21, 26A and 27 of, and Schedules 2 and 6 to, the 1993 Act'; and
        (ii) after the word '3,' there shall be inserted the words '6(1)(b)(i) and (iii),';
    (b) in sub-paragraph (4)(a), for the words from 'sections 15' to '37 of the 1997 Act' there shall be substituted the words 'sections 1A, 3A, 11 to 13, 15 to 21, 26A and 27 of, and Schedules 2 and 6 to, the 1993 Act';
    (c) in sub-paragraph (5), for the words 'Sub-paragraph (5)' there shall be substituted the words 'Sub-paragraph (6)'; and
    (d) in sub-paragraph (6), the words 'or Part III of the 1997 Act' shall cease to have effect and, in the Table, for the entry relating to the expression 'young offenders institution' there shall be substituted the following entry—

'Probation officer appointed for or assigned to such petty sessions area	Probation Officer appointed by the Probation Board for Northern Ireland'.

(7) In sub-paragraph (5) of paragraph 12, in the Table, the entry relating to the expression 'Prison rules' shall cease to have effect.

(8) In sub-paragraph (5) of paragraph 13, in the Table, the entry relating to the expression 'Prison rules' shall cease to have effect.

(9) In sub-paragraph (1)(a) of paragraph 17 (prisoners unlawfully at large), after the words 'section 49(1)' there shall be inserted the words 'and (5)'.

(10) In sub-paragraph (1) of paragraph 20, in the definition of 'supervision', after the word 'purpose' there shall be inserted the words 'or a detention and training order'.

136. In Schedule 2 to the 1997 Act (repatriation of prisoners to the British Islands), paragraphs 4 and 8 are hereby repealed.

137. In Schedule 4 to the 1997 Act (minor and consequential amendments), the following provisions are hereby repealed, namely—
    (a) in paragraph 6, sub-paragraph (1)(b);
    (b) paragraphs 9 and 11; and
    (c) in paragraph 12, sub-paragraph (4).

138.—(1)—In Schedule 5 to the 1997 Act (transitional provisions and savings), paragraphs 1 to 4 and 6 are hereby repealed and the following provisions shall cease to have effect, namely—
    (a) paragraph 5(2);
    (b) paragraphs 8, 9(1) and 10(1);
    (c) in paragraph 11, sub-paragraph (1), in sub-paragraph (2)(c), the words 'or Part III of the 1997 Act' and, in sub-paragraph (3), the words from the beginning to '1995; and'; and
    (d) in paragraph 12, sub-paragraph (1) and, in sub-paragraph (2)(c), the words 'or Part III of the 1997 Act'.

(2) In paragraph 11(2) of that Schedule—
    (a) in paragraph (a)—
        (i) for the words from 'sections 15 to '1997 Act' there shall be substituted the words 'sections 1, 1A, 3, 3A, 5, 6(1)(a), 7, 9, 11 to 13, 15 to 21, 26A and 27 of,

and Schedules 2 and 6 to, the Prisoners and Criminal Proceedings (Scotland) Act 1993 ("the 1993 Act")'; and

(ii)   for the words 'the 1989 Act' there shall be substituted the words 'the Prisons (Scotland) Act 1989 ("the 1989 Act"); and

(b)   in paragraph (b), for the words from 'sections 15' to '1997 Act' there shall be substituted the words 'sections 1A, 2(4), 3A, 11 to 13, 15 to 21, 26A and 27 of, and Schedules 2 and 6 to, the 1993 Act'.

(3)   In paragraph 12(2) of that Schedule—

(a)   in paragraph (a)—

(i)   for the words from 'sections 15' to '1997 Act' there shall be substituted the words 'sections 1, 1A, 3, 3A, 5, 6(1)(a), 7, 9, 11 to 13, 15 to 21, 26A and 27 of, and Schedules 2 and 6 to, the Prisoners and Criminal Proceedings (Scotland) Act ("the 1993 Act")'; and

(ii)   for the words 'the 1989 Act' there shall be substituted the words 'the Prisons (Scotland) Act 1989 ("the 1989 Act"); and

(b)   in paragraph (b), for the words from 'sections 15' to '1997 Act' there shall be substituted the words 'sections 1A, 2(4), 3A, 11 to 13, 15 to 21, 26A and 27 of, and Schedules 2 and 6 to, the 1993 Act'.

139.   In Schedule 6 to the 1997 Act (repeals), the entries relating to sections 33 to 51 and 65 of the 1991 Act are hereby repealed.

Crime and Punishment (Scotland) Act 1997 (c. 48)

140.   Section 4 of the Crime and Punishment (Scotland) Act 1997 (supervised release orders) is hereby repealed.

141.—(1)   In Schedule 1 to that Act (minor and consequential amendments), the following provisions are hereby repealed, namely—

(a)   paragraphs 1, 9(7), 10(2)(a), 13(3) and 21(3); and

(b)   in paragraph 14, sub-paragraphs (2)(a), (3)(e), (4) to (7), (9), (10)(a), (11)(b), (12), (13) to (15) and (17).

(2)   In paragraph 14 of that Schedule, for sub-paragraph (16) there shall be substituted the following sub-paragraph—

'(16)   In section 27(1) (interpretation), in the definition of "supervised release order" the words "(as inserted by section 14 of this Act)" shall cease to have effect.'

142.   Schedule 2 to that Act (transitional provisions) is hereby repealed.

143.—(1)   Schedule 3 to that Act (repeals) shall be amended in accordance with this paragraph.

(2)   In the entry relating to the Prisons (Scotland) Act 1989, in the third column, the words 'In section 39, subsection (7)' are hereby repealed.

(3)   In the entry relating to the Prisoners and Criminal Proceedings (Scotland) Act 1993—

(a)   the words relating to sections 1, 3(2), 5, 6(1), 7, 9, 12(3), 16, 17(1), 20, 24, and Schedule 1;

(b)   in the words relating to section 14, the words 'and in subsection (4), the words "short-term"';

(c)   in the words relating to 27(1)—

(i)   the words 'the definitions of 'short term prisoner' and 'long-term prisoner' and';

(ii) in the words relating to the definition of 'supervised release order' the words 'and the words from "but" to the end'; and

(d) the words relating to section 27(2), (3), (5) and (6), are hereby repealed.

(4) In the entry relating to the Criminal Procedure (Scotland) Act 1995, in the third column, the words relating to section 44 are hereby repealed.

Sex Offenders Act 1997 (c. 51)

144. In subsection (1)(a) of section 4 of the Sex Offenders Act 1997 (young sex offenders), after the word 'under' there shall be inserted the words 'a detention and training order or'.

Section 120(1)   SCHEDULE 9
TRANSITIONAL PROVISIONS AND SAVINGS

Presumption of incapacity

1. Nothing in section 34 of this Act shall apply in relation to anything done before the commencement of that section.

Effect of child's silence at trial

2. Nothing in section 35 of this Act shall apply where the offence was committed before the commencement of that section.

Sexual or violent offenders: extended sentences

3. Section 58 of this Act does not apply where the sexual or violent offence was committed before the commencement of that section.

Drug treatment and testing orders

4. Section 61 of this Act does not apply in relation to an offence committed before the commencement of that section.

Young offenders: cautions

5.—(1) Any caution given to a child or young person before the commencement of section 65 of this Act shall be treated for the purposes of subsections (2) and (4) of that section as a reprimand.

(2) Any second or subsequent caution so given shall be treated for the purposes of paragraphs (a) and (b) of subsection (3) of that section as a warning.

Abolition of secure training orders

6. In relation to any time before the commencement of subsection (7) of section 73 of this Act, section 9A of the 1997 Act shall have effect as if after subsection (1) there were inserted the following subsection—

'(1A) Section 9 above applies to periods of detention which offenders are liable to serve under secure training orders as it applies to sentences of imprisonment.'

Sentencing guidelines

7.—(1) Section 80 of this Act does not apply by virtue of subsection (1)(a) of that section in any case where the Court is seised of the appeal before the commencement of that section.

(2) In this paragraph 'the Court' and 'seised' have the same meanings as in that section.

Confiscation orders on committal for sentence

8. Section 83 of this Act does not apply where the offence was committed before the commencement of that section.

Football spectators: failure to comply with reporting duty

9. Section 84 of this Act does not apply where the offence was committed before the commencement of that section.

Power to release short-term prisoners on licence

10.—(1) Section 99 of this Act does not apply in relation to a prisoner who, immediately before the commencement of that section, has served one or more days more than the requisite period for the term of his sentence.

(2) In this paragraph 'the requisite period' has the same meaning as in section 34A of the 1991 Act (which is inserted by section 99 of this Act).

Early release: two or more sentences

11.—(1) Where the terms of two or more sentences passed before the commencement of section 101 of this Act have been treated, by virtue of section 51(2) of the 1991 Act, as a single term for the purposes of Part II of that Act, they shall continue to be so treated after that commencement.

(2) Subject to sub-paragraph (1) above, section 101 of this Act applies where one or more of the sentences concerned were passed after that commencement.

Recall to prison of short-term prisoners

12.—(1) Sub-paragraphs (2) to (7) below have effect in relation to any prisoner whose sentence, or any part of whose sentence, was imposed for an offence committed before the commencement of section 103 of this Act.

(2) The following provisions of this Act do not apply, namely—

(a) section 103;

(b) paragraphs 83(1)(b) and 88(3)(a) of Schedule 8 to this Act and section 119 so far as relating to those paragraphs; and

(c) section 120(2) and Schedule 10 so far as relating to the repeal of section 38 of the 1991 Act and the repeals in sections 37(1) and 45(4) of that Act.

(3) Section 33 of the 1991 Act has effect as if, in subsection (3)(b) (as amended by paragraph 80(1) of Schedule 8 to this Act), for the words 'section 39(1) or (2)' there were substituted the words 'section 38(2) or 39(1) or (2)'.

(4) Section 33A of the 1991 Act (as inserted by paragraph 81 of Schedule 8 to this Act) has effect as if—

(a) in subsection (1), for the words 'section 38A(1) or 39(1) or (2)' there were substituted the words 'section 38(2) or 38A(1)'; and

(b)   in subsection (3), for the words 'section 39(1) or (2)', in both places where they occur, there were substituted the words 'section 38(2)'.

(5)   Section 34A of the 1991 Act (as inserted by section 99 of this Act) has effect as if, in subsection (2)(g), for the words 'section 39(1) or (2)' there were substituted the words 'section 38(2)'.

(6)   Section 40A of the 1991 Act (as inserted by section 105 of this Act) has effect as if, in subsection (1), for the word '39' there were substituted the word '38'.

(7) Section 44 of the 1991 Act (as substituted by section 59 of this Act) has effect as if—

(a)   in subsections (3) and (4), after the words 'subject to' there were inserted the words 'any suspension under section 38(2) above or, as the case may be,'; and

(b)   in subsection (7), for the words 'sections 37(5) and 39(1) and (2)' there were substituted the words 'section 37(5), 38(2) and 39(1) and (2)'.

(8) Section 45 of the 1991 Act has effect as if, in subsection (3) (as amended by paragraph 88(2) of Schedule 8 to this Act), for the words 'section 39(1) or (2)' there were substituted the words 'section 38(2) or 39(1) or (2)'.

(9) For the purposes of this paragraph and paragraph 13 below, consecutive sentences, or sentences that are wholly or partly concurrent, shall be treated as parts of a single sentence.

Release on licence following recall to prison

13.   Section 104 of this Act does not apply in relation to a prisoner whose sentence, or any part of whose sentence, was imposed for an offence committed ,before the commencement of that section.

Release on licence following return to prison

14—(1)   Section 105 of this Act does not apply where the new offence was committed before the commencement of that section.

(2)   In this paragraph 'the new offence' has the same meaning as in section 40 of the 1991 Act.

Remand time: two or more sentences

15.—(1)   Where the terms of two or more sentences passed before the commencement of paragraph 11 of Schedule 8 to this Act have been treated, by virtue of section 104(2) of the Criminal Justice Act 1967, as a single term for the purposes of section 67 of that Act, they shall continue to be so treated after that commencement.

(2)   Subject to sub-paragraph (1) above, paragraph 11 of Schedule 8 to this Act applies where one or more of the sentences concerned were passed after that commencement.

Section 120(2)   SCHEDULE 10
                                      REPEALS

Chapter	Short title	Extent of repeal
30 Geo 3 c. 48.	Treason Act 1790.	The whole Act.
36 Geo 3 c. 7.	Treason Act 1795.	The whole Act.
36 Geo 3 c. 31.	Treason by Women Act (Ireland) 1796.	The whole Act.
57 Geo 3 c. 6.	Treason Act 1817.	The whole Act.
11 & 12 Vict c. 12.	Treason Felony Act 1848.	Section 2.
21 & 22 Geo 5 c. 24.	Sentence of Death (Expectant Mothers) Act 1931.	The whole Act.
23 Geo 5 c. 12.	Children and Young Persons Act 1933	In section 47(2), the words from the beginning to 'court; and'. In Schedule 2, in paragraph 15(a), the word 'shall', in the second place where it occurs, and, in paragraph 17, the words 'or, if a metropolitan stipendiary magistrate, may sit alone'.
1945 c. 15 (N.I.).	Criminal Justice Act (Northern Ireland) 1945.	Sections 32 and 33.
1967 c. 80.	Criminal Justice Act 1967.	In section 56, subsections (3), (6) and (13). Section 67(5)(c).
1968 c. 19.	Criminal Appeal Act 1968.	In section 10(2), the words '(other than a supervision order within the meaning of that Part)'.
1969 c.54.	Children and Young Persons Act 1969.	Section 12D. Section 13(2). In section 16, subsection (10) and, in subsection (11), the words 'seventeen or'. Section 23(14)(a). In section 34, in subsection (1), paragraph (a) and, in paragraph (c), the words '7(7), 7(8),'. Section 69(5). In Schedule 6, the entries relating to sections 55, 56(1) and 59(1) of the Children and Young Persons Act 1933.
1972 c. 71.	Criminal Justice Act 1972.	Section 49.

Chapter	Short title	Extent of repeal
1973 c. 62.	Powers of Criminal Courts Act 1973.	In section 1, in subsections (8)(b) and (8A) the words '37 or'. Section 1B(10). In section 1C(1), paragraph (b) and the word 'and' immediately preceding it. In section 2(1), the words 'by a probation officer' and the words from 'For the purposes' to 'available evidence'. Section 11. Section 14(8). In section 31, in subsection (3A), the words 'Subject to subsections (3B) and (3C) below,', subsections (3B) and (3C), in subsection (4), the words '4 or' and, in subsection (6), the words 'about committal by a magistrates' court to the Crown Court'. Section 32(5). Section 42(2). In Schedule 1A, paragraph 6(7). In Schedule 5, paragraph 35.
1976 c. 63.	Bail Act 1976.	In section 3(5), the words 'If it appears that he is unlikely to remain in Great Britain until the time appointed for him to surrender to custody'.
1980 c. 43.	Magistrates' Courts Act 1980.	Section 37. In sections 38(2) and 38A(2), the words ', in accordance with section 56 of the Criminal Justice Act 1967,'. In section 108(2), the words 'a probation order or'. In section 125(4)(c), the word 'and' at the end of sub-paragraph (ii). In section 126, the word 'and' at the end of paragraph (c). In Schedule 7, paragraph 120(b).

Chapter	Short title	Extent of repeal
1982 c. 48.	Criminal Justice Act 1982.	Section 1A(4A). Section 1B. In section 1C(2), the words 'but if he is under 18 at the time of the direction, only for a temporary purpose'. In section 3(1)(a), the words 'under section 1A above'. Section 18(7). In section 19, in subsection (3)(a), the words 'revoke it and' and, in subsection (5), the words 'revoke the attendance centre order and'. Section 66(3). In Schedule 14, paragraph 28.
1987 c. 42.	Family Law Reform Act 1987.	Section 8(1). In Schedule 2, paragraph 26.
1988 c. 33.	Criminal Justice Act 1988.	Section 69(2). In Schedule 15, paragraph 40.
1989 c. 45.	Prisons (Scotland) Act 1989.	In section 39(7), the words from 'and the foregoing' to the end.
1991 c. 53.	Criminal Justice Act 1991.	In section 6(4), the word 'and' immediately following paragraph (e). In section 31(1), in the definition of 'custodial sentence', in paragraph (b), the words 'or a secure training order under section 1 of the Criminal Justice and Public Order Act 1994'. Section 33(4). In section 37, in subsection (1), the words 'any suspension under section 38(2) below or, as the case may be,' and, in subsection (4), the words '(which shall include on his release conditions as to his supervision by a probation officer)'. Section 38. In section 45(4), the words 'any suspension under section 38(2) below; or'.

Chapter	Short title	Extent of repeal
		In section 61(1), paragraph (b) and the word 'or' immediately preceding that paragraph.
		Section 62.
		In Schedule 2, in paragraphs 3(1)(d) and 4(1)(d), the words 'revoke the order and' and, in paragraph 17(1), the words from 'and the court' to the end.
		In Schedule 11, paragraphs 10, 11 and 14.
		In Schedule 12, paragraph 17(3).
1993 c. 9.	Prisoners and Criminal Proceedings (Scotland) Act 1993.	Section 11(3)(b) and (4).
		Section 14(2) and (3).
		Section 16(7)(b).
		In paragraph 6B(1) of Schedule 6, the word 'and' after head (a).
1993 c. 47.	Probation Service Act 1993.	Section 17(5A).
1994 c. 33.	Criminal Justice and Public Order Act 1994.	Sections 1 to 4.
		Section 20.
		In section 35, in subsection (1), the words 'who has attained the age of fourteen years' and subsection (6).
		Section 130(4).
		In Schedule 10, paragraph 42.
1994 c. 37.	Drug Trafficking Act 1994.	Section 2(7)(a).
1995 c. 46.	Criminal Procedure (Scotland) Act 1995.	Section 118(4A)(c)(iii).
		In section 175(5C), the words 'paragraph (a) of'.
		In section 209(1), the words 'not less than twelve months but'.
1997 c. 43.	Crime (Sentences) Act 1997.	Section 1.
		Section 8.
		Sections 10 to 27.
		In section 31(2), the words '(which shall include on his release conditions as to his supervision by a probation officer)'.
		In section 35, in subsection (5), paragraph (c) and the word 'and' at the end of paragraph (d), and in subsection (8), in paragraph (a), the words 'to revoke the order and

Chapter	Short title	Extent of repeal
		deal with an offender for the offence in respect of which the order was made' and the word 'and' at the end of that paragraph. Section 43(4). Section 54(2). In Schedule 1, in paragraph 9(1), paragraph (a) and, in paragraph (b), the words 'to that and', paragraph 9(5), paragraph 10(4), in paragraph 11(6), the words 'or Part III of the 1997 Act', in paragraph 12(5), in the Table, the entry relating to the expression 'prison rules' and, in paragraph 13(5), in the Table, the entry relating to the expression 'prison rules'. In Schedule 2, paragraphs 4 and 8. In Schedule 4, paragraph 6(1)(b), paragraphs 9 and 11 and paragraph 12(4). In Schedule 5, paragraphs 1 to 4, paragraph 5(2), paragraph 6, paragraph 8, paragraph 9(1), paragraph 10(1), in paragraph 11, sub-paragraph (1), in sub-paragraph (2)(c), the words 'or Part III of the 1997 Act' and, in sub-paragraph (3), the words from the beginning to '1995; and', and in paragraph 12, sub-paragraph (1) and, in sub-paragraph (2)(c), the words 'or Part III of the 1997 Act'. In Schedule 6, the entries relating to sections 33 to 51 and 65 of the Criminal Justice Act 1991.
1997 c. 48.	Crime and Punishment (Scotland) Act 1997.	Section 4. Chapter I of Part III. In Schedule 1, paragraph 1, paragraph 9(7), paragraph 10(2)(a), paragraph 13(3), in paragraph 14, sub-paragraphs (2)(a), (3)(e), (4) to (7),

Chapter	Short title	Extent of repeal
		(9), (10)(a), (11)(b), (12), (13) to (15) and (17), and paragraph 21(3). Schedule 2. In Schedule 3, in the entry relating to the Prisons (Scotland) Act 1989, the words 'In section 39, subsection (7)', in the entry relating to the Prisoners and Criminal Proceedings (Scotland) Act 1993, the words relating to sections 1, 3(2), 5, 6(1), 7, 9, 12(3), 16, 17(1), 20, 24, 27(2), (3), (5) and (6) and Schedule 1, in the words relating to section 14, the words 'and, in subsection (4), the words "short-term" ', in the words relating to section 27(1), the words 'the definitions of "short term prisoner" and "long-term prisoner" and' and 'and the words from "but" to the end' and, in the entry relating to the Criminal Procedure (Scotland) Act 1995, the words relating to section 44.
1997 c. 50.	Police Act 1997.	In section 94(4), the word 'and' immediately preceding paragraph (c).

Index